RJM

Auctions
Law and Practice

'Ah, who can believe sellers!' said old Michael Mail in a carefully-cautious voice, by way of tiding-over this critical point of affairs.

'No one at all,' said Joseph Bowman, in the tone of a man fully agreeing with everybody.

'Ay,' said Mail, in the tone of a man who did not agree with everybody as a rule, though he did now; 'I knowed a' auctioneering feller once—a very friendly feller 'a was too. And so one hot day as I was walking down the front street o' Casterbridge, jist below the King's Arms, I passed a' open winder and see him inside, stuck upon his perch, a selling-off. I jist nodded to en in a friendly way as I passed, and went my way, and thought no more about it. Well, next day, as I was oilen my boots by fuel-house door, if a letter didn't come wi' a bill charging me with a feather-bed, bolster, and pillers, that I had bid for at Mr. Tayor's sale. The slim-faced martel had knocked 'em down to me because I nodded to en in my friendly way; and I had to pay for 'em too. Now, I hold that that was coming it very close, Reuben?'

''Twas close, there's no denying,' said the general voice.

Thomas Hardy *Under the Greenwood Tree* (1872).

Auctions

Law and Practice

Brian W Harvey, MA, LLM (Cantab)
Solicitor, Dean of the Faculty of Law,
University of Birmingham

Franklin Meisel, LLB
of the Middle Temple, Barrister, Lecturer in Law,
University of Birmingham

London
Butterworths
1985

United Kingdom	Butterworth & Co (Publishers) Ltd, 88 Kingsway, LONDON WC2B 6AB and 61A North Castle Street, EDINBURGH EH2 3LJ
Australia	Butterworths Pty Ltd, SYDNEY, MELBOURNE, BRISBANE, ADELAIDE, PERTH, CANBERRA and HOBART
Canada	Butterworth & Co (Canada) Ltd, TORONTO and VANCOUVER
New Zealand	Butterworths of New Zealand Ltd, WELLINGTON and AUCKLAND
Singapore	Butterworth & Co (Asia) Pte Ltd, SINGAPORE
South Africa	Butterworth Publishers (Pty) Ltd, DURBAN and PRETORIA
USA	Butterworth Legal Publishers, ST PAUL, Minnesota, SEATTLE, Washington, BOSTON, Massachusetts, AUSTIN, Texas and D & S Publishers, CLEARWATER, Florida

British Library cataloguing in publication data

Harvey, Brian W.
Auctions: law and practice.
1. Auctions — Great Britain
I. Title II. Meisel, Franklin
344.106'72 KD2517.E7

ISBN 0 406 52660 5

Typeset by Lin-Art, Ashford, Kent
Printed in Great Britain by Billings of Worcester

Foreword

'Eureka!' Such was Archimedes' exclamation of delight when he discovered gold; or, to be more precise, when he saw the practical means of testing for purity between the real and the alloyed.

The simple test which I have been able to apply to *Auctions: Law and Practice* is to read it and, in so doing, to recognise a golden discovery of a different sort: a wide-ranging, deeply-researched and exhaustive treatise on these twin components — law and practice — of this complex pursuit, the realisation of money's worth by the auction process.

Sales by open public competition, by various rules, methods and styles, emerge out of the mists of time into commonplace by the early seventeenth century, when 'inch of candle' or 'hour glass' were the acknowledged means of concentrating the bargaining process within time and space, before 'fall of the hammer' gained almost universal favour as the more practical way of determining the point of sale, whether at the end of an ascending, or of a descending, pattern of bidding.

For the last two hundred years or so, therefore, there has developed in the United Kingdom a corpus of some forty statutes and perhaps a thousand cases producing a sophisticated overlapping network of law and an elaborate web of commercial and professional convention within which the machinery and skills of the auction are required to operate, for the mutual benefit of vendor, purchaser and — necessarily — practitioners, both of law and of auctioneering.

It is to the unravelling and illumination of these essential realities, in all their considerable complexity, that Brian Harvey and Frank Meisel have addressed themselves with such energy over the last two years or so and it is we, their readers, who are the beneficiaries, to their great credit. Some of their expert conclusions and commentaries will raise a few eyebrows, I think, and perhaps temperatures as well, among experienced rostrum artists whose standard procedures and interpretations of law and practice are called into serious question; but then that is what a book like this is all about and it behoves each of us to assimilate its definitive instruction whilst responding to its occasional challenge.

During this Diamond Jubilee Year of The Incorporated Society of Valuers and Auctioneers, it is my great privilege to have been given this opportunity of contributing the Foreword to what will undoubtedly become a new standard work of reference on the law and practice of auctions.

To the authors, our thanks; to the public, my recommendation.

John M Phillips FRICS FSVA ACIArb
Diamond Jubilee President of
The Incorporated Society of Valuers and Auctioneers
London
February 1985

Preface

Despite the economic recession in the United Kingdom, London can still be said to be the centre of the auction market in fine art and other valuable commodities. Admittedly other major cities such as New York and Geneva are pressing hard on London's heels, but the whole history and development of large scale auctioneering has been and largely remains centred in London. Besides the companies who are household names operating in London there are numerous smaller firms who offer a service mainly confined to U K residents in all parts of England, Wales, Scotland and Northern Ireland. An auction sale of land can be organised by a firm which normally operates as estate agents or surveyors but which decides that on a specific occasion an auction sale of a house, and possibly the accompanying chattels, is in the best interests of the vendor. It is this situation which is most familiar to solicitors as well. But in addition to chattels sales and sales of land, there are numerous other specialised types of auction which have established a market of their own. To give an example, motor vehicle auctions have mushroomed in popularity in the U K — it being estimated that 750 000 vehicles were sold at auction in 1982, and that one in five of these was bought by a member of the general public. Similarly, perhaps as a sign of the times, auctions of plant and machinery have become an important way of disposing of commercial property where companies have cashflow difficulties or need to turn their stock into cash prior to liquidation.

In the light of the continuing development of the U K auction market and the increasingly bouyant returns shown by the large London auctioneers, it is surprising that there has been no recent comprehensive treatise solely confined to the law of auctions. The last edition of Bateman's *Law of Auctions* (11th edn) was published by the Estates Gazette in 1953. In the 30 years intervening since the publication of this book, not only has the common law of agency and contract been transformed by judicial decision-making but the legislature has been active, too, in promoting consumer-orientated legislation some of which has a direct bearing on the law of auctions. Modern textbooks which include a section on auction law, usually in the more general context of estate agency work, do not normally deal with specialist auctions such as sales of motor vehicles, livestock, plant and machinery and the like. Nor could we find anywhere an examination of such matters as export licensing or, beyond a brief mention, any analysis of the increasingly important law relating to trade descriptions and obtaining property by deception in the criminal law. These matters are all of vital interest to auctioneers and the legal practitioners who advise them and we therefore hope that our readers will agree that it is opportune to endeavour to write a reasonably exhaustive treatise on this topic which examines the law as it is now. Some matters, we know from our consultations with practitioners, are controversial and will undoubtedly cause dismay. We have in mind particularly potential criminal liability of auctioneeers under s 15 of the Theft Act 1968 in respect of property obtained by deception. But the Trade Description Act 1968 has an equally important, and often more directly threatening, bearing on auctioneer's activities and there have been recent prosecutions of auctioneers (who seem in some cases to think that the criminal law in this area does not apply to auctioneering activities) where auctioneers have been convicted. Normally problems are caused by ignorance of the law which in some cases can be avoided by adopting up-to-date Conditions of Sale or slightly altering saleroom practices. We hope that our work will assist professional practitioners in these areas, and in the Appendices we have included as much material directly useful in practice as there is space for.

The book is aimed to be of use primarily both to professional auctioneers and their staff and to practising lawyers. We hope that the book will also prove useful to law students and those studying for the professional examinations of the bodies to which auctioneers and estate agents belong. Professional dealers and others who make it a habit to buy at auction may also welcome a full-scale statement of the law which regulates such an important part of their business transactions.

As can be inferred from the acknowledgments which follow, the writing of the book (though inevitably hard labour) has been made exceptionally enjoyable by the very large degree of co-operation afforded to us by professional auctioneers. Whilst we both have experience in legal practice we do not pretend to be professional auctioneers, though we have observed a good many sales from the inside and from the outside. But without the help and encouragement of the auctioneering profession, together with their comments on much of our material, the book would have been the poorer. We must accept that there are likely still to be inadequacies and these will no doubt be brought to our attention. But it is our sincere hope that the book will prove genuinely useful both to auctioneers and lawyers since the importance of this area of economic activity in the United Kingdom cannot be overestimated. And finally, we should also like to thank the editorial staff of our publishers, Butterworths, who have taken an exceptional degree of trouble to convert our untidy manuscript into print.

Brian Harvey
Frank Meisel

Contents

Acknowledgments

We wish particularly to acknowledge the help of the staff of Sotheby's in London who, besides giving kind permission for their Conditions of Sale etc to be reproduced in this book, took great trouble to introduce the authors to the auctioneering business of their firm and answered many questions with tolerance and good humour. Exactly the same remark applies to Christie's International plc in London who have also given kind permission for their Conditions to be reproduced and dealt similarly with the authors' enquiries. We wish to stress that the copyright in these Conditions etc as reproduced remains in the respective firms and must not be infringed. The authors have appended a sample and simplified set of General Conditions which may be used as appropriate by readers.

We are also most grateful to John M Phillips Esq, Diamond Jubilee President of the ISVA, for his Foreword, the Solicitors' Law Stationery Society plc and the Law Society of England and Wales for permission to reproduce the relevant Conditions of Sale relating to land, those firms whose names appear in the Directory in Appendix 4 for the information given, and to those others, our colleagues, our secretarial staff and the long-suffering staff of our publishers, who have co-operated and made this venture possible we also extend our heartfelt thanks.

BWH
FM

Table of statutes

References in **bold** type indicate where sections of the Act are set out in part or in full.

Table of cases

Chapter 1

The evolution and economics of auction sales

DEFINITION OF AUCTIONS

It is perhaps surprising that there is no comprehensive definition of an auction in English statute law. The reason is, no doubt, that since no single statute deals with both the civil and criminal aspects of auction sales in their entirety, it has never been necessary to attempt a statutory definition. Such statutes as do relate to the topic may refer to the necessity of 'competitive bidding' (see Mock Auctions Act 1961) or may refer purely to a particular feature of auction sales, such as the general rule that the offer is made by the bidder and accepted by the auctioneer when he signifies his acceptance by fall of the hammer (see Sale of Goods Act 1979, s 57(2), Appendix 2). For present purposes, a satisfactory a definition as any is to be found in Halsbury:[1] 'An auction is a manner of selling or letting property by bids, usually to the highest bidder by public competition'.[2]

TYPES OF AUCTION

The Halsbury definition above has the virtue of making it clear that an auction 'usually' involves sale to the highest bidder by public competition. The method familiar in the British Isles, involving a system whereby prices are bid upwards until the last bidder eventually succeeds, is not the only method of auctioning. The following alternative methods also exist.

(a) The Dutch auction.This is a descending-price system whereby the auctioneer determines the starting figure and quotes prices at descending intervals until he finds a bidder at a particular price. Quite sophisticated methods exist to effect this scheme which may take those accustomed to the 'English' type of ascending-bid system somewhat by surprise. Whether or not the system results in a better price for the vendor is conjectural and depends upon market conditions. If a bidder is anxious to

1 2 Halsbury's Laws (4th edn) para 701.

2 See also *Frewen v Hays* (1912) 106 LT 516, PC at 518, 'The prices which the public are asked to pay are the highest prices which those who bid can be tempted to offer by the skill and tact of the auctioneer under the excitement of open competition' (per Lord MacNaghten). And in *Bexwell v Christie* (1776) I Cowp 395 at 397 Lord Mansfield asked, 'What is the nature of an auction? It is, that the goods shall go to the highest real bidder.'

secure a lot he will not risk not being the first to shout 'mine' (or otherwise signal acceptance) for fear of losing the lot. Had the bidding been competitive in an upwards direction, competition might have been weak and he might have secured the lot at a less high price. Under this system a bid is normally made orally in the way suggested above, though a more sophisticated system of accepting the auctioneer's offer is by the pressing of electronic buttons which stops a clock at a certain point and can assist with the identification of a buyer where more than one bid is made at almost the same time. This descending-price system emanates from Holland, though the ascending-bid system is now apparently well on the way to replacing it.[3]

(b) A sub-species of the Dutch auction involves a combination of the ascending-bid and descending-bid systems. The economic justification for this hybrid system existed where a precise market level for the lots being sold (e g miscellaneous antiques) could not clearly be established. Here the auction is conducted on an ascending-bid system first, on the understanding that the highest bidder's offer is not accepted unless he remains the highest bidder in the second, or descending, phase of the auction. The method fixes the top level from which the bidding will start in a downward direction. The cumbersome and somewhat time-consuming procedures involved have made this method obsolescent if not quite obsolete on the continent of Europe.[4]

(c) In commodity markets, particularly in the Third World, there are several varieties of essentially ascending-bid systems. The variants involve the method of communicating bids to the auctioneer. Bids may be communicated privately to the auctioneer either by handshake or by a whisper, in ignorance of the competition, and the auctioneer then chooses the highest bidder. The element of open competition is thus missing. (This is also so in the case of 'postal auctions' of, for instance, stamps, but these are more akin to tenders considered below.)

(d) Yet another variety of the ascending-bid auction is one which is combined with a time limit. Bidding must be completed before an interval of time elapses as determined in a specified way. This may be by burning a candle of a certain length, using a sand-glass or a clock. The sale of an estate in England in 1932 was described thus: 'After supper an inch of candle is lit, and the bidding continues until it dies out, the last [and thus highest] bid before the final flicker securing the tenancy for the ensuing year'.[5] It is difficult to see what advantages the setting of a time limit in this way can confer upon the vendor. A skilled auctioneer can effectively control the time that it takes to offer each lot without this device. Its only effect would seem to be to exclude some possible higher bidders who make their offers after the candle has expired. It may now be regarded as an obsolete method, at least in Great Britain.

3 These, and other non-standard forms of auctioning, are more fully discussed in Cassady *Auctions & Auctioneering* University of California Press (1967). There is discussion of an Australian sale after sunset by Dutch auction in *Ex p Hamilton* (1882) 3 LR (NSW) 89.

4 The Court of Appeal, Criminal Division, found it 'difficult, indeed impossible' to envisage a 'system of bidding which involved bidding up and bidding down — Dutch and English — simultaneously' in *R v Pollard* (1983) 148 JP 679, CA. See (1984) 92 Monthly Review 110 and below p 139.

5 Cassady (n 3 above) citing 'A curious survival . . . sale by candle' (1932) XVII Conveyancer (May) 138.

(e) Sealed bid arrangements. Although 'tenders' are not, in popular parlance, regarded as 'auctions', a sale by tender to the highest sealed bidder, the property having been publicly advertised, does comply with the definition advanced above. Equally, the definition cannot apply to the type of tender which is designed to find the lowest bidder, as is the case for tenders for building construction for public authorities. Selling real property by tender is quite common and an important method of disposing of property. Both from the point of view of the vendor and purchaser, there is likely to be more time for the careful consideration of a bid and for decisions as to its acceptance. Depending on the Conditions of Sale,[6] the vendor may not be obliged to accept any particular tender. The method does not, of course, involve 'competitive bidding' quite in the sense used in conventional auctions. One tenderer will not be aware of the level of the bid of his competitors. There will not, therefore, be the identification of the market price on the particular day of the property sale which is a key feature of the conventional auction. On the other hand, a tenderer may well offer either more or less for the property than he would have been obliged to do at a conventional auction. This method of selling property is primarily confined to sales of land (considered in further detail in ch 9). The contractual situation is that a statement inviting tenders is normally not an offer.[7] The person submitting the tender makes the offer, and the acceptance is at the option of the person inviting such tenders.[8]

HISTORY OF AUCTIONS

What follows is necessarily a selective account of a huge subject. The auction, particularly the ascending-bid 'English' auction which is the subject matter of this book, is such a straightforward and obvious way of obtaining money for goods by matching supply and demand at a particular time, that it is not surprising that its ancestry can certainly be traced to antiquity. Herodotus writes that auctions existed at about 500 BC in Babylon, the transaction being primarily concerned with the yearly sale of women of marriageable age. These auctions could apparently work also in an inverse way, unattractive women being assigned to buyers in exchange for a donation by the seller!

On historically firmer ground, there has been considerable juridical investigation of auction sales under Roman law. The Roman auction proceeded in a way familiar to present-day auction-goers. The intended auction was announced publicly by a praeco (herald) and by written proscriptio (notice). The sale would be held in an atrium auctionarium (auction hall). Lots were probably available for prior inspection and the praeco acted as auctioneer, putting up the lots for sale and intimating reserve prices. Eventually the lot would be knocked down to the successful bidder. It is thought that such auctions were held under the ascending-bid system, as the word 'auction' is connected to the Latin roots augere and auctum (to *increase*).

6 See *Spencer v Harding* (1870) LR 5 CP 561, 39 LJCP 332: a circular advertised stock in trade 'for sale by tender' as one lot. It was held that there was no contract to sell to the highest tenderer.
7 See *Spencer v Harding* (1870) LR 5 CP 561, 39 LJCP 332, n 6 above.
8 In June 1984 it was announced in the press that Agnews, the Bond Street picture dealers, had successfully experimented with tenders, involving sealed bids to be opened on a set date, when selling valuable paintings.

Examples are known of auction sales on bankruptcy and to meet state deficits. Roman soldiers allegedly auctioned their loot sub hasta ('under the spear').[9]

The Roman auction sale involved four parties: the dominus, or person on whose behalf the property was sold; the argentarius who organised the sale and in some cases financed it; the praeco in charge of advertising the sale and auctioning the lots; and the emptor, the buyer whose bid was successful. How far the relationships between these parties correspond to those under current English law, particularly the law of agency, is open to some doubt. The praeco *appeared* to be the agent of the dominus, though the law of agency in Roman times was undeveloped. Intermediate parties are thought to have charged a low, flat-rate commission for their services. There is, however, one interesting possible divergence from English law. It is thought that all bidders in succession became conditionally bound to the vendor and could not retract their bids otherwise than in actionable breach of contract. The vendor could, however, refuse to accept a bid.[10]

In England the recorded history of auctions is much more recent.[11] Chattel auctioneering as a profession can be traced back to shortly after the Restoration. Sales of pictures and furniture were held by entrepreneurs in coffee houses, public houses and the like. An early catalogue of February 1689/90 refers to the selling of 'paintings and limnings by auction' at the Barbadoes Coffee House, and to the fact that 'of late the worthy gentlemen who comprised the buyers had both by their presence and custom, promoted and encouraged' the institution of the auction. The notice also refers to the fact that printed Conditions of Sale together with an additional one, namely 'that no Person or Persons shall be admitted to bid for his, or their own Pictures etc' are to be displayed at the place of sale. Another catalogue of a roughly similar date refers to goods being 'exposed to sale, by way of Mineing, on Thursday 12, Friday 13th and Saturday 14th of this instant March, at Mrs Smythers coffee house in Thames Street, by the Custom House'. The reference to 'Mineing' appears to relate to the Dutch-auction method of sale, i e a system of decreasing bids until someone called out 'mine' (discussed above).

In his diary for 3 September 1662, Samuel Pepys refers to the 'candle' method of limiting the time for bids (also discussed above). He states: 'After dinner, we met and sold the Weymouth Successe and Fellowship Hulkes,[12] where pleasant to see how backward men are at first to bid and yet, when the candle is going out, how they bawl and dispute afterwards who bid the most first.' Apparently the successful bidder held his fire until he observed the smoke descending, which was an indication that the candle was about to expire!

Auctions of land appear to have become established at least by 1739 when an advertisement appeared in the London Evening Post for the sale of a

9 See in particular J A C Thomas 'The Auction Sale in Roman Law' (1957) I Jur R (April) 43, and T Frank (ed) *An Economic Survey of Ancient Rome* vol V: *Rome and Italy of the Empire* (1940) John Hopkins Press.

10 See J A C Thomas (n 9 above) at 65-6.

11 A useful source of information on the origins of sales by auction is Peter Ash 'The First Auctioneer', centenary supplement to (1958) 33 E G (3 May), to which article the authors are much indebted. See also D Baldock 'Focus on Auctions — A History of the London Auction House' (1983) 268 EG 458; and A Bailey 'The Learned Babble' (1983) 268 EG 464, in which George Robbins (born 1777) is regarded as 'the father of estate-agency English' — a doubtful honour. He was a successor to Christopher Cock's practice.

12 These were ships.

bankrupt's estate, including two houses at Paddington. If this indeed was amongst the first land auctions, the first such auctioneer was one Christopher Cock of the Great Piazza, Covent Garden. Certainly by 1740 he was advertising a series of landed estates to be sold 'on Whitsun Monday at Three in the Afternoon'.[13]

It is from the middle of the eighteenth century that perhaps the two best-known auction houses in London can trace their beginnings.

Sotheby's can trace its beginnings to the 1730s, the first recorded auction taking place in 1744. The founder was Samuel Baker, a bookseller and publisher. In 1778 on Baker's death his nephew John Sotheby was taken into partnership. Between 1861 and 1924 the firm expanded under the style of Sotheby, Wilkinson & Hodge, then becoming Sotheby & Co and then, from 1975, Sotheby Parke Bernet & Co.[14] Throughout the nineteenth century a wide variety of articles was sold, including books, pictures, jewellery, coins, wine and furniture. Removal of currency restrictions which existed until the mid-1950s enabled Sotheby's to pay the proceeds of auction sales in the consignor's own currency, and this in turn resulted in an expansion of business. As with the other great auction houses, turnover also expanded with the internationalisation of the fine arts auction market in particular. Great paintings tend to hold individual records for the sale of any type of single article. A record was established by a sale in 1983 when a consortium of West German public authorities paid £8·14 m at Sotheby's in London for a twelfth-century illuminated manuscript of the Gospels, a work commissioned in the 1170s by Henry the Lion, Duke of Saxony and Bavaria, and regarded as the most important surviving document of German medieval history. It is interesting to note that the buying consortium commissioned *two* of London's best-known antiquarian booksellers to bid on its behalf, thus reducing the risk of competition.[15]

Christie, Manson & Woods Ltd (Christie's) can be traced back to its founder James Christie (1730-1803), a Scotsman who established his auction house in Pall Mall in 1766. There were thought to be some 60 other auctioneers active in London at the time. Christie's 'Great Rooms' soon became a fashionable meeting place in London, and as he specialised in fine art auctioneering, the meeting place also for painters such as Gainsborough and Reynolds. He conducted studio sales not only of pictures by these artists but also sold many important collections belonging to British and French aristocrats. In the late

13 The first reported case concerning auctions, or rather an agent's failure to hold one of real property when so instructed by the vendor, appears to be *Daniel v Adams* (1764) Amb 495. The buyer was in these circumstances held disentitled to specific performance of the privately negotiated contract (see further ch 3). Another interesting economic indication of the growth of auction sales was the introduction of an indirect tax on auctions and sales in 1779.

14 For an extensive account of Sotheby's history, see Frank Hermann *Sotheby's* (1980) Chatto & Windus. 'Sotheby's' is now a private company after a successful takeover by an American consortium in 1983.

15 By April 1985 the world record for a single painting was the £8.1 m paid at Christie's, London, for a Mantegna. A further UK record of a different kind was established by Christie's (London) on 3 July 1984 in respect of the sale on that day of 71 old master drawings owned by the Duke of Devonshire. With the 8 per cent buyer's premium, £21 179 880 was realised. On the net sum it was estimated that the Duke could expect to pay capital gains tax of £5 881 620, thus realising net £13 729 380. Previously, the British Museum had unsuccessfully offered £5 250 000. The world record for a single collection was the £26.5 m paid at Sotheby's, New York, for the Gould collection of Impressionists, in April 1985.

eighteenth century some collections were auctioned following the execution of their ill-fated owners by the French Revolutionary Tribunal. The firm moved in 1823 to its present premises at King Street, London, while the partnerships with William Manson and Thomas Woods (1859) established the firm's present full name. In the case of both Sotheby's and Christie's, from starting as enterprises by single proprietors they became partnerships and then limited companies. More recently these companies went public (in 1973 Christie's offered 37 per cent of its shares on the stock market),[16] though Sotheby's reverted to a private company in 1983.

A third eminent firm, Phillips, Son & Neale can also trace its ancestry back to the late eighteenth century. The founder, Harry Phillips, had been James Christie's head clerk and he established himself on his own in 1796. He, too, proved a successful entrepreneur having by the time he died in 1840 dealt with goods belonging to Beau Brummell, the Duke of Buckingham, Marie Antoinette, Napoleon, Talleyrand and, in 1823, with the sale of the contents of Fonthill Abbey, the home of William Beckford (the sale taking 30 days). The firm had somewhat mixed fortunes until after the second world war when it was once again built up by the acquisition of Glendining & Co (specialising in coins and medals) and Puttick & Simpson (a firm specialising in the sale of musical instruments). As with Sotheby's and Christie's, Phillips is now an international auction house.

In 1983-84 the world turnover of Sotheby's was £401 m, an increase of 47 per cent on the previous year. The turnover of Christie's was £350.6 m, an increase of 53 per cent over the previous year; and that of Phillips, £44.1 m, an increase of 16 per cent over the previous year.[17]

Although these three firms have been singled out as being perhaps the best known in the UK in terms of fine art etc auctioneers, the directory in the *Auction Companion*[18] makes it clear that there is a large number of other very well-established auction-houses both in London and scattered throughout the UK, many of which can trace their history to the late eighteenth or early nineteenth century. These firms normally advertise in the local press or, on special occasions, in the national press. The *Antiques Trade Gazette* and *Art & Antiques Weekly* also carry extensive auction advertisements. Auction sales of land are described and advertised in the *Estates Gazette*, and *The Valuer* also contains much useful professional information.

As already indicated, displayed Conditions of Sale were from earliest times an important feature of the auction. Typical Conditions of Sale in the eighteenth century included at least the following six points:

(a) The buyer is the highest bidder, disputes as to his identity being resolved by putting the goods up for sale again.

16 Christie, Manson & Woods Ltd is one of a number of wholly-owned subsidiaries of Christie's International plc.
17 In 1984 Sotheby's achieved sales of £477 m and Chistie's, £373 m.
18 Daniel and Catherine Leab *Auction Companion* (1981) Macmillan, this being a most valuable guide both to the auction-houses that exist in the larger countries of the world and containing a layman's guide to selling or buying at auction. See also Klaster (ed) *Going, Going, Gone* (1982) Chartwell Books, a practical auction guide which also contains an international directory.

(b) The amounts by which another's bid may be advanced is stipulated by reference to a minimum sum.
(c) There is some warranty as to the condition of the goods, in earlier times this being more absolute than is the case today.
(d) Buyers are required to give their names and make a deposit if demanded.
(e) Goods must be cleared within a stipulated period, e g three days, at the buyer's expense.
(f) The offer is made to execute bids on behalf of buyers unable to attend the sale.[19]

ECONOMIC CONSIDERATIONS IN AUCTION SALES

Our main concern here is to analyse, in layman's terms, the comparative economic efficiency of selling land or chattels by auction as opposed to the normal alternative of some variety of private treaty sale.

With regard to private treaty sales of goods, typically they can either be on a take-it-or-leave-it basis, for instance in the supermarket where there is no opportunity to bargain with regard to the price, or where the pricing policy involves negotiation between buyer and seller. In the case of land to be sold by private treaty, for instance, the usual practice is for the estate agent to state either a particular price, or to use some vaguer expression such as 'offers around £50 000'. Following this advertisement there is likely to occur a series of offers and counter-offers until eventually a price acceptable to both buyer and seller is reached and a contract formed.

By contrast, if the auction is chosen as the means of disposal, competition between bidders for a particular lot is focussed at a particular time and place, supply and demand are at that time adjusted until they are in equilibrium by the emergence of the highest bid, and the sale is concluded. The price determinant here appears to be set by the buyer. The seller can have, however, a residual control by fixing a reserve price below which he is not prepared to sell. This will normally attract a penalty in the form of a commission to the auctioneer on a lower scale than if the buyer were successful, and this penalty tends to deter the fixing of too high a reserve. What the highest bidder will bid may vary from time to time and place to place even assuming the goods are identical. The presence of two or more eager potential buyers will force up the price of a lot beyond what might be regarded its 'market' value.[20] It is also well-known that a favourable ambiance, for instance the sale of the contents of a stately house in situ, may engender an atmosphere where psychological rather than economic reasons can predominate in fixing the price of what might not necessarily be particularly meritorious lots on their own. (A historic chattels sale which attracted high prices and total proceeds of £6 389 933 was that of the Rothschild-Rosebery Estate at Mentmore in 1977.)

19 See James Brough *Auction!* (1963), cited in Cassady (above, n 3).
20 Equally 'an auction which only produces one bid is not necessarily an indication that the true market value has been achieved' (per Lord Templeman in *T Kwong Lam v Wong Chit Sen* [1983] 3 All ER 54, PC at 60). See also *Davis v Artingstall* (1880) 49 LJ Ch 609, 42 LT 507.

In terms of general economic efficiency, if a particular selling scheme maximises returns and minimises the effort expended by buyers and sellers, its utility will be the greater. Whether a sale by auction will be the most appropriate way of disposing of particular goods may well depend on their type. Auctions of commodities in bulk are common throughout the world. As a means of market distribution this is obviously to be preferred in most cases over the alternative of the vendor seeking out individual buyers for small lots. The effort expended in the latter exercise would cost more than the possible difference between the aggregate prices so obtained and the price obtained at one point of time at the auction. Auctions are also a highly effective method of disposing of property for which there is no 'exchange' or readily available market. A private vendor of, let us say, antique furniture or antiquarian books or valuable paintings may approach individual dealers or retailers. However, it is difficult for him to judge whether or not he has got the best possible offer and the process can be time-consuming and expensive. The disincentive to him of the auction room is the auctioneer's commission, which varies between 10 and 20 per cent in the UK. In addition to this, the buyer's price may be depressed by the likelihood that under the Conditions of Sale he will also have to pay a 'premium' on top of the hammer price. Nevertheless, the auction's disadvantages may be outweighed by a surer sale. The facility is particularly useful to the private vendor or personal representatives of a deceased's estate. Some auctioneers refuse to accept lots other than from private sources.

Auctions of land provide a good barometer of the economics of this method of selling generally.[1] It is generally recognised that the auction is more appropriate in times of economic boom than of recession. Larger estates which claim to be unique as to their characteristics, rather than a standard semi-detached or terraced house, are also more likely to be suitable for auction. Potential buyers may be limited, but their funds may not be so limited and market value can perhaps be more accurately established on this basis. From the seller's point of view, the saving of time is an important consideration. From the buyer's point of view, though, auctions of real property can have substantial disadvantages. He is well advised to commission a survey and must do his local searches and pre-contract work without being assured that he will be the successful bidder. Furthermore in many cases a mortgage must be arranged in anticipation of a successful bid, and this is not in practice an easy or an inexpensive process. Once he has successfully bid for the land, the buyer must be prepared to pay a deposit of 10 per cent at the auction and complete within 28 days thereof. It is only rarely that the sale can be rescinded after the auction. Land auctions are discussed in more detail in ch 9.

Within the last two decades, auctions in England have been used to dispose of a wider variety of goods than formerly. Two examples may be given. Both in the United States and in the United Kingdom the growth of used-car auctions has been marked. In the USA the bulk of second-hand automobiles are sold in this way and used-car prices tend to be based on auction quotations. In England, such groups as British Car Auctions or Central Motor Auctions have streamlined the auction procedure for used cars so as to protect as far as possible the private motorist. It is estimated that in 1982 one in five of the

1 See 'Return of the Auctioneer' (1983) 268 EG 470 which takes a bullish view of the land auction market and refers to the era of the 'superauction' where real estate may be put up in lots of 200 over two days with a total realisation of several million pounds.

750 000 vehicles sold at auction in Britain was purchased by a member of the general public. 'End of the line' cars can also be auctioned by their manufacturers, as can showroom stock of dealers which has remained unsold for, say, 60 days and which is becoming a cash-flow burden.[2]

Another noticeable development in the UK recently has been the emergence of auction sales of plant and machinery. Typically, if an engineering company desires to move to new premises an auction of its machinery, machine tools, office furniture, factory equipment and motor vehicles which are surplus to requirements will be held on the site. An important Condition of Sale imposes an obligation on the buyer to remove lots from the site not later than the stipulated day, and failure to do this is penalised by heavy per diem storage charges. Plant auctions have obvious applications to firms with cash-flow difficulties who are wishing to turn their stock into cash prior to a liquidation. (The alternative of finding a purchaser for the shares, which will in part reflect an estimate of the value of the stock, can be a much less certain operation.) This type of sale, together with the Conditions of Sale applicable thereto, is considered further in ch 10.

2 See (1983) Times, 20 May p 23.

Chapter 2

Auctioneers: restrictions on trading

The profession of auctioneer is, as compared with the other professions today, relatively uncontrolled. The law does not require any minimum qualifications for practice, membership of a professional body is not obligatory, and there are no compulsory accounting rules designed to protect 'consumers'. However, there are some general restrictions on trading in connection with the form of business association utilised and as regards licence requirements.

QUALIFICATIONS

There is no requirement as to any particular qualification for practice as an auctioneer, nor is an auctioneer required to join any professional association. However, most auctioneers do in fact belong to one of the main bodies[1] and these have academic training programmes which, combined with relevant work experience, lead to professional qualifications. The absence of any minimum qualification requirement is perhaps surprising these days and, in the case of estate agent auctioneers, a change may be in the offing. The Estate Agents Act 1979[2] for the first time provides some statutory regulation of estate agents. Section 22 states (so far as is material):

> (1) the Secretary of State may by regulations made by statutory instrument make provision for ensuring that persons engaged in estate agency work satisfy minimum standards of competence.
> (2) . . . the regulations may . . .
> (a) prescribe professional or academic qualifications which shall also be taken to be evidence of competence;
> (b) designate any body or persons as a body which may itself specify professional qualifications the holding of which is to be taken as evidence of competence.

This provision is part of a package of controls over the activities of estate agents laid down by this Act. It may be that the consumer considerations

1 The main bodies are the Royal Institution of Chartered Surveyors; the Incorporated Society of Valuers and Auctioneers, the Rating and Valuation Association; and the Central Association of Agricultural Valuers.

2 The Act provides for the Director General of Fair Trading to prohibit unfit estate agents from carring on business. It also requires estate agents to keep separate client accounts and to maintain insurance cover against failure to account for a client's money. (For the sections dealing with accounting regulations, see Appendix 2.)

which gave rise to this statutory intervention are less pressing in the case of auctioneers and there is at present no move to provide similar controls, which are effected ultimately through the criminal law, for auctioneers generally.

LICENSING

The major prerequisite for acting as an auctioneer used to be that of possession of a licence. The Auctioneers Act 1845 required, save for special excepted cases provided for in s 5, every person 'who engages or carries on the trade or business of an Auctioneer' to take out a licence, renewable annually and costing £10.[3] Failure to produce the licence could result in imprisonment for up to one month. These provisions were more of a revenue-collecting device than any attempt at regulating the profession and they were repealed finally by the Finance Act 1949. However, one important section survives, relating to display of names (dealt with later in this chapter). Whilst no *general* trading licence is now required, an auctioneer must have a licence or be registered in order to effect sales of certain types of goods, outlined below.

(a) *Excise licences.* Certain commodities including wine, spirits and tobacco can only be sold if the seller possesses an excise licence. Until recently there were concessions obviating this requirement where an auctioneer sold by sample goods for an owner who held a requisite licence in respect of premises in the same locality. Further, and more generally, the Commissioners of Customs and Excise had power to dispense with the requirement of a licence where an auctioneer sold for a private person otherwise than by way of trade. These concessions, provided by the Customs and Excise Act 1952 and consolidated in the Customs and Excise Management Act 1979, s 105(2) and (3), were removed in 1982 by the Finance Act 1981. As from 1 July 1982, auctioneers selling such goods require the appropriate excise licence.[4]

(b) *Firearm registration.* Problems relating to sales of firearms at auction are considered in detail in ch 8. Registration as a firearms dealer is obviated if the auctioneer obtains a permit provided by the Chief Officer of Police in the area in which the auction is held. Whilst a certificate is normally required in order to possess a firearm or ammunition, none is needed by an auctioneer possessing such in the ordinary course of his business.[5]

(c) *Export licences.* The obtaining of these is an obligation of the exporter of specified goods, though this has implications for auctioneers who sell them to the exporter. They are considered below in ch 7.

DISPLAY OF NAME AND OTHER NOTICES

As mentioned above, one provision of the Auctioneers Act 1845 remains in force and is of practical importance. Section 7 states:

3 Auctioneers Act 1845, s 4.
4 Section 11(2)(a) and Sch 8, para 5 of the Finance Act 1981.
5 Firearms Act 1968, s 9.

> And be it enacted, that every Auctioneer, before beginning any Auction, shall affix or suspend, or cause to be affixed or suspended, a Ticket or Board containing his true and full Christian and Surname and Residence painted, printed or written in large letters publicly visible and legible in some conspicuous Part of the Room or Place where the Auction is held so that all Persons may easily read the same, and shall also keep such Ticket or Board so affixed or suspended during the whole Time of such Auction being held; and if any Auctioneer begins any Auction or acts as Auctioneer at any Auction, in any Room or Place where his Name and Residence is not so painted or written on a Ticket or Board so affixed or suspended, and kept affixed or suspended as aforesaid, he shall forfeit for every such Offence the Sum of Twenty Pounds.

The fine has been increased to £100 by the general 'inflation allowance' provision in the Criminal Law Act 1977.[6]

In addition, notices must also be displayed containing copies of the Auctions (Bidding Agreements) Acts 1927 and 1969. The effect of these provisions are considered in chs 8 and 9.

BUSINESS ASSOCIATION

There is no restriction as to the *type* of business association (i e sole trader, partnership or corporation) in which the auctioneer may practise. Major firms such as Christie's and Sotheby's are companies, but rules of professional conduct of professional bodies such as the RICS and the ISVA place restrictions on practising with limited liability and it is more common to find auctioneers practising in partnerships.

With regard to partnerships, certain restrictions are laid down as to numbers. Under s 434 of the Companies Act 1948 no partnership could be formed consisting of more than 20 members. However, the position was alleviated by the Companies Act 1967 and regulations made thereunder. Since 1968 there has been no such restriction on the size of partnerships of auctioneers, provided that not less than three-quarters of the partners are members of either the Royal Institution of Chartered Surveyors, the Chartered Land Agents Society, the Chartered Auctioneers and Estate Agents' Institute, or the Incorporated Society of Valuers and Auctioneers.[7] In this way a person dealing with the larger firms of auctioneers (i e exceeding 20 partners) will be assured that a considerable degree of professional qualification exists within it.

The keynote of partnership is that its members, unlike members of a registered company, have unlimited liability. Each partner is jointly and separately responsible for the whole of the partnership debts and obligations. However, since 1907 it has been possible to create a hybrid animal whereby some partners do enjoy limited liability. Under the Limited Partnership Act 1907 a firm can be formed in which one or more of the partners are designated 'general partners' liable for all the debts of the firm whilst the remainder may have liability limited to the extent of their capital contributions. Where this form of association is employed (and it has not proved a popular mode) there

6 See s 31(6), and Criminal Justice Act 1982, s 46. The fine is on level 2 of the scale.
7 See now Companies Act 1985, s 716; Partnership (Unrestricted Size) Regulations, SI 1968/1222.

is again a general ceiling as to numbers of members fixed at 20. However, a second category of dispensation is provided to auctioneers forming limited partnerships whereby the number may exceed 20 as long as two requirements are satisfied: first, not less than three-quarters of the partners must be members of either the RICS or the ISVA; and second, at least three-quarters of the partners must be general partners.[8] The Limited Partnership Act 1907 requires such firms to be registered and provides for the register to be available for public inspection.

FIRM NAME

Until recently it was necessary for every firm which carried on business under a name which did not consist of the names of the sole trader or partnership members to register the true surnames of those members in a Business Names Registry. This was required by the Registration of Business Names Act 1916. The Act was, however, much honoured in its non-observance and over a period the registry came to contain a large element of stale information as firms ceased trading. The government decided to cut its losses and the Act was repealed by the Companies Act 1981. With the abolition of the registry the desideratum of providing information as to the identity of partners is achieved by a self-regulating system. Now s 4 of the Business Names Act 1985 places a duty on each partner to state the name and address of every partner in the firm on all business letters, written orders, bills and the like. Where the number of partners exceeds 20, the names need not be given if the document recites the address of the firm's principal place of business and states that the names are listed and available there. A notice containing this information is required to be prominently displayed on the business premises. Finally, written notice of these particulars must be supplied on request to 'any person with whom anything is done or discussed in the course of business, who requests them'.

The new regime is enforced by a combination of criminal and civil sanctions, the former consisting of fines and the latter taking the form of a disability: the court is empowered[9] to dismiss an action brought by the firm if the defendant shows that he has suffered loss as a result of the plaintiff firm's breach of these obligations.

Despite these changes in the law, it appears that the business community is not convinced that the abolition of the register was a wise move. The London Chamber of Commerce and Industry set up its own private business names registry in 1982.

Where the firm trades as a company then the company is obliged to have its name:

(a) painted or affixed on the outside of every office or place in which the business is carried on, in a conspicuous position and in legible letters;
(b) engraved legibly on its seal; and

8 Limited Partnerships (Unrestricted Size) No 1 Regulations, SI 1971/782.
9 Business Names Act 1985, s 5.

(c) mentioned legibly in all business letters, publications etc.[10]

If the company is limited, the name includes the word 'limited' which must therefore similarly be published.

Where a company carries on a business under a name which does not consist solely of its corporate name it must again in all business correspondence and on a prominent notice at all business outlets display its corporate name and an address at which documents may be served on it.[11]

10 Companies Act 1985, part XI, ch 1.
11 Business Names Act 1985, s 4.

Chapter 3

Capacity and authority

INTRODUCTORY

An auctioneer is a particular kind of agent. Pre-eminently he is employed[1] by the vendor of property to effect a sale, but frequently, an auctioneer may also act as agent of the purchaser for limited purposes. In the course of transacting his business he may additionally act in some other legal capacity, e g as bailee with a duty to care for the property in his possession.[2] The fact that an auctioneer may also act as agent for the purchaser does not, it seems, prevent him from selling his own property and thus acting as a principal; as he is not an agent of the purchaser for all purposes, no conflict of interest arises.[3] However, in this chapter we are principally concerned with an auctioneer's position as agent of the vendor. (The ambit of the auctioneer's authority as agent of the purchaser is considered in ch 5 below).

There are few restrictions placed upon carrying on the business of auctioneer, and no special formal qualifications are required. The only limitations are those arising from the law of contract and certain general statutory provisions relating to companies, partnerships and the like.[4] Indeed, whereas there are factors which may render a principal incapable of contracting, e g infancy, the same defect in an agent will not prevent that agent from concluding a valid contract between his principal and a third party. The explanation is that the agent is regarded as a mere conduit through which a principal acts so that the only contractual capacity that is relevant is that of the principal himself.[5] Of course, one must distinguish between an agent's capacity to be constituted an agent and his capacity to contract for a principal once so constituted.

1 This word is not used here as a term of art. However, it is said in Halsbury that the agency of auctioneer is a true employment, and it has been held that he is employed not as a servant but rather as an independent contractor. *Walker v Crabb* (1917) 61 Sol Jo 219 at 220.

2 See e g *Williams v Millington* (1788) 1 Hy Bl 81. His right of possession also gives the auctioneer a lien over the goods for his charges and commission; see ch 4.

3 *Flint v Woodin* (1852) 9 Hare 618, 22 LJ Ch 92, though when selling as a principal he cannot sign the memorandum of sale as agent of the purchaser. However the auctioneer now probably owes a duty of disclosure by virtue of the Estate Agents Act 1979, s 21.

4 See generally, 2 Halsbury's Laws (4th edn) paras 702-706; and see ch 2.

5 In such a situation, however, the agent will not be liable *personally* on the contract and a third party will have to look exclusively to the principal. On the personal contractual liability of auctioneers to third parties, see ch 5.

AUTHORITY

Agency has been defined as:[6]

> The relationship that exists between two persons when one, called the *agent*, is considered in law to represent the other, called the *principal*, in such a way as to be able to affect the principal's legal position in respect of strangers to the relationship by the making of contracts for the disposition of property.

Thus we are concerned with a tripartite situation, and with the rights and duties inter se of these three parties. The pivotal concept which determines these rights and duties is *authority*. Only if an agent has authority will his acts bring about the desired relationship between the principal and the third party: in the case of an auction, the contract of sale. If the auctioneer exceeds his authority, the vendor will not be bound to the purchaser but the purchaser may then be able to recover from the auctioneer for breach of warranty of authority — i e for breach of a contractually binding promise as to the extent of his authority. Sometimes an agent will act outside his *actual* authority but the law nevertheless binds the principal to the third party; in such circumstances the principal will have recourse against the agent. Writers have traditionally regarded authority as the key concept by which to explain an agent's power to bring about a contract between his principal and a third party. It may be regarded as a somewhat artificial use of the term where the principal is held bound not because he did in fact empower his agent so to act, but because his actions merely led the third party to believe that the agent was so invested. Nevertheless it is convenient to explain and analyse the powers of an agent in terms of authority and, before examining the authority of auctioneers, we shall briefly outline the types of authority with which an agent may be clothed.

Varieties of authority

Having said that authority is a central concept, it needs to be added that classification of the varieties of authority is attended by difficulty and dispute. No two writers seem to agree, and the position is not helped by the looseness with which judges frequently use the terms. What follows must be regarded therefore as an attempt at providing a working classification but not, necessarily, a reconciliation of the various academic views.

There are essentially two kinds of authority, within which may be found sub-species. Authority may be:

(a) *actual* or *real*; or it may be
(b) *apparent* or *ostensible*.

Actual authority

Actual authority of an agent is that authority which he is *expressly* given.

6 Fridman *Law of Agency* (5th edn, 1983) Butterworths, p 9.

Express authority will usually present no difficulty. If the agent is employed under a contract, as is usually the case today, the court will discover the authority by construing the contract, applying the ordinary rules of construction in order to ascertain the intention of the parties. A helpful definition of 'actual' authority is provided by Diplock L J in *Freeman & Lockyer (a firm) v Buckhurst Park Properties (Mangal) Ltd*:[7]

> An 'actual' authority is a legal relationship between principal and agent created by a consensual agreement . . . Its scope is to be ascertained by applying ordinary principles of construction of contracts, including any proper implications from the express words used, the usages of the trade, or the course of business between the parties.

From this it will be seen that in addition to that which has been expressed, the agent will be invested with such power as may be *implied*. Thus implied authority is a sub-species of express authority. Implied authority probably encompasses those things which are incidental or reasonably necessary to the carrying out of that which is expressly authorised. An aspect of this may include usual or customary authority, namely that which an agent of that type normally has. Examples would probably be the auctioneer's power to sign the memorandum relating to a sale of land or to receive the deposit moneys. The first is probably implied in the sense of being necessary to the main purpose of effecting the sale. The second is probably better regarded as usual or customary. It must be emphasised that this authority is actual or real – the agent does in fact possess it. A difficulty arises here if a principal in fact restricts the agent's authority but fails to give notice to third parties of this fact. In such a case the principal will be bound to the third party; the law regards the agent as nevertheless possessing the authority. To regard the authority in this situation as implied and therefore actual, requires a straining of language. The alternative is to regard the authority as falling within the second category, namely apparent authority; the principal is bound because his omission to provide notice of the restriction of the authority that such an agent normally possesses, makes it *appear* as though the agent is so possessed.

Apparent authority

Before returning to this problem, we must outline the ambit of apparent authority. Apparent authority is the antithesis of actual authority in that the agent *in fact* has no authority but in law is regarded as being empowered to bind the principal and third party. It arises out of the conduct of the principal which amounts to a repesentation that the agent has authority. Where a third party acts upon such a representation, the principal is bound.[8] An example relating to the creation of the agency of an auctioneer was given by Lord Ellenborough C J in the old case of *Pickering v Busk*:[9]

> I cannot subscribe to the doctrine, that a broker's engagements are necessarily and in all cases limited to his actual authority . . . it is clear that he may bind his principal

7 [1964] 1 All ER 630, CA at 644.
8 *Bowstead on Agency* (14th edn, 1976), Sweet & Maxwell, ch 3. And see *Freeman & Lockyer (a firm) v Buckhurst Park Properties (Mangal) Ltd*, above.
9 (1812) 15 East 38 at 43.

> within the limits of the authority with which he has been apparently clothed by the principal . . . and there would be no safety in mercantile transactions if he could not . . . if one sends goods to an auction-room can it be supposed that he sent them thither merely for safe custody?

In this case Lord Ellenborough began his judgment with the conclusion that the agent had 'an implied authority to sell' but the case is, it is suggested, an example of apparent authority. Fridman[10] argues that apparent authority only arises where there is no express agency at all as mentioned above. Suppose that it is usual for an auctioneer to collect the deposit on a sale but that in fact the principal has instructed his agent not to collect the deposit, but to ensure that such be paid direct to him or, say, his solicitor. And suppose that he fails properly to notify potential buyers by for example, appropriate notice in the auction particulars. If a buyer pays the deposit to the auctioneer who then absconds, the principal will wish to deny that the payment to the auctioneer discharges such a buyer. It is clear that it does; or, to put it another way, the principal is bound. In such an instance it matters to the buyer not one jot whether the explanation is that the auctioneer had usual (implied) or apparent authority. Nor is it clear that it matters in practice vis-à-vis the principal and agent. So long as an agent acts within his actual authority, it cannot be said against him that he is in breach of contract. However, if he in fact exceeds his express instructions, the mere application of the term 'implied' to the authority he has exercised will not prevent his acts from amounting to a breach of contract. Moreover, an agent who acts within his authority is entitled to be indemnified by his principal against all losses and liabilities properly incurred by him in the execution of his authority. It cannot be supposed that an agent acting in defiance of his express instructions could enforce such an indemnity.

It may be, therefore, that arguments about the proper classification of these varieties of authority are purely academic. Be that as it may, it is suggested that in the example of a restriction upon the usual authority of an agent, we are dealing with apparent authority. The principal is liable because he has (by omission) held out his agent as having the usual authority without restriction. Fridman[11] counters: 'But in the cases under discussion the agent is *in fact*, not by virtue of an estoppel, an agent. His authority is *actual* not apparent even though in part it may be implied and not express.' This seems (with respect) to confuse two separate points: the agent with restricted usual authority is, it is argued, an agent in fact – that is not in dispute – but that does not mean that his authority, or all of it, must needs be actual. There is no reason why an actual agent may have both actual *and* some ostensible authority. Bowstead,[12] on the other hand, suggests that there is a strong case for treating usual authority as a third, separate form of authority, neither actual nor apparent, but concludes that the case law does not justify such a conclusion.

There are also other situations where an agency relationship may arise, and these are described below.

10 Fridman (n 6 above) p 60f.
11 Fridman (n 6 above) p 65.
12 Above, n 8.

Agency of necessity

This arises by operation of law. It may effect either the creation or the enlargement of an agency relationship and in the latter case clearly involves the question of authority. The classic situation in which it arises is that of a carrier of perishable goods who sells them when they are uncollected. The essence is some emergency relating to the goods coupled with an impracticality for the agent to communicate with his principal.[13]

Where the necessity enlarges the authority of the agent, it might be argued that it is really a question of implied authority to act in the emergency, but this may be questioned. It seems better to regard it as a separate species of authority created by law.[14]

Ratification[15]

Finally, for the sake of completeness we mention ratification by a principal of a hitherto unauthorised act. Ratification has the effect of giving ex post facto authority to the agent and is thus equivalent to antecedent authority. Some writers have doubted whether ratification can be regarded as consensual. Three conditions must be satisfied according to the classic explanation given by Wright J in *Firth v Staines*,[16] namely: (a) the agent whose act is sought to be ratified must have purported to act for the principal; (b) at the time the act was done the agent must have had a competent principal; and (c) at the time of the ratification the principal must be legally capable of doing the act himself.

THE AUTHORITY OF AUCTIONEERS

Having outlined the varieties of authority, it is proposed to detail the auctioneer's authority. Of course, as regards express authority this will depend upon his actual instructions. In this regard the courts will simply construe the agreement using the usual tools to ascertain what was intended. It is not clear whether the courts are astute to construe express authority generously or narrowly. It was suggested in one case[17] that, as a general rule, a liberal construction would be applied. However, in the Irish case of *Hawkins v Rogers*[18] it was argued by the purchaser of a race horse that the horse was sold with its engagements. The purchaser was the partner of the vendor and argued that it was understood by both of them that the horses were being sold with their engagements and that this factor was crucial. The vendor intended,

13 See eg *Springer v Great Western Rly Co* [1921] 1 KB 257, 89LJKB 1010, CA. And see *Sweeting v Turner* (1871) LR 7 QB 310, 41LJQB 58 where an auctioneer's claim to an agency of necessity re goods threatened by distress failed because although left on the vendor's premises they had become the property of the purchaser.

14 See *China Pacific SA v Food Corpn of India, The Winson* [1982] AC939, [1981] 3 All ER 688, HL and see the discussion in Fridman (n 6 above) p 120.

15 See generally *Bowstead on Agency* (n 8 above) arts 14-20.

16 [1897] 2 QB 70 at 75.

17 *Pole v Leask* (1860) 28 Beav 562, 29 LJ Ch 888.

18 [1951] IR 48.

however, to sell without engagements. The court held that the auctioneer is primarily an agent of the vendor and as such he sells what the vendor intends to sell and no more, in the absence of anything to the contrary. This suggests a somewhat restrictive approach. The case involved a claim by the purchaser against the vendor. Where there is a claim by the vendor as principal against his agent for exceeding his authority, the courts might take a more liberal approach where instructions are ambiguous. However, it is obviously sensible for the auctioneer to ensure that he properly understands his instructions and seeks clarification when necessary.

Subject to this kind of issue, there is little of a general nature that can be said about the content of express authority and we shall, therefore, concentrate upon consideration of various specific matters and on the meaning of certain instructions and the potential ambit of the implied and/or usual authority with which an auctioneer may be endowed.

Sale by auction

As we have seen,[19] if a person sends goods to an auctioneer, he will have apparent authority to auction those goods. More usually of course, his authority will be express. No doubt also those instructions will usually be explicit about the nature of the sale to be undertaken. But if it is sought to give an auctioneer authority to sell otherwise than by auction, e g by private treaty, perhaps after a lot has failed to reach its reserve price at the auction, such power must be given expressly. Authority to sell otherwise than by auction will not be implied. The classic case is *Daniel v Adams*,[20] decided in the eighteenth century, where a husband and wife instructed their steward to sell certain properties by auction and fixed a reserve of £120 per property. The agent believed he had power to sell privately so long as he achieved the reserve price, and he sold to the plaintiff for £150. Mrs Adams refused to effect the sale; she had given another first refusal on the property if it was sold privately. In an action by Daniel for specific performance of the contract of sale, the court held Mrs Adams not bound, the auctioneer lacking authority to sell otherwise than by auction. Similarly in *Marsh v Jelf*,[1] which involved a claim by an auctioneer for commission when he sold privately after the property had failed to achieve its reserve at the auction, it was denied that any such sale would bind the vendor in the absence of specific instructions and that there was no custom that commission was payable in such circumstances.

There are two decisions which might, at first sight, suggest that an auctioneer may have implied authority to sell otherwise than by auction. In *Else v Barnard*[2] there was a sale ordered by the court. The various lots were subject to secret reserves and the auctioneer was instructed that if they failed to achieve these prices they were to be bought in by him for the parties interested therein. The first lot did not reach its reserve and was bought in. Thereafter the successful bidder of a second lot discovered the reserve on the first. He agreed to buy it. It appears that this agreement was struck after the auction but before the

19 See above, pp 17-18.
20 (1764) Amb 495. And see also *Re Loft* (1844) 2 LTOS 397.
1 (1862) 3 F&F 234.
2 (1860) 28 Beav 228, 29 LJ Ch 729.

auctioneer had in fact left the rostrum. Subsequently the purchaser repudiated his purchase of the first lot and sought to resist the vendor's claim on the grounds that the auctioneer lacked authority to sell otherwise than by open bidding. The court held the sale to be good. However, it cannot be said that *Else v Barnard* is authority for the proposition that an auctioneer may, in the absence of express instructions, sell otherwise than by auction, because it is clear that the court (a) declined to decide whether this had in fact been a sale by auction, and (b) in any event held that the purchaser's actions prevented him from denying that it was. Romilly M R said:[3]

> I do not go into the question whether that is a sale by auction or not, but I think it is impossible for [the buyer] to say that it is not to be treated as a sale by auction for he signs a bidding paper by which he agrees that it shall be so treated; it is impossible for him afterwards to say he is not bound by it.

The second case, *Bousfield v Hodges*,[4] decided a few years later, similarly involved an auction sanctioned by the court. This was in order to bring about an end to litigation by compromise. An auctioneer was instructed to sell at a stated reserve. However, there were no bids and the auctioneer sold by private treaty at the reserve price. Once again the purchaser resiled from the bargain and sought to invoke the auctioneer's lack of authority to sell otherwise than by auction. The court held the purchaser bound. Murdoch[5] regards the decision in *Bousfield v Hodges* as representing a more liberal view of the auctioneer's authority, but it is submitted that such a conclusion is not justified. Romilly M R did, it is true, say that it was competent for the auctioneer to sell by private contract at the amount of the reserve bidding, but is is clear that he regarded the auctioneer in this case as having been expressly authorised to do so; as he said:[6]

> I do not dispute that where an agent or trustee is authorised to sell any property in a particular manner, the authority is limited to that particular mode of selling, and that he cannot exceed the scope of his authority. But that is not the case here.

The reason for this conclusion on the facts is that the whole object of the exercise was to achieve a sale at a certain figure and thereby bring about the desired compromise. Those interested in selling were unconcerned about the mode of sale employed.

It may be further observed that both of these cases involved claims by principals against third parties to enforce contracts made by agents. Provided the other requirements were satisfied, the vendors in both cases could, in any event, have simply ratified their agent's acts if no authority had antecedently been given. Therefore, apart from the objections already taken, it would have been unsafe to rely on these cases as authority for the proposition that a power to sell otherwise than by auction would readily be implied. Only if it were held that a vendor was bound by such a sale at the suit of the purchaser could such a proposition be advanced. The more recent case of *Garnier v Bruntlett*,[7] where

3 (1860) 28 Beav 228 at 231.
4 (1863) 33 Beav 90.
5 Murdoch *The Law of Estate Agency and Auctions* (2nd edn, 1984) Estates Gazette, p 385.
6 *Bousfield v Hodges* (1863) 33 Beav 90.
7 (1974) 236 EG 867.

vendors were held bound by a sale made by private treaty after the reserve was not reached at auction, is such a case. However here again, as in *Bousfield v Hodges*, it was held on the facts that whilst auction was the preferred mode of sale, of overriding importance was the need to achieve a minimum price, howsoever obtained, in order to discharge mortgages. If it is desired to give an auctioneer authority to sell by private treaty it must, therefore, be expressly provided.[8]

Sales without or below reserve

This area gives rise to a number of related problems. The issues are complex and have not, perhaps surprisingly, all been authoritatively ruled on by the courts. It will be necessary to discuss them in some depth.

The problem of authority

What is the position where an auctioneer purports to sell property without reserve or below the reserve in defiance of his express instructions? In *Rainbow v Howkins*,[9] one Dr Dukes instructed the auctioneer Howkins to sell his pony at Rugby Cattle Market. He placed a reserve on the pony of £25. Howkins forgetfully announced the sale as being without reserve and knocked the pony down at 15 guineas. Then, realising his error, he informed the purchaser and put it up for sale again. When the bidding this time stopped at 17 guineas Howkins bought the pony in. No memorandum in writing, as was at that time required under s 4 of the Sale of Goods Act 1893, was ever signed. The purchaser, Rainbow, claimed that the sale was valid at 15 guineas or alternatively, that he was entitled to damages from the auctioneer for breach of warranty of authority.

The Divisional Court held that the sale was unenforceable by virtue of the absence of the memorandum required by s 4 but that, apart from that point, there was here a valid contract. The auctioneer *had* authority to sell without reserve and thus there was nothing in the claim for breach of warranty of authority. The authority was 'an apparent authority'.[10] The conclusion that the auctioneer had apparent authority to sell without reserve seems to have been based on the assumption that it is part of the usual authority of an auctioneer to sell without reserve and that the vendor is thus at risk if he fails to give notice to potential purchasers of the restriction he has placed on that authority.

The finding that an auctioneer has usual authority to sell without reserve may seriously be questioned. That proposition, and the decision in *Rainbow v Howkins* itself, was roundly criticised by the Court of Appeal in *McManus v Fortescue* decided a few years later. Fletcher Moulton L J said:[11]

8 An early example is afforded by *Green v Bartlett* (1863) 14 CBNS 681, 32 LJCP 261. The simple expedient being to instruct the auctioneer to sell 'by auction or otherwise'.

9 [1904] 2 KB 322, 73 LJKB 641.

10 [1904] 2 KB 322 at 326.

11 [1907] 2 KB 1 at 7, CA.

> A principal, therefore, who gives authority to an auctioneer to sell subject to a reserve price gives no power to the auctioneer, either expressly or impliedly, to accept a less price. The case of *Rainbow v Howkins* so far as it is inconsistent with this view cannot be regarded as in harmony with well established principles . . . the auctioneer . . . could not make a contract so as to bind his principal to accept less than the reserved price.

In this case an auctioneer again knocked down a lot (a corrugated iron structure resting by its own weight on dwarf walls and thus goods within the Sale of Goods Act 1893) for less than its reserve price. Here the printed auction catalogue included a condition that each lot would be offered subject to a reserve price and reserved the right on the part of the vendors to bid up to such a price. Once again, the auctioneer realising his error refused to complete the sale and the highest bidder claimed either that there was a valid contract of sale to him which the auctioneer was obliged to effect by signing the requisite memorandum, or that the auctioneer was in breach of his implied warranty of authority. Both claims were rejected.

Despite the criticism levelled at *Rainbow v Howkins*, it must be stressed that in *McManus v Fortescue* the lots were expressly offered subject to a reserve. There could, therefore, be no question of any apparent authority to the contrary nor of any estoppel against the vendor. Nor could it be said that the auctioneer in accepting a bid lower than the reserve was, in effect, warranting that he had authority to sell without reserve. As was made clear, when an auction is conducted subject to a reserve, every bid is and remains only a conditional offer to buy and the acceptance of the highest bid by the auctioneer is only a conditional acceptance, the condition being that the reserved price has been reached.[12]

The vendor thus protects himself against the possibility of sales below the reserve price by the relatively simple expedient of ensuring that notification of the existence of a reserve is effected through the auction particulars.[13] He is also protected, though less assuredly, if it is made clear that the right to place a reserve on a property is provided. In these circumstances a purchaser is put on notice of the possibility that the auctioneer may in fact be limited as to his authority and thus becomes liable to enquire as to whether a reserve has in fact been fixed, or, perhaps, is saddled with constructive notice of such having been fixed if this is the case. In *Fay v Miller Wilkins & Co*,[14] the auctioneer who erroneously knocked down the property at below the reserve in these circumstances went further and signed a memorandum which satisfied the requirement of evidence in writing laid down in s 40 of the Law of Property Act 1925 relating to interests in land. Although the unwilling vendor was not forced to complete, the court allowed the claim against the auctioneer for breach of warranty of authority.[15]

12 But see *Fay v Miller Wilkins & Co* [1941] Ch 360, 110 LJ Ch 124, CA, where the condition ceased to attach once the auctioneer signed a memorandum of sale satisfying the Law of Property Act 1925, s 40.

13 The vendor's instructions to the auctioneer should be expressed. The courts will not be astute to deduce such instructions. In Canada the courts have refused to find instructions not to sell goods below an invoice price merely from the circumstance that the goods were sent together with invoices: *Nelson v Hicks* (1899) QR 15 SC 465.

14 Above, n 12.

15 The argument that the auctioneer had apparent authority to sign the memorandum as a transaction separate from the sale itself was rejected because the auctioneer did not have authority to make representations as to his own authority.

Whilst the decision in *Rainbow v Howkins* has been attacked, it can be argued that neither *McManus v Fortescue* nor *Fay v Miller Wilkins & Co* directly subvert it. Indeed it may be said that indirectly they support it; for both cases where the vendor was held not bound were decided on the basis that the purchasers had *notice* of the limited nature of the auctioneer's authority to sell; actual in the former case and constructive in the latter; and notice would only be crucial if, apart from notice negativing it, an auctioneer *did* have apparent authority to sell without reserve because that was part of his usual authority. It must be pointed out, however, that what is usual may vary with particular trades or types of property sold and may change over the years.

In the New Zealand case of *Hawke's Bay Farmers' Co-operative Association Ltd v Farquharson*[16] the New Zealand Court of Appeal entertained no doubt that an auctioneer could be sued for damages by his vendor-principal for selling below a fixed reserve.

Sales expressed to be without reserve[17]

More problematic is the case where the sale is expressed to be without reserve but in effect a reserve is fixed subsequently or, what amounts to the same thing, the owner bids highest so as to buy the property in. The case which has given considerable difficulty is that of *Warlow v Harrison*[18] where a horse 'the property of a gentleman, *without reserve* Janet Pride' was advertised to be sold by auction. Harrison, a Birmingham auctioneer and dealer, put up the horse and Warlow bid 60 guineas for her. The owner, one Henderson, then bid 61 guineas and when Warlow discovered that the owner had intervened, he withdrew from the sale. The property was knocked down to the owner. Warlow thereupon claimed the horse as the highest bona fide bidder. Subsequently he brought an action against the auctioneer for breach of contract in failing to complete the sale to him. On a technicality relating to the way the claim was framed, both at first instance and on appeal, the court found for the defendant auctioneer. However, in a reserved judgement the majority of the judges hearing the appeal suggested, strictly obiter, that the plaintiff could on these facts succeed in an action against the auctioneer for breach of a collateral contract – that is one collateral to the sale – to sell without reserve. Martin B said:[19]

> . . . it seems to us that the highest bona fide bidder at an auction may sue the auctioneer as upon a contract that the sale shall be without reserve. We think the auctioneer who puts up the property for sale upon such a condition pledges himself that the sale shall be without reserve; or in other words contracts that it shall be so; and that this contract is made with the highest bona fide bidder.

The difficulties stemming from this analysis are considerable and it raises fundamental questions as regards the law relating to auctions.[20] It also presents problems concerning contractual theory generally and it may,

16 [1916] NZLR 917.
17 See generally, Slade (1952) 68 LQR 238; Gower (1952) 68 LQR 457; Slade (1953) 69 LQR 21; C G Cox 'Auctions Without Reserve: A Schematic Approach' (1982) 132 NLJ 716.
18 (1858) 1 E&E 295, 29 LJQB 14 (page references will be to the first-named report).
19 (1858) 1 E&E 295 at 316.
20 Scots law takes a different view. See *Fenwick v Macdonald Fraser & Co* 1904 6 F (Ct of Sess) 850, 41 Sc LR 688.

therefore, be useful at this juncture to enunciate some propositions of a basic nature before returning to examine this dictum.

Contractual analysis of auction sales

It has traditionally been said that a contract consists of a promise by one party — frequently called an offer — and acceptance of that offer plus the necessity of consideration from the promisee, that is some 'benefit' to the promisor or 'detriment' to the promisee, with which the promise is bought. English law does not, save when the contract is by formal deed, recognise gratuitous promises. As regards sales by auction, it has long been established by the courts and has subsequently been given statutory endorsement that:

(a) the advertising of an auction sale does not amount to an offer to sell any property;[1]
(b) the bid is the contractual offer which is capable of being accepted or refused and that, as a corollary, the bid is capable of being withdrawn as is any contractual offer[2] before acceptance;[3]
(c) the contract is completed when the bid is accepted, classically by the fall of the hammer.[4]

Conceptual analysis of contracts

As suggested above, contracts can be analysed as comprising offers and acceptances cemented by consideration. Contracts can also be classified according to whether they are:

(a) *bilateral* or *synallagmatic*: these are the most common kind of contract, imposing obligations on both (or all) parties to the contract; both parties are under a contractual duty to perform.
(b) *unilateral*: here only one party is bound to perform although that performance typically only becomes due on the satisfaction of a condition by another. A classic example is the so called 'reward' situation where a promise to pay is conditioned on, say, finding stolen goods. But there is no question of the finder being under any contractual duty to act.

We can now return to the troublesome case of *Warlow v Harrison*. The statement quoted above[5] raises the following difficulties.

1 *Harris v Nickerson* (1873) LR 8 QB 286, 42 LJQB 171; Sale of Goods Act 1979, s 57(2) (Appendix 2).
2 Except perhaps certain types of unilateral offer where the courts may imply a term that it shall not be revoked in appropriate circumstances; see e g *Daulia Ltd v Four Millbank Nominees Ltd* [1978] Ch 231, [1978] 2 All ER557, CA.
3 *Payne v Cave* (1789) 3 Term Rep 148; Sale of Goods Act 1979, s 57(2) (Appendix 2).
4 Above, n 3. See also *Dennant v Skinner & Collom* [1948] 2 KB 164, [1948] 2 All ER 29 where a provision that title to a car sold at auction would not pass to the purchaser until his cheque was cleared was ineffective because the provision was not incorporated until after the car had been knocked down.
5 From *Warlow v Harrison* (1858) 1 E&E 295 at 316; see p 24.

The nature of the bid

We have said that the bid is the contractual offer and also that it can be withdrawn at any time until it is accepted. Yet in *Warlow v Harrison*[6] it is suggested that a contract is made by an auctioneer with the highest bidder in a 'without reserve' sale then the highest bidder will be the buyer. This sounds perilously close to saying that the bid, or at any rate the highest bid, acts as an *acceptance* of a contractual offer to accept it. In Bateman it is said that this 'is not in accordance with well accepted and well established principles of the law of contract'.[7] However, what Martin B appears to be suggesting is that selling without reserve amounts to a quite separate offer to the class of bidders that on condition that they become the highest bidder the property will be knocked down to them; and that acceptance is by bidding. The offer is conditional on the bidder becoming the highest bidder; only by satisfying that condition does the bidder accept the offer.[8] The separate collateral contract made by the auctioneer is, therefore, a unilateral contract; the auctioneer is bound if the condition is satisfied but no one is bound satisfy it — no one is bound to bid.[9] If this is correct then the bid by a prospective purchaser fulfils two quite separate functions: it is an offer to make a contract of sale, and it is an acceptance of a separate offer to sell to whomsoever becomes the highest bidder.

If this is the correct analysis, then surprising results seem to flow. Whereas there is no breach of contract if the auctioneer simply withdraws the goods from the sale *(Harris v Nickerson*[10]*)* if he instead allows bidding to commence and then announces there is a reserve, he is in breach.[11]

Be that as it may, there is a further, perhaps more difficult obstacle in the way of such an analysis. It is difficult to see what consideration supports this collateral promise to sell to the highest bidder.

Consideration

The problem here is: how can it be said that the act of bidding, which amounts to acceptance, can also be the consideration for which the offer is given? Now it is perfectly possible for an act to provide both signification of acceptance and consideration; indeed it typically does in a unilateral contract,[12] but what benefit is it to the auctioneer or what detriment is it to the bidder that he bids? A number of possibilities have been canvassed,[13] including the argument that the bidder suffers detriment by bidding: he runs the risk of being bound by the contract of sale and the auctioneer benefits as the bidding is driven up. But it

6 Above, n 5.
7 Bateman *Law of Auctions* (11th edn, 1953) Estates Gazette, p 152.
8 See Cox (above, n 17).
9 Bateman (above, n 7) objects that for the auctioneer to be bound but for the bidder to be free to withdraw his bid offends against a principle of mutuality (p 158) but it is denied that any such principle obtains with a unilateral contract.
10 Above, n 1.
11 Under the American Uniform Commercial Code s 2-328 (3) goods put up without reserve cannot be withdrawn.
12 Slade's objection (68 LQR 238 at 241) that 'the mere making of a bid is no more consideration for the promise than the effort of saying or even writing the words "I accept"...' is not taken.
13 See e g Gower 68 LQR 457; Treitel *Outline of the Law of Contract* (3rd edn, 1984) Butterworths, p 9.

is difficult at first sight to see how an act which is revocable and may immediately be revoked can be of benefit to the auctioneer or be any real detriment to the bidder. This perhaps explains the not uncommon provision in auction conditions of a stipulation that bids may not be withdrawn. However, we have already suggested that, in a sense, it is only with the person who becomes the highest bona fide bidder that the auctioneer really contracts, and that person, ex hypothesi, will not have withdrawn his bid. It also must be admitted that there are many commercial situations where the law recognises a contract but where it is impossible without great artificiality either to analyse the relationship in terms of offer and acceptance or to find real consideration.[14]

The problems considered above are the main ones raised by the notion of a collateral contract between the auctioneer and the highest bona fide bidder, but there are others. In particular it may be difficult for the court in any given case to quantify the loss flowing from the breach by the auctioneer. We have suggested that the highest bidder is the only person who contracts and therefore suffers any loss. But as Slade points out:[15]

> At any time until the hammer has fallen it is always open to other persons to bid. The plaintiff at most therefore can argue that as the highest bidder pro tempore he has been deprived of the chance of obtaining the goods at the price which he actually bid. If this chance had any value at all, the court would not reject his claim to damages simply on the grounds that these were difficult to assess. The defence however will merely have to produce one witness who satisfies the court that he intended or was instructed to make a higher bid at the moment when the goods were withdrawn to make proof of damage impossible.

One must accept, therefore, that there are a number of difficulties in the way of accepting the collateral contract idea. However, it is surely permissible to ask what would be the legal effect of advertising a sale as being without reserve if there were no collateral contract. Since the sale is not complete until the fall of the hammer, and since there would be no liability for subsequently imposing a reserve after the bidding had progressed, the statement that the sale was without reserve would be of absolutely no legal significance to the bidder. Two judges in *Warlow v Harrison*[16] suggested that the auctioneer would be in breach of an implied warranty of authority in such circumstances. However, it is difficult to understand how this could be so. The fact is, the auctioneer *was* authorised to sell without reserve; it is simply that his authority was subsequently revoked. This leads us to the final problem raised by the case. All along it has been discussed on the basis that the auctioneer in contracting to sell to the highest bidder does so, not as agent for the vendor so as to make him liable on the collateral contract, but as a principal. Indeed Martin B continued the dictum quoted above with these words:[17]

> We entertain no doubt that the owner may, at any time before the contract is legally complete, interfere and revoke the auctioneer's authority: but he does so at his peril; and, if the auctioneer has contracted any liability in consequence of his employment and the subsequent revocation of conduct of the owner, he is entitled to be indemnified.

14 See the observations of Lord Wilberforce in *New Zealand Shipping Co Ltd v A M Satherthwaite & Co Ltd* [1975] AC 154 at 167 and the several examples given of which the first is 'Sales at auction'.
15 Above, n 12.
16 (1858) 1 E&E 295, 29 LJQB 14.
17 (1858) 1 E&E 295 at 316.

This is in accordance with well established principles that the vendor can normally terminate the auctioneer's authority at any time before sale.[18] But if the statement 'without reserve' amounts to a collateral contractual offer, there seems little reason in theory why the principal should not be bound by it and thus unable to resile from it once it has been accepted by bidders. After all, the auctioneer states that the sale is without reserve because those are his instructions; he is *authorised* so to state. It may be said that there is no practical difference between the formulation in *Warlow v Harrison* that the auctioneer is personally liable but can look to the vendor for indemnification, and one that renders the vendor primarily liable on the contract; but if an advertisement of a sale without reserve is made on the instructions of the vendor there seems nothing in principle to prevent the court from holding that this constitutes an offer by the vendor, as principal, to sell to the highest bidder made through the auctioneer merely as agent. If however, as in this case, the identity of the principal is not disclosed, it may be that the auctioneer remains personally liable for non-delivery of the article.[19]

Signing the contract

It has been suggested that the classic example of implied authority as it applies to auctioneers is the authority to sign the contract of sale or the memorandum thereof. This today only arises in respect of sales of land by virtue of s 40 of the Law of Property Act 1925. We shall deal with this in later chapters.[20]

Collecting payment

Two related questions are involved here. First, is the purchaser discharged if he pays the agent? Second, is the agent liable to the principal if he fails to recover the proceeds or part of them from the purchaser? The first question turns on the extent of the agent's authority, whilst the second more properly involves the question of his duty, but it will be convenient to deal with the two questions together here.

Early cases[1] suggested that agents generally, and therefore auctioneers, had implied authority to collect the price from the purchaser, but these authorities have subsequently been doubted.[2] However the position is not entirely free from doubt. In the old case of *Williams v Millington* Lord Loughborough observed: 'In the common course of auctions there is no delivery without actual payment; if it be otherwise the auctioneer gives credit to the vendee entirely at his own risk.'[3] This dictum was recently cited with approval by

18 We discuss termination of authority later in this chapter. See pp 35-37 below.
19 On this question see ch 5.
20 See chs 5 and 9.
1 See e g *Capel v Thornton* (1828) 3 C&P 352; *Howard v Chapman* (1831) 4 C&P 508.
2 *Butwick v Grant* [1924] 2 KB 483 per Horridge J at 488 citing with approval a dictum of Lush J in *Drakeford v Piercy* (1866) 7 BS 515 at 522: 'that an agent authorised to sell has as a necessary legal consequence authority to receive payment is a proposition utterly untenable and contrary to authority.'
3 (1788) 1 Hy Bl 81 at 84 and see *Woolfe v Horne* (1877) 2 QBD 355, 46 LJQB 534; *Davis v Artingstall* (1880) 49 LJ Ch 609, 42 LT 507; *Wood v Baxter* (1883) 49 LT 45; *Consolidated Co v Curtis & Son* [1892] 1 QB 495, 61 LJQB 325.

Lord Denning in *Chelmsford Auctions Ltd v Poole,* where the then Master of the Rolls said:[4]

> The vendor entrusts the auctioneer with the possession of the goods for sale by auction. The understanding is that the auctioneer should not part with the possession of them to the purchaser except against the price or, if the auctioneer should part with them without receiving payment, he is responsible to the vendor for the price.

This, said Lord Denning, was the common law position apart from any express conditions. If the auctioneer is responsible to the vendor for the price, it must be that he authorised to collect it. It cannot be that he has a duty without a power to perform it. On the other hand, there appears to be no case directly in point. Both *Williams v Millington* and *Chelmsford Auctions Ltd v Poole* concerned actions by auctioneers against defaulting purchasers and in both cases it was held that, by virtue of the lien which possession of the goods gives to the auctioneer, the auctioneer may recover the price. In the latter case the purchaser had refused to take the goods but the auctioneers had paid over the full price to the vendor. Thus the question whether the auctioneer was *authorised* to receive the price so as to discharge the purchaser vis-à-vis the vendor, did not arise. However in the recent case of *Fordham v Christie Manson & Woods Ltd*[5] the defendants auctioned a painting and knocked it down to a bidder who refused to take it or pay for it. After the death of the vendor, his estate brought an action against the defendant auctioneers. It was held that there was no general duty at common law to get in the purchase money although here the auctioneers did have authority to receive it and account to the owner.[6] It is suggested, therefore, that the better view is that there is no implied authority to receive payment of the purchase price.

The absence of conclusive authority on the question is probably explained by the fact that it is usual for the contract between the vendor and auctioneer expressly to provide the requisite powers. In sales of goods it is normal for the auctioneer to be authorised to complete the sale and collect the purchase price from the buyer.[7] Where land is sold it is generally provided that the auctioneer has authority to receive the deposit but not the full purchase price.

Where the auctioneer is authorised to collect the purchase money or the deposit, the question then arises as to whether there are restrictions as to the mode of payment permissible. Again, there may be express instructions but in their absence the common law has generally refused to discharge a purchaser who has paid otherwise than in cash. In *Howard v Chapman*[8] for example, a purchaser who sought to pay in kind, by giving the agent a quantity of horse hair, was held still liable to pay the price to the vendor. Moreover an agent who accounted for less than the full price where he had been persuaded to allow a set-off claimed by the purchaser against the vendor was held liable to the vendor for the balance.[9]

4 [1973] QB 452, CA at 548.
5 (1977) 121 Sol Jo 529.
6 See also *Hardial Singh v Hillyer* (1979) 251 EG 951 – not negligent in failing to ensure that a purchaser of land signs the memorandum *immediately* after the fall of the hammer.
7 For an early example see *Brown v Staton* (1816) 2 Chit 353.
8 (1831) 4 C&P 508.
9 *Brown v Staton* (above, n 7).

There are a number of old cases which are said to indicate that receipt of payment of the price by bill of exchange is inappropriate, but these may not be reliable. In *Sykes v Giles*[10] a purchaser was held liable to the vendor for the balance of the purchase price on a sale of timber when he had paid the auctioneer by accepting a bill of exchange drawn in favour of the latter who then endorsed it for value and disappeared. But here the conditions provided that only the deposit was to be paid to the auctioneer. It is true that Parke B said that even if the auctioneer had had authority to receive the whole of the purchase money 'he had no authority to receive it in this way by means of a bill of exchange. Cash payment was intended'.[11] However the better ground for the decision is that given by Abinger C B, namely, that once the deposit moneys had been paid the authority of the auctioneer was at an end. He therefore had no authority whatsoever to accept anything from the purchaser thereafter.

Williams v Evans[12] is a stronger authority in that there were no express conditions, but here the vendor specifically instructed the purchaser not to pay the auctioneer at all, but to account directly to him. In these circumstances it is hardly surprising that the court held the purchaser, who paid the auctioneer with a bill of exchange, not discharged. However the court did expressly rely on *Sykes v Giles* as authority for the proposition that payment by bill of exchange was not valid. There is authority for saying that an auctioneer may, when authorised to collect the *deposit*, take a cheque from a purchaser[13] and that it is reasonable to do so. As Baggallay L J pointed out,[14] 'persons cannot be expected to come to sales with large sums of money in their pocket'. A cheque is, of course, a special kind of bill of exchange. It seems hardly conceivable today that an auctioneer authorised to collect the price of goods sold at an auction would not, in the absence of express instructions to the contrary,[15] be entitled to receive a cheque. Where an auctioneer does receive the deposit there may be arguments in favour of his taking it as *agent* for the vendor and not as *stakeholder*, since receipt in the latter capacity may in certain situations jeopardise his lien.[16]

Describing the property: authority to warrant

An auctioneer will, almost inevitably, apply some sort of description to the lots as he puts them up. Later in this book we shall consider the potential liability of an auctioneer for any misdescription.[17] For the present, our concern is the question whether, in the absence of express authority from the vendor to give warranties about the property, such may be implied so as to give the purchaser rights against the vendor in the event that the warranty is proved false. A

10 (1839) 5 M&W 645, 9 LJEx 106.
11 (1839) 5 M&W 645 at 651.
12 (1866) LR 1 QB 352, 35 LJQB 111
13 *Farrer v Lacy Hartland & Co* (1885) 31 Ch D 42, 55 LJ Ch 149, CA
14 (1885) 31 Ch D 42 at 46.
15 See e g *Earl of Ferrers v Robins* (1835) 2 Cr M & R 152, 4 LJ Ex 178.
16 *Skinner v Trustee of the Property of Reed (Bankrupt)* [1967] Ch 1194, [1967] 2 All ER 1286; and see further on this, ch 5.
17 See chs 6 and 8.

warranty, in this context, may be defined somewhat loosely as some representation of fact (which may include a opinion — see *Smith v Land and House Property Corpn*[18]) made before or at the time of the sale intended or tending to induce a party to enter into a contract.

That there is no implied authority to warrant was emphatically stated in *Payne v Lord Leconfield*[19] where a mare was sold by auction. A by-stander (presumably officious!) noted that the mare was suffering from a discharge from her nostrils. The auctioneer, in the presence of the plaintiff who subsequently bought the horse, said: 'you need not be afraid. The mare comes from Lord Leconfield; she has only got a cold upon her, and I shall sell as only having a cold.' Unfortunately, it turned out that she was suffering from chronic glanders and had to be destroyed, as had other of the purchaser's horses which were allegedly infected by her. The plaintiff's action against Lord Leconfield on the warranty failed on the ground that the auctioneer had neither express nor any implied authority to give warranties. However recent decisions have cast doubt upon whether an auctioneer has not implied authority to warrant.

In *Mendelssohn v Normand Ltd*[20] a car-park attendant employed by the defendant company insisted on being given the car keys and represented that he would look after the contents of the plaintiff's car. When a bag left in the car disappeared, the plaintiff sued the company. A written term of the contract contained in the ticket issued to the plaintiff purported to exclude any responsibility for loss. Nevertheless it was held that the company was liable; whilst the employee had no actual authority to give promises (warranties) it was within his authority to do so, and this overrode the written term of the contract subsequently entered into. Now this case, of course, has nothing to do with auctions. However, it was considered in the subsequent case of *Overbrooke Estates Ltd v Glencombe Properties Ltd*,[1] the facts of which were as follows.

The plaintiffs instructed auctioneers to sell certain property. Before the sale the auctioneers gave representations as to the absence of certain slum clearance or compulsory purchase plans affecting or likely to affect the property, and the purchasers bought it. Subsequently, however, they discovered that the representations were untrue and sought to resile from the contract. The vendors sued for specific performance of the contract and the purchasers resisted on the ground, inter alia, that they had been induced to enter into the contract by a material mis-representation which the auctioneers had ostensible authority to make. The auction had been conducted subject to printed conditions of sale which provided so far as material: 'The vendors do not make or give and neither the auctioneers nor any person in the employment of the auctioneers has any authority to make or give any representation or warranty in relation to these properties.' Brightman J granted specific performance of the contract. He distinguished *Mendelssohn v Normand Ltd* in that the printed conditions advertised the restriction on the authority of the auctioneers before the representation was made and said:[2]

18 (1884) 28 ChD 7, 51 LT 718, CA.
19 (1882) 51 LJQB 642, 30 WR 814.
20 [1970] 1 QB 177, [1969] 2 All ER 1215, CA.
1 [1974] 3 All ER 511, [1974] 1 WLR 1335; approved in *Collins v Howell-Jones* (1980) 259 EG 331.
2 [1974] 3 All ER 511 at 516.

> It seems to me that it must be open to a principal to draw the attention of the public to the limits which he places on the authority of his agent and this must be so whether the agent is a person who has, or has not, any ostensible authority. If an agent has prima facie some ostensible authority, that authority is inevitably diminished to the extent of the publicised limits that are placed on it.

'Prima facie . . . ostensible authority' is perhaps an odd expression but it is thought this refers to that implied or usual authority which is actual unless and until limited and thereafter is thus apparent or ostensible unless, as happened here, the principal takes steps to give notice of the limitations he has placed upon it. As was said earlier in another context, if the reason for the absence of implied authority is the fact of notification of an express limitation, it can be concluded that in the absence of such a limitation the auctioneer would have been clothed with authority and that authority must therefore be implied.

If a vendor makes it clear that he is inviting an auctioneer to attach particular descriptions to goods it is the auctioneer's duty so to describe them in terms, and the measure of damages for breach will be the difference between the price the goods would probably have fetched had they been sold under that description and the prices actually achieved.[3]

Delegating authority

The question whether an auctioneer can delegate any of these duties or powers has tended to arise in relation to his authority to sign memoranda evidencing the sale. The general rule is *delegatus non potest delegare:* one who is himself a delegate may not delegate to another. It is well settled that an auctioneer has implied authority from both the vendor and the purchaser to sign any memorandum required to be signed by or for either party in order that a contract of sale may be enforceable. The requirement of such written evidence of certain contracts originated in the Statute of Frauds 1677. The contracts involved were those for the sales or other dispositions of an interest in land and sales of goods for a value of £10 or above. As regards sales of goods, the relevant provision was re-enacted by s 4 of the Sale of Goods Act 1893 but was abolished by the Law Reform (Enforcement of Contracts) Act 1954. However, with regard to land, the requirement of written evidence to be signed by the parties to be bound continues and now finds expression in s 40 of the Law of Property Act 1925.

The question for consideration now is: to what extent does an auctioneer have implied authority to delegate the signing of the requisite memorandum, typically, to his clerk? It is possible that one must distinguish the position vis-à-vis the vendor from that as it affects the purchaser. In the Irish case of *Dyas v Stafford* Chatterton V C said:[4]

> There is, I think, a difference between the agency of the clerk in the case of a vendor from that of a purchaser. In the latter case the agency is only constituted on the

3 *Brown v Draper* (1975) 233 EG 99. However auction conditions not infrequently reserve to the auctioneer the right to apply his own descriptions to lots offered for sale. In such circumstances he would not be liable to the vendor. Such description must not, of course, be a false trade description — see ch 8.

4 (1881) 7 LR Ir 590 at 601.

moment by the bid of the purchaser who thus authorises the clerk to enter his name and bidding, and to bind him by signature. The agency for the vendor is of a more deliberate character, and arises from the employment of the auctioneer which by the usages and mode of such sales carries with it the employment of his clerk. The vendor must be presumed to have been aware of and to have adopted these usages, and thus to have given an authority to the clerk when the occasion should arise to act as his agent directly in doing those acts which it was necessary for the clerk to do.

Binding the vendor

This dictum suggests that an auctioneer has usual (a species of implied) authority to delegate his authority to sign a memorandum so as to bind his principal to an enforceable contract of sale. However there are to be found fairly categorical statements to the contrary. Bateman asserts baldly that 'there is certainly no power to delegate the signing the memorandum under s 40 Law of Property Act, 1925 to a clerk',[5] but cites no authority for this. Halsbury concurs with this view and gives a number of authorities which now fall to be considered. The first is *Coles v Trecothick*[6] where Lord Eldon L C certainly said that there was no usage that an auctioneer's clerk was an agent of the principal, but the case is weakened by the fact that here there was an express authority, the auctioneer having warned the vendor that he would not be able to attend and the vendor having assented to the auctioneer's clerk acting, and also the fact that, in the result, the sale was concluded by private treaty. Thus the question of implied authority did not arise. Another case was *Gosbell v Archer*[7] where it was held that there was not an enforceable contract when the clerk signed the memorandum. But here it was clear that the clerk merely signed as a witness and *Coles v Trecothick* was expressly distinguished on that ground. The clearest statement that there is no implied authority was made in *Peirce v Corf*[8] in 1874. This case concerned the sale of a mare for a price in excess of £10 and Blackburn J said:[9]

> The memorandum, to be a good memorandum, must be signed in such a manner that when the auctioneer attaches his signature it authenticates the contract as to the price and conditions of sale. I have already said that the usage of sales by auction which we must take notice of is, that the auctioneer is the person who has authority to sign, and generally he does wisely if he signs upon the catalogue . . . but I take it as quite clear that the auctioneer's clerk has no authority to sign by the general custom.

The objection here, however, was that the clerk signed only a sales ledger and even assuming, which was not decided, that the clerk could be regarded as the agent of the *purchaser*, the memorandum was defective in that it made no reference to conditions of sale. Finally Halsbury refers to *Bell v Balls*,[10] but this case too involved the issue whether the auctioneer can delegate the signing of the memorandum so as to bind the purchaser and, if the statement by Chatterton V C in *Dyas v Stafford* is correct, different considerations may apply

5 Bateman *Law of Auctions* (11th edn, 1953) Estates Gazette, p 23.
6 (1804) 9 Ves 234, I Smith KB 233.
7 (1935) 2 Ad & El 500, 4 LJKB 78.
8 (1874) LR 9 QB 210, 43 LJQB 52
9 (1874) LR 9 QB 210 at 214.
10 [1897] 1 Ch 663, 66 LJ Ch 397.

in such a case. With regard to that point, it might be thought unsatisfactory if the practice of an auctioneer permitting his clerk to sign were upheld or disapproved depending upon the circumstance of whether it was the vendor or the purchaser who happened to wish subsequently to resile from the sale.

Be that as it may, even if it is felt that English authority against an auctioneer having usual authority to delegate the signing of a memorandum so as to bind the vendor is not particularly strong, it would clearly be unsafe for an auctioneer to entrust such to his clerk in the absence of express authorisation.

Binding the purchaser

The position vis à vis the purchaser appears to be free from doubt. Despite the somewhat ambiguous wording used in *Dyas v Stafford* ('who *thus* authorises the clerk . . . to bind him by signature'),[11] *Bell v Balls*[12] is clear authority for the proposition that the auctioneer has no implied authority to delegate the signing of the memorandum as agent for the purchaser. That case involved the auctioning of freehold land and the auctioneer invited the defendant to give him a bid. The defendant obliged and the property was knocked down to him. Thereupon the defendant maintained that he thought he was being invited to 'puff' for the auctioneer and that he had not intended bidding for the property for himself. The auctioneer's clerk subsequently signed the memorandum and the vendor sought to enforce the contract. Stirling J refused to accept that the purchaser was bound.[13] Having expressly approved *Peirce v Corf*,[14] his Lordship said that there was no ground for the contention that the auctioneer should be held entitled to delegate his authority to his clerk.

There are cases where the clerk's signature has been held to bind the purchaser, but these appear to have been decided on the basis that the particular circumstances lent themselves to the conclusion that the clerk was authorised directly by the purchaser so that no question of delegation arose. In *Bird v Boulter*[15] the purchaser of wheat at an auction was prevented from resiling from the contract of sale where the requisite memorandum was signed on his behalf by the auctioneer's clerk. After each property was knocked down, the clerk called out the name of the purchaser and, if the party assented, entered his name in a sale book. Denman C J said: 'the clerk was not acting merely as an automaton, but as a person known to all engaged in the sale, and employed by any who told him to put down his name.'[16]

Finally, in *Wilson & Sons v Pike*[17] it was decided that when an auctioneer who is a partner in a firm employed to auction property signs the memorandum, he does so qua agent in his own right and not as a delegate of the firm.

11 (1881) 7 LR Ir 590 at 601, emphasis added.
12 Above, n 10.
13 [1897] 1 Ch 663 at 668: the judge also said, in argument, that where the auctioneer does himself sign as agent for the purchaser this is 'not a matter to be put off'. Cf *Hardial Singh v Hillyer* (1979) 251 EG 951.
14 Above, n 8.
15 (1833) 4 B&Ad 443, 1 Nev & MKB 313.
16 (1833) 4 B&Ad 443 at 497. See also *Sims v Landray* [1894] 2 Ch 318, 63 LJ Ch 535.
17 [1949] 1 KB 176, [1948] 2 All ER 267, CA.

Termination of authority

An agency will determine on the death or insanity of either party or the bankruptcy of the principal. Leaving aside those general rules, an auctioneer's authority may terminate in one of two ways: either (a) naturally, where the auctioneer performs all that he is authorised to do; or (b) artificially, by the principal taking positive steps to bring it to an end by revoking the authority previously given. We shall deal with each mode separately.

Natural termination

Once the auctioneer has performed the duties he is employed to perform, his authority comes to an end: he is *functus officio*. When this occurs will obviously depend upon the precise extent of his express and implied authority. Generally we can say that, unless otherwise agreed, his authority will determine after the sale has been completed, including, in the case of sales of land, signature of the memorandum evidencing the contract. So, for example, he will not be able to deal with the terms on which title is to be made.[18] Whether he has power to rescind the contract of sale is not settled. In *Nelson v Aldridge*[19] an auctioneer at the insistence of the highest bidder, who claimed his horse was not 'fresh and active' or otherwise as described, agreed to take back the horse and return the purchase moneys. In an action against the auctioneer, the vendor recovered damages for breach of contract. Best J was emphatic: 'It was the duty of the auctioneer to sell and not to rescind, to do and not to undo.'[20]

On the other hand, in *Stevens v Legh*[1] a vendor failed in a similar action against his auctioneer who had returned the purchase price to the purchaser after the latter had discovered fraud. The answer may be that, where rescission is justified, it is circuitous not to give the auctioneer power to rescind since he would be liable directly to the purchaser and could then claim indemnification from the vendor. This is all very well when the purchaser's purported rescission is justified, but it does not follow that auctioneers have *authority* to rescind (or accept rescission of) the contract of sale and it is suggested that they should not do so. It is better that they refuse and look to their principal for indemnity, than take the risk involved in a possibly unjustified act which would lead them open to an action by the vendor. However, Conditions of Sale often make specific provision for rescission, e g if the lot is a deliberate forgery as defined and proved pursuant to the General Conditions. In this case, the auctioneer has specific authority to rescind the contract and return the price paid to the buyer.

Revocation

We have already alluded to the right of the principal to revoke the auctioneer's authority in dealing with sales expressed to be without reserve.[2] The dictum of

18 See *Seton v Slade* (1802) 7 Ves 265; *Strachan v Auld* 1884 11 R (Ct of Sess) 756, 21 Sc LR 747.
19 (1818) 2 Stark 435.
20 (1818) 2 Stark 435 at 437. See also *Farquhar v Billman* (1901) 40 NSR 289.
1 (1853) 2 CLR 251, 22 LTOS 84.
2 See above, pp 24-28.

Martin B in *Warlow v Harrison*[3] that the principal can revoke his agent's authority at any time is generally correct. However there is one situation where the authority is irrevocable, namely where the agent has an agency 'plus an interest'. This arises where, for example the auctioneer is to recoup sums advanced to the vendor out of the sale of his property; the vendor cannot revoke the authority to sell while the auctioneer's interest in the goods remains extant. An illustration is provided by *Charlesworth v Mills.*[4] There an owner of goods who was subjected to a writ of execution against them by a sheriff, agreed in writing with the plaintiff-auctioneer that if the latter paid out the sheriff he could sell the goods thus recovered and recoup himself out of the proceeds. The auctioneer did as he was asked, whereupon the vendor purported to revoke his authority to sell. The House of Lords decided in favour of the auctioneer. The authority to sell was 'irrevocable except upon terms of paying back the money'.[5] The courts are not astute to extend this idea of an agency coupled with an interest. In *Taplin v Florence,*[6] such was held not to exist in the form of licence to enter the premises of a vendor and there to carry out the auction sale. Creswell J said that it was clear that an auctioneer who was employed to sell goods on the premises of a third party has no such interest in the goods as will make the licence to enter the premises for the purpose of selling the goods irrevocable.

For the revocation to be effective, it is not necessary that the purchaser is made aware of it. As it was put in one case where the vendor told the auctioneer that a right of way was to be reserved over land to be sold but the auction particulars previously produced were not amended:[7]

> It was said in argument that, if there were any mistake, that mistake was all on the part of the vendors, and that all that had passed was, as regards the plaintiff, res inter alios, and not binding upon him. But that argument proves too much. If admitted, it would deprive a vendor of a power to revoke an authority to sell, unless he could prove that the revocation was actually known to the party who chanced to become the purchaser. This cannot be successfully contended for. The revocation of the authority of the auctioneer is operative per se, and therefore, like a deed, is binding upon persons not parties to or conusant of it.

Thus the purchasers could not resist an action by the vendor for specific performance. In this case the auctioneer had read the altered particulars before commencing the sale but the purchaser's evidence that he had not heard this was accepted. The auctioneer risks being sued for breach of warranty of authority in such circumstances, and a warning given by Wigram V C that he should 'pointedly have called their attention to the fact that they had been altered and in what way'[8] is well taken.

It has been said that an auctioneer's authority is revocable at any time until sale. This means, in the case of sales of land, that once the hammer has fallen the vendor cannot revoke the auctioneer's authority to sign the memorandum.[9]

3 (1858) 1 E&E 295, 29 LJQB 14.
4 (1892) AC 231, 61 LJQB 830, HL. Contrast *Chinnock v Sainsbury* (1860) 30 LJ Ch 409, 3 LT 258.
5 [1892] AC 231 at 243.
6 (1851) 10 CB 744, 20 LJCP 137.
7 *Manser v Back* (1848) 6 Hare 443 at 449-50.
8 (1848) 6 Hare 443 at 446.
9 See e g *Phillips v Butler* [1945] Ch 358, [1945] 2 All ER 258.

Despite the right of the vendor to revoke his auctioneer's authority, where the auctioneer retains the goods and in fact sells them by auction, it is arguable that the bona fide purchaser without notice of the lack of authority will get a good title to the goods, leaving the vendor with a right of action against the auctioneer. This is argued on the basis that an auctioneer falls within the definition of a 'mercantile agent' under the Factors Act 1889 whereunder, by s 2(1) it is provided:

> Where a mercantile agent is, with the consent of the owner, in possession of goods or the documents of title to goods, any sale pledge or other disposition of the goods made by him when acting in the ordinary course of business of a mercantile agent shall subject to the provisions of this act, be as valid as if he were expressly authorised by the owner of the goods to make the same; provided that the person taking under the disposition acts in good faith, and has not at the time of the disposition notice that the person making the disposition has not authority to make the same.

And the fact that the vendor has revoked the authority of the auctioneer does not mean that he is not selling with the consent of the goods owner; see sub-s (2). This point does not, however, appear to have come before our courts for consideration.

Chapter 4

The rights of an auctioneer

RIGHTS AGAINST THE VENDOR

An auctioneer has a number of rights which may be exercised against the vendor, the most important being his right to be paid for his work. Also of significance is his right to be indemnified in respect of any losses or liabilities incurred in performing his mandate. An auctioneer has other subsidiary rights, such as his right to a lien over the property of his principal, which may be exercised to enforce his right to remuneration. We shall deal with these in turn.

The right to remuneration and expenses

The right to remuneration includes both the right to agreed commission and, rarer in these days of more or less standardised forms of contract, the right to be paid a reasonable sum where the contract is silent as to the commission to be paid or where the work done is outside that provided for by the contract (a quantum meruit).

Commission

Whether the auctioneer is entitled to his commission will depend upon the terms of his contract.[1] It is necessary to determine what are the conditions upon satisfaction of which the contract provides that commission is payable, and secondly, whether they have been satisfied. The first element involves a legal question, and the second a factual one.[2]

Construction of the contract

The conditions to be satisfied before an agent, including an auctioneer, becomes entitled to his commission will depend, therefore, upon the precise

1 Where the auctioneer is also an estate agent (as he frequently will be where land is sold by auction) he will be unable to recover charges as estate agent unless he has notified the vendor as to his rate of commission etc: Estate Agents Act 1979, s 18.

2 Bowen L J in *Beningfield v Kynaston* (1887) 3 TLR 279, CA, seems to suggest that the first question is also one of fact but that is doubted.

terms of his contract. The contract must in each case be construed to ascertain the intention of the parties. There is a plethora of case law on commission contracts, but as Lord Russell of Killowen pointed out in *Luxor v Cooper*:[3]

> Commission contracts are subject to no particular rules or principles of their own; the law which governs them is the law which governs all contracts and all questions of agency. No general rule can be laid down by which the rights of the agent or the liability of the principal under commission contracts are to be determined. In each case these must depend upon the exact terms of the contract in question, and upon the true construction of those terms.

There is thus little to be gained from a detailed cataloguing of the cases; it is evident that a different decision may be expected when the contract as construed provides for commission to be paid:

(a) upon the introduction of a person able and willing to enter into a contract of purchase
(b) upon the introduction of a person who enters into a binding contract of purchase
(c) upon the introduction of a person who completes a contract of purchase.[4]

A few illustrative examples may however be given. In *Peacock v Freeman*[5] the defendant auctioneers claimed to retain commission in the following circumstances: the contract provided that commission was to be paid if the property were sold at auction but if the property 'should...not be sold we shall charge an auction fee of 30 guineas.' At auction the property was knocked down to a purchaser who paid a deposit to the auctioneer. Subsequently the purchaser raised certain requisitions and, as provided for in the conditions of sale, the vendors rescinded the contract of sale and repaid the deposit amount. Thereupon they demanded the deposit moneys retained by the auctioneers claiming that all that the latter were entitled to retain was the 30 guineas allowable where the property was not sold. The Court of Appeal held that on the true construction of the contract, commission was only payable upon completion when the purchaser paid or came under a liability to pay the purchase moneys. Lord Esher M R said:[6]

> Land could only be said to be sold when the conveyance was complete not when there was a mere contract to sell. Therefore in this case the commission was not earned under the terms of the contract itself...It could never be supposed that there was an implied contract with...the auctioneers, that the plaintiffs should not do what that contract authorise them to do.

On the other hand, in *Skinner v Andrews and Hall*[7] in substantially similar circumstances it was held that the auctioneers were entitled to their commission. Here the correspondence, which formed the contract, referred to a 'sale...under the hammer'. Vaughan Williams LJ emphasised that the

3 *Luxor (Eastbourne) Ltd v Cooper* [1941] AC 108 at 124.
4 The classification is that of Bateman *Law of Auctions* (11th edn, 1953) Estates Gazette, ch 7, where numerous cases, most involving estate agents' contracts, are discussed.
5 (1888) 4 TLR 541, CA.
6 (1888) 4 TLR 541 at 542.
7 (1910) 26 TLR 340, CA.

agreement in this case involved a 'very different contract'[8] to that in *Peacock v Freeman*.

In both these cases the vendor justifiably prevented the *completion* of the contract of sale. More common a problem arises where the auctioneers are prevented from bringing about an auction sale by the revocation of their authority by the vendor. In such circumstances the auctioneers will wish to claim either, (a) that there is an implied term in their contract of agency precluding such revocation, and giving rise to a right to damages for its breach, or (b) that where there is a subsequent sale of the property, the terms of their contract entitle them to commission.

Implied term

The argument that there was an implied term in the agency contract, that the vendor shall not prevent the auctioneer from earning his commission by himself selling or simply revoking the authority of the auctioneer before sale or completion, was raised in *Peacock v Freeman* but was rejected because of the express term in the conditions of sale that in certain circumstances, one of which obtained, the vendor could rescind the contract of sale. It is axiomatic that a term cannot be implied in the face of an express term to the contrary. And it is not necessary in order to exclude the implication of a term of the kind argued for, to find an express term such as that in *Peacock v Freeman*; it seems that the express provision for commission to be paid on a certain event will be fatal both to the implication of any term to pay on any other event and to the implication of a term not to prevent that event from materialising. In *Luxor v Cooper* Lord Russell of Killowen said:[9]

> I can find no safe ground on which to base the introduction of any such implied term. Implied terms, as we all know, can only be justified under the compulsion of some necessity. No such compulsion or necessity exists in the case under consideration. The agent is promised a commission if he introduces a purchaser at a specified or minimum price. The owner is desirous of selling. The chances are largely in favour of the deal going through, if a purchaser is introduced. The agent takes the risk in the hope of a substantial remuneration for comparatively small exertion.

And he continued:[10]

> My Lords in my opinion there is no necessity in these contracts for any implication; and the legal position can be stated thus: If according to the true construction of the contract the event has happened upon the happening of which the agent has acquired a vested right to the commission...then no act or omission by the principal or anyone else can deprive the agent of that right; but until that event has happened the agent cannot complain if the principal refuses to proceed with or carry to completion, the transaction with the agent's client.

What was said was in the context of a claim by an estate agent, but the statement of principle is arguably wide enough to apply to an auctioneer who has been prevented from earning his commission. If an auctioneer wishes to

8 (1910) 26 TLR 340 at 341.
9 [1941] AC 108 at 125.
10 [1941] AC 108 at 128-29.

protect himself he must provide expressly in his agreement with the vendor for the circumstances in which he is to receive commission or to be paid expenses incurred in preparing for a sale which he is prevented from effecting.[11] However, one must distinguish the case where the principal has justifiably prevented the agent from bringing about the event upon the happening of which the commission is payable, of which *Peacock v Freeman* is an example, from that where the principal prevents that event from happening by breaking his contract with the purchaser. In such a case, the Court of Appeal has recently decided, there will be a term implied on the basis of necessity that the principal will not so act.[12]

Express provision where sale otherwise than by the agent

It is not uncommon, particularly with regard to estate agents' contracts, to find express provision for payment to be recoverable even though the sale is not effected directly by the agent but perhaps as a result of something done by him. This frequently gives rise to difficult questions as to whether the advertisements or introductions of the agent actually caused the sale. The notion of 'cause' may involve philosophical questions but the courts tend to take a more robust factual approach. A number of cases have come before the courts where it has been necessary to construe the agency contracts and decide, whether, on the facts found, the agent has effectively caused the sale. Once again, since these cases have turned on their own particular facts, they must be treated with some caution; it is not possible to deduce wide statements of principle from them. The line drawn between one decision and another has frequently been thin.

In *Bayley v Chadwick*[13] the House of Lords held auctioneers entitled to their commission when the property, a ship, was sold to one whose agent had been introduced by the auctioneers. There the contract specifically provided:

> In case the ship is not sold by auction, she is forthwith to revert to the custody of the owners for private sale, but in case a subsequent sale be effected to any person or firm introduced by you or led to make such offer in consequence of your mention or publication for auction purposes, you to be entitled to the...commission on such sale.

This clause is quite wide, but even if there is such a clause and even if the purchaser is originally introduced to the vendor by the agents, it will not follow that a subsequent sale was by their intrumentality. In a case where a purchaser bought a lot two and a-quarter years after the abortive auction, having attended there and bought other lots, the jury found that the sale had not been brought about as a result of the introduction of the auctioneers.[14] There is some ancient authority for the proposition that it is *customary* for the auctioneer to be paid commission if the vendor sells his property privately without the auctioneer's intervention before the auction or after an abortive

11 The position is similar in New Zealand see *Sinclair v Stuart* (1886) 5 N Z L R 85.
12 *Alpha Trading Ltd v Dunnshaw-Patten Ltd* [1981] QB 290, [1981] 1 All ER 482.
13 (1878) 39 LT 429, 4 Asp MLC 59, H L. See also *Green v Bartlett* (1863) 14 CBNS 681, 32 LJCP 261.
14 *Lumley v Nicholson* (1886) 34 WR 716, 2 TLR 711. The judge stressed that this was a question for the jury and that there was evidence that the sale was a separate transaction although he would have found the other way.

auction sale. Such was found in *Rainy v Vernon*[15] where three experienced auctioneers gave evidence to that effect. But the existence of such a custom was not accepted in the more recent case of *Williams v Tucker,*[16] and the plaintiff auctioneer's reliance on *Rainy v Vernon* was unsuccessful.

Thus auctioneers have been astute to include the kind of express conditions we have been discussing. Moreover, auctioneers may not wish to make their entitlement to remuneration depend upon a finding that they effectively caused the sale or introduced the purchaser. It is simpler and safer to provide that they should be paid their commission if the property is sold before auction or within a certain time thereafter. However, even the most widely-drawn clause of this kind can prove unavailing; it is difficult to provide for every possible eventuality that can intervene and defeat the auctioneer's expectation of commission. In *John Meacock & Co v Abrahams*[17] the facts were as follows: the defendant, who was the second mortgagee of five houses, instructed the plaintiff auctioneers to sell them by auction in exercise of his remedies as an unpaid mortgagee. The contract was on the terms of the Chartered Auctioneers' and Estate Agents' Institute conditions which provided:

> Sale before auction. If a sale of the property whether arranged by the auctioneer or not, is effected between the date of acceptance of instructions and the date of the auction, commission is payable to the auctioneer on the same scale as for a sale by auction.

The auctioneers made all the necessary preparations for the sale, but at the same time the mortgagor of the properties negotiated their sale to the sitting tenants and, the day before the projected auction, succeeded in redeeming the mortgage. Thus there was nothing for the principal-second mortgagees to sell. The auctioneers claimed to recover their scale commission. At first instance they were held entitled to do so. The objection, that the clause could not be intended to cover a situation as here, where the property was sold by one other than the vendor, was not taken. The County Court judge thought that if it were so restricted it was open to abuse:[18]

> It is argued that this does not apply because the sale that was effected was made not by the mortgagee but by the mortgagor, though in substance the mortgagee's interest was greater than the mortgagor's. There is nothing which states expressly by whom the sale must be made. Anyone can sell land taking the risk of being unable to make a title before completion. A wife could sell and get her husband to come in as vendor. A tenant could sell but he would have to get in the landlord's interest before completion. A partner could sell and attempt to do the auctioneer out of commission by getting his partner to assume the character of vendor. If 'sale' is limited to a sale by the person who instructed the auctioneer there would be a number of holes through which vendors could slip out of the network of the liability for commission...As a matter of language the word 'sale' is wide enough to cover a sale by anyone, wide enough to cover a sale by the mortgagor. Mr Clauson, who argued attractively on behalf of a client whose conduct has not been wholly attractive, says that I should read into the clause after the word 'sale' the words 'by the vendor'. There might be cases where the purpose of the clause pointed to a

15 (1840) 9 CP 559.
16 (1900) Times, March 9.
17 [1956] 3 All ER 660, [1956] 1 WLR 1463, CA.
18 [1956] 3 All ER 660 at 669, [1956] 1 WLR 1463 at 1475.

> restrictive interpretation. Here it is the other way about. The purpose of the clause is to prevent people doing the auctioneer out of payment for his work. The people who framed the clause were aiming at a sale by anyone. There is no reason to apply a restrictive interpretation.

The principals appealed to the Court of Appeal. The judges there were divided. The majority, Lords Justices Denning and Hodson, found against the auctioneers. They preferred a restrictive interpretation of the commission clause and held that its natural construction covered only a sale by the client;[19] they did not believe that the framers of the clause ever addressed their minds to the possibility of a sale by any person other than the client. Morris L J dissented. He looked to the purpose of the condition and said:[20]

> It seems to me...that the purpose of the clause was to ensure that the auctioneer should not be deprived of payment for his work once he has accepted instructions from someone in a position to give those instructions...If the property is sold before auction, it is but reasonable and fair that the auctioneer should be paid, and the language is wide enough to refer to a sale by anyone entitled to sell the freehold.

And further, 'The purpose of the clause is to prevent people doing the auctioneer out of payment for his work.'[1]

Whilst Morris L J and the County Court judge were clearly more sympathetic to the auctioneer's plight, it is suggested that the decision of the majority in this case is correct. The abuse of sales with the connivance of the client can be dealt with by 'lifting the veil' and ascertaining that in truth the sale was by an agent of the client. If, as in this case, a mortgagor is entitled to redeem his mortgage or sell the mortgaged property at any time, it can hardly be regarded as 'doing the auctioneer out of payment for his work'; it is simply that the client has lost his right to sell the property. And if the auctioneer wishes to protect himself against such an eventuality he must provide specifically for it.

An auctioneer can, however, protect himself against the property being sold by another agent and provide for his full commission to be payable in such an event. In *Gross Fine & Krieger Chalfen v Gaynor*[2] auctioneers were appointed sole agents for the sale of a house and prepared to sell it by auction. Before the proposed sale could be effected, however, the clients sold it through another firm of estate agents by private treaty. The auctioneers were held entitled to commission at the contractually agreed rate on the price achieved in the private sale. Technically, of course, the sum was awarded as damages for breach of the contract of sole agency rather than as commission and the court also allowed a small sum as special damages to cover the costs of printing the auction sale brochure.

The amount of the commission

Assuming commission to be payable, the next question to be determined is what is the amount of the commission to which the auctioneer is entitled. In a

19 A similar view had been suggested in the earlier case of *Murad v Hearts of Oak Society* (unreported, 4 November 1955).
20 [1956] 3 All ER 660 at 670, [1956] 1 WLR 1463 at 1476.
1 [1956] 3 All ER 660 at 669, [1956] 1 WLR 1463 at 1475.
2 (1974) 233 EG 1015, QBD.

properly drawn contract, this should pose no difficulties; but the question sometimes arises because either there is a dispute as to the terms of the contract, or the contract does not specify a sum and the courts have to imply a term into the contract.

Dispute as to the incorporation of a term

Where a contract is formed by correspondence it sometimes happens that a party to a contract argues that terms have been assented to by the other party because the latter has not objected to or varied them. As Lord Denning put it recently: 'In some cases the battle is won by the man who fires the last shot. He is the man who puts forward the latest term and conditions: and, if they are not objected to by the other party, he may be taken to have agreed to them.'[3] This sort of problem tends to arise where both parties trade on standard forms and one then encounters a 'battle of the forms', but it is not restricted to that situation. If an agent and a client enter into negotiations in the form of a series of letters, it may fall to be determined whether a particular provision is incorporated into the final agreement.

In *John E Trinder & Partners v Haggis,*[4] Mr Haggis put his house in the hands of a firm of estate agents for sale. Later, his wife (with, as the county court judge found, the authority of the husband) orally engaged the plaintiff firm, although nothing was at that time said about commission. Subsequently the plaintiffs wrote detailing their commission, but neither Mr Haggis nor his wife responded to that letter. The plaintiffs who had been engaged to introduce a person willing to sign a contract to purchase at an agreed price did so, but the clients refused to sign the contract of sale which had been drafted by their solicitors. In these circumstances the judge awarded the agents their commission at the rate specified in their letter. The Court of Appeal, by a majority, dismissed the defendants' appeal. Lord Evershed MR concluded that the defendant had by his conduct unambiguously bound himself to the terms of the letter. Denning L J dissented; he said that silence could not make a new agreement nor could it add terms to an existing agreement. However, it seems clear that his view was in fact based on the finding that the agents had not established the existence of a binding agreement prior to the letter. It is well established that once there is a contract, a failure to respond to a letter setting out the terms will have a confirmatory effect; the dictum of Lord Denning in the *Butler Machine Tool* case is clear about that.[5]

If an auctioneer seeks to rely on a scale charges clause, or for that matter, any other clause as forming part of his contract, he must show that he has taken sufficient steps to bring it to the attention of his principal. In the recent case of *Bernard Thorpe & Partners v Snook,*[6] the plaintiff auctioneers were instructed to sell the defendants' farm by auction subject to a reserve of £275 000. They sent a form to the defendants which contained their scale fees. On the reverse was a further clause which provided:

> Sale After Auction. If a sale of the property, whether arranged by the auctioneers or not is effected within three months after the auction commission on the price

3 *Butler Machine Tool Co Ltd v Ex-Cell-O Corpn (England) Ltd* [1979] 1 All ER 965, CA at 968.
4 [1951] WN 416.
5 [1979] 1 All ER 965, [1979] 1 WLR 401, CA. See also *Way & Waller Ltd v Ryde* [1944] 1 All ER 9, CA.
6 (1983) 266 EG 440.

> realised shall be payable to the auctioneers on the same scale as for a sale by auction in which event any fee for non-sale shall merge in the commission then payable.

This was an adaptation of the standard clause contained in the Royal Institute of Chartered Surveyors' scale of fees booklet. At the auction the property failed to reach its reserve and the defendant, within three months, sold the property by private treaty for £285 000. The auctioneers duly claimed their commission of £5 700 and their principals claimed that they had not agreed to the condition quoted above. Whether a condition has become incorporated into contract of agency depends upon whether the party to be bound had notice of it. Nolan J said:[7]

> The plaintiffs do not have to establish that Mr Snook actually read the critical clause. The question is whether they did all that was reasonably sufficient to give Mr Snook notice of it. The question falls into two parts: first did they adequately inform Mr Snook of the significance of the scale charges and of their reliance on it. Secondly, if so, was the supply of that document enough to convey to him the whole of its contents?

Although there was nothing on the front of the form referring to the conditions on the back, the judge found that in all the circumstances of the case the auctioneers had established that the clause had become a condition of the contract and they were entitled to their commission.

No contractual provision as to commission

If the contract is silent as to the amount of the commission payable, either because the parties have not addressed their minds to this, or because the auctioneer has failed to show that a provision as to his charges has been incorporated into the agreement, the court will readily imply a term to pay a reasonable sum. As Jessel M R observed in *Miller v Beal*:[8]

> In ascertaining what amount was due...allowance should be made for a reasonable commission which he was entitled to charge,...the manifest object generally which auctioneers had in view when they entered into transactions of such a kind was to earn their commission, and it would be doing an injustice not to allow it.

What is 'reasonable' will be a matter of evidence and will normally be based upon standard charges generally operating in such a transaction. In *Newman v Richardson*,[9] an agent claimed five per cent commission on the sale of a dry dock in Swansea. The court accepted evidence from other agents that there were no special rates for the sale of such property, and said that a reasonable sum was to be ascertained on the then prevailing scales of the professional bodies.[10]

Loss of commission

Where the auctioneer has, prima facie, earned his commission, i e satisfied the condition on which it is payable, he may nevertheless lose his right to it by

7 (1983) 266 EG 440 at 443.
8 (1879) 27 WR 403 at 404. See also *Re Page (No 3)* (1863) 32 Beav 487, 8 LT231. The common law position has now been confirmed by statute; see the Supply of Goods and Services, Act 1982, s 15 (see Appendix 3).
9 (1885) 1 TLR 348. See also *Maltby v Christie* (1795) 1 Esp 339 below, p 83.
10 On the appropriate scales where sales are by order or with the authority of the courts, see ch 11. Where an auctioneer is instructed to sell by the court there is no custom or practice to allow commission when the property is not so sold but is later sold by private treaty: *Re Maitland, Pickthall v Dawes* (1903) 47 Sol Jo 709.

reason of negligence or other misconduct. There are few reported cases concerning loss of commission and those that exist are rather ancient.[11] Omission to take a step which in common usage an auctioneer would take will amount to negligence. An example is a failure timeously to obtain the purchaser's signature to the memorandum of sale in respect of land.[12] In Canada, an auctioneer has been deprived of his commission when he caused loss to his principal by concealing material facts from him.[13]

Quantum meruit

We have seen that there is no room for an implied term that the principal will not prevent his agent from earning his commission save where he does so by breaking his contract with the purchaser (as in *Alpha Trading Ltd v Dunnshaw-Patten Ltd*,[14] where a contract was concluded but the principal then refused to deliver the goods to the buyer). Can the disappointed agent however claim a quantum meruit sum, i e a sum to recompense him for the work done short of performance of that upon which the commission was payable? In *Luxor (Eastbourne) Ltd v Cooper*, Lord Russell said:[15]

> As to the claim on a quantum meruit, I do not see how this can be justified in the face of an express provision for remuneration which the contract contains. This must necessarily exclude such a claim unless it can (upon the facts of a particular case) be based upon a contract subsequent to the original contract, and arising from some conduct on the part of the principal.

It will be recalled that that case involved an estate agent's contract and the question arises as to whether an auctioneer's contract of agency is in *pari materia*. In some respect it may be, but there is some judicial opinion that in this situation it is not. In *Frank Swain (a firm) v Whitfield Corpn Ltd*,[16] the plaintiff auctioneer's instructions to sell properties of a company were revoked at 'the eleventh hour and fifty-ninth minute' and the judge at first instance awarded them a quantum meruit sum based upon the agreed commission calculated on the reserves that had been placed on the properties. It does not appear to have been argued that a quantum meruit claim was impermissible. However, Upjohn LJ, with whom Pearson and Ormerod LLJ agreed, did briefly advert to this question and asserted that a quantum meruit claim was available:[17]

> That that is the law is not now in dispute. It is clear that an auctioneer is in a different position from an estate agent who contracts with his principal to introduce a purchaser. Until he introduces a purchaser he has no right to any commission whatsoever; but with an auctioneer the law is different, if the properties are withdrawn from auction he is entitled to a quantum meruit for the services thrown away.

Whilst this dictum by a senior judge in the Court of Appeal must be accorded respect, it must also be treated with some caution. The opening sentence may

11 See e g *Denew v Daverell* (1813) 3 Camp 451; *Jones v Nanney* (1824) 13 Price 76, M'Cle 25.
12 See *Hardial Singh v Hillyer* (1979) 251 EG 951.
13 *Ring v Potts* (1903) 36 N B R 42.
14 [1981] QB 290, [1981] 1 All ER 482.
15 [1941] AC 108 at 125. See also per Lord Wright at 141 where his Lordship gave as an additional ground the fact that the principal had not obtained any benefits.
16 (1962) 183 EG 479.
17 (1962) 183 EG 479 at 479.

be merely a reference to the fact that the issue was not specifically argued by the defendants in this case. It certainly would not be true to say that the legal position is not in dispute. Indeed the point had been authoritatively decided against an auctioneer by a differently constituted Court of Appeal just six years earlier in *John Meacock & Co v Abrahams*.[18] There Hodson L J said:[19]

> The alternative way in which the claim has been put — and often it is put in this class of case where there is difficulty in complying with the express terms of the contract — is upon a quantum meruit. We have had put before us, I think, every argument which could be put, supported by the correspondence showing the late date at which the defendant withdrew his instructions for the auction, and showing that, so far as he could, he confirmed the instructions and insisted, almost to the very last, that the auction should go forward... Of course once the debt had been redeemed, they had nothing to sell. Notwithstanding the attraction of the argument that after all the plaintiffs had done their work, or a substantial part of their work, and it is hard on them that they should not be paid because the auction never took place, yet I feel that this class of case is in pari materia with estate agents cases where a professional man enters into a contract on which he is only to be paid commission, usually based on a percentage rate. If commission is to be paid on the happening of an event, there being a specific contract which goes off, he cannot claim a quantum meruit.

Faced with these two irreconcilable Court of Appeal decisions, we suggest that the decision in *John Meacock & Co v Abrahams* is more reliable. It does not appear to have been considered by the court in the later case where the point did not strictly arise for decision. In both cases the judges took judicial notice of the fact that commission rates are fixed high in recognition of the fact that auctioneers may do a lot of work on abortive sales for which they do not get paid.[20] However, there is nothing to prevent an auctioneer expressly providing for the payment of a reasonable sum for his work in such an event.

Assuming there is such an entitlement, the next question is: how much is recoverable? The question of quantification was the substantial point in issue in the *Frank Swain* case,[1] where the judge had ordered a payment to the auctioneers based on the commission rate applicable to the reserve prices. The defendants objected that those commission rates did not necessarily reflect the work done. Lord Upjohn pointed out that with a quantum meruit, one was not concerned with precise sums. There was always an element of approximation. The judge had not been in error in taking into account that the properties had been withdrawn from sale a matter of minutes before they would have come under the hammer and that there were many anxious bidders waiting in the auction rooms. The properties might well have exceeded their reserves resulting in a higher commission for the auctioneers.

Expenses

An auctioneer not infrequently provides expressly that he shall be paid his out-of-pocket expenses incurred in selling the property. If he does not, but earns

18 [1956] 1 WLR 1463.
19 [1956] 1 WLR 1463 at 1469. See also Denning LJ at 1466-8 and per Morris LJ at 1476.
20 In *Luxor (Eastbourne) Ltd v Cooper* [1941] AC 108, 110 LJKB 131, the agent stood to earn £10 000 for 8 or 9 days' work. Lord Russell's observation (at 126) that this was equivalent to the then annual salary of a Lord Chancellor may explain their Lordships' reluctance in that case to award damages or any quantum meruit sum!
1 Above, n 16.

his commission, he recoups himself thereout. There is however a paucity of authority on the question whether he can claim his expenses where he is prevented from earning his commission. In *Gross Fein & Krieger Chalfen v Gaynor*,[2] where the auctioneer recovered damages for breach of a sole agency provision, a separate award of special damages in respect of his expenses was made. However the contract in that case had expressly provided for expenses up to £300 to be chargeable. Where no claim for breach of contract arises, and assuming that there is no claim for a quantum meruit maintainable, it is arguable that an auctioneer may nevertheless claim reimbursement of his expenses. Bateman[3] opines otherwise, but such judicial opinion as has been expressed on the subject is in favour of such a claim. In *Chinnock v Sainsbury* Romilly M R said:[4]

> Where a person agrees with auctioneers for the sale by them of property in a particular manner and he then changes his mind, the rule is — *subject to the claims of auctioneers for their expenses incurred* — this court will not enforce such an agreement.

This dictum is echoed by Lord Denning in *John Meacock & Co v Abrahams*.[5] Both dicta were obiter but there seems nothing inconsistent in denying an auctioneer commission or a quantum meruit, i e payments in the way of *remuneration* when he is unable to satisfy the particular precondition, but allowing him to recoup his out-of-pocket expenses incurred at the behest of or on behalf of his principal. However, it is safest if an auctioneer expressly provides for this in his contract with his client. Both Sotheby's and Christie's reserve the right to charge the vendor in respect of withdrawn lots at a fee calculated by reference to a percentage of the reserve price or valuation of the property together with expenses.

Indemnity

An auctioneer may in the course of acting for his client incur liabilities to third parties. If he does so he will wish to recover from his principal. As we have suggested in other contexts, an auctioneer will be well advised to make express provision in his contract with his client. However, in the absence of express provision, the law may imply a promise by the principal to indemnify his agent. The circumstances in which such an implied term will be found now fall to be considered.

It can as a general proposition be stated that the existence of an agency relationship is enough for an indemnity to be implied. In *Adamson v Jarvis*, Best C J said:[6]

> ...every man who employs another to do an act which the employer appears to have the right to authorise him to do undertakes to indemnify him for all such acts as would *be lawful* if the employer had the authority he pretends to have.

2 Above, p 43, n 2.
3 Bateman *Law of Auctions* (11th edn, 1953) Estates Gazette, p 304.
4 (1860) 30 LJ Ch 409, but only as reported in (1860) 3 LT at 259, emphasis added.
5 [1956] 1 WLR 1463 at 1467.
6 (1827) 4 Bing 66 at 72.

There is an immediate limitation on the principle as expressed by Best C J, namely that the act must be one which would have been lawful if the principal had the authority he purported to have. If the act is known to the agent to be tortious or otherwise illegal, the auctioneer is unable to claim an indemnity in respect of losses incurred as a result of it. In such a case the agent is independently liable.[7]

The situations in which an auctioneer may seek indemnification are varied.[8] We have referred already to the right to indemnity where, for example, the principal revokes the auctioneer's authority. Disputes have, however, most commonly arisen where an auctioneer has been subjected to a claim for conversion of or trespass to goods because it has been alleged that his principal was not the true owner. *Adamson v Jarvis* itself involved a claim of this nature. In order for an auctioneer to be liable to the true owner it is necessary that he receives the property and delivers it to the purchaser with a view to passing title in it to him. The agent's ignorance of his principal's lack of title is no defence. But if the auctioneer merely acts as a intermediary in, e g, settling the price between the parties, no such liability is incurred.[9]

The principle enunciated in *Adamson v Jarvis* was wider than the decision there required. The agent was said to be entitled to an indemnity in respect of all authorised acts save those which were known by him to be unlawful. This would mean that a principal would invariably be liable to indemnify his agent where his instructions were lawful but nevertheless caused his agent to incur losses. However, it has been suggested that a principal should not have to indemnify his agent when he, the principal, has not been at fault. In *Halbronn v International Horse Agency and Exchange Ltd*,[10] the unusual facts were as follows: the plaintiff auctioneers, carrying on business in France, were instructed by the defendant to sell his mare 'Pentecost'. She was entered and described under that name in the English stud book. One Delavan, a French horse-breeder, had earlier imported a thoroughbred mare of the same name into France and claimed, and was subsequently awarded, damages from the plaintiffs on the ground that their advertising of another mare of the same name had reduced the value of his own animal. The auctioneers' claim for an indemnity against their client was dismissed on the ground that their loss was not incurred by virtue of any wrong done by the principal. Bruce J said:[11]

> It was contended by Mr Vaughan Williams that the mere fact of the employment of the plaintiff as auctioneer by the defendants involved an obligation on the part of the defendants to indemnify the plaintiff against all claims arising out of the plaintiffs' conduct as auctioneer in respect of acts done by him within the scope of his authority. I am not prepared to assent to that proposition...

Here, since the damages recovered in the French court arose not from any act of the plaintiffs in the performance of their duty but because of a mistake as to the identity of the mare, and since that mistake was not attributable to any

7 See *Dugdale v Lovering* (1875) LR 10 CP 196, 44 LJCP 197, per Brett J, citing with approval Tindal CJ in *Toplis v Grane* (1839) 5 Bing NC 636, 9 LJCP 180.

8 Where an auctioneer wishes to seek an indemnity in proceedings being brought against him, he may serve a third-party notice on his principal under RSC Ord 16. (Appendix 3.)

9 See *Barker v Furlong* [1891] 2 Ch 172, 60 LJ Ch 368. The auctioneer's potential liability for conversion is discussed in ch 5.

10 [1903] 1 KB 270, 72 LJKB 90.

11 [1903] 1 KB 270 at 272.

misdescription by the defendant, there was no right to recover an indemnity. This conclusion was tested by the learned judge by hypothecating the case where a genuine Constable was auctioned but a jury subsequently mistakenly concluded that the painting was a fake. In such circumstances, said the judge, the 'auctioneer would have no claim to recover, against the person who had entrusted him with the sale of the picture'. It is, with respect, difficult to follow the reasoning of the judge. There is a dictum of the Privy Council which, in terms, says that if an agent suffers loss as a result of a court decision it matters not whether that decision is erroneous in law[12] and, in any event, it is submitted that where the loss is suffered by the auctioneer in the course of carrying out his instructions an indemnity should be implied; one is not apportioning *blame*; it is simply a question of deciding upon whom a loss should fall. And if a loss arises as a result of an authorised act, he who authorises it should bear the loss.

The observations made in the *Halbronn* case were expressly disapproved by the Court of Appeal in *Williams v Lister & Co.*[13] There Lister and Co as auctioneers had been instructed by third parties, who had let out furniture to the plaintiffs on hire purchase, to seize and to sell the furniture. This the auctioneers did and were duly sued by the plaintiffs for wrongful seizure. The auctioneers set about defending this action which was subsequently dismissed for want of prosecution after long delays by the plaintiffs. The auctioneers were held entitled to an indemnity in respect of their costs in defending the action. Since there was no successful action for wrongful seizure it cannot be said that the principals were guilty of any wrongful act in instructing them to seize and sell the furniture. Vaughan Williams LJ, who had been counsel for the unsuccessful auctioneers in the *Halbronn* case,[14] said:[15]

> It is perfectly clear that this case falls within the common indemnity which arises where the agent is injured in carrying out his master's instructions, and because he has carried them out. In these circumstances the agent is entitled to be indemnified by his principal notwithstanding the observations of the learned judge in *Halbronn v International Horse Agency and Exchange Ltd.*

Buckley LJ was less restrained; he said:[16]

> The defendants acted rightly as agents in defending the action, and in so doing incurred costs, and for these costs I think they are entitled to be indemnified. The case of *Halbronn v International Horse Agency and Exchange Ltd* is cited as a denial of that right. I must say that I do not understand that decision, but if it contains anything inconsistent with the present judgements, I am clearly of the opinion that it is wrong.

So long, therefore, as the auctioneer acts within his actual or implied authority, he may recover an indemnity in respect of losses incurred as a result of his performance thereof. If, however, he goes beyond that which he is authorised to do, he will not be able to claim at common law on any implied indemnity.

12 *Frixione v Tagliaferro & Sons* (1856) 10 Moo PCC 175 at 200.
13 (1913) 109 LT 699, CA.
14 Above, n 10.
15 (1913) 109 LT 699 at 700.
16 Above, n 15.

In *Sweeting v Turner*,[17] where the defendant auctioneer paid rent on premises owned by the vendor where goods he had auctioned were kept, in order to avoid the goods being levied for distress, it was held that no indemnity was available since his act was unauthorised. His claim that he had an agency of necessity failed because the goods had at that time ceased to be the property of the vendor-principal.

Whereas, as we have seen, an agent is entitled to defend an action, e g, in conversion,[18] arising out of the performance of his agency, he is not entitled to be indemnified as regards the costs of defending an action where the allegation against him was, substantially, that he was in *breach* of his agency. In *Tomlinson v Liquidators of Scottish Amalgamated Silk Ltd*,[19] the estate of a deceased director of a company in liquidation failed to recover on an indemnity claim either at common law or on the basis of a clause in his company's articles in respect of the expenses of (successfully) defending both criminal and civil charges of fraud brought against him in connection with his running of the affairs of the company. In answer to the estate's submission that the expenses arose by reason of acts done in the discharge of his duties as an agent of the company, Lord Tomlin in the House of Lords said:[20]

> In my view the expenses incurred by reason of the allegations made against the deceased being allegations of matters which would have been a breach of his duty and which were held to be disproved or non-proven, are not expenses incurred by him by reason of an act done by him as a director in the discharge of his duties.

It has been held that where an auctioneer by virtue of his own mistake of the law incurs a liability, he will be unable to recover from his principal.[1] Similarly, where the auctioneer is negligent there will be no implied indemnity.[2] Finally, as with any implied term, there can be no implication in the face of an inconsistent express term in the contract.

Lien

Grove J in *Hammonds v Barclay*[3] provided the classic definition of a lien arising at common law thus: 'A lien is a right in one man to retain that which is in his possession belonging to another until certain demands of him the person in possession are satisfied.'[4]

Property attached

An auctioneer has by virtue of the possession of his principal's property, a lien over it for his charges and remuneration. The right of retention of those goods

17 (1872) LR 7 QB 310, 41 LJQB 58. Above, ch 3.
18 Unless, perhaps he defends without the consent of his principal; see *Spurrier v Elderton* (1803) 5 Esp 1, sed quaere.
19 1935 SC (HL) 1.
20 1935 SC (HL) 1 at 6.
1 *Capp v Topham* (1805) 6 East 392, 2 Smith KB 443 where the auctioneer failed to take precautions to avoid auction duty being payable on an abortive sale under the candle. Contrast *Brittain v Lloyd* (1845) 14 M&W 762, 15 LJ Ex 43.
2 *Jones v Nanney* (1824) 13 Price 76, M'Cle 25.
3 (1802) 2 East 227.
4 (1802) 2 East 227 at 235.

(and documents of title in the case of land)[5] thus gives the auctioneer a security interest. This valuable right is established by custom and is independent of any right specifically provided for in his contract with his client. As long ago as 1788 it was said by the Lord Chief Justice:[6]

> I entertain no doubt that an auctioneer has a possession coupled with an interest in goods which he is employed to sell, not a bare custody...an auctioneer also has a special property in him with a lien for the charges of the sale and the commission.

This dictum has since been endorsed in numerous cases.[7] The custom, as with most customs developed in commercial law, was established 'for the convenience of trade' and, in this area, with a view to encouraging 'factors to advance money upon goods in their possession or which must come into their hands as factors'.[8]

It is perhaps obvious that if an auctioneer is to have a lien over his principal's property, he must be entitled not only to retain it as against his principal but he must also be entitled to withhold the property from the *purchaser*. We shall see later that, independently, an auctioneer has rights against the purchaser with regard to the price and in this connection has a lien against him over the property; but, equally, in support of his rights against his vendor-principal, the auctioneer may resist a claim by the purchaser of the property in tort for wrongful intereference with the goods knocked down to him.[9] The lien is a *possessory* right, however, and once the auctioneer parts with possession of the goods he loses his right.

In *Coppin v Walker*,[10] which involved an action by the auctioneer against the purchaser for the price, the court held that the auctioneer had disentitled himself from claiming the price which the purchaser sought to avoid paying, relying on a set-off against the vendor. The judges suggested that by parting with possession without giving the purchaser notice of his lien, the auctioneer lost it. However the auctioneer can, and usually will, let the purchaser take the property in return for the price since it is also well settled that he has a lien over the proceeds of sale. In *Robinson v Rutter* Lord Campbell CJ said: 'As auctioneer the plaintiff must be supposed...to have had a lien upon the horse for the price and to have a right of lien on the price when paid for his commission and charges.'[11]

An auctioneer may also be protected if he takes merely a deposit rather than the whole price, provided that this is sufficient to cover his commission etc. However, the capacity in which he receives the deposit may be crucial. An auctioneer should perhaps take the deposit as agent of the vendor.[12] If the contract provides for him to receive it as 'stake-holder' (a provision regarded by Lord Denning MR as 'odd' and as a 'falsa demonstratio' in *Chelmsford*

5 Which, it has been held in Canada, do not include plans of the property. *Blackburn v Macdonald* (1857) 6 UC CP 380, CA.
6 *Williams v Millington* (1788) 1 HyBl 81 at 85 per Lord Loughborough LCJ.
7 See e g *Lane v Tewson* (1841) 12 AD&El 116 n; *Woolfe v Horne* (1877) 2 QBD 355, 46 LJQB 534; *Benton v Campbell, Parker & Co Ltd* [1925] 2 KB 410, 94 LJQB 881; *Chelmsford Auctions Ltd v Poole* [1973] QB 542.
8 *Houghton v Matthews* (1803) 3 Bos&P 485 at 486, 127 ER 263 at 264.
9 *Lane v Tewson*, n 7 above.
10 (1816) 7 Taunt 237, 2 Marsh 497.
11 (1855) 4 E&B 954 at 956, 119 ER 355 at 356; see also *Drinkwater v Goodwin* (1775) 1 Cowp 251; *Webb v Smith* (1885) 30 Ch D 192, 55 LJ Ch 343, CA.
12 Whether this is advantageous will depend on the circumstances. This matter is more fully discussed in ch 5.

Auctions Ltd v Poole[13]), then in certain situations he will be unable to maintain a lien over the moneys vis-à-vis his principal. One example arose in *Skinner v Trustee of Property of Reed (Bankrupt)*,[14] where an auctioneer was instructed by a mortgagee of a farm to sell it free from the encumbrances. The property was sold to Skinner who paid the auctioneers a deposit of £3 000 as stake-holder. Before the sale was completed the vendor-mortgagees went bankrupt. Subsequently the contract of sale was completed and the auctioneers asserted a claim over the deposit monies in their hands. However the plaintiff-purchaser sought to have the money applied in or toward the discharge of the encumbrances which, contrary to the contract, had not been discharged. Cross J explained the position thus:[15]

> If, as in this case, the stake-holder is an auctioneer who has a lien on the deposit for his commission and his disbursements, the question whether he can exercise his lien must, I think, depend on the trust on which in the event he holds the deposit. If the contract has gone off owing to the vendor's default, then clearly the auctioneer cannot exercise his lien for his charges because the deposit has never become the property of the vendor and is returnable in toto to the purchaser. If, on the other hand, the contract has gone off owing to the purchaser's default, it is quite obvious that the auctioneer can exercise his lien against the vendor because the deposit has become the absolute property of the vendor. But what is the position if the contract is completed... When the purchaser affirms the contract the vendor cannot in my judgement claim payment for the deposit in the hands of a stake-holder so long as there are outstanding encumbrances on the property sold which it is the vendor's duty to discharge...if a stake-holder is an auctioneer his lien will only attach to so much of the deposit as is not needed to discharge the encumbrance.

This is not a question of the auctioneer's right of lien being postponed in favour of other prior rights but rather that the deposit moneys, held as stake-holder, did not, in that character, ever become the property of the vendor so as to be capable of being affected by the lien which the auctioneer has over the vendor's property.

The question of priorities did arise however in *Webb v Smith*.[16] In this case the defendant auctioneers sold a brewery on behalf of a vendor who owed certain sums to the plaintiff-purchaser. The vendor by letter charged the proceeds of sale including certain deposit moneys in favour of the purchaser to the extent of this indebtedness. The auctioneers however claimed their lien in respect of their commission over the same fund. It was held that their lien took priority over the charge in favour of the purchaser. Here the charge in favour of the plaintiff was posterior to the lien. If the charge had effectively pre-dated the sale and the receipt of the deposit, it is thought that it would, on general principles, have taken priority.

Nature of the lien

A further aspect in *Webb v Smith*[17] concerned the nature of the lien possessed by an auctioneer: can it be exercised only over the specific property in respect of

13 [1973] QB 542, [1973] 1 All ER 810, CA.
14 [1967] 3 WLR 871.
15 [1967] 3 WLR 871 at 874-6.
16 Above, n 11.
17 Above, n 11.

which the charges are incurred, or is it in the nature of a general lien attaching to a general balance in the hands of the auctioneer? The question arose because the auctioneers had also, as a distinct transaction, sold furniture belonging to the vendor and retained the balance of the proceeds of sale thereof. Webb claimed that where a creditor held two separate funds he should pay himself out of that fund which did not prejudice the rights of another creditor. This is known as the doctrine of marshalling. The Court of Appeal held, in this case, that the doctrine was inapplicable because the auctioneers had subsequently accounted to their principal for the proceeds of sale of furniture and thus had no lien over it. Lindley L J:[18]

> The vice of the argument for the plaintiff is that in truth there were not two funds to which the defendant could resort, that is, two funds standing upon an equal footing. The defendants had a superior right of lien as to the funds produced by the sale of the brewery.

He added however:

> I think, however, that they could not have deprived the plaintiff of the benefit of his charge, if there had been two funds to which they might have resorted under equal circumstances.

This last comment begs a rather important question. If an auctioneer sells independently, under separate instructions, two items of property and their sale gives rise to separate claims for commission etc, can he exercise a lien over one item in respect of his commission earned on the sale of the other? A negative answer seems, generally to be correct. It is true that in *Palmer v Day & Sons*[19] an auctioneer was held entitled to retain commission on the sale of a house out of the proceeds of sale of certain pictures, but this case turned on the application of a specific right of set-off provided by the Bankruptcy Acts.[20] The judge at first instance had held in favour of the auctioneer on the ground that there was one entire indivisible contract, but the Divisional Court found that the evidence did not support that contention. Lord Russell of Killowen L J said:[1]

> The case appears to us the ordinary one of auctioneers being instructed to sell first, the furniture and secondly the house...It therefore becomes necessary to consider whether his judgement can be supported on the other ground, that of mutual dealings [under] s 38 of the Bankruptcy Act 1883.

No lien will be available in respect of work done before the agency contract comes into being,[2] or for work outside the auctioneer's normal duties,[3] or where the auctioneer has waived his lien,[4] or where the auctioneer is estopped

18 (1885) 30 ChD 192, CA at 202-3.
19 [1895] 2 QB 618, 64 LJQB 807.
20 Section 38 of the Bankruptcy Act 1883. See now s 3 of the Bankruptcy Act 1914. See also *Miller v Hutcheson and Dixon* (1881) 8 R (Ct of Sess) 489; *Houghton v Matthews* (n 8 above); *Scarfe v Morgan* (1838) 4 M&W 270, 7 LJ Ex 324.
1 [1895] 2 QB 618 at 620-21.
2 *Houghton v Matthews*, n 8 above.
3 *Sanderson v Bell* (1834) 2 Cr&M 304, 3 LJ Ex 66.
4 *Scarfe v Morgan* (n 20 above) where the court declined to hold that seeking to retain a mare for a general balance amounted to a waiver of his particular lien thereon for the charge on the particular occasion.

from setting it up by having previously denied the owner's title.[5] It is also possible that if an auctioneer exercising a lien accepts some other form of security instead — e g a promissory note — he will be taken to have abandoned his lien. Whether or not abandonment has occurred is a question of intention. In the case of an agent such as a solicitor, the prima facie inference is that he abandons his lien if he takes an alternative security from his client. That is because a solicitor has a special duty of disclosure vis-à-vis his client, but if the agent has no such special duty the inference will not be taken.[6] It is thought that an auctioneer is in this latter category.

Enforcement of lien

Where the lien sought to be enforced against the principal is over his goods the auctioneer may be put to the expense of keeping them properly. In the case of livestock there will be costs involved in feeding, and in the case of other goods possibly warehousing charges.[7] Since the auctioneer is a bailee of the goods in his possession, it is his responsibility to care for them properly.[8] This duty may be onerous but, unless there is express provision in the contract of agency, the right of lien carries with it no right of sale; it is merely a passive interest giving rise only to a right to retain possession.[9] Auctioneers should, therefore, make express provision for a right of sale in such circumstances. Failing that, the court has discretion to allow a sale. In *Larner v Fawcett*[10] the Court of Appeal considered the ambit of its discretion under the precursor of the present rule: RSC Ord 29 r 4.[11] The court declined to lay down any principles but upheld the discretion of the judge at first instance who had ordered a sale of a filly in the hands of a racehorse trainer whose expenses had not been paid, there being a dispute as to ownership. However, the court did say that the mere fact that the person claiming a lien would be inconvenienced by having to retain the chattel pending determination of the issues was not, ipso facto, a reason for ordering a sale.

No problem of this sort arises where the lien is exercised against funds. An auctioneer retaining proceeds of sale as against his vendor can, and perhaps should, invest the sum and retain a proportion of the income derived therefrom. However, if pending a dispute between vendor and purchaser as to entitlement to a deposit, the auctioneer is required to pay the money into court, there is authority for the proposition that he is allowed to deduct his costs and expenses first and not wait until the determination of potentially protracted litigation.[12] The court may order the property subject to the lien to be released on the provision of security: RSC Ord 29, r 6.[13]

5 *Dirks v Richards* (1842) 4 Man & G 574, 5 Scott NR 534.
6 *In Re Taylor, Stileman, and Underwood*, ex p *Payne Collier* [1891] 1 Ch 590, 60 LJ Ch 525.
7 In practice a lien over livestock is unlikely to arise; livestock auctioneers invariably deliver up these goods to the purchaser and, indeed, allow a week to a fortnight for payment.
8 See e g *Scarfe v Morgan* (n 20 above) and further ch 5.
9 *Bartholomew v Freeman* (1877) 3 CPD 316, 38 LT 814; and see *Thames Iron Works Co v Patent Derrick Co* (1860) 1 John & H 93, 29 LJ Ch 714; *Larner v Fawcett* [1950] 2 All ER 727, CA.
10 Above, n 9.
11 See Appendix 3.
12 See *Annersley v Muggridge* (1816) 1 Madd 593; *Yates v Farebrother* (1819) 4 Madd 239; *Blenkhorn v Penrose* (1880) 29 WR 237.
13 See Appendix 3.

Other rights

There may be many other rights which an auctioneer may wish to reserve to himself in the contract with the vendor. For example, it is common to find in auctioneers' contracts provisions whereby the auctioneer is given: (a) complete discretion as to the description to be applied to the property to be sold; (b) reservation of the right to seek expert advice and to illustrate lots in literature at the seller's expense; (c) the exclusive right to bid on behalf of the seller when there is a reserve placed upon the property; (d) rights relating to insurance and warehousing; and (e) a right to accept rescission of the contract of sale where the lot is a deliberate forgery (as defined).

RIGHTS AGAINST THE PURCHASER

An auctioneer enjoys a number of rights against the purchaser. We have already stated that he has a lien on his principal's goods which may be enforced against the purchaser in so far as he may retain possession of them and successfully defend an action for their delivery up or for damages for their detention. Perhaps of fundamental importance, however, is an auctioneer's right to sue the purchaser for the price of goods sold.

Action for the price of goods

Normally, unless an agent contracts personally, he cannot be sued or sue on the contract made by him, because the contract is that of the principal.[14] However, an auctioneer has long been held able to sue the purchaser for the price of goods.[15] The right was first enunciated in *Williams v Millington*,[16] and has subsequently been reiterated many times. However the exact principle upon which this right is based is uncertain. A number of explanations have been given: namely that it is based on his lien, or upon his special property in the goods, or on some collateral contract with the purchaser. It may be important to establish the precise basis, where for example, the lien has been lost or waived but it is in any event clear that when the auctioneer sues the purchaser, e g for the price, he does not do so in enforcement of the contract of sale itself. In *Benton v Campbell Parker & Company Ltd*,[17] Salter J said:[18]

> The auctioneer has a special property in the chattel delivered to him for sale, he has a lien on it and on the price of it. These rights...do not arise from the contract of sale which binds only the buyer and the principal. They arise from the contract which the auctioneer makes on his own account with the buyer... It is clear therefore that the auctioneer does not sue for the price by virtue of the contract of sale.

If the true explanation is that he sues on some separate personal contract, then an auctioneer's right to sue for the price of goods provides no special exception

14 See e g *Bowstead on Agency* (14th edn, 1976) Sweet & Maxwell, arts 112-128.
15 But not land. See below.
16 (1788) 1 Hy Bl 81. The position is the same in Canada. See *Coate v Terry* (1875) 24 C&P 571; and in Scotland, see *Mackenzie v Cormack* 1950 SC 183, 1950 SLT 139.
17 [1925] 2 KB 410, 94 LJKB 881.
18 [1925] 2 KB 410 at 415-416.

to the principle that an agent cannot sue on his principal's contract. That this is the true explanation was expressly left open by the Court of Appeal in *Wilson & Sons v Pike*[19] where recovery by the auctioneer was on behalf of the vendor-principal whose contract the auctioneer was enforcing. In *Chelmsford Auctions Ltd v Poole*[20] Lord Denning MR emphasised that a sale by auction involved three contracts: not only those between the principal-vendor and the auctioneer and between the vendor and the purchaser, but a third[1]

> between the auctioneer and the highest bidder (the purchaser). The auctioneer has possession of the goods and has a lien on them for the whole price. He is not bound to deliver the goods to the purchaser except on receiving the price... If he does allow the purchaser to take delivery without paying the price...the auctioneer can sue in his own name for the full price.

The reference to the 'full price' is significant. In this case the auctioneers knocked down a car to Poole for £57. Poole paid a deposit of £7 which sufficed to cover the auctioneer's charges and commission but he refused to accept or take delivery of the vehicle on the grounds that it was unroadworthy. Poole sought to meet the auctioneer's claim for the price with the defence that since their charges were covered, their interest had been satisfied, and they had suffered no loss; thus they had no cause of action. In fact, the auctioneers had accounted to their principal for the price realised. The conditions of sale expressly provided that the auctioneers could recover the price from a purchaser, but Lord Denning held that, apart from the express provision, the common law recognised such a right and that the right was not barred by receipt of a deposit covering the auctioneers' commission. When it is recalled that the auctioneer is generally under a duty in sales of goods to obtain the price for the vendor, the conclusion reached by the Court of Appeal in this case seems correct.

The next question which arises is whether the purchaser can successfully defend an action for the price brought by the auctioneer by showing that he has already paid the principal-vendor. Consonant with the principle that the auctioneer has a separate contract with the purchaser for the price (but not perhaps with the commercial considerations upon which it is based), the answer seems to be that payment to the vendor does not avoid the purchaser's liability to the auctioneer. Such was laid down in *Robinson v Rutter*.[2] The report of this case is not very full and it is unclear whether the plaintiff auctioneers had received their commission etc. If they had not, the decision is justifiable since the auctioneer by delivering up the goods (here a horse) to the defendant-purchaser gave up his lien therefor in exchange for the promise to be paid. However, if the auctioneer has received his commission, payment of the price to the vendor should avoid liability since the auctioneer's interests are fully satisfied and he is not at risk of a suit by the principal for the price.

This last proposition seems to be supported by two cases distinguished by Lord Denning in *Chelmsford Auctions Ltd v Poole*, viz *Holmes v Tutton*[3] and *Grice v*

19 [1949] 1 KB 176, [1948] 2 All ER 267, CA.
20 [1973] QB 542.
1 [1973] QB 542 at 548.
2 (1855) 4 E&B 954, 24 LJQB 250.
3 (1855) 5 E&B 65, 24 LJQB 346.

Kenrick.[4] In *Holmes v Tutton* the question arose whether, in an action by auctioneers for the price of goods sold and delivered, the purchaser could resist the claim by showing that he had a set-off against the vendor. Lord Campbell C J, who had also given judgment in *Robinson v Rutter*, said:[5]

> There may be some doubt whether the auctioneer, not having the possession of the goods, and it not appearing whether he sold in his own name, and his lien for the price having been covered by the money he received, so that he might be found to have paid himself out of the proceeds received could have sued the plaintiffs for the price of the goods.[6] But if he could, we think that in an action for the price of the goods so sold it would be a good answer...to show for the defendant that the lien of the auctioneer was satisfied *and that he was suing merely for the principal*, and that there was a set-off as between the principal and the vendee of the goods.

The italicised words allow for a different conclusion, it is suggested, where there is such a set-off but the auctioneer is out of pocket by reason of having accounted to his principal for the price; in such a situation the auctioneer is suing on his own account and not 'merely for the principal'. In *Grice v Kenrick* the vendor had by prior arrangement agreed that the purchaser could set-off the price against debts he was owed. This was unknown to the auctioneers who, having deducted their charges, paid a sum on account to the vendor for the proceeds of sale of certain lots. The purchaser then warned the auctioneers of the arrangement he had with the vendor and told them not to pay any further sums to him. However the auctioneers failed to take heed and paid over the balance then in their hands. On these facts the court held that the purchaser could resist a claim for the price brought by the auctioneers. Hannen J said:[7]

> By the terms of the original agreement between the defendant and [the vendor] the defendant was to have the goods without payment; and it appeared that as between the plaintiff and [the vendor] the plaintiff's charges...had been satisfied before action. If the plaintiff were to recover the amount in the present action he would be bound to hand over the whole proceeds to his employer, who, however, by agreement between him and the defendant, was not entitled to receive anything. Any facts, therefore, which show that [the vendor] would not be entitled to recover, established a defence to an action brought by the plaintiff.

A few comments need to be made in respect of this dictum. First, the apparent breadth of the last sentence is clearly limited by the context of the preceding words. Second, the bar to recovery only operated in this case on the finding that the auctioneers, having been satisfied, were effectively seeking to recover for their vendor-principal. If there had been a question of potential liability of the auctioneers to their client for the price or if they had paid the price to him, the position would, it is suggested, have been different for it could then not be said that they would be bound to disgorge the fruits of their action.[8] Similarly, if an auctioneer has been instructed to defray debts due to other creditors of the

4 (1870) LR 5 QB 340, 39 LJQB 175.
5 (1855) 5 E&B 65 at 81-2, emphasis added.
6 A doubt resolved in favour of the auctioneer in *Chelmsford Auctions Ltd v Poole* [1973] QB 542 [1973] 1 All ER 810, CA.
7 (1870) LR 5 QB 340 at 345.
8 See also *Traynor v Larkin* (1916) 50 ILT 17 to a similar effect.

vendor out of the proceeds of sale, a set-off claimed by a purchaser will not be a good defence to an action by the auctioneer for the price save only to the extent of any balance payable to the vendor.[9]

Where a principal agrees that another may take goods at auction in satisfaction of a prior claim, the analysis may be that there is in fact no sale at auction at all. This is what occurred in the unusual case of *Bartlett v Purnell.*[10] The defendant was granted a legacy of £200 in the will of a testator whose estate was disposed of at auction. The executor of the will agreed before the sale that the defendant could take goods up to the value of her legacy in satisfaction thereof. The auction particulars provided for part payment to be paid on sale and the balance on delivery. The defendant 'bought' goods to the value of £145 and refused to pay for them. The auctioneers were held unable to sue her for the price. Coleridge J held that had she been a purchaser she would have been liable but that on the facts she did not buy at auction: 'she was to take the goods; but they were to be reckoned at the highest price bidden for them. The auctioneer wrote the name down but that was merely the necessary way of fixing such price.'[11]

We said earlier that the precise basis of the auctioneer's rights against the purchaser has been the subject of differing formulations. Whilst it is clear that an auctioneer has a lien on the goods and on the proceeds of sale for his charges and commission, it cannot be that the lien itself is the basis upon which the auctioneer may sue for the price. A lien is a *possessory* security which in itself confers no right of action. If possession of the goods were a pre-requisite to recovery of the price, no such action would lie once the auctioneer had delivered the goods to the purchaser. There are dicta which suggest that possession is necessary. In *Coppin v Walker,*[12] the plaintiff auctioneer sold goods of one Appleton in the latter's house. However he also included certain goods belonging to Appleby without disclosing this fact. The defendant purchased certain of these goods and took them away without paying but without demur by the auctioneer. The defendant was a creditor of Appleton and refused to pay. The court refused the auctioneer's claim for the price. Park J said:[13]

> The plaintiff [sic] had a clear right of set-off against Appleton; and the auctioneer has parted with his lien, without giving the defendant notice of any claim which he had on the price, and therefore it would be gross iniquity to say that the defendant is not entitled to his set-off.

And Burrough J opined that 'it is enough for the court to decide on, that the auctioneer has parted with his lien.'[14]

The marginal note to this report states that there is no implied contract to pay on the auctioneer giving up his lien by delivery of the goods. However, in *Coppin v Craig,*[15] a subsequent case arising on the same facts, the courts suggested that an action for the price did arise on such an implied promise to

9 *M Manley & Sons Ltd v Berkett* [1912] 2 KB 329, 81 LJKB 1232.
10 (1836) 4 Ad&El 792.
11 (1836) 4 Ad&El 792.
12 (1816) 7 Taunt 237, 2 Marsh 497, above.
13 (1816) 7 Taunt 237 at 241-2.
14 Above, n 13.
15 (1816) 7 Taunt 243, 2 Marsh 501.

pay, the consideration therefor being the foregoing of the lien by delivery without payment.

In many of the cases discussed above, the auctioneer is suing for the price just because he has parted with possession without payment; it is submitted that the better view is that the right to sue does not depend upon the continuing existence of the lien itself, but rather on a implied contract arising from the delivery up of possession without payment. *Coppin v Walker* is better explained by treating the act of the auctioneer as expressly negativing such an implication, as suggested by Dallas J in that case. In other words, there will be no contract arising out of the relinquishment of the lien if, in the circumstances, the auctioneer *waives* it; but merely allowing the purchaser to take the goods will not, of itself, amount to waiver.[16]

Thus the right to sue for the price does not depend upon the continued existence of the lien but *arises out* of the lien or special property in the goods.[17] Therefore, the auctioneer must originally have possessed such an interest; and a prerequisite for this is possession of the goods. For this purpose it is settled that an auctioneer has possession when he sells goods in situ at the owner's premises. Such was expressly stated in *Williams v Millington*[18] itself and was approved in *Mackenzie v Cormack*[19] where furniture and plenishings of Keiss Castle were sold by auction at the castle. Moreover, it has been held that an auctioneer had sufficient possession to maintain an action for the price when a vendor-principal himself sold a horse at the auction rooms after buying it in at a previously abortive auction, the auctioneer's contract providing for commission to be payable in such circumstances and the auctioneer having paid the price to the vendor.[20]

In cattle auctions[1] it quite frequently occurs that private sales are effected by the owners outside the ring but on the auction premises before or after the auction sale is conducted, and the sale is then 'booked' with the auctioneer. Such sales have only relatively recently been the subject of judicial analysis. In *Murphy v Howlett* Diplock J (as he then was) described the practice thus:[2]

> If the auctioneer accepts the booking he pays the seller...the amount of the price agreed between the seller and the intending buyer... As regards the cattle, the subject matter of the booked sale, the seller upon receiving his cheque or cash from the auctioneer is no longer interested in the transaction [and] the auctioneer...exercises all the rights of the owner...including the right of retaking possession if he has parted with it, and the right of re-sale.

In this type of sale the true legal analysis is that there are two concurrent sales of the cattle: a sale by the owner to the auctioneer at the agreed price less

16 See eg *Jarvis v Chapple* (1815) 2 Chit 387; *Maxwell v Coyle and Wadsworth* (1889) 33 ILT 131.
17 The special property or interest in the goods is, of course, derived from the interest of the vendor. If, therefore, the vendor has no title or right to sell the goods, the auctioneer cannot sue for the price: *Dickenson v Naul* (1833) 4 B&Ad 638, 1 Nev&M KB 721.
18 (1788) 1 Hy Bl 81.
19 1950 SC 183, 1950 SLT 139.
20 *Freeman v Farrow* (1886) 2 TLR 547.
1 On which see ch 10.
2 (1960) 176 EG 311 at 312.

commission and one by the auctioneer to the buyer at the agreed price. Here the auctioneer suing for the price does so not on any implied contract arising from delivery but on a quite separate contract of *sale* in which he is a principal.

There is another situation in which the auctioneer sues in fact on a quite independent contract and that is where he 'advances' money to the purchaser by taking an IOU[3] or a cheque.[4] When an auctioneer takes payment in this form he may be doing so in accordance with his instructions or without the consent of the vendor-principal. *Cleave v Moore*[5] is an example of the former situation and the court held the auctioneer entitled to sue on the IOU. In such a case the obligation owed by the purchaser to the vendor to pay e g the deposit is extinguished. Where, however, the auctioneer accepts an instrument instead of cash in breach of the Conditions of Sale and without express consent, the purchaser remains liable to the vendor but this does not preclude the auctioneer from suing on the note. As Palles C B explained in *Hodgens v Keon*:[6]

> The agreement by the auctioneer involved a warranty by him of authority to [accept] it;... By accepting it without...consent he plainly incurred a liability to [the vendor]. There is evidence that this acceptance was at the request of the defendant, and it therefore constituted a sufficient consideration for a promise by the defendant to the plaintiff from whom the consideration moved.[7]

Hodgens v Keon and *Cleave v Moore* both involved claims by auctioneers in respect of a deposit but there have been similar decisions in connection with claims for the price[8] and auction fees.[9]

The significance of the fact that recovery by the auctioneer is on a quite separate and independent contract lies, in the case of sales of goods, in the fact that this contract is unaffected by factors which may vitiate the contract of sale. In *Hindle v Brown*,[10] for example, the auctioneers were held entitled to sue on a cheque given them in respect of the sale of pictures notwithstanding that the sale was induced by fraudulent misrepresentations made by the vendor. Here it was found by the jury that the auctioneers, who had accounted to the vendor for the price, were entirely innocent of the fraud. Had it been otherwise, their contract for the cheque would have been tainted with the fraud and voidable. It has recently been held that the auctioneer's right to sue on a cheque given for the deposit survives the vendor's justifiable rescission of the contract of sale.[11]

It is frequently the case these days that auctioneers expressly reserve to themselves a right to resell property upon the failure of the purchaser to accept it, a right not concomitant with a lien at common law. If such a right is exercised the auctioneer may no longer sue for the price but can maintain an

3 *Hodgens v Keon* (1894) 2 IR 657.
4 *Hindle v Brown* (1908) 98 LT 791.
5 (1857) 28 LT OS 255, 3 Jur NS 48.
6 [1894] 2 IR 657 at 660.
7 See *Pollway Ltd v Abdullah* [1974] 2 All ER 381, [1974] 1 WLR 493 for a more recent formulation.
8 *Hindle v Brown* (1907) 98 LT 44; affd (1908) 98 LT 791, CA; *Trapp v Prescott* (1912) 17 BCR 298, 50 SCR 263.
9 *Gillen v Gibson* (1909) 44 ILT 17; *Montgomery v Fleming* (1905) 39 ILT 229.
10 Above, n 8; and see *Campbell v Smith* (1887) 13 VLR 439.
11 *Pollway Ltd v Abdullah* (n 7 above).

action for damages for the difference, if any, between the auction price and the price on resale.[12] However, unless the court construes the right of sale as a duty to sell, the purchaser will be unable to resist an action for the price where the auctioneer declines to re-sell. In *Robinson, Fisher and Harding v Behar*[13] the auction particulars provided: 'All lots uncleared within [the stipulated time] shall be re-sold by public or private sale and the deficiency (if any) attending such re-sale shall be made good by the defaulter at this sale.' The court declined to construe this provision as a mandatory order to sell (despite the use of the word 'shall') and held that the condition merely gave the auctioneers an option.

Sales of land

Sales of land are in many respects not treated by the law in the same way as contracts for the sale of goods. In the context of claims by auctioneers for the price or for the deposit, the law does not permit an auctioneer in his own right to recover from a defaulting purchaser where the sale concerns land.[14] We have seen that in the case of sales of goods, the auctioneer sues not on the contract for sale itself but on a separate contract arising from his relinquishment of the lien or from his special property in the goods which possession gives him. In the case of land there can be no such special property. In the Irish case of *Cherry v Anderson*, Palles CB explained:[15]

> . . . upon the sale of real estate the auctioneer has no right to sue in his own name, analagous to his right in the sale of goods. In the latter case he has, or is deemed to have, a possession of the goods and a qualified property in them. On the sale of real property the right to sue depends upon the written contract alone: and unless that contract be so framed as to render the auctioneer the ostensible vendor . . . he cannot on the sale of real estate maintain in his own name an action against the purchaser.

This case concerned an action for fees in connection with the sale of leasehold property which, under the conditions of sale, were payable to the auctioneer by the purchaser. The auctioneer was held unable to recover those fees. Whilst the distinction between land and goods renders an auctioneer unable to sue for the price or for the deposit in the case of land, it seems hard on the auctioneer that he cannot recover his fees from a purchaser who contracts with a vendor that he shall pay them. Moreover, it seems that in such circumstances the auctioneer will be unable to claim on a quantum meruit from his vendor principal since his contract with the vendor is inconsistent therewith. An auctioneer of land will, therefore, be well advised always to insist in his contract with the vendor that the latter be responsible for his fees. This would still leave the vendor free to make whatever agreement he wishes with the purchaser in respect thereof but will not affect the auctioneer's contractual rights against his principal.

If the auctioneer contracts *personally* for the sale he may, of course, sue for the price.[16] He may also recover in those circumstances where the court treats him

12 *Lamond v Davall* (1847) 9 QB 1030, 16 LJQB 136.
13 (1927] 1 KB 513, 96 LJKB 150. See comparable clauses in Appendix 1.
14 He can however be joined as a plaintiff with the vendor in an action for specific performance of the contract of sale. For joinder of parties to an action, see RSC Ord 15, r 4 (Appendix 3).
15 (1876) IR 10 CL 204 at 209. And see also *Evans v Evans* (1835) 3 Ad & El 132, 1 Hat & W 239.
16 See e g *Fisher v Marsh* (1865) 6 B&S 411, 34 LJQB 177.

as having advanced money to the purchaser as for example, when he accepts a promissory note or a cheque. In view of the foregoing it is perhaps not surprising that of those cases discussed above, *Cleave v Moore, Hodgens v Keon, Pollway Ltd v Abdullah* and *Montgomery v Fleming*[17] all involved auctions of interests in land where, therefore, the only way in which the auctioneer could recover was by establishing a separate and independent contract.

RIGHTS AGAINST THIRD PARTIES

An auctioneer, although in no direct relationship with third parties, does have certain rights against them or in relation to them whereby he may protect his interest in the goods in his possession. These take the form of a positive right to bring actions against persons who unlawfully interefere with the goods in his possession, and immunities from certain otherwise lawful actions which may be taken against him. In addition, an auctioneer may avail himself of procedural remedies when adverse claims are brought by two or more persons to the goods in his possession or to the proceeds of sale thereof.

Wrongful interference with goods

We have seen that an auctioneer's special property in or possession of the goods gives rise to certain rights against both vendor and purchaser of them. Similarly, it gives him rights against third parties who wrongfully interfere with the goods. Thus, although not the owner, the auctioneer may maintain an action in respect of the torts of trespass, conversion and detinue[18] committed against the goods in his possession. The right was expressly recognised in *Williams v Millington*,[19] where it was said that it makes no difference whether the goods are located in the auctioneer's own premises or sold on the premises of the owner. Once, of course, the auctioneer parts with possession, the right is lost.[20]

It is perhaps obvious that the kind of interference predicated consists commonly of a wrongful damaging or taking away of the goods; and whilst trespass for land is possible, land cannot be converted or detained. Thus the auctioneer's rights here under discussion are only available with respect to goods. However, some goods may be affixed to land or buildings thereon. Depending upon the degree and purpose of affixation, items may be regarded in law as either goods or land. If a third party interferes with such property, an auctioneer will be unable to sue in tort if the true legal analysis is that the property in question is land, for then he has no right of possession. Such a situation arose in *Davis v Danks*,[1] where an auctioneer was employed to sell certain machinery and other items attached to the owner's house. The defendant, to whom certain of these items had been knocked down, removed

17 See above, nn 3, 5, 7 and 9.
18 Now, since 1977, abolished as a nominate tort. See Torts (Interference with Goods) Act 1977.
19 (1788) 1 HyBl 81.
20 See e g observation of Lord Campbell CJ in *Holmes v Tutton* (1855) 5 E&B 65 at 82.
1 (1849) 3 Exch 435, 18 LJ Ex 213.

them without paying. The auctioneer sued in trespass but was held unable to recover. Park B said:[2]

> [The auctioneer] cannot be considered to have such possession of the house and fixtures as would entitle him to maintain an action of trespass . . . against a party for an injury to them . . . He was only authorised at the time of his employment to sell the right of detaching and removing the fixtures, and he had no possession of them as materials and he was not in possession of the freehold.

The position would be otherwise if it was contemplated by the parties that the auctioneer was to sever the fixtures and sell them as chattels. The question of when an item will be held to be part of the land and therefore not 'goods' is beyond the scope of this book, but a few examples may indicate that no easy answer can be given (and see further, ch 10):

(a) The following have been held to remain goods:
   (i) pictures fixed with screws into panelled walls in recesses made for them when the panelling was installed,
   (ii) a life-size statue weighing half a ton placed on a plinth forming an integral part of the elevation of a house,
   (iii) large tapestries up to 14 feet in length attached to walls and tacked onto canvas-covered wooden frames nailed to the walls.

(b) The following became land:
   (i) sculptured marble vases placed on plinths inside a house,
   (ii) a picture and tapestry attached as part of a scheme to make a room into a specimen of an Elizabethan room.

Privilege from distress

Distress is an ancient common law self-help remedy whereby a creditor is permitted to seize goods belonging to his debtor to be held as a pledge to compel the satisfaction of a debt or other obligation. There are certain specific statutory rights of distress, but most commonly it was a remedy employed by landlords in respect of rent owed by a tenant.[3] In general a landlord could distrain on any goods found on the premises out of which the rent issued, whether the goods were the property of the tenant or not. However, the common law developed a number of important exceptions to this somewhat Draconian rule, the most important, for our purposes, being a general privilege relating to goods delivered to a person exercising a public trade.

In *Adams v Grane and Osborne*,[4] it was held that this immunity applied to goods sent to an auctioneer for the purpose of sale, where a landlord had sought to distrain goods which had been delivered to an auctioneer, the goods being on premises sub-let as auction rooms to the auctioneer by a tenant who was in arrears for rent. The privilege is grounded in public policy, namely: 'For the convenience and benefit of trade . . .'[5] It appears that the quality of the

2 (1849) 3 Exch 435 at 437.
3 See generally 13 Halsbury's Laws (4th edn) para 201 f.
4 (1833) 1 Cr&M 380, 2 LJ Ex 105.
5 (1833) 1 Cr&M 380 at 387 per Bayley B. See also per Blackburn J in *Lyons v Elliott* (1876) 1 Q B D 210 at 214. The immunity extends to goods kept in the yard outside the premises: *Williams v Holmes* (1853) 8 Exch 861, 22 LJ Ex 283.

auctioneer's possession of the premises in question is immaterial. In *Brown v Arundell*,[6] it was alleged that the auctioneer was trespassing on the property in which he carried out the auction. The Chief Justice found that the evidence did not support that allegation but, even if it had, it would not affect the privilege.

Thus far, we have been concerned with distraints against goods found on the auctioneer's premises pursuant to claims against the owners or occupiers of those premises. Where distress is levied against a person's goods on his *own* premises, there will be no immunity by virtue of the fact that the owner has happened to put them into the hands of an auctioneer for sale. So was held in *Lyons v Elliott*.[7] As Lush J observed:[8]

> If therefore we were to hold this plate privileged, we must necessarily hold that as soon as a tenant gets into difficulties he has nothing to do but call in an auctioneer, and so oust the landlord of his remedy by distress, although he could not remove the goods for the same purpose. That, it seems to me, would be a very strange extension of the doctrine, and one by no means justified either by convenience or authority.

These old cases help to explain the policy behind the privilege but the law is now governed by the Law of Distress Amendment Act 1908. This Act simply provides, so far as is material, that a goods-owner not being a tenant or having any beneficial interest in premises in which his goods are, whose goods are being distrained upon, may serve notice of these facts upon the landlord and that if a landlord disregards the notice he shall be guilty of an illegal trespass. The goods-owner may, inter alia, obtain restoration of his goods and bring action against the landlord or his agent for trespass thereto.

Interpleader

Where an auctioneer is faced with adverse claims from two or more persons, it would be inconvenient to leave him to elect whom to satisfy. The unsatisfied claimant would presumably seek redress against him. Where the auctioneer himself claims no interest in the subject matter of the dispute, it would be more efficient for the real disputants to claim against each other. The rules of court[9] provide a simple procedure in these circumstances, known as 'interpleader', whereby the person in this position says: 'I have a fund in my possession in which I claim no personal interest, and to which you the defendants set up competing claims; pay me my costs and I will bring the fund into court, and you shall contest it between yourselves.' This was the formulation given by Lord Cottenham L C in *Hoggart v Cutts*,[10] a case which well illustrates both the kind of difficulty an auctioneer can find himself in and the fact that as an essential prerequisite, the two or more claims must be truly adverse or competing. In this case an auctioneer was instructed to sell an estate belonging to one Thodey. The property was knocked down to the defendant Cutts who duly paid a deposit to the auctioneer. Disputes then arose between vendor and

6 (1850) 10 CB 54, 20 LJCP 30.
7 Above, n 5.
8 (1876) 1 QBD 210 at 216. The authority of this decision is probably not weakened by the fact that the chattels in question belonged to neither the owner of the premises nor the auctioneer but to a third person who had sent them to the house for auction.
9 In the High Court by RSC Ord 17 and in the County Court by CCR Ord 33, r 6 (see Appendix 3).
10 (1841) Cr&Ph 197 at 204.

purchaser and Thodey, alleging the contract was at an end and the deposit forfeited, instructed the auctioneer to re-sell. Subsequently the property was re-sold to Vickers, who also paid a deposit.

Cutts sought specific performance of his contract whilst Vickers sought the return of his deposit. Thodey, as vendor, claimed the deposits in respect of both sales. The Lord Chancellor, after describing interpleader proceedings in the words quoted above, held that for interpleader relief to be appropriate: 'The case must be one in which the fund is a matter of contest between the two parties, *and in which the litigation between those parties will decide all their respective rights with respect to the fund*'.[11] His Lordship held that Vickers' claim and the claims by Cutts and Thodey were not susceptible of interpleading; Vickers' claim to a return of his deposit could not possibly settle the questions between the other parties. Thus he was not a proper party to these proceedings. The proceedings were proper, however, with regard to the claims involving Cutts and Thodey.

Similarly, interpleader by an auctioneer has been disallowed when the claims made against him were one by the vendor of a horse for the price and another by the purchaser thereof for damages for breach of warranty concerning the condition of the animal.[12]

The mode of application for interpleader relief is laid down in RSC Ord 17, r 3, for the High Court, and CCR Ord 33, r 6, for proceedings in the county court. The court has a discretion whether to grant the relief sought. One of the matters on which the applicant must adduce evidence is that he has not 'colluded' with any of the claimants. Collusion does not necessarily connote any moral wrong-doing — it suffices if the applicant has placed himself in the position of being sued at the request and in the interests of one of the claimants.[13] Collusion, however, will only be a bar if raised by the *other* claimant. In *Thompson v Wright*,[14] auctioneers were instructed to sell goods by Wright. They advertised them for sale and were notified by Thompson that the goods were his. Wright gave the auctioneers an indemnity and instructed them to sell. This they duly did and then sought to interplead as to the rival claims to the proceeds of sale between Wright and Thompson. The vendors objected, but it was held that interpleader lay; the taking of an indemnity did not deprive the applicants of the benefits of interpleader — it did not amount to collusion — and, in any event, collusion could not be raised by the person who was a party to it.

11 (1841) Cr & Ph 197 at 205, emphasis added.

12 *Wright v Freeman* (1879) 48 LJQB 276; see also *Ingham v Walker* (1887) 3 TLR 448, CA. For a case where two firms of auctioneers were *defenfdants* in an interpleader action which failed, see *Greatorex & Co v Shackle* [1895] 2 QB 249, 64 LJQB 634.

13 *Belcher v Smith* (1832) 9 Bing 82, LJCP 167.

14 (1884) 13 QBD 632, 54 LJQB 32.

Chapter 5

Duties and liabilities of the auctioneer

DUTIES TO THE VENDOR

We have seen that the authority of an auctioneer and his rights will depend ultimately upon the precise terms of the contract with his principal within the framework of the general rules of common law, in particular, the law of agency. The same is true as regards his duties and liabilities. Some specific duties will be provided for expressly in his contract but, in addition, the law lays down a number of general obligations concomitant with the agency relationship. These may conveniently be classified as:

(a) duties relating to performance,
(b) fiduciary duties,
(c) the duty to account for goods or proceeds,
(d) the duty to care for the goods.

Duties relating to performance

To act in accordance with his instructions

It is axiomatic that an auctioneer, like any agent, may only perform those acts which are authorised. If he fails to obey his instructions he will be liable to his principal for any loss arising. This liability will be an additional consequence to that of failing to bring about a contract between his principal and a third party with the resultant loss of commission. Thus, as we have already seen in dealing with authority to receive payment of the price or deposit, if an auctioneer is expressly instructed to obtain cash only and he takes some other form of payment he will be liable to his vendor.[1]

Of course, if the auctioneer acts within his implied or usual authority he will incur no liability notwithstanding that he does something which has not been expressly authorised.

If the auctioneer is in doubt as to his instructions he should seek clarification. In the unusual case of *Re Bishop, ex p Langley, ex p Smith*[2] it was stated that on

1 See above, ch 3.
2 (1879) 13 Ch D 110, 49 LJ Bcy 1. If the auctioneer only receives notice of an injuction after the sale although before receipt of the proceeds, the court will not set aside the sale. See *Freehold Permanent Building Society v Choate* (1871) 3 Chy Chrs 440.

receipt of a telegram from solicitors advising that an injunction restraining sale had been issued by the Bankruptcy Court an auctioneer was under a duty to communicate with his principal although it was not incumbent upon him to communicate with the court. In this case the auctioneer communicated with his client, the sheriff levying execution on the goods of a judgment debtor who had subsequently filed a liquidation petition. Having received instructions to proceed with the sale, and bona fide believing the telegram to be a ruse by the debtor, he was held not liable in contempt of court when he went ahead with the sale.

To act with skill and care

An auctioneer, as a professional, is under a general duty under the common law to exercise proper skill and care in and about the sale of his principal's property. As Lord Ellenborough long ago put it in an oft-cited dictum:[3]

> In the present case the plaintiff appears to have been guilty of gross negligence and the defendant has suffered an injury instead of deriving any benefit from employing him... I pay an auctioneer, as I do any other professional man for the exercise of skill on my behalf and I have a right to the exercise of such skill as is normally possessed by men of that profession.

That case decided that an auctioneer lost his right to commission in circumstances where he had had to return the purchaser's deposit due to the failure of the vendor of a lease to show his lessor's title. It was found that it was usual practice in such cases for the auctioneer to insert a proviso in the conditions of sale that the vendor was not to be called upon to show the title of the lessor and the auctioneer's negligence consisted of the failure to include such a provision. Whilst this case concerned only the auctioneer's liability to forego his commission, he will also be liable in damages for loss occasioned to his principal by reason of his negligence. It is impossible to provide an exhaustive list of the circumstances in which such a liability may arise, but a number of instances are given below.[4]

Duty to secure a binding agreement

There is a number of old cases which establish that an auctioneer is liable in negligence if he fails to ensure that a binding contract has been entered into by the purchaser. Frequently the default of the auctioneer has consisted of a failure to ensure that a contract evidenced in writing sufficient to satisfy the requirements of the Statute of Frauds 1677 and subsequent enactments based thereon, has been procured. These requirements still obtain with regard to sales of land by virtue of s 40 of the Law of Property Act 1925,[5] but no longer

3 *Denew v Daverell* (1813) 3 Camp 451 at 452-3. This has recently been made the subject of statutory provision: Supply of Goods and Services Act 1982, s 13 (Appendix 2).

4 Several examples are given by May J in *Fordham v Christie Manson & Woods* (1977) 244 E G 213 at 219-20. It has recently been decided at first instance in *Balsamo v Medici* [1984] 2 All ER 304, [1984] 1 WLR 951, that a sub-agent can be liable in negligence to an owner of goods for damage thereto (but not for misapplication of the proceeds of sale). Thus an auctioneer instructed to sell by one who is merely the agent of the owner will owe a duty of care to that owner although there is no contractual relationship between them.

5 See the discussion in ch 9, Sales of land by auction or tender.

apply to sales of goods.[6] With regard to land sales the duty owed by an auctioneer was explained in an Irish case as follows:[7]

> [An auctioneer] ... impliedly by undertaking a work undertakes to bring reasonable care, skill and diligence to the doing of it. An important part of an auctioneer's work, when he sells real estate, on the very lowest estimate of his legal obligation to his employer is to take reasonable care to have a binding contract, under the Statute of Frauds, entered into by the person who purchases the property at the auction. It may be that he does not undertake without any qualification to make a binding contract.

The explanation of the last sentence of this dictum may be that an auctioneer will not be liable for failing to make a binding contract if the failure is caused by, e g defects in title or other similar vitiating elements for which he is not responsible. We have already seen that an auctioneer will frequently include a power to accept rescission of a contract — e g in the case of fraud, but that he probably has no authority to do so in the absence of such express provision.[8]

There are, however, other ways in which an auctioneer may fail to bring about a contract binding the purchaser: he may for example simply fail to accept a bid. In the New Zealand case of *Logie v Gillies & Hislop*[9] the reserve placed on an estate at Dunedin was £2000. A bid of that amount was made, but inexplicably, the auctioneer did not accept it and the property was bought in at £2100. After several subsequent abortive auctions at decreasing reserves, the estate was eventually sold for £1250. It was held that the auctioneer was liable to his principal-vendor for damages, the proper measure of which was the difference between the wrongfully unaccepted bid and the true market value of the property at that time, the subsequent sale price achieved being only one means of ascertaining that value. In this case the court found the market price to have been £1775 so that the loss was £225 plus £12 regarding the expenses of the abortive sale. It is clear then that a negligent failure to accept the bid will render an auctioneer liable in damages for any loss arising. Many auctioneers' Conditions of Sale reserve the right to refuse any bid, but it is questionable whether such a provision would protect an auctioneer in this type of situation where he does not exercise a discretion to refuse a bid but carelessly fails to accept it to the detriment of the vendor.

In these days when international auctions have become more commonplace it appears that an auctioneer is at risk of a negligence suit if his, or his audience's linguistic skills are lacking so that a mistake is made as to the price which a lot has reached, entitling a purchaser to set aside the contract. This occurred in the quite recent case of *Friedrich v A Monnickendam Ltd*,[10] where the chairman of Christie's himself conducted a major jewellery auction in Geneva. According to the law of Geneva the auction had to be conducted in French. Many of the potential purchasers invited to the sale were from England and the United States of America. The auctioneer's French was not good and a genuine mistake occurred whereby the defendant purchaser thought that a lot had reached 190 000 Swiss francs, whereas it had in fact reached 290 000 Swiss

6 Law Reform (Enforcement of Contracts) Act 1954, s 2.
7 *Kavanagh v Cuthbert* (1874) IR 9 CL 136 per Dowse B at 140.
8 See above, ch 3.
9 (1885) 4 NZLR 65.
10 (1973) 228 EG 1311.

francs, an extravagantly high price. Under Swiss law the purchaser, an English diamond-cutter, was held entitled to avoid the contract on the grounds of mistake. The case involved an action by a vendor against the purchaser but the question of negligence by the auctioneer was considered. Lord Denning said:

> There was concurrent negligence on the part of the auctioneer. He should have known that the bid of 290 000 Swiss francs was not such a sum as Mr Monnickendam the expert diamond-cutter would knowingly bid. The auctioneer should therefore have assured himself by the clearest words in English that Mr Monnickendam appreciated that the figure was 290 000 Swiss francs.

Stamp L J was of the view that the lack of care consisted not so much in the imperfection of the auctioneer's French as in a failure to give the bids in English as well, given that the auction particulars were printed in both English and French and that English-speaking people were specifically solicited to attend.[11]

Duty to describe the property accurately

If the auctioneer describes the property he must be careful to do so accurately and not in such a way as to cause harm to his vendor-principal by virtue of losing the sale or necessitating that he compensate the purchaser. In *Parker v Farebrother*[12] an auctioneer engaged to sell certain properties described them as three-storey buildings. In fact they only comprised of two storeys. The vendor was liable to compensate the purchaser as a result of this misdescription and the auctioneer was held bound to indemnify him.

Conditions of Sale frequently make express the right of the auctioneer to apply his own description to the properties offered for sale.[13] In the absence of such, an auctioneer will be liable in damages to his principal if he departs from his descriptions to the detriment of the vendor in circumstances where the vendor expressly or impliedly instructs him to sell under his descriptions. In *Brown v Draper & Co*[14] the vendor handed the auctioneer a box of items together with a list describing them. The auctioneers sold them under different descriptions and the vendor sued in negligence. He recovered damages being the difference between the prices which the goods would probably have achieved had they been sold under the vendor's descriptions, and the prices they actually fetched.

It is important, therefore, that auctioneers expressly reserve the right to sell under their own descriptions. However, if they do, it is equally important that they take care to describe the property accurately to its best advantage. Failure to do so, so that the sale fails to attract the appropriate class of bidders, or the optimum price, may render the auctioneers liable in negligence. The leading case is *Cuckmere Brick Co Ltd v Mutual Finance Ltd*,[15] which involved a dispute

11 The third Lord Justice of Appeal, James L J criticised the lack of clarity in the conduct of the auction but declined to categorise the auctioneer as negligent.
12 (1853) 21 LTOS 128, 1 C L R 323.
13 See e g Christie's Conditions of Acceptance, condition 2 (Appendix 1).
14 (1975) 119 Sol Jo 300, 233 E G 929.
15 [1971] Ch 949, [1971] 2 All E R 633. For observations as to valuation evidence see *Johnson v Ribbins* (1975) 235 E G 757 per Walton J at 761.

between mortgagors and mortgagees of certain development land. The plaintiff mortgagors obtained finance to develop a site with 100 flats and obtained planning permission therefor. Subsequently, due to financial difficulties, they resolved instead to build 33 houses, a less lucrative, but less expensive scheme. They obtained planning permission for this revision. Subsequently they defaulted on the mortgage. The defendant bankers entered into possession and, in exercise of their power of sale under the mortgage, put the site up for auction. The auctioneers described the property as having planning permission for 33 houses but omitted to mention the permission for the more valuable flat development scheme. The main reason for this omission was that they took a pessimistic view as to the economic value of such a development and decided that it was not an attractive proposition. The sale of the site as described, realised £44 000. The judge at first instance awarded damages against the mortgagees on the basis that, properly described to include the planning consent for 100 flats, the land would have realised £65 000. Although this was not in issue in this decision it seems clear that the auctioneers would be liable to indemnify their principals in such a case. The Court of Appeal upheld the decision although there was some disagreement about the proper method of computing the true value of the property. Two of the judges considered that the conscious omission of the auctioneers amounted to negligence but one, Cross L J, considered it to be merely an error of judgment. However, whilst the pessimistic evaluation of the property was not itself negligent, Cross L J held them negligent in being so confident of its correctness as not to see to it that the earlier planning permission for flats was mentioned in the particulars in the hope at least of attracting some developers prepared to bid more for the property for that purpose.

Duty to obtain the deposit and price

We have already briefly adverted in ch 3 to the question whether an auctioneer is liable to his principal if he fails to obtain the proceeds of sale or part of them or obtains them otherwise than in cash. In *Hibbert v Bayley*,[16] a ship was put up for sale by auction upon certain conditions including that the highest bidder should forthwith sign the contract and pay a deposit. The ship was knocked down at £2950 and the bidder gave his name as 'Shaw & Co.' Bristol. The purchaser then excused himself from signing the contract and paying the deposit asking for half an hour to arrange matters. He disappeared and the ship was subsequently sold, after intervening lots, for £2600. The plaintiff vendors claimed the difference i e £350 from the defendants alleging negligence, inter alia in failing to procure the deposit. Earle C J directed the jury as follows:[17]

> The question is, whether you think that there was a breach of duty — that is, a want of due care, in letting the purchaser go away without signing or paying, and without declaring the bidding to be void and putting the ship up again for sale *instanter*. By the conditions of sale ... the purchaser was to pay a deposit immediately.

The jury found for the plaintiff vendor but awarded only 40 shillings nominal damages. It is not clear whether the breach of duty consisted of not obtaining the deposit or not putting the ship up for sale again immediately or whether the

16 (1860) 2 F&F 48.
17 (1860) 2 F&F 48 at 50.

two defaults were regarded as interlinked, but it would be wrong to assume that, in the absence of express instructions to procure the deposit immediately as here were present, it would always be negligent to permit a purchaser time to pay and to leave the auction rooms without doing so. In this case evidence was given that such practice was common when the purchaser was known to the auctioneer or left an address, known to be genuine, in London.

Auction Conditions of Sale today frequently give auctioneers a discretion whether to allow the purchaser credit. In *Cyril Andrade Ltd v Sotheby & Co*,[18] a case involving some famous personnel, the auctioneers knocked down a fine suit of armour belonging originally to Count Von Trapp to a Mr Bartel who had previously acted, and they believed presently to be acting, for the American newspaper tycoon William Randolph Hearst. The sale price was £5000 and, acting on this belief, the auctioneers allowed Mr Bartel to depart without taking a deposit from him. The conditions of sale provided that a deposit was payable 'if required'.[19] The sale was repudiated by Mr Hearst who said that Mr Bartel was not his agent and the auctioneers returned the armour to their clients. The plaintiff-vendors claimed £2500 being the 50 per cent deposit they alleged ought to have been taken. Sotheby's gave evidence that they did not normally demand deposits unless they did not know or trust the purchaser. On these facts it was held that there was no breach of duty by the auctioneers.

Fiduciary duties

Inherent in the agency relationship is the notion that it is based upon trust. An agent is in a fiduciary position vis-à-vis his principal and, as a consequence, owes him certain duties.[20] These may variously be described as duties of loyalty or duties of good faith. Essentially this means that an agent must not so place himself that his personal interests may conflict with his duty to his principal. The main instances include:
(a) taking commission from both parties,
(b) purchasing the principal's property,
(c) obtaining a secret profit.

Taking commission from both parties

The practice of auctioneers charging buyers a commission or premium on sales in addition to that payable by the vendor is commonplace today.[1] As such it is much objected to by buyers but it may also act to the detriment of the vendor-principal. As Sargeant L J explained in a case involving an hotel broker who sought to charge both his principal and the buyer commission:[2]

> He is seeking to impose an onerous condition on the purchaser which might very well prevent the purchaser ever taking advantage of the order to view; and to impose

18 (1931) 47 TLR 244.
19 Contrast Sotheby's current condition 6(b) and Christie's condition 5(c) (Appendix 1).
20 For a detailed analysis of the fiduciary relationship see *Bowstead on Agency* (14th edn, 1976) Sweet & Maxwell, arts 45-51.
1 See e g Sotheby's Conditions of Business, condition 3, and Christie's Conditions of Sale 5(A) (Appendix 1).
2 *Fullwood v Hurley* [1928] 1 KB 498 at 505, 96 LJKB 976.

> such a condition would be in flagrant violation of his duty to the vendor which is to bring along any purchaser who can be found on the terms of the vendor paying ... the agreed commission ... [The] condition ... might have the effect of stalling off a purchaser and preventing the plaintiff from securing for the vendor such a purchaser as would be acceptable to the vendor.

As regards auctions, it is clear that the imposition of a buyers' premium could have the effect of, at least, depressing the price which a buyer would be prepared to pay and this is obviously contrary to the vendor's interests.

It is not a situation, however, where the auctioneer's interests and duty conflict since it will be likewise in his and his vendor's interests to obtain the highest possible price and, therefore, taking commission from the buyer will not involve a breach of fiduciary duty provided that the auctioneer fully discloses to his vendor-principal the existence of a contractual provision entitling him so to do.[3] The position would be otherwise if the agent's interest was to obtain a low price as occurred in *Rhodes v McAlister*,[4] where a buyer had promised an agent the difference between the top price which the buyer was prepared to pay and the price at which it was sold to him. Here the agent arranged with the vendor for commission on the sale and was held unable to recover from the buyer. Whether, in fact, the principal suffers any detriment is here irrelevant.[5]

Another situation where there may appear to be a potential conflict of interest is where an auctioneer, for gain or otherwise, agrees to bid on behalf of a prospective purchaser; for then he is acting as agent for two parties whose interests are antithetical. As to whether such activity is lawful is nowadays not a matter for much doubt. In *Bexwell v Christie*[6] Lord Mansfield suggested that it was, although there the question did not strictly arise for decision. However in *Fullwood v Hurley*,[7] which concerned the taking of remuneration from both sides, Lord Hamworth M R stated categorically: 'If and so long as the agent is the agent of one party he cannot engage to become the agent of another principal without leave of the first principal with whom he has originally established his agency.'[8] The crucial words are 'without leave'. It is thought that provided the auctioneer notifies the vendor and obtains his consent, actual or tacit, the practice will not involve a breach of fiduciary duty.

Sotheby's (Condition 32) provide that they will execute bids for buyers (whilst discouraging the practice somewhat by warning them that their interests are best served by personal attendance). Christie's notify their willingness to accept 'commissions' in the 'Information for Sellers and Buyers' section of their particulars.[9]

Purchasing the principal's property

The purchase by an auctioneer of his principal's property is another activity giving rise to a potential conflict of interest and duty, and once again he is

3 Above, n 2.
4 (1923) 29 Com Cas 19, CA.
5 See e g per Scrutton L J (1923) 29 Com Cas 19 at 27.
6 (1776) 1 Cowp 395 at 397.
7 Above, n 2.
8 Above, n 2.
9 The practice was commented on with approval (albeit obiter) in *Fordham v Christie Manson & Woods Ltd* (1977) 244 E G 213 at 215 per May J.

enjoined from so doing unless he has made the fullest disclosure of all relevant facts to his principal. As it was put by a textbook writer in the nineteenth century:[10]

> If then, the seller were permitted as the agent of another, to become the purchaser, his duty to his principal and his own interest would stand in direct opposition to each other; and thus a temptation, perhaps in many cases too strong for resistance by men of flexible morals or hackneyed in the common devices of worldly business, would be held out, which would betray them into gross misconduct ...

If an auctioneer does, without the requisite disclosure and consent, buy his client's property,[11] two consequences may flow. First, he will not be able to keep the property purchased but will hold it as a trustee on trust[12] for his principal the sale will be set aside at whose suit. In *Oliver v Court*[13] where an auctioneer who had also valued an estate carelessly omitting to take account of valuable timber thereon, bought it himself after an abortive auction, the principal was held entitled to set the sale aside even after a lapse of 13 years. However, whilst delay may not, of itself, preclude the setting aside of the sale, it was stressed in *Wentworth v Lloyd*[14] that where the principal delays and as a result, evidence may have been lost, the defendant agent is 'entitled to every fair and reasonable presumption that may be drawn in favour of the direct testimony [he] adduces.'[15] This case also shows that the burden of proving that he made full disclosure and that the vendor acquiesced in his purchase lies on the agent.[16] The second consequence of such a breach of his fiduciary duty is that the auctioneer will be disentitled to his commission and this will be so whether the principal has elected to set the sale aside or has affirmed it. As Pollock C B put it in *Salomons v Pender*:[17]

> The argument has failed to convince me that a person can, in the same transaction buy in the character of a principal, and at the same time charge the seller as his agent. I cannot agree that, because the seller has chosen to abide by the sale he is therefore to be held to have acknowledged the claims of the plaintiff both as agent and purchaser.

This seems a correct result. If the auctioneer has not shown that he made full disclosure to the vendor and that the latter acquiesced in the sale to him, he has simply acted outside his authority and thus, on general principles,[18] not earned his commission; he was employed to sell to third parties and has sold instead to himself.

Given these consequences, it is obviously vital that an auctioneer ensures that he does satisfy the disclosure requirements and obtains the express consent to

10 *Story on Agency* p 262 para 210, cited in *Salomons v Pender* (1856) 3 H&C 639 at 643-4. And see per Coram Richards L T B in *Oliver v Court* (1820) 8 Price 127 at 160-61.

11 By himself or in consortium with others see *Wentworth v Lloyd* (1863) 32 Beav 467; *Dunne v English* (1874) LR 18 Eq 524, 31 LT 75.

12 See *Lees v Nuttall* (1829) 1 Russ and M 53, affd (1834) 2 My&K 819.

13 Above, n 10.

14 (1863) 32 Beav 467.

15 (1863) 32 Beav 467 per Sir John Romilly M R at 474.

16 See also *Dunne v English* (n 11, above) where it was said that it is not enough merely for the agent to disclose that he has an interest, leaving the principal to make enquiry as to the extent thereof.

17 (1856) 3 H&C 639 at 641.

18 See ch 4 above.

his purchase from his client. However, in one situation he will be free to buy, namely when his agency has terminated. In the New Zealand case of *Young v Hill Ford & Newton*[19] the facts were as follows. Young bought a property with the aid of a loan secured thereon. He then instructed Ford & Newton to prepare plans for the division up of the land into small parcels for sale. Having defaulted on the mortgage, he instructed Ford & Newton to auction the properties. Thereafter the mortgagees instructed the auctioneers to sell on their behalf in enforcement of the mortgage. Young was informed but continued to try to re-schedule his loan repayments. The auctioneers put up the properties for sale but received no bids. Fourteen days later they made an offer to the mortgagees to buy them and this was accepted. Young thereupon sought to recover the properties claiming that the auctioneers remained his agents and thus held the properties on trust for him. The Court of Appeal held that the onus of proof that the auctioneers had divested themselves of their fiduciary character lay on them and that once an agency existed subsequent purchases by an agent would be strongly scrutinised. However, in the circumstances of this case, the agency had terminated and the auctioneers' purchase of the property was, vis-à-vis Young, unobjectionable. Here the auctioneers had subsequently become agents for the mortgagees from whom they had bought. As to this Williams J said:[20]

> It appears that they were employed by the mortgagees to sell the property by auction; the auction proved abortive as no bid was received, and the agency of Ford & Newton so far as regards the mortgagees had therefore determined. An auctioneer is agent *pro hac vice*, and whether he succeeds in effecting the sale or not his agency is determined after the auction.

Such a categorical statement has to be treated with some caution. Much will depend upon the circumstances of the auctioneer's appointment, his conduct of the auction and so on. In *Oliver v Court*,[1] for example, it was held that the agency of the auctioneer continued after he had descended from the rostrum and that he had in any event already determined to purchase the property himself when he commenced conduct of the auction. On that basis, his agency was extant when he purchased the estate and the sale to him was set aside.

Obtaining a secret profit

It is an inexorable rule, derived from the law of trusts, that an agent must not use his position to acquire for himself any secret profit from a third party. This is so even if the principal has suffered no actual loss. There are numerous circumstances in which a 'secret profit' can arise. At one extreme the notion will include a bribe, and at the other, the relatively innocent receipt of commission from a third party for the introduction of the principal's business. The leading case as regards auctioneers is *Hippisley v Knee Bros*.[2] There the defendant auctioneers had been instructed to sell goods on terms that they were to be paid a lump sum by way of commission together with disbursements, including the costs of printing and advertising. The auctioneer

19 (1883) 2 NZLR 62.
20 (1883) 2 NZLR 62 at 88.
1 (1820) Dan 301, 8 Price 127.
2 [1905] 1 KB 1.

contracted with printers for posters and catalogues and newspaper advertisements for which they were invoiced at the normal rate. However, the auctioneers were allowed, in fact, a 10 per cent discount. When accounting to their client, however, the auctioneers charged these expenses at the normal invoice price. On discovering these facts the plaintiff sued to recover the discounts and also the commission paid. As regards the discounts it was held that these were repayable to the client. The auctioneers' claim to a trade custom entitling them to such discounts did not succeed. Lord Alvestone C J adverted to 'an extraordinary laxity in the view taken of the earning of secret profits by agents' within commercial circles.[3] Whilst the auctioneers' honest belief in their right to retain these discounts as additional profit for themselves did not affect their duty to account for them to their principal, their bona fides in this regard was relevant in the context of the claim for return of the commission. The Chief Justice said:[4]

> If the court is satisfied that there has been no fraud or dishonesty upon the agent's part, I think that the receipt by him of a discount will not disentitle him to his commission unless the discount is in some way connected with the contract which the agent is employed to make or the duty which he is called upon to perform. In my opinion the neglect by the defendants to account for the discounts in the present case is not sufficiently connected with the real subject-matter of their employment. If the discount had been received from the purchasers the case would have been covered by *Andrews v R Ramsey*[5] but here it was received in respect of a purely incidental matter: it had nothing to do with the duty of selling. It cannot be suggested that the plaintiff got one penny a lower price than he would otherwise have got. Therefore I come to the conclusion that, so far as the £20 commission is concerned, the plaintiff is not entitled to succeed.

Whilst the bona fides of these auctioneers was accepted by the court, there can no longer be any doubt that agents are not entitled to retain discounts or share commissions in these situations and auctioneers must ensure that they disclose and account for such to their clients.

Duty to account

The duty to account is one of the duties owed by an agent to his principal which arises out of the fiduciary relationship which exists between them. However, it is convenient to deal with it under this separate heading. It is the duty of every agent to keep the property and money of his principal separate from his own and to preserve and keep accounts of all his dealings in the course of his agency. He must also be prepared to produce all relevant books and documents relating to his principal's affairs.[6] If an agent fails to keep proper accounts or fails to pay or transfer to his principal money or property received for him the agent is liable to an action for an account,[7] normally brought in the Chancery Division of the High Court.

The significance of the fact that the duty to account arises out of the fiduciary relationship between the agent and his principal lies in the remedies available

3 [1905] 1 KB 1 at 7.
4 [1905] 1 KB 1 at 8.
5 [1903] 2 KB 635.
6 See generally *Bowstead on Agency* (14th edn, 1976) Sweet & Maxwell, art 53.
7 See Supreme Court Act 1981, s 61(1) and Sch 1. The relevant rules are to be found in RSC Ord 43 (Appendix 3).

against a defaulting agent, namely that the principal can *trace* the property belonging to him in the hands of his agent in priority to that agent's ordinary creditors. Thus in *Re Cotton, ex Cook*,[8] the deceased was instructed in cattle sales in Bromsgrove and four other towns. It appears that he generally sold in his own name and made himself personally liable for all money received. Occasionally he gave credit to purchasers and allowed sets-off to those who were also vendors. Cook instructed him to sell certain cattle and this was duly effected but the proceeds were not immediately collected. Thereafter the auctioneer committed suicide but his son obtained outstanding payments due and paid the money into a separate bank account. The auctioneer's estate being insolvent, the question arose whether a sum of £40 17s 6d in respect of the proceeds of sale of Cook's cattle was recoverable by the latter or whether it was properly kept by the trustee in bankruptcy as part of the general assets of the estate into which Cook could prove his debt together with the other creditors. The Divisional Court held that the auctioneer had established a course of dealing in which he became a principal, buying and selling on his own account and that Cook merely looked to him as a debtor. The Court of Appeal, however, found such a course of dealing negatived by the express conditions of business of the auctioneer and held that the question was whether Cook was entitled to say: 'These cattle of mine were entrusted to you for a particular purpose, as commission agent to sell for me. That is a fiduciary position and the fiduciary relation applies to the money received from the sale of the cattle entrusted to you for sale'.[9] This question was, on the facts, answered in the affirmative; the proceeds belonged to the principal and he could trace into the insolvent auctioneer's estate ahead of the general creditors by virtue of the fiduciary relationship existing between them. If, however, the facts had been as the Divisional Court had found them — that the auctioneer in fact sold as principal on his own account, having bought them from his client — no fiduciary relationship would have existed nor attached to the proceeds and the seller would merely have been an unpaid creditor. This kind of arrangement is not uncommon in cattle auctions where sales are effected outside the ring and booked with the auctioneer.[10]

The right to trace property exists both at law and in equity. The latter remedy is more efficacious when money is involved because at common law the right to trace is lost when the true owner's property is no longer identifiable. Equity however is prepared to unscramble bank accounts containing moneys belonging to several persons. It is beyond the scope of this book to examine the remedy in any detail, but the right to trace would be lost if the property were taken by another without notice of the rights of the true owner, having given value for it. So, in *Marten v Rocke Eyton & Co*,[11] unpaid vendors were held unable to trace into the bank account of the defaulting auctioneer when the bankers had taken the balance therein in satisfaction of an overdraft, without notice that the balance comprised moneys due to the vendors.

The fact that the auctioneer holds his principal's property in a fiduciary character and is not merely a debtor may have serious consequences in other

8 (1913) 108 L T 310.
9 (1913) 108 L T 310 at 311 per Cozens-Hardy M R.
10 See e g *Murphy v Howlett (a firm)* (1960) 176 E G 311, and ch 10 below.
11 (1885) 53 L T 946, 34 WR 253.

contexts. In *Crowther v Elgood*[12] an auctioneer found himself committed to prison having failed to account for proceeds of sale of farming stock sold on behalf of a deceased. Whilst imprisonment for debt has largely been abolished by the Debtors Act 1869, there remain some cases of debt where imprisonment is still possible. By s 4 of the Act committal is available in the case of 'default by a trustee or a person acting in a fiduciary capacity and ordered to pay by a Court of Equity any sum in his possession or under his control'. Cotton LJ was in no doubt that a defaulting auctioneer was caught by this provision:[13]

> In the first place, was the appellant acting in a fiduciary capacity in the transaction? In my opinion he was. He was an auctioneer, and as such he held the goods in trust to sell them for the benefit of the person who entrusted them to him; and if any deposit was paid at the time of the sale, he held it in trust for the vendor...and when he has received the money produced by the sale he holds that as the money of his principal.

It is clear therefore that an auctioneer is at risk if he fails properly to account and he will in the absence of express authority to the contrary only escape liability if he does so direct to the principal himself. There is no implied authority to pay proceeds or a deposit to his client's solicitors.[14] The auctioneer must remain willing and able to account to his principal. In *Lowe v Gallimore*[15] it was held that a principal could enforce this duty after having revoked an earlier instruction to pay proceeds of sale into a bank account pending resolution of a dispute surrounding them. Further, in *Crosskey v Mills*[16] the defendant auctioneer was instructed to sell goods by one W Crosskey the brother of a deceased who had given the plaintiff a bill of sale. The deceased's widow instructed the auctioneer to hold the proceeds to satisfy all the creditors of the deceased. It is unclear whether the plaintiff concurred in such an arrangement,[17] but in any event he subsequently instructed the auctioneer to account to him. It was held that the auctioneer was bound to do so: '...the plaintiff was the person who originally employed the defendant to sell. Therefore prima facie, the defendant was bound to account to the plaintiff.'[18]

The problem in these cases can be regarded as stemming from conflicting instructions from the principal. However, the major area of difficulty for an auctioneer exists where a third party lays claim to the goods or their proceeds. As we shall see later, if the third party's claim is justified, the auctioneer is exposed to an action in tort for conversion of the true owner's property. The auctioneer may, therefore, be caught on the horns of a dilemma but in certain circumstances may be able to escape liability for failing to account to his

12 (1887) 34 Ch D 691, CA.
13 (1887) 36 Ch D 691 at 696.
14 See *Brown v Farebrother* (1888) 58 LJ Ch 3 at 4 per Kekewich J, although in that case auctioneers instructed to sell by the plaintiff acting under a court order and under a duty to pay proceeds into court were held discharged when they paid the proceeds over to solicitors for the vendor for that purpose. It seems that in this case the auctioneers *did* have actual authority so to do.
15 (1851) 18 LTOS 63, 241.
16 (1834) 1 Cr M&R 298, 3 LJ Ex 297.
17 The marginal note to the law report, (1834) 1 Cr M&R 298, suggests that he did. Parke B at 302 says that the evidence does not bear this arrangement out but then says that the plaintiff may have been a trustee for the general creditors. Whilst the auction catalogue was headed 'For the benefit of creditors' it does not appear that this was ever submitted to the plaintiff for approval. On the other hand, it is suggested in the report that a sale for the creditors generally did at one time represent the plaintiff's intentions.
18 (1834) 1 Cr M&R 298 at 301-302 per Parke B.

principal where he invokes the right and title of a third party: the 'jus tertii' defence.

The jus tertii defence

In *Crosskey v Mills*[19] it was expressly held that there no third party had shown any title to the money but that if such had been shown the auctioneer might have had a defence to an action by the principal. The precise circumstances where this defence will be available now fall to be considered. The common law position has been affected by the Torts (Interference with Goods) Act 1977. The Act does not represent a masterpiece of clear draftsmanship and it may well be that its provisions do not apply at all to cases where a principal sues an agent for failure to account to him for the proceeds of sale. We shall therefore first outline the position at common law, and then consider the impact of the statute.

Common law

In *Hardman v Willcock*[20] an auctioneer was instructed by the plaintiff to sell certain goods he possessed. Before the sale the auctioneer was given notice by assignees of an insolvent that the goods belonged to them and that the plaintiff had obtained them from the insolvent under a fraudulent arrangement devised to defeat their claim. Having subsequently sold the goods, the auctioneer refused to account to the plaintiff for their proceeds. The plaintiff duly brought an action for money had and received to his use and the auctioneer pleaded the defence of jus tertii, that is, the right of the assignees as third parties entitled to the property. The court accepted the general proposition that an agent is under a duty to account to his principal, but held the defence good on the ground that the principal had taken the goods as part of a fraudulent scheme to defeat the rights of the true owners. A defence based on a notion of fraud by the client is somewhat narrow and the principle was explained and extended a few years later in *Biddle v Bond*[1] where an auctioneer refused to account to his principal, a landlord selling a tenant's goods under distraint for rent. Here again, the auctioneer received notice just before the sale from the tenant claiming that the distress was void. The court held that the defence of jus tertii was available against the principal. Blackburn J explained the rationale thus:[2]

> We do not question the general rule that one who has received property from another as his bailee or agent or servant must restore or account for that property to him from whom he received it... But the bailee has no better title than the bailor and consequently if a person entitled as against the bailor to the property claims it, the bailee has no defence against him.

Whereas normally, an agent is estopped from denying the title of his principal, the estoppel ceases when the possession on which it is founded is determined by the agent being 'evicted' by someone with a better title. There must be

19 Above, n 16.
20 (1831) 9 Bing 382n.
1 (1865) 122 ER 1179, 6 B&S 225.
2 (1865) 122 ER 1179 at 1181.

something in the nature of an eviction or dispossession (although this need not be physical); mere *notice* of another's claim does not suffice. The agent can set up the jus tertii only if he defends by virtue of the title and on the authority of the true owner.[3] And the defence is not restricted to cases where the principal has been guilty of fraud on the true owner. Blackburn J pointed out that the position is precisely the same whether the bailor was honestly mistaken as to the rights of the third person or fraudulently acting in derogation of those rights.[4]

An auctioneer then, in order to have a valid defence to an action brought by his principal for failure in his duty to account must prove two things: first, he must prove the title of the adverse claimant by whose authority he is defending the claim and, second, he must show that he has not by his conduct estopped himself from setting up that adverse claim. Where an auctioneer knows of an adverse claim but disregards it and sells for his principal he cannot then deny his principal's title by invoking that of the third party whose claim he has disregarded. This was the difficulty into which the auctioneer placed himself in *Re Sadler, ex p Davies*.[5] Here the auctioneer with due notice of two claims effectively took sides. He was held to be estopped from denying the title of one of two persons who had concurrently instructed him to sell. This case is distinguishable from *Biddle v Bond*,[6] where the notice of the conflicting claim came only a short time before the sale was due to be commenced so that it could not properly be said that the auctioneer made an election. The obvious course for an auctioneer who has notice of rival claims to property is to interplead.[7]

Statutory modifications

The Law Reform Committee considered the law relating to the jus tertii defence to be unduly complex and restrictive. The Committee favoured relaxation of the rules in order to avoid multiplicity of actions. They recommended that whenever a wrongful interference with goods was alleged the defendant should have power to apply to join any third parties claiming competing rights. The Committee's proposals were largely enacted in 1977 by the Torts (Interference with Goods) Act. Section 8 provides:

> (1) The defendant in an action for wrongful interference shall be entitled to show, in accordance with rules of court, that a third party has a better right than the plaintiff as respects all or any part of the interest claimed by the plaintiff, or in right of which he sues, and any rule of law (sometimes called jus tertii) to the contrary is abolished.
>
> (2) Rules of court relating to proceedings for wrongful interference may —
>
> (a) require the plaintiff to give particulars of his title.
> (b) require the plaintiff to identify any person who, to his knowledge, has or claims any interest in the goods,

3 See *Rogers Sons & Co v Lambert & Co* [1891] 1 Q B 318, 60 LJQB 187, CA.
4 (1865) 122 E R 1179 at 1181.
5 (1881) 19 Ch D 86, 45 LT 632, CA.
6 Above, n 1.
7 On interpleader see above, ch 4.

(c) authorise the defendant to apply for directions as to whether any person should be joined with a view to establishing whether he has a better right than the plaintiff, or has a claim as a result of which the defendant might be doubly liable,

(d) where a party fails to appear on an application within paragraph (c), or to comply with any direction given by the court on such an application, authorise the court to deprive him of any right of action against the defendant for the wrong either unconditionally, or subject to such terms or conditions as may be specified.

(3) Subsection (2) is without prejudice to any other power of making rules of court.

There is an immediate difficulty over the parenthesis in sub-s (1). It is not the defence based on the invocation of the jus tertii that is abolished, but the *limitations* on that defence outlined above. Thus, if the Act applied in the situations under consideration, the basic rule laid down by the common law — that generally a bailee cannot deny the title of his bailor — is abrogated. *Rogers Sons & Co v Lambert*[8] is therefore no longer good law and an auctioneer defendant would always be able to invoke the defence of jus tertii.

But does the Torts (Interference with Goods) Act 1977 apply where the auctioneer fails to account for proceeds of sale to his principal? Section 8 refers to the rights of a defendant 'in an action for wrongful interference'. Section 1 defines such as:

(a) conversion of goods (also called trover),
(b) trespass to goods,
(c) negligence so far as it results in damage to goods or to an interest in goods,
(d) subject to section 2, any other tort so far as it results in damage to goods or an interest in goods.

The problems with this definition are two-fold. First, it is doubtful whether a fund representing proceeds of sale of goods would be regarded as 'goods' within the definition.[9] Second, and more difficult to surmount, is the fact that a vendor seeking such proceeds could invariably bring an action for breach of *contract*. A right to the proceeds of sale is usually expressly provided and if it is not, such will be implied. Thus the action would not be one for conversion, trespass, negligence or any other tort.

One is driven to the conclusion that the Act simply does not apply to a retention by the auctioneer of the proceeds of sale.[10] This is rather unfortunate; the consequence is that an auctioneer who before sale learns of a rival claim to goods may freely invoke the jus tertii and enjoin the rival in any action against him for their return. Whereas if he sells the goods and seeks to set up the jus tertii as a defence to an action in respect of the proceeds, framed in contract, he can only invoke the jus tertii subject to the strict common law rules outlined above.

It is thought that despite the very general wording of s 8(1) of the Torts (Interference with Goods) Act 1977, even where the Act does apply, a specific estoppel such as that which was found in *Re Sadler*[11] could still operate to

8 Above, n 3.
9 Money is specifically excluded: Torts (Interference with Goods) Act 1977, s 14(1).
10 Murdoch *The Law of Estate Agency and Auctions* (2nd edn, 1984) Estates Gazette, p 428, is of a similar view.
11 Above, n 5.

prevent the auctioneer setting up the defence. The Act seeks to ameliorate the position of a defendant who finds himself subject to two or more rival claims. If he has chosen to throw in his lot with one of the rivals he should account to him and face the legal wrath of the other.

Where the provisions of the Act are available to the defendant he is permitted to name any interested rival, and apply for his being joined. The rules of court referred to in s 8(2) are to be found in RSC Ord 15, 10A(2) for the High Court, and CCR 1981, Ord 15, 4(1) for the county court.

An auctioneer will also have a defence to an action for money had and received where his receipt of the proceeds of sale or deposit is only conditional so that the purchaser's claim to its return is valid. In *Hardingham v Allen*[12] for example, a horse was sold at auction under the contractual condition that if it was warranted quiet in harness it could be returned within a prescribed period as not answering the warranty given. The horse was then to be tried and examined by an impartial person whose decision would be final. A purchaser returned a horse under this condition and the auctioneer duly paid back the purchase money. The vendor-plaintiff's claim for the purchase price as money had and received failed. Coltman J held: 'With regard to the money received by the defendant as the price of the horse [it] was received conditionally only and never in fact became money had and received to the use of the plaintiff.'[13]

The decision in *Murray v Mann*[14] where the purchaser justifiably rescinded the contract for fraud is to similar effect. However, we have already noted[15] that the question whether an auctioneer is entitled, in the absence of express authority, vis-à-vis his principal to accept rescission of a contract is not entirely free from doubt. If he unjustifiably does so he will be liable to account for the money he ought to have received and retained.[16]

Interest

We have already seen that, by virtue of his fiduciary relationship with his principal, an auctioneer may not make any profit out of his agency. It is perhaps obvious therefore that where an auctioneer holds money which belongs to his principal, any interest which it earns must be accounted for to him.[17] The question arises whether an agent holding money for his principal is under a *duty* to invest it so that it yields interest and is liable for such interest as could have been earned if he fails to do so. At common law the position was as follows:

(a) If an agent not expressly under a duty to invest his principal's money merely allows it to remain dead in his hands he is not liable to account for any interest it could have earned.[18]
(b) If, however, the agent mixes his principal's money with his own or makes any use of it he is liable to pay interest.[19]

12 (1848) 5 C B 793.
13 (1848) 5 C B 793 at 797-8.
14 (1848) 2 Exch 538, 17 LJ Ex 256.
15 See above, ch 3.
16 See *Nelson v Aldridge* (1818) 2 Stark 435 and contrast *Stevens v Legh* (1853) 2 CLR 251, 22 LTOS 84.
17 The general principles are discussed in *Bowstead on Agency* (14th edn, 1976) Sweet & Maxwell, art 56.
18 *Rogers v Boehm* (1798) 2 Esp 701.
19 Above, n 18.

(c) Similarly if an agent wilfully withholds accounts or money or is guilty of any fraudulent dealing with his principal's money he will be liable for interest.[20]

The common law has now been rendered somewhat obsolete by the Law Reform (Miscellaneous Provisions) Act 1934 which gives the court a wide general discretion to award interest on any debt or damages between the date when the cause of action arose and the judgment.[1]

Duty to care for the goods

The main legal relationship between a vendor and an auctioneer is that of agency, but in addition there exists in connection with goods a relationship of bailment. Bailment is a legal institution of some antiquity and complexity and it is possible within the scope of this book to discuss its impact in the field of auctions only in rather brief and general terms.[2] As a leading author has noted, 'bailment stands at the point at which contract, property and tort converge.'[3]

The salient feature of bailment involves the delivery of goods by the bailor into the custody of another, the bailee. Bailment is usually but not invariably for reward. Although an auctioneer will generally be a bailee for reward there are situations where the bailment may be gratuitous — as where he is in possession of a prospective vendor's goods for valuation purposes if he does not charge for such or, vis-à-vis the purchaser, after a sale but before collection by him.[4] Originally it was thought that bailment presupposed redelivery by the bailee but this is no longer so. A bailment can clearly exist where it is envisaged, as is the case with auctions, that the bailee will deliver the goods to a third party — the purchaser after the sale. But if the sale is abortive, the auctioneer will again be holding the goods as a bailee for the vendor with the concomitant rights and duties created by the relationship. A failure to return such goods without lawful excuse such as in exercise of his lien, or pleading the jus tertii, will render the auctioneer liable in conversion.

In the case of auctions the bailment will usually be contractual and its terms will depend upon the precise terms of that contract. Subject to such provisions, the duty of the auctioneer at common law will be to take reasonable care of the goods in his custody. In the old case of *Maltby v Christie*[5] an auctioneer was instructed to sell a quantity of plate glass. A dispute arose as to whether the auctioneer was entitled to deduct commission at the rate of 7½ per cent. No commission had been agreed between the parties but the defendant claimed there to be a trade custom that such an amount was usual in view of the extraordinary risks attending the sale of such goods. Lord Kenyon in denying the auctioneer's claim said that he was of the opinion that the auctioneer as

20 *Turner v Burkinshaw* (1867) 2 Ch App 488, 17 LT 83.
1 Questions relating to interest earned on deposits received by auctioneers are dealt with separately below.
2 The major modern work of reference is N E Palmer *Bailment* (1979) Law Book Company. See also 2 Halsbury's Laws (4th edn) para 1501 f.
3 Palmer (above, n 2) p 1.
4 The classic classification of the various sorts of bailment is to be found in *Coggs v Bernard* (1703) 2 Ld Raym 909, 1 Com 133 per Holt C J, viz: (a) custody of goods without reward, (b) loan of goods, (c) hire of goods, (d) pawn or pledge of goods, (e) carriage of goods or other performance of service for reward, and (f) the same, without reward.
5 (1795) 1 Esp 340.

bailee was only bound to take such care of the goods as he would exercise in respect of his own, and that for a loss arising from misfortune or unavoidable accident he was not liable.

Such a general statement as to the duty and standard of care must be treated with some caution. Some bailments involve benefit to both bailor and bailee, some create benefits only to the bailor, and some create benefits only to the bailee. According to Halsbury, 'an ordinary degree of care and skill is usually required where both benefit from the transaction; slighter diligence, perhaps, where the benefit is wholly that of the bailor... and greater diligence where the benefit accrues only to the bailee.'[6] However, in *Houghland v R R Low (Luxury Coaches) Ltd,*[7] the Court of Appeal preferred simply to say that the standard of care depended upon the circumstances of the particular case, it being artificial frequently to try to fit a particular case into the various rigid categories.[8] Moreover it has been held that where the bailment is contractual, as with auctions it usually is, if the bailee deals with the property entrusted to him in an unauthorised manner, he takes upon himself the risks of so doing. Thus if, for example, an auctioneer were to warehouse his principal's goods with a third person, in breach of contract whereupon the goods become destroyed by fire, the auctioneer will be liable.[9] This raises the question whether in the absence of express provision, a bailee may sub-contract out his duties. The answer turns on whether the contract involved is one, the essence of which is the personal skill and care of the bailee employed. As Denning LJ put it in *Edwards v Newland & Co:*[10]

> There are many bailments in which the bailee is entitled to make a sub-bailment: the repairer of a motor-car, for instance, can often quite reasonably send away a part of it to another firm for repairs; a carrier of goods may need to entrust them to another carrier for part of the journey; a hirer may himself often, quite lawfully, sub-hire the goods. It all depends upon the circumstances of the particular case. The contract here is a contract for the storage of furniture. In such a case, in my opinion, the personal skill and care of the contractor is of the essence of the contract. Much skill and care is necessary in appointing the men who are to handle the goods, in selecting the place where they are to be stored, in seeing that it is reasonably fireproof and burglarproof and in choosing the caretakers. The owner of the goods is entitled in these respects to the personal skill and care of the contractor. If the contractor employs a sub-contractor, he does it at his own risk...

A final problem in relation to the duty of care concerns the question whether a bailee is responsible for the loss of the bailor's goods due to their theft or other depredations by an employee. There are two possible bases for such a liability: first, the bailee may be liable personally in so far as his selection of the employee may have been neglegent.[11] Auctioneers frequently deal with very valuable merchandise and it is incumbent upon them to select and supervise their staff with care. In the absence of negligent selection, will he be liable, secondly, for the depredations of his employee — i e *vicariously?* Broadly speaking, an employer will be vicariously liable for the torts of his servant

6 2 Halsbury's Laws (4th edn) para 1503.
7 [1962] 1 Q B 694, [1962] 2 All ER 159, CA.
8 For a detailed consideration of this question see Palmer (above, n 2) pp 288-302.
9 See e g *Lilley v Doubleday* (1881) 7 Q B D 510, 51 LJQB 310; *McMahon v Field* (1881) 7 Q B D 591, 50 LJQB 552, CA.
10 [1950] 2 K B 534, CA at 542.
11 See *Jobson v Palmer* [1893] 1 Ch 71, 62 LJ Ch 180.

acting within the course of employment. Thus a bailee will be liable for the theft or conversion of his bailor's goods committed by an employee where such is employed in some part to perform taks involving care of the goods. He may not however be liable if, say, the goods are stolen by a tea-lady.[12]

As we have said, these duties are subject to express contractual variations. Auctioneers' contracts frequently make some provision for their potential liability and both Christie's and Sotheby's[13] provide for their right as auctioneers to insure the seller's goods, and state that if they are not so insured on the instructions of the seller that the latter shall be liable for all risks whether caused by negligence or otherwise. As such, the contracts provide exclusion of liability clauses and their efficacy depends upon the ordinary rules of common law and the provisions of the Unfair Contract Terms Act 1977 discussed more particularly elsewhere.[14]

DUTIES AND LIABILITIES OWED TO THE PURCHASER

An auctioneer may be liable to the purchaser of lots in a variety of ways. To a limited extent he is the purchaser's agent. More significantly, he will in certain circumstances be personally liable in contract. Finally, the general law imposes certain duties on auctioneers in and about the conduct of their business.

The auctioneer as agent of the purchaser

We have mentioned in passing that the auctioneer, whilst primarily of course the agent of the vendor, is also, to a limited extent, the agent of the purchaser. It seems to have been well settled by the early nineteenth century[15] that the auctioneer is the agent of the purchaser for the purpose of signing the memorandum required to make enforceable certain contracts of sale. Both contracts for the sale etc of land and those for the sale of goods, where the value exceeded £10, were required to be evidenced in writing but today only contracts for the sale of land are significant in this context and these are discussed in detail in ch 9.

The agency of the auctioneer vis-à-vis the purchaser has been described as follows:[16]

12 There may be some doubt whether the employer's duty is here properly categorised as vicarious; it may be that it is better regarded as personal liability, he being answerable for the way in which his employee carries out a duty of care which the employer has delegated to him. See the alternative formulations in *Morris v C W Martin & Sons Ltd* [1966] 1 Q B 716, [1965] 2 All ER 725, CA.

13 See Christie's Conditions of Acceptance 7; Sotheby's Conditions of Business 20 (Appendix 1).

14 See ch 6.

15 See *Emmerson v Heelis* (1809) 2 Taunt 38; *White v Proctor* (1811) 4 Taunt 209; *Farebrother v Simmons* (1822) 5 B & Ald 333; *Eden v Blake* (1845) 13 M & W 614, 14 LJ Ex 194.

16 *Sims v Landray* [1894] 2 Ch 318 per Romer J at 320.Cf *Chaney v Maclow* [1929] 1 Ch 461, 98 LJ Ch 345, CA; *Bell v Balls* [1897] 1 Ch 663, 66 LJ Ch 397; *Van Praagh v Everidge* [1902] 2 Ch 266, 71 LJ Ch 598 (revsd [1903] 1 Ch 434, 72 LJ Ch 260, CA, on the ground that there was no sufficient memorandum).

> Where there is a sale by public auction and the property is knocked down by the auctioneer to the highest bidder, the auctioneer is not only the agent of the vendor, but he is also the agent of the purchaser, the highest bidder; and ... he is the purchaser's agent clearly to this extent, that he is entitled to sign in the name and on behalf of the purchaser, a memorandum sufficient to satisfy the provisions of the Statute of Frauds ...

Most of the cases where this agency has been invoked have involved claims by vendors or auctioneers against defendant purchasers seeking to resile from their bargains. The question arises, however, to what extent if at all, this agency involves obligations on the part of the auctioneer to the purchaser. In other words, does this agency involve *duties* to sign the memorandum on the part of the purchaser so that he can insist that he becomes a party to the contract, and, if so, does it follow that he can further insist that the auctioneer sign on behalf of the vendor so that the contract becomes enforceable? It is clear from the cases cited earlier that the authority to sign on behalf of the purchaser is irrevocable after the property is knocked down to him[17] and it would be surprising, not to say commercially unfortunate, if an irretrievably bound purchaser could not be certain that the vendor too would be bound or that if he was not, a remedy would lie against him or through his agent, the auctioneer. However Halsbury[18] suggests that the agency imports no liability on the part of the auctioneer either for failing to sign on the purchaser's behalf or to let him sign, or for failing to bind the vendor by providing a signature on his behalf.

It must be accepted that there is no conclusive authority on these important questions. In *Johnston v Boyes*[19] a freehold inn, the White Hart at South Mimms, was put under the hammer. The Conditions of Sale provided that the highest bidder would be the purchaser and pay immediately a deposit of 10 per cent and sign the requisite memorandum. The plaintiff deputed her husband to bid for her but did not trust him to the extent of furnishing him with cash. When the property was knocked down to him he sought to sign the memorandum and, having no cash for the deposit, offered his own cheque. Unfortunately, by coincidence, the solicitor to the vendor, who sat as registrar of the local county court recognised the husband as one who, the previous week, had sworn to be penniless. He therefore instructed the auctioneer not to permit the husband to sign in any capacity. The would-be purchaser was denied an injunction restraining the sale of the property to any other persons. The court was prepared to accept that a vendor could be liable in damages in such circumstances, not on the contract of sale itself which remained unenforceable but on an agreement that a contract of sale would be effected with the highest bidder. However in the event, the action failed because, since the pre-condition of payment of a deposit of 10 per cent in cash had not been fulfilled, there was no breach of the agreement contained in the Conditions of Sale. A similar case is *McManus v Fortescue*[20] where the purchaser claimed against the auctioneer for his refusal to sign the memorandum of sale relating to personal property then required by s 4 of the Sale of Goods Act 1893. Here the auctioneer, having knocked down the property to him, refused to complete the memorandum because he had erroneously knocked it down below a reserve to

17 *Chaney v Maclow*, n 16 above. And see (1929) 45 L Q R 289.
18 See 2 Halsbury's Laws (4th edn) para 752.
19 [1899] 2 Ch 73, 68 LJ Ch 425; injunction proceedings are reported at 14 T L R 475.
20 [1907] 2 KB 1, 76 LJ KB 393, CA.

which the item had been expressly subject. The Court of Appeal in affirming the decision at first instance, held the auctioneer not liable on the grounds that, in such circumstances, all bids and all acceptances thereof are subject to the condition that the reserve has been reached. Thus the fall of the hammer did not produce a sale at all. This analysis is, it is submitted correct, but it leaves unanswered the contention that an auctioneer is liable for failing to sign a memorandum where the sale *is* completed unconditionally by the fall of the hammer either where the sale is without reserve or the fixed reserve is reached.

The judgments in these two cases are, it is argued, consistent with the proposition that an action will lie when a purchaser is prevented from signing the memorandum or the auctioneer declines to do so as his agent in circumstances where the purchaser has fulfilled all the required conditions. However, as was recognised in *McManus v Fortescue*,[1] the existence of a right to sign is not enough to protect the purchaser: he must also be able to insist that the auctioneer completes the memorandum as agent of the vendor or that the vendor himself signs. Without such a reciprocal duty on the part of the auctioneer, the purchaser will only be able to bind himself, leaving the vendor to decide whether he wishes to be bound. Yet in the relatively modern case of *Richards v Phillips*,[2] Pennycuick J, responding to the contention that the auctioneer was bound to sign on behalf of the vendor rendering the contract enforceable at the suit of the highest bidder, said:[3]

> The ... contention raises a question of law which has been the subject of one or two inconclusive dicta, but ... not of any actual decision ... An auctioneer is primarily the agent of the vendor ... there is no doubt that he becomes also the implied agent of a purchaser to sign the memorandum on behalf of the purchaser. But it is not at all clear to me how this implied agency on behalf of the purchaser can make it part of his duty to the purchaser to sign the memorandum on behalf of the vendor.

In this case again the question did not in the result arise for decision because it was held that there had been a genuine dispute about rival bids justifying the withdrawal of the lot and its re-offer for sale. On this aspect of the case, the decision was upheld on appeal.

The duty, it is suggested, can be regarded as arising in this way: the purchaser, as highest bidder impliedly or expressly authorises the auctioneer to effect an enforceable contract by adding his signature to the requisite memorandum. As part of this agency relationship, and impliedly imported into it to give it business efficacy, is a corresponding duty to ensure that the contract is mutually enforceable; that the purchaser effectively is the purchaser by obtaining or supplying the vendor's signature. And it is submitted that cases such as *Johnston v Boyes*[4] and *McManus v Fortescue*[5] are entirely consistent with such an analysis. The auctioneer has power to sign on behalf of and to bind both parties. This authority is, as regards each party irrevocable after the property is knocked down. It is difficult to see why a purchaser should be left without a remedy if the vendor is not bound (as we have seen, a vendor can recover from the auctioneer if he fails to secure an agreement binding the

1 Above, n 20.
2 [1969] 1 Ch 39.
3 [1969] 1 Ch 39 at 52.
4 Above, n 19.
5 Above, n 20.

purchaser).[6] Were it otherwise, the agency between auctioneer and purchaser would largely be, as Murdoch describes it, a 'spurious agency'[7] enuring exclusively to the benefit of the vendor.

Personal contractual liability to the purchaser

An auctioneer may be personally liable to the purchaser in contract[8] in three distinct ways, and we shall consider each in turn.

Breach of warranty of authority

If an agent, including an auctioneer, sells property without or in excess of his authority he will be liable to the purchaser in damages for breach of the implied warranty that he does, in fact, possess the authority exercised. The simplest situation is where the agent has no authority to sell at all. In *Anderson v John Croall & Sons Ltd*[9] auctioneers sold a mare after a selling race, the trainer's lad having failed to remove her from the paddock after the weighing up so that the auctioneers were misled into believing that she was being offered for sale. The owners refused to deliver her and the purchaser claimed against the auctioneer for 35 guineas being the difference in price between that at which she had been knocked down to him and the price which she had fetched six months later. The Court of Sessions in Scotland allowed such a claim being damages for breach of the warranty that they were authorised to sell, 10 guineas being deducted in respect of costs of upkeep.

More problematic is the position where the auctioneer has some authority to sell but exceeds it. The obvious case where this may arise is where the auctioneer is instructed to sell subject to a reserve and sells below it. We have already discussed this problem in ch 3 from the point of view of the auctioneers's ability to bind his principal. If, as we have suggested, the seller is not bound on the contract of sale because the bids and any acceptance remain conditional, the question arises whether the auctioneer is liable to the purchaser for breach of warranty of authority. If the fact that a reserve is or may be fixed is notified to purchasers, as it usually is through the auction particulars, the auctioneer will not normally be liable for breach of warranty because the purchaser has notice of the restriction on that authority, or notice of the possibility that it may be restricted and he is put on enquiry as to whether it has been. That was decided in *McManus v Fortescue*.[10] However in *Fay v Miller Wilkins & Co*[11] auctioneers were held liable to the purchaser because they went further than merely knocking the property down; they proceeded to sign the requisite memorandum on his behalf. This was held to amount to a waiver of the condition that the property was sold subject to the

6 See the discussion in the first section of this chapter, 'Duties to the vendor'.
7 Murdoch *The Law of Estate Agency and Auctions*. (2nd edn, 1984) Estates Gazette, p. 431.
8 Liability for breach of warranty of authority may alternatively lie in tort where it is negligent or fraudulent: *Bowstead on Agency* (14th edn, 1976) Sweet & Maxwell, art 121.
9 1903 6 F (Ct of Sess) 153, 41 Sc LR 95.
10 Above, n 20.
11 [1941] Ch 360, CA.

reserve. Since now only dispositions affecting interests in land require to be evidenced in this way, an auctioneer may be liable for breach of warranty of authority when he sells land below reserve but not when he sells goods. It is questionable whether such a distinction should exist. The difficulty for the purchaser is that even if he knows that there is or may be a reserve placed on the property, he will not know whether it has in fact been reached. Should he not be entitled to assume that it has if the auctioneer knocks the property down to him, or, at any rate, should he not have redress against the auctioneer in such circumstances? The liability would not attach for falsely representing that he had authority to sell without reserve but for representing that the reserve had been reached. In *Fay v Miller Wilkins & Co* the auction conditions empowered the vendor to fix a reserve. Clauson LJ, after reiterating that in such circumstances the purchaser took the risk that in selling at the knock-down price the auctioneer might be exceeding his authority, went on to say that the purchaser relies: '... in practice on the care and honesty of the auctioneer as a professional man, and in law on his ... right to sue the auctioneer on the warranty of authority implied in the fact of his selling on the principal's behalf at the figure named in the note.'[12] Whilst this dictum is not entirely free from ambiguity it lends some judicial support to the proposition that an auctioneer, in concluding the formalities required for the sale of the property which is or may be subject to a reserve, represents that the property has reached or exceeded the reserve price and, that if it has not, whilst he cannot enforce the sale against the vendor, the purchaser can sue the auctioneer on that representation. Since the only 'formality' required in a sale of goods is that the property be knocked down, such an action should lie in the case of chattel auctions on the fall of the hammer without more.

Liability on the contract of sale

Whilst the general rule is that an agent is not liable on the contract which he makes on behalf of his principal, there is a number of exceptions. Liability may attach because of particular strict rules relating to certain kinds of contract. Thus an agent will be liable where he makes a contract by deed and himself executes it. He is liable even though he is described as acting for and on behalf of his principal.[13] Additionally an agent will also be liable if his principal is undisclosed. This is axiomatic in that, in such circumstances, the *fact* of his agency is not revealed to the purchaser at all. Here the purchaser may also sue the principal once he discovers his existence. It might have been arguable that an auctioneer could never sell for an undisclosed principal in that, qua auctioneer, he inevitably sells only the property of another. Indeed there have been judicial suggestions to this effect.[14] Unfortunately, however, this is not the case. It has been settled, at least since the case of *Flint v Woodin*[15] in 1852 that there is no objection to an auctioneer selling his own property to the purchaser. In such a case, clearly, the auctioneer sells as principal.

12 [1941] Ch 360 at 367.

13 See *Bowstead on Agency* (above, n 8) art 113, and see also art 114 re liability on bills of exchange etc.

14 See e g per Blackburn J in *Mainprice v Westley* (1865) 6 B&S 420 at 429 reporting the opinions of Cockburn C J and Shee J: 'In the employment of an auctioneer the character of an agent is necessarily implied and the party bidding at auction knowingly deals with him as such....' See also in similar vein at first instance in *Anderson v John Croall & Sons Ltd* 1904 6 F (Ct of Sess) 153, 41 Sc LR 95.

15 (1852) 9 Hare 618, 22 LJ Ch 92.

More uncertain, however, is the question whether an auctioneer may be liable personally in contract if the fact of his agency is disclosed but the *identity* of his principal is not. It is very important here to distinguish between the case where the principal is undisclosed, where the agent will always be liable, and the case where the existence of the principal is disclosed but his identity is not.[16] In such circumstances it is not possible to be dogmatic as to whether the agent incurs personal liability on the contract. In some cases the identity of the vendor may be important to the purchaser so that a purchaser who contracts with an agent who declines to name his principal may be taken to do so only on the basis that the agent undertakes some concurrent liability. In other circumstances the identity of the seller may be of no interest. In *Teheran-Europe Co Ltd v S T Belton (Tractors) Ltd* Diplock L J said:[17]

> A person may enter into a contract through an agent whom he has actually authorised to enter into the contract on his behalf or whom he has led the other party to belief he has so authorised but we are concerned here only with actual authority. Where an agent has such actual authority and enters into a contract with another party intending to do so on behalf of his principal it matters not whether he discloses to the other party the identity of the principal or even that he is contracting on behalf of a principal at all, if the other party is willing or leads the agent to believe that he is willing to treat as a party to the contract anyone on whose behalf the agent may have been authorised to contract. In the case of an ordinary commercial contract such willingness of the other party may be assumed by the agent unless either the other party manifests his unwillingness or there are other circumstances which should leave the agent to realise that the other party was not so willing.

However, there are several cases involving auctions which suggest that where the name of the principal-vendor is not given, the auctioneer invariably incurs contractual liability to the purchaser. As long ago as 1792,[18] Lord Kenyon held an auctioneer liable where a bond was not assigned to the purchaser within the contractual period. Although it is not clear from the brief report of this case, it appears[19] that the fact of agency was disclosed but the name of the principal was not. The purchaser was said to be entitled to look to the auctioneer 'personally for the completion of the contract'. In *Franklyn v Lamond*[20] it was held that the auctioneer was liable for the non-transfer of certain company shares sold at auction. Here the judge, Wilde C J, opined that the auctioneer had contracted personally. The auctioneers were described as such in the catalogue and they argued unsuccessfully that this sufficed as an indication of agency absolving them from personal liability. The case is not particularly strong on the question of personal liability where the fact of agency is disclosed because the Chief Justice observed that 'their character as agents was no [sic] otherwise intimated to the purchaser' and that 'this is the simple case of parties who have sold as principals, turning round and saying that they are merely agents.' However, more modern cases have reiterated the principle that: 'Where an agent purports to make a contract for a principal, disclosing the fact

16 Regrettably, the judges have not always made such distinctions with care: 'the case [is] one of disclosed agency and undisclosed principal', *Benton v Campbell Parker & Co* [1925] 2 KB 410 per Salter J at 414; and per Blackburn J in *Mainprice v Westley* (above, n 14) at 429 where, speaking of the sale in *Warlow v Harrison* (1859) 1 E&E 309, 27 LJQB 14 (involving the sale of a horse sold as 'the property of a gentleman') his Lordship said 'the principal was not disclosed ... he was a concealed principal'.

17 [1968] 2 Q B 545, CA at 555.

18 *Hanson v Roberdeau* (1792) Peake 120.

19 Per Salter J in *Benton v Campbell Parker & Co* [1925] 2 KB 410 at 417.

20 (1847) 4 CB 637, 16 LJCP 221.

that he is acting as an agent, but not naming his principal the rule is that, unless a contrary intention appears, he makes himself personally liable on the authorised contract.'[1]

The nature and scope of this personal liability falls to be considered. In *Wood v Baxter*[2] the purchaser of wheat and straw sold by a tenant sued the auctioneers when the landlord refused to allow him to remove the straw, invoking a custom that such was to remain on the land. It was held that the claim failed because the auctioneer had done all he could to effect delivery and was not responsible for the vendor's lack of title (if such there was) to sell. Williams J said:[3]

> What is the character and extent of the contract entered into by the auctioneer when he sells without disclosing the name of his principal? The answer to this is, that it depends upon the conditions of sale, upon what is said by the auctioneer at the time, upon the surrounding circumstances, and upon the nature of the subject matter of the sale. In the first place, it would certainly be going too far to say that an auctioneer, selling without disclosing the name of his principal, makes himself a contracting party in the same way and to the same extent that another agent acting for an undisclosed principal does. The auctioneer sells, not as an owner having a right to sell by virtue of his own right of property, but as an auctioneer empowered and entrusted by his employer to sell. If he is selling livestock or implements in the market place or furniture in a room, the extent of his contract would ordinarily be to deliver the goods to the buyer; if he was selling shares in a joint stock company, it would be to procure a transfer to the purchaser; if he was selling timber stacked in a yard or loaded on board ship or growing crops on a farm, it would be in each case to give such constructive delivery as according to the nature of the subject matter was practicable and usual. Upon making such delivery, his obligation would ordinarily be fulfilled.

Thus it appears that the liability of an auctioneer is essentially only for non-delivery. Despite that Williams J says that 'his contract is very nearly that of an ordinary vendor,'[4] it is clear from the decision in that case, and also from *Benton v Campbell, Parker & Co*[5] that no liability attaches to the auctioneer for any want of title (logically, because as an expressed agent he does not claim to have any). The earlier cases of *Hanson v Roberdeau*[6] and *Franklyn v Lamond*[7] are consistent with a limited liability to deliver, since failure to deliver was in each case the complaint, but the question arises whether such a limitation is consonant with principle. If the rationale of fixing the auctioneer with personal liability is that given by Salter J in *Benton*'s case,[8] namely that 'a purchaser is willing to contract with an unknown man ... but only if the agent will make himself personally liable if called upon to perform the contract,'[9] there seems little justification or commercial logic in limiting the duty of performance to delivery only. Should not the purchaser have recourse against the auctioneer if the goods are defective or unfit for their purpose too?

1 *Benton v Campbell Parker & Co* [1925] 2 KB 410 per Salter J at 414.
2 (1883) 49 L T 45.
3 (1883) 49 L T 45 at 46. See also *Payne v Elsden* (1900) 17 T L R 161.
4 Above, n 2.
5 [1925] 2 K B 410.
6 Above, n 18.
7 Above, n 20.
8 [1925] 2 K B 410.
9 [1925] 2 K B 410 at 414.

It is suggested, however, that the reason for rendering the auctioneer liable is not because of any assumption that the identity of the vendor is crucial, but simply because the duty to deliver is the reverse of the coin that an auctioneer may sue for the price.[10] We concluded in ch 4 that the auctioneer's right to sue for the price is based upon his implied contract arising out of the delivery up of possession of the goods sold, and that this contract is quite separate from the contract of sale. Although Williams J suggested in *Wood v Baxter*[11] that the auctioneer could be sued upon the contract of sale, the better view is that expressed in *Benton v Campbell, Parker & Co* that:[12]

> These rights and liabilities do not arise from the contract of sale which binds only the buyer and the principal. They arise from the contract which the auctioneer makes upon his own account with the buyer ... The duty to deliver and the right to receive the price are usually expressed in the conditions of sale. But whatever its terms may be, the contract is entirely independent of the contract of sale.

If it is right that the duty to deliver is the correlative of the right to sue for the price, then it is obvious that liability should not extend beyond a duty to deliver. Normally delivery causes no problem in practice since chattels sold are in the sale room and available for removal by the buyer. But occasionally large chattels such as a grand piano are sold 'off site' and it is in this sort of situation that non-delivery could arise. It is, however, difficult to see why such a duty is then only imposed, in the absence of express provisions,[13] where the principal is unnamed or unidentified.[14] Moreover, there is a difficulty concerning sales of land. In such cases unless the auctioneer contracts as vendor, we have argued that he has no right to sue for the price and, therefore it would follow, that there could be no correlative personal liability to deliver. The absence of such liability would strengthen the argument in favour of rendering the auctioneer liable as agent of the purchaser to complete the necessary memorandum binding the vendor, advocated in the earlier part of this section.

Finally, it could be argued that the best reason for making the auctioneer personally liable where he declines to name the vendor is that if the auctioneer fails to identify him, the purchaser will be unable to bring actions against the vendor. However, we suggest that this practical obstacle can be overcome by an action for discovery. Normally, discovery will not be available save against a party to an action. There, of course, lies the problem because if the auctioneer is not personally liable — where the action is for something other than non-delivery — he cannot be made a party to the action. However, recently there has been developed, or perhaps revived, a right to bring an action for discovery against a non-party. In *Norwich Pharmacal v Customs and*

10 See e g per Field J in *Woolfe v Horne* (1877) 2 Q B D 355 at 360, and per Rowlatt J in *Page v Sully* (1918) 63 Sol Jo 55.

11 Above, n 3.

12 [1925] 2 K B 410 at 415-16.

13 An example of a case where the duty to deliver was expressed in the Conditions of Sale is *Woolfe v Horne* (above, n 10) where the relevant provision read 'if any deficiency shall arise, or from any cause the auctioneers shall be unable to deliver any lot or portion of a lot, then in such a case the purchaser shall accept compensation for the same...' On the other hand in *Page v Sully* (above, n 10) McCardie J suggested that the liability could be excluded by appropriate provisions.

14 A principal remains unnamed where the property is described as 'the property of a gentleman' as in *Warlow v Harrison* (1859) 1 E&E 309, 29 LJQB 14, and also it seems where the sale is expressed to be 'By order of Mr J Spurling and Others' (even if it later transpired that the named person was the seller of the particular lot) as in *Page v Sully* (above, n 10).

Excise Comrs[15] a plaintiff who owned a patent for a chemical compound was held entitled to seek discovery from the defendants as to the names and addresses of importers who had infringed their patent. The defendants to this action — an action for discovery only — were of course in no way implicated in the infringement. Lord Reid said that if through no fault of his own a person gets mixed up in the tortious acts of others so as to facilitate their wrong-doing he may incur no personal liability but he comes under a duty to assist the person who has been wronged by giving him full information and disclosing the identity of the wrongdoers. If an innocent party is so enjoined then a fortiori an auctioneer unreasonably refusing to disclose the identity of his principal should be. The only difficulty with this principle is that Lord Reid refers expressly to tortious acts of others, whereas in our situation the claim will normally be in contract. Other judges, e g Lord Morris,[16] refer simply to persons who have information about 'wrongdoers'. It seems to us that the *Norwich Pharmacal* case lays down a principle of fairly general application and that it would be unreasonable to assume that it was restricted to cases involving torts. We say this because of the rationale behind this recently revived action: it was thought that discovery would never lie save against a party to proceedings because of the so-called 'mere witness' rule, namely that you cannot obtain information by discovery from the person who will in due course be compellable to give that information as a witness. But as was pointed out in the *Norwich Pharmacal* case, if the information in the possession of the commissioners was not to be made available by discovery, no action could ever be begun because the identity of the wrongdoers would remain unrevealed. Similarly, discovery against the auctioneer would be justified simply because without it the purchaser would be unable to bring an action against the wrongdoer, e g a seller in breach of implied terms under the Sale of Goods Act 1979. In these circumstances no hardship is involved in limiting the auctioneer's liability to non-delivery.

Other liability

Under the general law an auctioneer may incur liability to the purchaser in a variety of circumstances. Generally speaking, the liability will arise from a failure to take proper care either of the purchaser's goods, or his person, or for mis-statements in and about the sale of the property.

Duty with regard to the goods purchased

When specific goods are sold to a purchaser ownership of them will, unless a contrary intention appears, pass to the purchaser when the contract is made,[17] i e on the fall of the hammer. Thereafter they are the purchaser's goods. If the auctioneer retains possession of them, he will become the bailee of the purchaser. As such he will be under a duty to take reasonable care of them, apart from any express exclusion of liability provision which will be subject to the test of reasonableness under the Unfair Contract Terms Act 1977.[18] In

15 [1974] A C 133, [1973] 2 All ER 943, HL.
16 Above, n 15.
17 Sale of Goods Act 1979, s18, r1. (Appendix 2).
18 See generally ch 6.

practice, however, it is rare to find that title to property passes to the purchaser on the sale. Both Sotheby's and Christie's conditions provide that ownership shall not pass until payment and that credit may be given. Sotheby's give the buyer five days in which to remove the goods purchased where they have been paid for or where credit has been given, and provide further that after collection or the five-day period the buyer will be responsible for any loss. This leaves open the potential liability of the auctioneers during the collection period. Christie's on the other hand state that the risk shall be on the buyer 'in all respects from the fall of the hammer.'[19] The effect of such a clause requires consideration. Where the ownership passes to the buyer and the auctioneer retains possession during a period when the purchaser may collect, the auctioneer is the bailee of the purchaser and, as such, owes him a duty to take reasonable care of his goods. Where the property does not pass to the purchaser pending payment, the analysis is different. Neither ownership nor possession passes to the buyer and, therefore, he cannot be a bailor although he has an interest in the preservation of the goods. Until very recently the law was clear that such a person could not, in the absence of a contract with the person in whose custody they were – e g carrier or warehouseman – sue in negligence for any failure to take care of them. This is because in order to maintain such an action a party has to be their owner; if he is not then none of *his* property is damaged or lost and his loss is purely economic and not recoverable. However, in *Schiffahrt und Kolen GmbH v Chelsea Maritime Ltd, The Irene's Success,*[20] a buyer to whom the risk but not title in goods had passed was held able to sue a carrier for negligent damage to them. In many such situations the buyer will have no contract with the person in whose custody and possession they are, and this decision closes a gap in the protection afforded to him by the law. However, in the case of auctions, there is a separate contract with the buyer on the terms of the Conditions of Sale. Whether such a contract would include an implied term, in the absence of the exclusions commonly found, to care for the goods of a purchaser who has not become their owner, is however doubtful, and the recasting of the law by the judge in *The Irene's Success* may, therefore, have significance for auctioneers. It may be questioned whether a provision such as that found in Christie's Conditions of Sale that the risk shall in all respects pass to the buyer is intended as a clause or notice excluding liability; its purport is in the main undoubtedly to allocate the risk between the vendor and purchaser. However, in the light of the first instance decision in *The Irene's Success,* the clause may amount to a notice excluding liability for negligence. If it does so then it must satisfy the test of reasonableness laid down in the Unfair Contract Terms Act 1977.

Liability for physical injury

An auctioneer may be liable in negligence if those attending the auction are damaged by goods, e g by a frisky horse, or by the state of the auctioneer's premises. The duties of care are owed not only to one who becomes a purchaser but to all those who are lawfully present at the auction, and we shall consider the ambit of this liability briefly in the following section of this chapter, 'Duties and liabilities to third parties'.

19 Christie's Conditions of Sale 9; Cf Sotheby's Conditions of Business 9, 10 and 12. (Appendix 1).

20 [1982] QB 481, [1982] 1 All ER 218; and see A M Tettenborn 'Sellers Buyers and Negligent Damage to Goods' [1983] JBL 459. In *Leigh & Sillavan Ltd v Aliakmon Shipping Co Ltd, The Aliakmon*[1985] 2 All ER 44, [1985] 2 WLR 289, two judges in the Court of Appeal doubted the correctness of *The Irene's Success* at least in so far as the shipping context was concerned.

Liability for misrepresentations

In considering the effect of auction houses' Conditions of Sale (below, ch 6) we make the point that whereas the vendor may be liable for misrepresentations, including those made quite innocently, under the Misrepresentation Act 19XX, no liability thereunder attaches to the auctioneer. However, an auctioneer may still render himself civilly liable to the purchaser for mis-statements made in the auction particulars or orally from the rostrum, under the common law. What follows is necessarily a truncated account. Readers are referred to the standard works on contract and tort for detailed consideration. There are three separate possible bases of liability, and these are given below.

In deceit

A person who causes loss to another by means of fraud will be liable to an action in tort for deceit. Fraud is a serious charge to be levelled at anyone but especially at a professional person and, in order for it to be made out, fairly stringent tests have to be satisfied. The House of Lords has held that it cannot be proved unless it can be said of a person that: 'he knowingly made a false statement or one which he did not believe to be true, or was careless whether what he stated be true or false'.[1] A prerequisite to a successful action against an auctioneer under this tort is, therefore, that it be shown that he did not honestly believe what he said was true. If he did have that honest belief, however foolish, credulous or negligent he might have been, he will not be liable to the purchaser for deceit.

In negligence

For 70 years after the decision in *Derry v Peek*[2] it was thought that no liability could attach for mis-statements if they were made merely negligently. In 1963 however, the House of Lords delivered a judgment of exceptional importance for professional men in *Hedley Byrne & Co Ltd v Heller & Partners Ltd.*[3] That case concerned a banker's reference on which another party relied but the decision is of very wide scope. The House of Lords said that a person could owe a duty of care to another in giving information or advice and that such a duty would exist where there was some 'special relationship' between the parties. The precise circumstances when such a special relationship will be held to exist have not been exhaustively stated, but in general it can be said to arise whenever someone possessed of special skill undertakes to apply it for the assistance of another person who relies upon it.[4] There appears to be no reported instance of an auctioneer being held liable under the *Hedley Byrne v Heller* doctrine, probably because purchasers will normally prefer to take

1 *Derry v Peek* (1889) 14 App Cas 337, 58 LJ Ch 864; HL.
2 Above, n 1.
3 [1964] A C 465, [1963] 2 All ER 575, HL.
4 The more restrictive test suggested by the majority in the Privy Council in *Mutual Life and Citizens' Assurance Co Ltd v Evatt* [1971] A C 793, [1971] 1 All ER 150, PC, that the advisor should be in business as the supplier of information or advice or expressly have claimed to possess special skill, has not been regarded as conclusively limiting the English authority. However, even on the basis of such a narrow interpretation, an auctioneer would normally be, prima facie, regarded as owing a duty of care.

recourse against the vendor in cases of negligent mis-statement made by the auctioneer as his agent. The reason for this is that the vendor's liability under s 2(1) of the Misrepresentation Act 1967 is somewhat easier to establish, because under the Act it is for the vendor positively to disprove negligence, whereas at comon law the onus would be on the purchaser to prove it. However, there can be little doubt that an auctioneer is in a special relationship vis-à-vis a purchaser.

A difficulty arises as to exclusion of liability. We discuss elsewhere the impact of the Unfair Contract Terms Act 1977,[5] and it is clear that a vendor seeking to rely on the exclusion of liability clauses commonly found in auctioneers' conditions would have to show that such reliance was reasonable. As regards the auctioneer seeking to avoid liability for negligent mis-statements, the position is slightly different. In *Hedley Byrne v Heller* the bank were, in the result, held not liable because they had expressly disclaimed liability by heading their advice 'without responsibility'. Normally a person cannot avoid liability for negligence simply by broadcasting that he does not incur it, but the basis of the duty in this area is that the defendant has expressly or impliedly *undertaken* that he will give his advice or information with care. Obviously if he says in advance that he undertakes no such thing, no duty will arise. This kind of disclaimer differs from exclusion clauses as traditionally construed in that it does not seek to avoid the loss arising from a breach of duty but, rather, prevents the duty arising in the first place: 'a man cannot be said voluntarily to be undertaking a responsibility if at the very moment that he is said to be accepting it he declares that he is not.'[6] The Unfair Contract Terms Act 1977, s 2(2), subjects to a test of reasonableness a term or notice excluding or restricting 'liability for negligence' and it is arguable that this does not cover a term which negates the existence of the duty. It is true that s 13(1)(c) of the Act includes within the definition of an exemption clause those 'which exclude or restrict the relevant obligation or duty' but this provision relates to clauses excluding or restricting rules of evidence or procedure. At present the effect of the Unfair Contract Terms Act 1977 on disclaimers under *Hedley Byrne v Heller* remains to be settled.

On a collateral warranty

As stated, whilst tort imposes liability on auctioneers for deceit or negligence, there is no liability for purely innocent mis-statements. However, such liability may be imposed contractually on the basis that the auctioneer has made a collateral warranty.[7] Essentially the collateral contract is construed on this basis: the auctioneer effectively says to the successful purchaser 'if you will make the contract of sale with the vendor I promise that (e g) the horse is sound etc.' Thus the promise by the auctioneer is said to be part of a contract collateral to the main contract of sale which contains a representation which induces the formation of that contract, though it may not become incorporated in it. In such a way an auctioneer can be made liable for a representation, including one made innocently, which induces the formation of the main contract. Since the representation amounts, independently, to a term of a

5 See ch 6.
6 Per Lord Devlin in *Hedley Byrne v Heller* [1964] AC 465 at 533.
7 See e g *Webster v Higgin* [1948] 2 All E R 127; *Andrews v Hopkinson* [1957] 1 Q B 229, [1956] 3 All ER 422.

separate, collateral contract, the auctioneer will be liable for breach of it unless he can point to an exclusion clause which is apt to protect him. Once again, therefore, he will have to show that such a clause is reasonable.

Duties relating to the deposit

Invariably, in the case of sales of land by auction, and sometimes in chattel auctions, the Conditions of Sale require the purchaser to pay a deposit to the auctioneer. In such cases the auctioneer incurs certain liabilities with regard to the sums so paid. The requiring of a deposit has a two-fold purpose: first, to provide a part-payment of the purchase price — provided that the sale goes ahead to completion — but secondly and primarily, it is to 'guarantee that the purchaser means business' or to provide 'a security for the performance of the contract.'[8]

When such a deposit is paid to an auctioneer, the duties and liabilities which ensue depend largely upon whether he receives it as agent for one of the parties (usually the vendor) or as a stakeholder. The capacity in which the auctioneer holds the deposit is usually made clear by the contract;[9] but, if it is not, the law presumes that an auctioneer receiving a deposit does so as stakeholder whereas an estate agent and e g a solicitor do so as agent for the vendor.[10] The significance of the distinction was explained by Bowen L J in *Ellis v Goulton* as follows:[11]

> When a deposit is paid by a purchaser under a contract for the sale of land, the person who makes the payment may enter an agreement with the vendor that the money shall be held by the recipient as agent for both vendor and the purchaser. If this is done, the person who receives it becomes a stakeholder, liable in certain events to return the money to the person who paid it. In the absence of such agreement the money is paid to a person who has not the character of stakeholder; and it follows that, when the money reaches his hands it is the same thing so far as the person who pays it is concerned as if it had reached the hands of the principal. If so, it is impossible to treat money paid under these circumstances and remaining in the hands of the agent as there under any condition or subject to any trust in relation to the payer.

Thus as a stakeholder the duty of the auctioneer is to hold the deposit money as agent for both parties and not to part with it until the event upon which it becomes payable to one party or the other takes place. If he pays the money over to the vendor before completion or while a dispute is continuing relating to the contract of sale, he will be liable for it as money had and received to the purchaser's use;[12] whereas if he received it as *agent* it is the vendor who will be accountable to the purchaser in the event that the sale falls through, since payment to the agent is virtually payment to the principal.[13]

8 *Soper v Arnold* (1889) 14 App Cas 429, HL, per Lord MacNaghten at 435, and Lord Herschell at 433.
9 Both the National Conditions of Sale and the Law Society's Conditions of Sale provide for the deposit to be made to the auctioneer as stakeholder.
10 Conceded in *Furtado v Lumley* (1890) 54 JP 407, 6 T L R 168, but if the receipt for the deposit is signed by the auctioneer as agent for the vendor, he will hold it as such: *Bamford v Shuttleworth* (1840) 11 Ad & El 926; *Ellis v Goulton* [1893] 1 Q B 350.
11 [1893] 1 Q B 350 at 352-3.
12 *Edwards v Holding* (1854) 5 Taunt 815, 1 Marsh 377; *Burrough v Skinner* (1770) 5 Burr 2639, 98 E R 387.
13 *Bamford v Shuttleworth* (above, n 10).

An auctioneer holding as stakeholder should, therefore, not pay over any deposit to his vendor until he has satisfied himself that the sale has been satisfactorily completed. Most of the old cases cited so far concerned protracted disputes about title. If, however, his vendor is importunate for payment to him of what is, after all, part payment of the price, the auctioneer may pay it over but he should ensure that he obtains an indemnity from him.[14] The basic duty of the auctioneer as described above is well settled. Two important questions remain, however, as to which a certain degree of doubt may be entertained. The first relates to liability to pay interest on the deposit, and the second concerns responsibility where the deposit is lost.

Interest on the deposit

This subdivides into two separate concerns: whether the auctioneer is liable to invest the deposit money so that it yields interest and, in default, is liable for sums which could have been earned to the party ultimately entitled; and secondly, even where the answer to that question is no, whether if the auctioneer does in fact invest the deposit, he is entitled to keep the interest yielded.

Liability for non-investment

The first question has frequently arisen for decision, and it is clear that no interest is payable on deposit moneys whilst properly in the auctioneer's hands as stakeholder. In *Lee v Munn*[15] a purchaser claimed back his deposit with interest from the auctioneer when the vendor was unable to make the title. The court held that no interest could be recovered by him since negotiations for the sale had been continuing throughout but it was suggested, obiter, that the auctioneer could be liable for interest if the contract was rescinded and the auctioneer wrongly retained the deposit after demand had been duly made.[16] In *Gaby v Driver*[17] the purchaser's contention that interest would automatically run from the contractual completion date when the vendor failed to meet it was rejected, but again it was suggested that a claim for interest could be maintained after a valid demand and refusal. The purchaser's remedy, where the vendor is in breach of contract, is to sue the vendor and claim loss of income on the deposit moneys as special damages.[18]

Liability for interest earned

Less certain is the position where the auctioneer does, in fact, invest the deposit moneys. Here there is some division of opinion amongst the judges. Since deposits on sales of land are usually at least 10 per cent of the purchase price, the sums earned by a busy land auctioneer may not be insignificant. The earliest case in which the question seems to have received detailed

14 An appropriate form may be found in 2 Forms & Precedents (4th edn), Form 11.
15 (1817) 8 Taunt 45.
16 (1817) 8 Taunt 45 per Dallas J at 54 and per Burrough J at 55.
17 (1828) 2 Y & J 549.
18 See *Curling v Shuttleworth* (1829) 6 Bing 121, 3 Moo & P 368.

consideration is *Harington v Hoggart*[19] in 1830. Here the auctioneer was requested by the vendor's solicitors to invest the deposit in certain government securities and the vendor offered an indemnity in case such investment caused loss. The auctioneers, who held the deposit as stakeholders, said they would do as asked but only if the purchaser concurred. He did not, and the fund was not invested. In the result the sale was only completed some eight years after the deposit had been paid, due to protracted title disputes. The purchaser claimed interest on the deposit. Lord Tenterden the Chief Justice was clear that the auctioneers as stakeholders dealt correctly with the request of the vendors to invest the money. However he went on to consider what the position would have been had the sum yielded interest, and concluded that if a stakeholder chose to invest the funds he would be liable for any loss accruing, and 'if he is to answer for the loss it seems to me he has a right to any intermediate advantage which may arise.'[20] Moreover, whilst it was in the stakeholder's possession, the deposit fund belonged to neither vendor nor purchaser so that any interest yielded belonged to the stakeholder. This last point is not thought to be compelling: there is no reason why a stakeholder should not hold the interest as an accretion to the principal sum for whomsoever of the parties ultimately becomes entitled to it. Moreover, the notion that the right to any profit is the corollary of his potential loss is also objectionable. There are many situations where an agent may be liable to disgorge profits made even though he would be also liable to make good losses. The real question is whether the stakeholder should be distinguished from one who holds a fund as an agent. Such a distinction has been carefully maintained with regard to basic duties relating to the deposit. On the other hand it might be argued that the stakeholder is, as has frequently been stressed, the agent of *both* vendor and purchaser and that as such he should never be able to keep profits yielded by a fund which belongs to one of them. However a rationale for such a distinction was suggested in the modern case of *Potters (a firm) v Loppert*, viz:[1]

> The interest represents not merely a reward for the agent's trouble but also as a recompense for the sterilisation of the property vis-à-vis the estate agent during the period between payment of the deposit and the conclusion of the contract or its breakdown with the consequences that the agent has no prospect of earning a commission on its sale to any other party so long as the property remains sterilised.[2]

As will be obvious, all this was said in connection with an estate agent's position but it is arguable that similar reasoning can be applied to that of an auctioneer engaged to sell property; a vendor's solicitor, e g instructed to receive a deposit as agent, is in an entirely different position. But the simplest rationale is that given by Harman J in *Smith v Hamilton*, namely that 'the stakeholder is not bound to pay interest. He retains the benefit of it: that is his reward for holding the stake.'[3]

In the course of his judgment in *Potters v Loppert*[4], the Vice-Chancellor expressly approved *Harington v Hoggart*[5] and stressed that a stakeholder was

19 (1830) 1 B & Ad 577.
20 (1830) 1 B & Ad 577 at 586-7.
1 [1973] Ch 399, [1973] 1 All E R 658. This case concerned a pre-contract deposit paid to an estate agent but much of the discussion concerned the liability of an auctioneer-stakeholder of a contract deposit.
2 [1973] 1 All ER 658 at 669 per Pennycuick V-C.
3 [1951] Ch 174 at 184.
4 Above, n 1.
5 Above, n 19.

not in a position of a fiduciary agent under a duty to account to his principal for profits made. Contrary views have been expressed, most notably by Sachs L J in *Burt v Claude Cousins & Co Ltd*[6] to the effect that a stakeholder is a trustee for whomsoever becomes entitled to the fund, but the better view is that the stakeholder's liability sounds in contract or quasi contract for money had and received, and that whilst he retains it he does not do so as trustee for either party so as to disentitle him from profits earned by it. It is here that the significance of receiving the deposit as stakeholder rather than merely as agent of the vendor is most potently marked.[7] In this connection we should point out that where the auctioneer is an estate agent his duties as to the holding of clients' money are now governed by the Estate Agents Act 1979. It is clear that where he holds a deposit as agent for one party, he is liable to pay and account for interest, but that where he holds as stakeholder he is not.[8]

Loss of the deposit

The argument in favour of permitting the auctioneer when stakeholder to retain profits made out of the deposit moneys is based, at the end of the day, on the maintenance of a distinction between the capacity of the stakeholder and that of one who is merely an agent. A final question arises as to upon whom the liability should fall in the event that the auctioneer, through infraction or otherwise, causes the deposit to be lost, usually by reason of his insolvency. If he is the agent of one party one would expect that the risk of loss would fall on that party and, indeed, that is the position. Conversely, if the auctioneer is a stakeholder and as such is liable 'to hold it in medio pending the outcome of a future event,'[9] one might have expected the risk of loss to fall equally on either party, vendor or purchaser, who subsequently becomes entitled to it; he is equally the agent of both. However, it appears[10] to be the law that the vendor will bear the risk of loss so that he will be liable to recompense a purchaser who becomes entitled to its return and must give credit for it as part payment once it has been paid to the auctioneer. So was stated in *Fenton v Browne*,[11] but this case concerned a private sale where the deposit was paid to an estate agent who absconded and went bankrupt. The decision that the vendor was liable for the loss of the deposit is explicable in that the money had been paid to the estate agent qua agent of the vendor. As such, as we observed earlier, the fund is treated as having been paid to the vendor himself. What was said about auctioneers was necessarily obiter therefore. An unusual case is *Smith v Jackson & Lloyd*,[12] where a purchaser who was allowed into possession pending

6 [1971] 2 Q B 426, [1971] 2 All ER 611, CA. See also per Cross J in *Skinner v Trustee of Property of Reed (Bankrupt)* [1967] Ch 1194, [1971] 2 All ER 1286. The decision of the House of Lords in *Brown v I R C* [1965] A C 244, [1964] 3 All ER 119, HL, that a professional adviser is in a fiduciary relationship and as such cannot make a profit out of his client's money when entrusted with it, is not doubted but only begs the question when that person is a stakeholder.

7 Whilst in that situation it is advantageous for the auctioneer to be a stakeholder, it is necessary to bear in mind that in one situation he is in a stronger position if he acts as agent in receiving the deposit moneys — namely where he is seeking to exercise his lien against a vendor who has become bankrupt. The auctioneer can only exercise his lien against the vendor's property and the deposit will only have that character when the auctioneer holds it as his agent. See ch 4.

8 See Estate Agents Act 1979, ss 14-15 (Appendix 2), and Estate Agents (Accounts) Regulations 1981, r7. On the Act generally see Murdoch *The Law of Estate Agency and Auctions* (2nd edn, 1984) Estates Gazette, ch 9.

9 Per Denning M R in *Burt v Claude Cousins & Co Ltd* [1971] 2 Q B 426.

10 Murdoch (above, n 8) p 442, but the authorities are not entirely convincing and are of some age.

11 (1807) 14 Ves 144.

12 (1816) 1 Madd 618.

completion sought an order that the rent to be assessed by the court have deducted from it interest on the deposit he had paid. This was allowed by the court which rested on *Fenton v Browne* on the grounds that it was reasonable that the vendor be treated as having had the benefit of the stake because it amounted to part payment of the purchase price and because he could require the auctioneer to invest the money for his benefit. Neither of these reasons are, it is submitted, convincing. The part payment is only conditional pending completion which there had not taken place; and the notion that the vendor could require investment of the sum for his benefit is denied by *Harington v Hoggart.*[13] Finally there is the decision in *Rowe v May,*[14] where a mortgagee refused to complete until the purchaser of his interest paid him the balance of a deposit which the purchaser had already paid to a defaulting auctioneer. The court held that the mortgagee must take the risk of its loss. Romilly M R said:[15]

> Where a purchaser pays a deposit on his purchase-money to the auctioneer and it is lost, on whom does the loss fall? If the matter goes off, because the vendor cannot make a good title it is the vendor's duty to repay the deposit and the loss occasioned by the non-completion; and in case an action were brought against him for breach of the contract, the amount of deposit not repaid would be part of his loss, and the purchaser would be entitled to add it to the damages; so if the contract be completed and the deposit cannot be recovered from the auctioneer, *who for this purpose is the agent of the vendor,* it will be the vendor's loss, and not that of the purchaser.[16]

The italicised words are crucial. It appears that the Master of the Rolls was treating the auctioneer as agent rather than stakeholder. If the auctioneer were the vendor's agent, the result would be unremarkable. If however the courts are assimilating the position of stakeholder and agent, it is contrary to principle. There is however one explanation for this line of cases which can, we suggest, be supported: in the first of this quartet of cases, *Fenton v Browne,* Sir William Grant M R rationalised the decision thus: 'Upon a sale by auction the vendor determines who is to receive the deposit. The auctioneer is not a stakeholder of the purchaser: at least not of his choice... Under these circumstances it would be to hard to throw [the] loss upon this purchaser.'[17]

Where the parties are put at risk as to the honesty or financial stability of the auctioneer-stakeholder it is justifiable to render the vendor liable for any loss, since it is the vendor who selects the stakeholder — the purchaser has no choice but to entrust the auctioneer with the stake. The antiquity of the cases in this area may be a happy sign that today these risks are minimal.

13 (1830) 1 B & Ad 577. *Smith v Jackson & Lloyd* (n 12 above) was followed the same year in a case where it was held that a vendor was entitled to have the money paid into court and not repaid to a purchaser dissatisfied with the vendor's title, pending settlement of that dispute: *Annesley v Muggridge* (1816) 1 Madd 593.

14 (1854) 18 Beav 613.

15 (1854) 18 Beav 613 at 616-17, emphasis added.

16 In the case of an estate agent auctioneer the remedies available to his client are greatly enhanced by the Estate Agents Act 1979. Section 13 provides that a client's money is held in trust thus taking it out of the bankruptcy pool and rendering available the rules relating to tracing etc.

17 (1807) 14 Ves 144 at 148. Approved in *Burt v Claude Cousins & Co Ltd* [1971] 2 QB 426 at 450 per Sachs LJ.

DUTIES AND LIABILITIES TO THIRD PARTIES

Conversion and acts amounting to conversion

An auctioneer may owe a number of general duties — for example under the law relating to negligence (which we consider briefly below) — and he may also incur liabilities to a third party who is not either a seller or buyer concerned with the sale. The prime example of the latter is the liability which attaches when an auctioneer wrongly converts the property of another. This will arise if the auctioneer *sells* the property on behalf of a principal who is not entitled to sell, or where he wrongfully *delivers* property to one who is not entitled to receive it with notice of that fact, or where he *retains* property to which a third party is entitled. A conversion may be defined as an unlawful act of interference with goods inconsistent with the right of a third party whereby the latter is deprived of their use and possession. It is a tort for which the remedy is primarily damages; but where goods are detained by a person being sued, the court may order their return. Where such a remedy is available, the court may give the defendant the option of retaining them and paying damages instead.[18] Damages will be assessed by reference to the value of the goods, which in the case of a sale by auction will not necessarily be the price realised.[19] In addition, damages may be awarded for any consequential loss arising out of the conversion.

Sale without the authority of the true owner

The principal may simply have stolen them, or he may have a right of possession but not yet become their owner. Old cases frequently involved sales on behalf of vendors who had transferred the goods previously under a bill of sale in order to give security for a loan. A more modern manifestation concerns goods, typically cars, 'sold' under a hire-purchase agreement. Where a car is sold in this way, the 'buyer' in fact is given possession and the intention is that the property will become his. However, the legal analysis is that unless and until the hirer exercises an option to purchase, on paying the final instalment, he remains simply a hirer. As such he is entitled only to possession. The finance company which finances the deal is the true owner of the vehicle. If the hirer during the currency of the agreement 'sells' the car, the finance company will be able to maintain an action in conversion against him and if he sells through an auctioneer, the latter too will be liable if the purchaser gets title or if the auctioneer delivers the car to the purchaser with the intention of transferring title.[20]

18 Torts (Interference with Goods) Act 1977, s 3.

19 *Davis v Artingstall* (1880) 49 LJ Ch 609, 42 LT 507: 'the plaintiff is entitled to the real value of the goods sold, and not merely to what they fetched at auction, which cannot be assumed to be the real value of the goods' (per Fry J at 610).

20 Although conversion is essentially a wrong against possession, the finance company by law has a right to possession if, prior to the wrongful sale, it exercises the right to terminate the hiring, for e g non-payment of an instalment, normally contained in the contract. It also seems that he can establish a sufficient right to possession as a result of the hirer's delivery up of the vehicle to the auctioneer for sale since this is anathematic to the bailment. See *Union Transport Finance Ltd v British Car Auctions Ltd* [1978] 2 All E R 385, CA; *North Central (or General) Wagon & Finance Co Ltd v Graham* [1950] 2 K B 7, [1950] 1 All E R 780, CA.

It must be emphasised here that the liability of the auctioneer does not depend upon any deliberate or negligent wrongdoing: he is liable in conversion to the true owner even if he is totally innocent and acts in complete good faith. In *Union Transport Finance Ltd v British Car Auctions Ltd*[1] as recently as 1978 it was argued that auctioneers acting in good faith were incapable in law of converting goods when merely selling for a principal who, it transpired, had no title. However the Court of Appeal in that case were clear that the point had been established by the House of Lords in *Hollins v Fowler*[2] and it cannot now be seriously questioned. In 1971 the Law Reform Committee considered whether the 'innocent handler' (as opposed to the innocent acquirer, i e the purchaser) should be protected but concluded, on balance, that he should not. It was felt that auctioneers and others in a similar position carry on a business in which this risk is incidental and for which insurance is available.

There may remain, however, an argument open to the auctioneer that in certain circumstances he did not in fact effect the sale at all but merely acted in a lesser capacity to bring the seller and buyer together. In *Cochrane v Rymill*[3] one Peggs borrowed money from Cochrane and the loan was secured on a number of cabs and carriage horses, the borrower effecting a bill of sale in favour of Cochrane. Subsequently Peggs instructed the defendant auctioneer to sell the charged goods. The auctioneer gave the seller an advance on the proceeds of sale, sold the goods and, after deduction of the advance, paid the proceeds to Peggs. The holder of the bill of sale sued the auctioneer in conversion. Notwithstanding that Cochrane had been at fault in failing to register the bill of sale, the auctioneers were held liable. Bramwell L J held that here there had been a clear dealing with the property and an exercise of dominion over it coupled with its delivery to another. However, he distinguished such a dealing by auctioneers from one where the auctioneer would not be liable in conversion thus:[4]

> Supposing a man were to come into an auctioneer's yard holding a horse... and say 'I want to sell my horse; if you will find a purchaser I will pay commission' and the auctioneer says: 'Here is a man who wants to sell a horse; will anyone buy him?' If he then and there finds him a purchaser and the seller himself hands over the horse there could be no act on the part of the auctioneer which could render him liable for conversion.

This dictum has given rise to no little difficulty. The fact that in this case the auctioneer, having made the vendor an advance, had a lien on the goods sold, clearly, of itself, took the case out of the 'mere conduit' example given, but it would not be correct to conclude that where the auctioneer does not have such an interest in the sale, he will automatically be within its scope. In a subsequent case against the same auctioneer a couple of years later,[5] the court held the defendant not liable in conversion. There the horses were sold by private contract before the auction and the auctioneer took his commission and gave a delivery order to the purchaser. The Court of Appeal found the auctioneer to have not converted the goods as against the rights of the holder of a bill of sale relating to the horses. The auctioneer was held to be a mere

1 See previous footnote.
2 (1875) L R 7 H L 757, 44 LJQB 169.
3 (1879) 40 L T 744, 43 JP 572, CA.
4 (1879) 40 L T 744 at 746.
5 *National Mercantile Bank v Rymill* (1881) 44 L T 767, CA.

conduit. *Cochrane v Rymill*[6] was distinguished on the ground that here there was no question of the auctioneer selling for his own benefit but the salient distinction must be simply that the auctioneer did not effect the sale at all.[7] The case of *Turner v Hockey*[8] does, at first sight, suggest that whenever the auctioneer sells without having a personal interest in the sale, he does so merely as a conduit pipe but that decision has been doubted and explained on the basis that there all the auctioneer did was to communicate an offer, the sale being concluded privately by the vendor with the purchaser. Whether, in such circumstances, the auctioneer generally escapes liability must again be doubted however.

This situation arose in somewhat special circumstances in *R H Willis & Son (a firm) v British Car Auctions Ltd*,[9] the facts of which require some elaboration. Here a hire-purchase buyer in breach of his agreement placed the car in the hands of the defendant auctioneer for sale subject to a reserve. The property did not reach its reserve and the auctioneers, in pursuance of the usual practice, invited the purchaser and vendor to join them at their 'provisional bid office', where the vendor agreed to accept the bid. It was argued that here the auctioneers had done something less than effect the sale; no sale at auction had been concluded because since the goods had not reached their reserve the bids and acceptance remained conditional nor, it was argued, had they sold the property themselves by private treaty; they had merely introduced a prospective purchaser to the vendor. However, the Court of Appeal rejected that argument. The judges looked to the business purpose behind the fairly elaborate provisional bid procedure, namely that it was to bring about a sale, and to the fact that in such cases, as also in those where a sale is effected through the fall of the hammer, the buyer is required to pay an indemnity fee[10] and he concludes a contract on the terms of the Conditions of Sale. In all these circumstances the court held the auctioneer liable for conversion of the car since they had effectively sold it. The court doubted the correctness of both *National Mercantile Bank v Rymill*[11] and *Turner v Hockey*.[12]

We can conclude, therefore, that where the auctioneer effects the sale (whether at auction or by private treaty) of property which his principal is not entitled to sell, he will be guilty of conversion. Now it is a general principle of commercial law that where the seller is not the true owner, the purchaser from him will not get title: nemo dat quod non habet.[13] However, the desirability of protecting commercial transactions is also a crucial concern of the law. Thus the law permits certain exceptions to this general principle. If the auctioneer knocks down goods to a bidder he will be liable in conversion if he couples that act with a dealing, with intent to pass the title whether or not the purchaser does in fact get title to them. If the purchaser *does* get a good title so that the true owner is divested of his goods, then a fortiori the auctioneer will incur

6 Above, n 3.
7 See observations of Collins J in *Consolidated Co v Curtis & Son* [1892] 1 Q B 495 at 501-2.
8 (1887) 56 LJQB 301.
9 [1978] 2 All ER 392, [1978] 1 WLR 432, CA. See the discussion of this case in ch 10, below.
10 The insurance point pressed heavily on Lord Denning in particular, as did the fact that the auctioneers took their commission (albeit at a reduced rate).
11 Above, n 5.
12 Above, n 8.
13 The rule is partially set out in the Sale of Goods Act 1979, s 21(1).

liability in conversion. But in such a case the purchaser will not also be liable — he gets title and cannot be sued by the former owner. Where he does not get title both he and the auctioneer will be potentially liable. And it may be in the interests of the auctioneer to show that the purchaser does not become the owner of the goods, because if the true owner elects to sue the purchaser rather than the auctioneer, the latter may escape. A purchaser liable in conversion to the true owner may seek to sue the auctioneer in turn. However, the appropriate cause of action here would be for breach of warranty of authority. But an auctioneer will only be liable for such a breach if he has *expressly* warranted the vendor's title, for we have already seen that no such warranty will be implied: *Benton v Campbell Parker & Co.*[14] (Failing a remedy against the auctioneer, a purchaser who finds himself answerable to the true owner in conversion will be left with a right of action against the vendor himself on the contract of sale. In every contract for the sale of goods there is an implied condition that the seller has title or the right to sell them by virtue of s 12 of the Sale of Goods Act 1979 and that term cannot be excluded in any contract whether the sale is a consumer or non-consumer sale.)

Thus it is important to be aware of those circumstances where the purchaser will get a good title, leaving the auctioneer alone[15] liable to the former owner of the goods. Both the common law and statute have provided exceptions to the basic principle that the rights of the true owner should remain inviolable, and these will now briefly be noted.[16]

Estoppel

Section 21(1) of the Sale of Goods Act 1979 provides that a purchaser shall obtain on a sale no better title than the seller had, 'unless the owner of the goods is by his conduct precluded from denying the seller's authority to sell.' The quoted words indicate that a fairly general exception arises by way of estoppel when the true owner's conduct has led the purchaser to believe that the seller is entitled to sell. Many of the other specific statutory exceptions appear to be based on this notion too. It is a question of fact whether an owner of goods has sufficiently invested the seller with the indicia of property as opposed merely to possession.[17]

Sale in market overt

Another general common law exception, again now enshrined in the Sale of Goods Act 1979[18] is where property is sold in market overt. Market overt is 'an open, public and legally constituted market.'[19] Such a market may be set up by

14 [1925] 2 KB 410, 94 LJKB 881 (above). Even if the purchaser has no contractual claim against the auctioneer he has a right to *contribution* (Civil Liability (Contribution) Act 1978, s 1), but the amount of such is entirely at the discretion of the court.

15 His client the non-owner seller will also be liable and the auctioneer will be entitled to join him as co-defendant or claim an indemnity but, in many of these cases, recovery against the vendor will, in practice, prove difficult.

16 For a detailed account, readers are directed to Benjamin *Sale of Goods* (2nd edn, 1981), Sweet & Maxwell, paras 461-570.

17 Estoppel was successfully pleaded in *Eastern Distributors Ltd v Goldring* [1957] 2 QB 600, [1957] 2 All ER 525, CA, a case involving a complicated hire-purchase swindle.

18 Section 22. (Sections 21-25 of the Sale of Goods Act 1979 are to be found in Appendix 2.)

19 Per Jervis CJ in *Lee v Bayes & Robinson* (1856) 18 CB 599, 25 LJCP 249.

statute or under a charter. It is also established by custom that every shop within the city of London is market overt. There is nothing in the character of auction sales that make them, ipso facto, sales in market overt and relatively few will be.[20] The sale must take place between the hours of sunrise and sunset. Market overt is more usually a pertinent factor when the *vendor*, against whom it is alleged that he is not the owner, claims he became such because he bought the goods previously in market overt.

Sale under a voidable title

Where the seller has a voidable title, e g where he has obtained the property in the goods by fraud, the owner may take steps to avoid the title of the seller but until he does so the seller may pass a good title to a *bona fide* purchaser. However if the seller has obtained title by inducing a material mistake, the sale to him is absolutely void and he will have no title to pass to such a purchaser.

Sale by a mercantile agent

Section 2(1) of the Factors Act 1889 provides:

> Where a mercantile agent is, with the consent of the owner, in possession of goods, or of the documents of title to goods, any sale, pledge or other disposition of the goods made by him when acting in the ordinary course of business of a mercantile agent shall, subject to the provisions of this Act be as valid as if he were expressly authorised by the owner of the goods to make the same; and provided that the person taking under the disposition acts in good faith and has not at the time of the disposition notice that the person making the disposition has not authority to make the same.

An auctioneer is such a mercantile agent but in this context the provision is of no avail to a purchaser of stolen goods, for the auctioneer is not in possession of them or their documents of title 'with the consent of the owner'. However, where an auctioneer is in possession of goods with the consent of the true owner he may pass a valid title to a purchaser of them under this section even if the possession was given to him for a purpose other than sale. As Denning L J explained in *Pearson v Rose & Young Ltd*:[1]

> ... the owner must consent to the agent having them for a purpose which is in some way or other connected with his business as a mercantile agent. It may be for display or to get offers, or merely to put in his showroom; but there must be a consent to something of that kind before the owner can be deprived of his goods.

This section may be relevant where an auctioneer receives goods for sale *from* a mercantile agent, and we consider this briefly below.

Sale by seller remaining in possession

Where a seller sells goods to a purchaser but retains possession of them or their documents of title, a second sale to another purchaser will effectively pass title

20 For a case where it was argued, unsuccessfully, that in accordance with the custom of the market, the sale *had* to be by auction, see *Bishopsgate Motor Finance Corpn Ltd v Transport Brakes Ltd* [1949] 1 KB 322.
1 [1951] 1 KB 275, CA, at 288.

to the latter if he acts in good faith and without notice of the prior sale. This exception was provided by s 8 of the Factors Act 1889 and substantially reproduced by s 24 of the Sale of Goods Act 1979. It is immaterial in what capacity the seller has been left in possession. So for example, it suffices if the original buyer leaves the goods with the seller merely as bailee to care for them.

Sale by buyer in possession

Somewhat more complicated is the position where a buyer is given possession of the goods although the title in the property is not passed to him until some later date. This is covered now by s 25(1) of the Sale of Goods Act 1979 which provides that a sale by such a buyer shall 'have the same effect as if the person making the delivery or transfer were a mercantile agent in possession of the goods or documents of title with the consent of the owner'. A sale by a mercantile agent in such circumstances will, as we have seen, pass a good title to the purchaser under s 2(1) of the Factors Act 1889 provided the purchaser acts in good faith and without notice of any restriction on the agent's authority to sell. A sale under a hire-purchase agreement does not fall within s 25(1) of the Sale of Goods Act 1979, and special provisions are made for sales by hirers under certain such contracts. Also excluded is a 'Condition of Sale' where the price is payable by instalments with title to the property remaining in the seller until payment of the last instalment.

Where,however, the original sale to the buyer is merely conditional upon e g the price being paid but the buyer is given possession of the goods, a subsequent sale by that buyer is within the exception. Section 25 of the Sale of Goods Act 1979 does not provide that the effect of the sale is as if the buyer had the authority of the owner, as it does under s 24, but rather that the effect is the same 'as if' the original buyer was selling as a mercantile agent. This rather odd provision has been construed to mean that the subsequent purchaser only gets a good title and is thus immune from an action for conversion if the original buyer in possession sold to him *in the manner* in which a mercantile agent would have sold in the ordinary course of his business. Thus if an original buyer sells a car without releasing the log-book, the subsequent purchaser from him will not get a good title vis-à-vis his seller because a mercantile agent would, selling in the ordinary course of business, have delivered up the log-book.[2]

Sales of motor vehicles subject to hire-purchase agreements

Sales of motor vehicles under hire-purchase agreements are dealt with separately because they became especially prevalent in the 1950s and 1960s. It is relatively easy for hirers to pass themselves off as owners and sell the cars to unsuspecting purchasers. Section 27 of the Hire-Purchase Act 1964 as re-enacted by the Consumer Credit Act 1974 provides that where the purchaser of the car from the hire-purchase 'buyer' is a 'private purchaser' as defined,

2 See *Newtons of Wembley Ltd v Williams* [1965] 1 QB 560, [1964] 3 All ER 532, CA; *Lambert v G & C Finance Corpn Ltd* (1963) 107 Sol Jo 666.

acting in good faith and without notice of the hire-purchase (or conditional sale) agreement, that purchaser will get a good title to the vehicle.

It must be reiterated that the effect of all these exceptions is to protect the purchaser who thereby gets a good title. They do nothing to prevent the auctioneer from being liable in conversion for selling the particular goods. Indeed they place it beyond doubt that he is liable since the sale and delivery not only has the intention of passing the property to the purchaser but is actually effective to do so. The only way in which an auctioneer could protect himself from suit would be if he could show that the delivery to him of the goods in question amounted to a disposition under those exceptions whereby he, the auctioneer, got title; a subsequent sale or retention would then be of the auctioneer's own property and not that of another. Such an argument was advanced on the basis of the Factors Act 1889 in *Shenstone v Hilton*[3] where the buyer under a conditional sale agreement, before he acquired title, sent the goods, a piano, to the defendant auctioneers for sale. The auctioneers duly sold and the true owner — the seller under the conditional sale agreement — sued them in conversion. The auctioneers claimed to be protected by s 9 of the Factors Act, the precursor of s 25(1) of the Sale of Goods Act, in that they had received the goods from a buyer in possession. Bruce J construed the section as including a delivery to the auctioneers for sale. He said: 'I should be prepared to hold that a delivery of goods on the terms that they should be sold by the person to whom they were delivered for the benefit of the person delivering them was a "disposition" ... [within the section].'[4]

It is difficult to see how such a mere transfer of possession could be regarded as a disposition so as to protect the auctioneer from a conversion action in these circumstances. The 'disposition' (if indeed such it would be) in any event, on the terms of the section, only has 'the same effect as if the person making the delivery or transfer were a mercantile agent'. The effect of a delivery by a mercantile agent would be to give the auctioneers at most a right to possession but it would not, it is submitted, give them any *title,* so that any subsequent sale by them would still interfere with the title of another; the true owners would have an immediate right to possession against the conditional sale buyer on his delivering the goods to the auctioneers for sale, by parity of reasoning with the hire-purchase cases discussed earlier.

In *Waddington & Sons v Neale & Sons*[5] an owner entrusted goods, again a piano, to a dealer to sell for cash or to hire out. The dealer, a mercantile agent, took it to the defendant auctioneers for sale and when this was duly effected the owners sued them in conversion. The auctioneers relied on s 2(1) of the Factors Act 1889 contending that the delivery to them for sale by the dealer was a sale or pledge within the subsection. In fact, since the auctioneers advanced a sum to the dealer in contemplation of selling it, this might have been a rather stronger case than that of *Shenstone & Co v Hilton.*[6] However, the court held that the Act did not protect them. Phillimore J was clear that this was neither a sale nor a disposition, and it seems that the main argument was that it was a pledge. However this too failed, the true analysis being that it was merely a

3 [1894] 2 Q B 452.
4 [1894] 2 Q B 452 at 456.
5 (1907) 96 L T 786, 2 B T L R 464.
6 Above, n 3.

deposit of goods incidental to a transaction that was not authorised.[7] It is submitted that this is the correct approach.

Whilst it may seem hard on the auctioneer that he is exposed to liability by the wrongful act of others even where he is totally innocent,[8] we repeat that insurance is available to cover such business risks. Moreover in one of the more notorious areas, sales of motor vehicles subject to hire-purchase agreements, the auctioneers can usually ascertain whether the vehicle is let on hire-purchase by checking with the body known as HPI (Hire-Purchase Information) with which finance companies normally register vehicles whose purchase they finance.[9]

Refusal to deliver up to the owner

It is well settled that conversion can be committed by a wrongful refusal to deliver up possession of goods to the person entitled to them upon his demand. An auctioneer may obviously be in some difficulty if goods are being claimed by both his principal and a third party. In appropriate cases the auctioneer should interplead.[10] However, short of such action, an auctioneer is entitled to make reasonable enquiries to ascertain the true ownership of the goods. In *Lee v Bayes & Robinson* Jervis C J said:[11]

> As between master and servant, or perhaps as between Principal and Agent, where the servant or agent receives from his master or Principal goods which belong to a third person, on their being demanded of him by such a third person he is entitled to say 'I received them from my ... Principal and I require a reasonable time to ascertain whether the party making the demand is the real owner'; and such qualified refusal would not be evidence of a conversion ... But if, as in this case, and in most other cases cited, the man who holds the goods chooses to set up the title of his bailor, and to rely on it, he is doing an act which is foreign to ... his duty. He asserts a title adverse to the title of the real owner and is guilty of conversion.

Thus a refusal pending the obtaining of instructions from the vendor-principal would be a justifiable qualified refusal,[12] but a refusal to release goods until expenses incurred had been paid, would not.[13]

Other acts short of a sale[14]

For the sake of completeness we mention that conversion can be committed by the transfer of possession without sale. A re-delivery to the vendor after notice

7 See also *Kendrick v Sotheby & Co* (1967) 111 Sol Jo 470: Auctioneers held not entitled to retain goods which were sent to them for sale and on which they had made an advance, by a person merely instructed to keep them in order to obtain photographs.

8 He is of course, a fortiori, liable if he has notice of the seller's want of title: *Hardacre v Stewart* (1804) 5 Esp 103.

9 There is no legal duty on finance companies to do so and failure will not amount to an estoppel: *Moorgate Mercantile Co Ltd v Twitchings* [1977] A C 890, [1976] 2 All ER 641, HL.

10 We have discussed interpleader in ch 4, above.

11 (1856) 18 CB 599 at 607. See also *Turner v Ford* (1846) 15 N W 212.

12 *Alexander v Southey* (1821) 5 B & Ald 247.

13 *Loeschman v Machin* (1818) 2 Stark 311.

14 Although not a conversion as such it is convenient to mention here that if an auctioneer accepts instructions to deal with goods of a deceased, which do not emanate from the properly-appointed personal representatives, he may find himself liable for any losses suffered by the estate as an 'executor de son tort': *Nulty v Fagan* (1888) 22 L R Ir 604.

of a third-party's title would probably amount to such. Additionally, although it is difficult to conceive of many situations in which such depredations might occur in the context of auctions, a deliberate destruction of goods is also conversion, but if loss is caused simply negligently, it is not. However in such a case, the ordinary law of negligence would provide a remedy against the careless auctioneer.

All the foregoing discussion assumes that the sale by auction has been on the instructions of one who has not the right to sell them. If he has, no question of conversion can arise. So, even if the goods had previously been stolen, if the principal had obtained them in circumstances rendering him the true owner, for instance where he bought them in market overt, the auctioneer will be able to sell them with impunity. Usually of course the question whether the vendor had, or had acquired, the right to sell will be determined by the English law principles discussed above but occasionally foreign law is involved.

In the recent case of *Winkworth v Christie Manson & Woods Ltd*[15] the rather unusual facts were as follows. Winkworth had owned certain works of art in England and these were stolen. They found their way to Italy where they were bought by an Italian. Subsequently this buyer sent them to Christie's for auction and some were sold. Winkworth, having obtained an undertaking from Christie's that they would not part with the remaining articles or the proceeds of sale, sued the Italian vendor in conversion. A preliminary question of law arose before the High Court in England, namely whether English or Italian law should be applied to the issue whether the Italian defendant had title to the goods and the proceeds of sale. The court decided that, using English principles of private international law, on these facts the appropriate law to be applied was Italian.

Thus the rights of a true owner of English goods, situated in England, can be defeated by a transaction in another country in accordance with the law of that country, even though the owner had never consented to their going there.

The implications of the *Winkworth* case in the context of the seller's right to sell are discussed in ch 6.

Other duties to third parties

Negligence

As mentioned above, an auctioneer may be liable under the tort of negligence for carelessly damaging a person's goods or for injuring him. There is little to be gained from an attempt at listing the variety of instances in which such a liability might be incurred, but there is one area worthy of special — albeit brief — mention, namely the liability attaching to the occupier of premises.

Although all persons are under a general duty to take reasonable care not to injure those who would with reasonable forseeability be harmed if care were

15 [1980] Ch 496, [1980] 1 All E R 1121.

not taken, statute has provided specially for the liability of those who occupy or control premises. The Occupier's Liability Act 1957, as amended provides that the 'occupier' owes to all his visitors (which include those permitted to enter under a licence) a common duty of care. This duty of care is defined by s 2(2) of the Act as: 'a duty to take such care as in all the circumstances of the case is reasonable to see that the visitor is reasonably safe in using the premises for the purpose for which he is invited or permitted to be there.' The duty relates both to the state of the premises themselves and also to activities carried on there. So an auctioneer might, not too fancifully, be liable if improperly penned cattle injured persons attending the auction or if a bidder were injured falling as a result of a defective step in the auction rooms.

Whilst the Act applies not only to those who actually occupy premises but also to those in control of them, it is thought that an auctioneer would not be regarded as having sufficient control of e g the principal-vendor's house or place of business in which he is conducting the auction.[16] In *Walker v Crabb*,[17] however, where a mare which was being auctioned on the vendor's premises injured the plaintiff, the vendor himself was held not liable in negligence on the ground that the control of the entire sale and responsibility for the chattels lay on the auctioneer.

It is open to an occupier to satisfy the duty imposed on him by strategically placed warning notices where such a warning given is in fact sufficient to render the visitor safe. However, *exclusion* of a liability is a different matter. The Occupier's Liability Act 1957 permitted an occupier to modify the common duty of care 'so far as he is free to'. This has now been greatly affected by the Unfair Contract Terms Act 1977 which makes any purported exclusion of liability for negligence causing death or personal injury wholly ineffective,[18] and, as we have seen renders any other type of exclusion subject to a test of reasonableness. On the other hand a warning notice is still useful since, even if it does not render the duty of care satisfied, it may make it easier to point to some contributory negligence by the visitor with the result that any compensatory damages will be apportioned under the Law Reform (Contributory Negligence) Act 1945.

Nuisance

A nuisance is a use of land so that the use and enjoyment of neighbouring land by another is diminished. Clearly, the business of auctioneering may constitute a nuisance to others and may be actionable. In the nineteenth century the owner of a coffee-house near Covent Garden succeeded in an action against a defendant auctioneer when the latter's vans obstructed the door and the stench from the horses rendered the coffee-shop 'incommodious and uncomfortable'.[19] This lone reported case may be somewhat outmoded on its facts, but doubtless in appropriate circumstances an action would lie today.

16 Pre-Act this was the position laid down in Scotland: *Nelson v Scott, Croall & Sons* 1892 19 R (Ct of Sess) 425, 29 Sc LR 354.
17 [1916] W N 433, 33 TLR 119.
18 Section 2.
19 *Benjamin v Storr* (1874) L R 9 C P 400, 43 LJCP 162.

Chapter 6

Conditions of Sale affecting buyers

INTRODUCTION

The importance of Conditions of Sale in the conduct of an auction cannot be overestimated. Conditions of Sale form the flesh on the bones of the law of auctions. Their primary purpose, traditionally, has been to govern the relationship between the seller (and his agent, the auctioneer)[1] on the one hand and the successful buyer on the other. It is this relationship, imposed primarily by the law of contract and of sale of goods (in cases other than land) between the seller and the buyer that needs particularly careful exploration. Modern Conditions of Sale very often include conditions particularly appropriate to the relationship between the auctioneer and the *seller* as well. The contractual effect of these is reached by a different route. They form part of an ordinary business contract, between the seller and the auctioneer as his agent, made well before the auction. The contractual stipulations, if binding, will confirm or modify the position of the seller as it would have been according to ordinary principles of the law of agency and contract explored earlier in this book. We shall now focus on the Conditions of Sale affecting *buyers* and examine their effect in typical sales of chattels. Chattel sales of a less usual nature and which can pose special problems will be dealt with separately.

THE CONTRACTUAL FRAMEWORK

The Sale of Goods Act 1979, reproducing a similar provision in the 1893 Act, provides the basic contractual framework of the auction sale by stating as follows:

> 57(1) Where goods are put up for sale by auction in lots, each lot is prima facie deemed to be the subject of a separate contract of sale.
>
> (2) A sale by auction is complete when the auctioneer announces its completion by the fall of the hammer, or in other customary manner; and until the announcement is made any bidder may retract his bid.
>
> (3) A sale by auction may be notified to be subject to a reserve or upset price, and a right to bid may also be reserved expressly by or on behalf of the seller.

1 The problems involved in a buyer suing a seller whose identity is not disclosed, are explored above, p 92.

(4) Where a sale by auction is not notified to be subject to a right to bid by or on behalf of the seller, it is not lawful for the seller to bid himself or to employ any person to bid at the sale, or for the auctioneer knowingly to take any bid from the seller or any such person.

(5) A sale contravening subsection (4) above may be treated as fraudulent by the buyer.

(6) Where, in respect of a sale by auction, a right to bid is expressly reserved (but not otherwise) the seller or any one person on his behalf may bid at the auction.

The effects of s57(4) and (5) are: (a) to prohibit the seller or his agent to bid and the auctioneer to take any such bid unless the right to bid is so reserved, in practice in the relevant Conditions of Sale; and (b) to allow the buyer to treat any sale contravening s 57(4) as fraudulent. He may thus rescind the sale at his option and would also seem to be entitled to damages in respect of the fraud. The general position is discussed in more detail in the context of the similar provisions in the Sale of Land by Auction Act 1867, in ch 9.

In essence, the function of the Conditions of Sale is to regulate the position of the buyer once he has made a successful bid which is accepted 'by the fall of the hammer'. A collateral purpose, which may give rise to much more difficulty when analysing enforceability of the appropriate conditions, is to regulate the conduct of persons present at the auction generally even where they are *not* successful buyers. But before considering questions of the validity of Conditions of Sale, it is first essential to establish that the potential defendant who is alleged to be in breach of a particular condition has in fact been bound by that condition.

INCORPORATION INTO THE CONTRACT OF CONDITIONS

It is a basic and well known principle of contract law that a clause can be incorporated into a contract by *notice* or by *course of dealing*.

With regard to whether the potential defendant, typically the buyer, has notice of the contractual terms, a great deal of authority exists on this problem in the context of exemption clauses. These cases are of limited value when considering the typical auction situation where buyers will normally have acquired a catalogue and where the catalogue reproduces the relevant Conditions of Sale or draws attention to where they are on display. It is, of course, essential that notice of the relevant conditions is given before or at the time of contracting. They cannot be successfully incorporated into a contract after the contract has been made.[2] Where there is any doubt as to whether sufficient notice has been given, the court will take into account such factors as whether the conditions in question are of a standard nature. It is then probable that annexation of the conditions to catalogues issued to buyers would be held sufficient. If, on the other hand, the condition is an unusual one, the court

2 See e g *Olley v Marlborough Court Ltd* [1949] 1 KB 532, [1949] 1 All ER 127, CA.

would require far more effort to bring the condition in question to the buyer's notice. In *Thornton v Shoe Lane Parking Ltd*, Lord Denning said: 'Some clauses I have seen would need to be printed in red ink on the face of the document with a red hand pointing to it before the notice could be held to be sufficient'.[3]

In the case of auctions, it was held as long ago as 1801 that where the Conditions of Sale are printed and posted up under the auctioneer's box, and the auctioneer declares that the conditions are as usual, there is sufficient notice to purchasers of the conditions.[4] In the Scottish case of *Laing & Sons v Hain*,[5] it was held that at sale by auction where the Conditions of Sale empowered the vendor to resell in certain circumstances, it was not necessary to show that the conditions were read or exhibited at the sale.

Where there is a possibility that the purchaser might be able to argue that he has no notice of the relevant conditions, an alternative way in which he could still be bound is by reference to a course of dealing. This simply means that a clause may be incorporated in the contract, despite a lack of specific notice, where previous dealings between the parties can be proved to have taken place and it can be inferred from these dealings that similar clauses would apply in each case.[6] The relevance of this to auctions is obvious, thought it may seldom be necessary to resort to this principle. However in essence the auctioneer would argue that although a buyer might not have specific notice of a relevant condition because, for instance, he did not purchase a catalogue with the Conditions of Sale annexed, nevertheless because he had attended previous auction sales he must be taken to be aware of the fact that Conditions of Sale exist and of their nature.

ARE BIDDERS OTHER THAN THE BUYER BOUND?

This question most often arises in the context of discussion of the problem of 'without reserve' sales. Here, typically, the auctioneer either refuses to accept the bid of the highest bidder or, as in *Warlow v Harrison*,[7] accepts a bogus bid from the seller himself. We have already fully discussed the implications of *Warlow v Harrison*,[8] and it must be re-emphasised that there are two possible views. One is that there can be no contract with the highest bidder since he merely makes an offer which is not accepted by fall of the hammer. Just as a bidder may withdraw his bid before the fall of the hammer, it follows that the seller is equally entitled to withdraw the goods before this point of time.[9] The alternative view is that an advertisement that a sale should be without a reserve is a conditional offer to the whole world capable of acceptance by anyone who, relying on the advertisement, attends the auction and bids. The

3 [1971] 2 QB 163 at 170 (a case concerning an exemption clause referred to in a parking ticket). See also *Spriggs v Sotheby Parke Bernet & Co Ltd* (1984) 272 EG 1171, where it was held that a document containing the instructions of sale was not a receipt but a contract containing an exclusion clause valid to exempt the defendant auctioneers against liability for loss of the vendor's unmounted diamond, though on the facts they were held not to be negligent.

4 *Mesnard v Aldridge* (1801) 3 Esp 271.

5 1853 15 Dunl (Ct of Sess) 667, 25 Sc Jur 405.

6 See e g *Hardwick Game Farm v Suffolk Agricultural and Poultry Producers' Association Ltd* [1969] 2 AC 31, [1968] 2 All ER 444, HL.

7 (1859) 1 E & E 309, 29 LJQB 14.

8 See above, p 24f.

9 This was the view taken in *Fenwick v MacDonald, Fraser & Co Ltd* 1904 6 F (Ct of Sess) 850, 41 Sc LR 638.

consideration for the contract is said to be found in the rule that 'an act done at the request of another, express or implied, is sufficient consideration to support a promise'.[10] The difficulties in accepting this view of a 'collateral contract' with buyers generally, are explored above.[11]

However, it is of interest that the Full Court of the Natal Provincial Division of the S African Supreme Court was prepared to accept the idea in principle that such collateral contracts are capable of arising, though it will be noted that the analysis which follows does not deal with the difficult question of consideration. In *Shandel v Jacobs*,[12] an auction sale was held under conditions which included the following:

> (1) Each bid will be an offer to purchase and the party making the highest accepted bid will be the purchaser, the sale to become complete on acceptance of the bid by the auctioneer as indicated by the fall of the hammer or otherwise. The advance in the bidding will be regulated by the auctioneer who will have the sole right of deciding who was the last bidder. In the event of a dispute between two or more bidders the lot in dispute may be put up and resold at the discretion of the auctioneer.
>
> (2) The auctioneer may, at his discretion and without assigning any reason therefor, refuse a bid or withdraw an article either before or after it has been put up for auction.

The plaintiff made the highest bids for various articles but his bids were refused by the auctioneer, apparently out of malice. The articles were in fact knocked down to other persons attending the sale. The disappointed plaintiff therefore sued the auctioneer for damages. Carlisle J stated:[13]

> The action, as I understand it, is founded upon a breach of an implied term of the contract between the plaintiff and the auctioneers, the contract itself being embodied in the Conditions of Sale . . .
>
> The questions that arise are, I think, twofold:
> (a) Do the Conditions of Sale constitute a contract between the auctioneer and a bona fide bidder for any article which is put up?
> (b) If so, is it implied in such conditions that the auctioneer shall carry them out without mala fides?
>
> It seems to me that the first question must be answered in the affirmative. In the case of *Estate Francis v Land Sales (Property) Ltd*, Broome J said:[14]
>
> 'An auction is a form of competitive bargaining with the object of a contract of sale resulting carried out in accordance with certain rules. These rules are the Conditions of Sale. They are framed by the seller to represent the terms upon which he is prepared to submit his property to competition. They are, so to speak, the rules of the game and they bind all the players. . .'
>
> The question then arises, who are the players who are so bound? The Conditions of Sale are agreed upon in the first instance between the seller and the auctioneer and

10 See LCB Gower (1952) 68 LQR 458.
11 See above, pp 24-28.
12 1949 (1) SA 320, cited in George (1949) 65 LQR 310.
13 1949 (1) SA 320 at 325.
14 [1940] NPD 441 at 457.

> between these two they rest upon a contractual basis. When goods are offered for sale pursuant to them, they form the basis of the bargaining carried on between the auctioneer and the bidders. That the bidders are, as Broome J put it, the players, I have no doubt and, since an auctioneer usually acts for an undisclosed principal, the rules as between him and the bidder may bind the auctioneer personally. In *Warlow v Harrison*,[15] Martin B pointed out that in a sale by auction there were three parties, namely: the owner, the auctioneer and the portion of the public who intended to bid. He further pointed out that, in most cases of sale by auction, the owner's name is not disclosed and he remains a concealed principal. The name of the auctioneer only is published and where the sale is announced by them to be without reserve, that, according to all the cases of law and equity, meant that the property should be sold to the highest bidder whether the sum bid be equivalent to the real value or not. This judgment goes on to say that 'the highest bona fide bidder at an auction may sue the auctioneer as upon a contract that the sale shall be without reserve'.[16]

Carlisle J concluded that all the Conditions of Sale form a contractual relationship between the auctioneer and the bidding public,[17] and held that it was an implied term that the auctioneer should carry out the conditions without mala fides.

The significance of this is that it shows a willingness by the courts to give validity to stipulations, in this case in Conditions of Sale, outside the strict contractual nexus between seller, auctioneer and buyer. There are a number of conditions besides a possible one relating to sales 'without reserve', which fall into this category. For instance it may be stipulated that the auctioneer shall have the right to refuse any bid which does not exceed the previous bid by a specified percentage and, by the same token, there may be a condition stipulating that no bidder shall withdraw his bid. In the absence of modern and conclusive authority we can only reiterate that the willingness of a court to imply a collateral contract in these circumstances remains to be verified, at least in the United Kingdom.

VULNERABILITY OF CONDITIONS OF SALE

Assuming that it has been established that the Conditions of Sale in question are binding contractually on the potential defendant and cover the problem that has arisen, it is then necessary to consider whether the condition is open to attack as being 'unreasonable'. Prior to 1973, any person arguing that a contractual stipulation which excluded or limited the liability of the other party was not binding on him had to argue that there was a fundamental breach of contract, or that the stipulation was not incorporated in the contract and therefore not binding on him. The courts struggled with this problem for many years and although the case law thus generated is now far from irrelevant it is realistic to assume, in the light of recent dicta, that the courts will look primarily for guidance at the statutory provisions now incorporated

15 (1859) 1 E & E 309, 29 LJQB 14, [1843-60] All ER Rep 620

16 (1859) 1 E & E 309, 29 LJQB 14, [1843-60] All ER Rep 620 at 622.

17 *Shandel v Jacobs* 1949 (1) SA 320 at 326.

in the Unfair Contract Terms Act 1977,[18] though it must always be remembered that such clauses are construed contra proferentem and any inadequacies in wording may resolve the problem in the buyer's favour without further ado.

The full scope of this complex Act is explored in the standard works on contract.[19] Its object is to make void or make subject to 'the reasonableness test' relevant exemption clauses. The main provisions, ss 2-7, apply only to 'business liability' as defined. A number of contracts, such as contracts of insurance, are exempted from the scope of the Act altogether. Only two aspects of the Act will be dealt with here, these being those aspects most relevant to Conditions of Sale in auctions.[20]

Conditions relating to the title to, compliance with, description of, and quality of the goods sold

It is necessary to start with the implied conditions dealing with the above matters in the Sale of Goods Act 1979. Sections 12-15 contain the following implied conditions, of which this is a summary:

(a) That the seller has the right to sell the goods (s 12);
(b) That where there is a contract for the sale of goods by description, the goods will correspond with the description (s 13);
(c) That where the seller sells goods in the course of a business, that the goods supplied under the contract are of merchantable quality, except as regards defects specifically drawn to the buyer's attention before the contract is made; or if the buyer examines the goods before the contract is made, as regards defects which that examination ought to reveal (s 14(2));
(d) Where the seller sells goods in the course of a business and the buyer, expressly or by implication, makes known to the seller any particular purpose for which the goods are being bought, that the goods are reasonably fit for that purpose except when the buyer does not rely, or it is unreasonable for him to rely, on the skill or judgment of the seller (s 14(3));
(e) Where the sale is by sample, inter alia, that the bulk shall comply with the sample (s 15).

With regard to the implied conditions of merchantability and fitness foı purpose (above), it is the implied condition of merchantability which is likely

18 See Lord Denning's graphic review of these developments in *George Mitchell (Chesterhall) Ltd v Finney Lock Seeds Ltd* [1983] 1 All ER 108, CA, at 111, in which he described such developments as the Unfair Contract Terms Act 1977 as heralding 'a revolution in our approach to exemption clauses'. In *Spriggs v Sotheby Parke Bernet & Co Ltd* (see n 3 above) the judgment in the High Court proceeded on the basis that, as a matter of construction, there had been no fundamental breach such as to negate the exemption clause, following *Photo Production v Securicor Ltd* [1980] AC 827, [1980] 1 All ER 556, HL. The events occurred in 1977, whereas the Unfair Contract Terms Act 1977 did not come into force until 1 February 1978. Section 2 thereof, relating to purported exclusion of negligence liability, was not reproduced from previous leglislation and if negligence had been established, might otherwise have been relevant.

19 See e g Cheshire and Fifoot *Law of Contract* (10th edn, 1981) Butterworths p 159.

20 The relevant sections of this Act, of the Sale of Goods Act 1979 and of the Misrepresentation Act 1967 are to be found in Appendix 2.

to be of importance in the auction situation. This is because it is unlikely that in an auction sale the buyer would either expressly or by implication make known to the seller the purpose for which the goods are being bought, or place any reliance on the seller's skill or judgment.[1]

It will also be noted in the context of the two conditions of merchantability and fitness that they apply only to sellers selling goods *'in the course of a business'*. Section 14(5) states:

> The preceding provisions of this section apply to a sale by a person who in the course of a business is acting as agent for another as they apply to a sale by a principal in the course of a business, except where that other is not selling in the course of a business and either the buyer knows that fact or reasonable steps are taken to bring it to the notice of the buyer before the contract is made.

The significance of this sub-section (introduced in 1973) is often overlooked. It means that where an auctioneer is selling goods on behalf of a private vendor *and due notice is given to bidders of that fact*, s 14 will not apply at all since the sale will not be 'in the course of a business'. Experience suggests that few auctioneers do this,[2] although some do specifically restrict themselves to selling goods entered by private sellers only. If this fact is known to bidders it would probably be sufficient to make s 14 inapplicable in the first place. Those auctioneers who accept goods from all sources and fail to discriminate in the catalogue or otherwise between those entered by private and those entered by business vendors will be deemed to sell goods 'in the course of a business' and s 14 will apply except insofar as it can validly be negated or modified.[3]

The question now arises as to how far the Conditions of Sale may seek to negate or limit these important implied conditions in sales of goods. The position is dealt with by s 6 of the Unfair Contract Terms Act 1977 as amended, which runs as follows:

> (1) Liability for breach of the obligations arising from —
> (a) section 12 of the Sale of Goods Act 1979 (seller's implied undertakings as to title, etc.);
> (b) section 8 of the Supply of Goods (Implied Terms) Act 1973 (the corresponding thing in relation to hire-purchase),
> cannot be excluded or restricted by reference to any contract term.
>
> (2) As against a person dealing as a consumer, liability for breach of the obligations arising from —
> (a) section 13, 14 or 15 of the 1979 Act (seller's implied undertakings as to conformity of goods with description or sample, or as to their quality or fitness for a particular purpose);

1 Conditions of Sale often stipulate that buyers 'should exercise and rely on their own judgment' (see e g Sotheby's Condition 16 in Appendix 1). It would thus presumably be 'unreasonable' within s 14(3) above, to rely on the seller's skill or judgment.

2 Specific lots may be described eg as 'The Property of a Lady'. This statement with its aura of gentility would probably imply that the seller was a private one; the antithesis of a 'trader'. If, as in *Friedrich v A Monnickendam Ltd* (1973) 228 EG 1311, the lot is falsely stated to be 'sold by order of Executors' and this description is regarded as false to a material degree (since there is evidence that such descriptions encourage bids), there is likely to be an offence contrary to s 1 of the Trade Descriptions Act 1968.

3 This policy was suggested by the Law Commission Report No 24, First Report on Exemption Clauses (1969) paras 53-55.

(b) section 9, 10 or 11 of the 1973 Act (the corresponding things in relation to hire-purchase),

cannot be excluded or restricted by reference to any contract term.

(3) As against a person dealing otherwise than as consumer, the liability specified in subsection (2) above can be excluded or restricted by reference to a contract term, but only in so far as the term satisfies the requirement of reasonableness.

(4) The liabilities referred to in this section are not only the business liabilities defined by section 1(3), but include those arising under any contract of sale of goods or hire-purchase agreement.

As will be seen from the above, much depends on whether a bidder at an auction can be described as 'a person dealing as a consumer' or as 'a person dealing otherwise than as a consumer'. The answer to this is made clear by s 12(2) of the Unfair Contract Terms Act 1977, which states, 'But on a sale by auction or by competitive tender the buyer is not in any circumstances to be regarded as dealing as a consumer.' This policy decision[4] to exclude auction sales from being categorized as consumer sales, despite the fact that many individual buyers will in fact be, in the economic sense, consumers rather than intermediaries intent upon re-sale, makes it clear that the Sale of Goods Act obligations in ss 13, 14 and 15 of the 1979 Act *can* be excluded or restricted by reference to a contract term, 'but only in so far as the term satisfies the requirement of reasonableness'.

If Conditions of Sale therefore purport to exclude the seller's liability for, for example, goods which prove to be unmerchantable (i e, broadly speaking, materially defective), by what criteria is the reasonableness of the exemption clause in question to be judged? The answer to this question lies in s 11 and Sch 2 of the Unfair Contract Terms Act 1977. Section 11 stipulates that the requirement of reasonableness is 'that the term shall have been a fair and reasonable one to be included having regard to the circumstances which were, or ought reasonably to have been, known to or in the contemplation of the parties when the contract was made'. Section 11(2) goes on specifically to state that for the purposes of s 6, discussed above, whether a contract term satisfies the requirement of reasonableness shall be determined by having regard to the matters specified in Sch 2. Schedule 2 stipulates the following matters:

(a) the strength of the bargaining positions of the parties relative to each other, taking into account (among other things) alternative means by which the customer's requirements could have been met;
(b) whether the customer received an inducement to agree to the term, or in accepting it had an opportunity of entering into a similar contract with other persons, but without having to accept a similar term;
(c) whether the customer knew or ought reasonably to have known of the existence and extent of the term (having regard, among other things, to any custom of the trade and any previous course of dealing between the parties);
(d) where the term excludes or restricts any relevant liability if some condition is not complied with, whether it was reasonable at the time of the contract to expect that compliance with that condition would be practicable;
(e) whether the goods were manufactured, processed or adapted to the special order of the customer.

4 The policy was the one recommended by the Final Report of the Molony Committee (Cmnd 1781, 1962) para 445; and Law Commisssion Report No 24 (1969), paras 110, 114-119.

To summarise, s 6 of the Unfair Contract Terms Act 1977 provides:

(a) that the implied condition that the seller has the right to sell may not be excluded at all;

(b) that the implied conditions relating to description, merchantability and (where appropriate) fitness and compliance with sample (ss 13, 14 and 15 respectively) may be excluded or restricted only insofar as the contract term in question complies with the reasonableness test. However, in each case it must be considered whether the sale is 'in the course of a business'. If the vendor is a private seller and this is known to or notified to buyers, no conditions as to merchantability and fitness are implied in the first place. (It should be added that s 15 of the 1979 Act, which is subject to similar restrictions on exemption clauses, is not generally appropriate to *chattel* auctions since it deals with sales by sample.)

There is a further section of the Unfair Contract Terms Act 1977 which may, in some circumstances, need consideration. Section 3 runs as follows:

> (1) This section applies as between contracting parties where one of them deals as consumer or on the other's written standard terms of business.
>
> (2) As against that party, the other cannot by reference to any contract term —
> (a) when himself in breach of contract, exclude or restrict any liability of his in respect of the breach; or
> (b) claim to be entitled —
> (i) to render a contractual performance substantially different from that which was reasonably expected of him, or
> (ii) in respect of the whole or of any part of his contractual obligation, to render no performance at all,
>
> except in so far as (in any of the cases mentioned above in this subsection) the contract term satisfies the requirement of reasonableness.

It is conceivable that a buyer alleging a breach of contract other than a breach of one of the implied conditions already described and dealt with by s 6 of the Unfair Contract Terms Act 1977, might argue that though he does not deal 'as a consumer', he does contract on the seller's 'standard terms of business'. Accordingly any Condition of Sale excluding or restricting any liability for breach of contract by the seller or affecting the performance of the seller's obligations as described in s 3(2)(b) must be subject to the requirement of reasonableness, the test for which is explained under 'Misrepresentations' below. In fact it is doubtful if s 3 could be applied to the auction situation. Although the auctioneer's Conditions of Sale are his 'standard terms of business' within the meaning of this section, and although he is the seller's agent, a court (it is submitted) would be unlikely to hold that these conditions are the *seller's* 'written standard terms of business', since the seller may have to rely on them on a single occasion only and, even if a trader, may well have distinct standard term contracts for sales taking place in the ordinary course of his business rather than through the auction house. It is these which would be his 'written standard terms of business', not the auctioneer's Conditions of Sale.

Misrepresentations

Conditions of Sale may attempt to disclaim liability for misrepresentations made by the vendor or his agent, the auctioneer, and this problem is extensively discussed in the context of sales of land.[5] Similar principles apply to auctions of chattels. Any attempt to exclude the buyer's rights to rescind the contract or claim damages for material misrepresentations is, by s 8 of the Unfair Contract Terms Act 1977 (replacing s 3 of the Misrepresentation Act 1967) made subject to the requirement of reasonableness. It will be for the vendor to show that the term in question satisfies this requirement, namely that the term 'shall have been a fair and reasonable one to be included having regard to the circumstances which were, or ought reasonably to have been, known to or in the contemplation of the parties when the contract was made' (s 11(1)).[6]

COMMON PROBLEMS CONCERNING BUYERS, DEALT WITH BY CONDITIONS OF SALE

Throughout the ensuing discussion, reference will be made to the Conditions of Business of Sotheby's and to the Conditions of Acceptance, Notices and Conditions of Sale of Christie, Manson & Woods Ltd. With regard to the conditions of Sotheby's, those considered will be such as are applicable *except* to their Fast Sale Service. Those of Christie's relate to the sale of works of art.[7]

The seller's title

It has already been pointed out that s 12 of the Sale of Goods Act 1979 lays down, for the purposes of auction sales, an unequivocal condition that the seller has the right to sell the goods in question. Furthermore, the Unfair Contract Terms Act 1977 precludes the exclusion or restriction of this implied condition in any circumstances (s 6(1)). It cannot be over-emphasized that a sale by auction does not confer legitimacy on the title to goods where the seller has none. If the goods are stolen or otherwise belong to someone different from the seller, the buyer at auction will get no better title than the seller had — i e usually none at all. Since nothing can be done by way of a contract term to modify this position, both Sotheby's and Christie's content themselves by imposing a condition upon the seller that he is entitled to sell.[8] Should it transpire that the seller has no title to sell, the buyer is entitled to rescind the sale and recover the price paid.[9]

The above paragraph is subject to caveats. Firstly, in *Benton v Campbell Parker & Co*[10] it was stated that the position was that whilst not warranting the title

5 See ch 9.

6 A misrepresentation may also amount to a *contractual* misrepresentation. Where there is no effective exclusion clause and the catalogue misdescribes the goods — e g table napkins 'the authentic property of Charles I' worth £105 instead of the £787 bid — the buyer may either annul the contract or claim damages under s 13 of the Sale of Goods Act 1979 as in *Nicholson and Venn v Smith-Marriott* (1947) 177 L T 189.

7 The conditions in question and the other material reproduced in Appendix 1 are the copyright of the auction houses to whose sales they refer, and have been reproduced in this book by kind permission.

8 See Sotheby's Condition 17; Christie's Condition of Acceptance 1.

9 See *Rowland v Divall* [1923] 2 KB 500; *Butterworths v Kingsway Motors Ltd* [1954] 2 All ER 694, [1954] 1 WLR 1286. (The *auctioneer's* potential liability for conversion is discussed in ch 5.)

10 [1925] 2 KB 410.

of the seller the auctioneer, in a sale of specific goods, impliedly does warrant that he knows of no defect therein. Secondly, in deciding whether or not the seller has title to sell, careful account must be taken of the legal system which must decide such matters. The point is important where goods are auctioned which were sold previously abroad. This occurred in the *Winkworth v Christie, Manson & Woods Ltd.*[11] Here the goods in question were stolen in England from W. They were subsequently taken to Italy and sold and delivered by a third party to the present vendor. The contract in question was made in Italy and the contractual rights of the parties were governed by Italian law, the goods being at the time of such sale and delivery physically situated in Italy. The vendor had subsequently delivered them to Christie's in England for sale by auction on his behalf. When W discovered these goods not already sold, in the possession of Christie's, Christie's gave an undertaking not further to part with possession of the unsold goods pending determination of the ownership as between W and the vendor. The crucial issue was, therefore, whether the sale in Italy had the effect of conferring on the vendor a title to the goods valid even against W, from whom they had been stolen. In *Cammell v Sewell*,[12] Pollock CJ had held that if, as here, property was disposed of in a manner binding according to the law of the country where it was, that disposition was binding everywhere. The view of Pollock CJ was subsequently affirmed by the Court of Exchequer Chamber and had subsequently been accepted as a principle of private international law. Accordingly, Italian law applied to govern the situation and it was irrelevant that the goods had been brought back for sale in England or that the former owner was a British subject. The moral of this case is that since under many continental systems of law bona fide purchasers of chattels will get a good title even to stolen goods, it should not be assumed that English domestic law can exclusively be relied upon to answer vital questions of title.

Non-compliance with description

Auction sales are clear examples of sales by description within s 13 of the Sale of Goods Act 1979. Section 13(3) reinforces this point by stating that 'a sale of goods is not prevented from being a sale by description by reason only that, being exposed for sale or hire, they are selected by the buyer'.[13] Where the buyer finds that the goods he has bought at auction do not comply with the catalogue description, his first line of attack will be to sue the seller for breach of the implied condition of compliance with description.[14] This is a situation which most standard Conditions of Sale seek to guard against by an appropriate disclaimer. Condition 16(a) of Sotheby's is typical, and runs:

> Goods auctioned are usually of some age. All goods are sold with all faults and imperfections and errors of description. Illustrations in catalogues are for identification only. Buyers should satisfy themselves prior to sale as to the condition of each lot and should exercise and rely on their own judgment as to whether the lot accords with its description. Subject to the obligations accepted by Sotheby's under

11 [1980] Ch 496, [1980] 1 All ER 1121, also discussed above, p 110.
12 (1858) 3 H & N 617 at 638, Pollock CJ.
13 There are a number of decided cases holding that sales in shops or by reference to advertised descriptions are sales by description. See *Godley v Perry* [1960] 1 All ER 36, 1 [1960] 1 WLR 9, and *Beale v Taylor* [1967] 3 All ER 253, [1967] 1 WLR 1193, CA.
14 See *Nicholson and Venn v Smith-Marriott* (1947) 177 LT 189, mentioned above p 121.

> this Condition, none of the seller, Sotheby's, its servants or agents is responsible for errors of description or for the genuineness or authenticity of any lot, no warranty whatever is given by Sotheby's, its servants or agents, or any seller to any buyer in respect of any lot and any express or implied conditions or warranties are hereby excluded.[15]

The effect of a Condition of Sale purporting to preclude reliance on a catalogue description is not easy to assess. It could be argued that the description must be read in the light of the appropriate condition and as part of it. This, in turn, would make the description so qualified as to make it difficult for a buyer to argue that the property had actually been misdescribed. On the other hand, the courts are more likely to see this type of condition as an exclusion or restriction falling within the Unfair Contract Terms Act 1977. As has been explained above, the courts are then obliged to consider whether the condition complies with the test of 'reasonableness'. The analogous position where a Condition of Sale purports to disclaim liability for misrepresentations is fully considered in ch 9. If such decisions as *South Western General Property Co Ltd v Marton*[16] are any guide, there is a marked tendency in modern decisions to lean against the effectiveness of these disclaimers. On the other hand, there is a case for broad disclaimers as to descriptions in the context of auctions, particularly where the error is one of omission and the description is not fundamentally misleading. Auctioneers have to deal with a very large variety and volume of goods of which a guaranteed description and provenance is not always possible — as Christie's state, 'many lots are of an age and nature which precludes their being in pristine condition'.[17] On the other hand, a disclaimer of such a fundamental and careless misdescription that would, for instance, give rise to prima facie criminal liability under s 1 of the Trade Descriptions Act 1968 (see ch 8) would probably fall victim to the reasonableness test as well. The latter remains to be tested in the auction context, but the practical advice to the auctioneer is to exercise extreme caution over descriptions applied. In this connection it must also be remembered that it is for the buyer to show that there has been a misdescription, and where experts themselves can differ this may not be easy.

Both Sotheby's and Christie's make specific provision for any lot which proves to be a 'deliberate forgery'. This phrase is usually only apt to describe fake works of art, postage stamps, musical instruments and their labels, and similar items. The phrase is defined in Sotheby's Condition 38 (g) as follows: ' "Deliberate forgery" means an imitation made with the intention of deceiving as to authorship, origin, date, age, period, culture or source which is not shown to be such in the description in the catalogue and which at the date of the sale had a value materially less than it would have had if it had been in accordance with that description.' References in the Conditions of Sale to a 'deliberate forgery' must be read in this context.[18] In the case of Sotheby's, where Condition 16(b) is included, the buyer is given the right to return the forged lot within a stipulated period of the date of the auction in the same condition in which it was at the time of the auction, accompanied by a statement of defects and other details. If Sotheby's is then satisfied that the

15 See also Christie's Condition of Sale 2.
16 (1982) 263 EG 1090, discussed in ch 9.
17 Condition 2 of Christie's 'Notice'.
18 See also Condition 3 of Christie's 'Notice' to similar effect. The word 'deliberate' seems otiose. A forgery could hardly be other than deliberate.

item is a 'deliberate forgery' as defined, and that the buyer has and is able to transfer a good and marketable title to the lot free from any third-party claims, the sale will be set aside and any amount paid in respect of the lot will be refunded. The period during which the buyer has this right varies from five years in the case of fine art to 21 days in the case of a postage stamp. Christie's Condition 3 stipulates a similar right to return the purported 'deliberate forgery' within five years of the date of the sale.

This type of condition is by no means unique to the large London auction rooms. Its virtue is that it provides an opportunity to the buyer of goods at auction where the type of goods is peculiarly subject to the problem of forgery, to rescind the sale. From a business point of view it therefore removes a major potential disincentive to the less expert or more nervous bidder. On the other hand, the potential cost of implementing this policy by the auction houses, particularly where the time limit is lengthy, can be high.[19] It must nevertheless be borne in mind that where the buyer has the right to sue in respect of a breach of the condition of compliance with description (assuming that it has not been effectively disclaimed) at common law and under the Sale of Goods Act 1979, he would have the right to reject the goods before acceptance takes place and thereafter to sue for damages. When does acceptance take place? Section 35 of the Sale of Goods Act 1979 provides (inter alia) that this occurs 'when after the lapse of a reasonable time the buyer retains the goods without intimating to the seller that he has rejected them.' There is little authority on the meaning of 'a reasonable time' in this particular context, but it may be that the only effect of 'the deliberate forgery' condition discussed above is to give the buyer much longer than he would normally have to rescind the sale. His rights otherwise would take the form of a claim to damages which would be assessed by reference to the difference between the lot as it was described and the lot as it actually is, as measured by reference to the time when the buyer, acting with reasonable diligence, could have discovered the position.[20] This course of action is extinguished after the expiration of six years from the date on which the cause of action arose, i e normally the date of the sale, by virtue of the Limitation Act 1980, s 5.

In order to guard against the possibility of forgery, the major auction-houses adopt a policy of caution when attributing valuable artefacts to particular artists or makers. The catalogue description must be read by reference to the definitions in the Conditions of Sale of such phrases as 'attributed to...' 'with signature...' and the like. It should also be noted that the right to reject a 'deliberate forgery' is modified by: (a) a 'state of the art' defence of accuracy by the standards of the time of the description, and (b) a restriction of the right to reject to the actual purchaser and not his assignee. But an unreasonable failure by the auctioneer to comply with the requirements of such a condition, perhaps by a denial that an object is a deliberate forgery in the teeth of supporting expert evidence, would lay the auctioneer open both to an action for damages and possible criminal liability under the Trade Descriptions Act 1968, s 14 (false statements as to services).

19 Neither set of Conditions entitle the auctioneer to recover the amount paid to the buyer from the seller once the sale proceeds have been remitted to the seller. Sotheby's Condition 22 in effect annuls the sale if the lot is agreed to be a deliberate forgery *before* the sale proceeds have been paid out (usually one month from sale).

20 See e g *East Ham Borough Council v Bernard Sunley & Sons Ltd* [1966] AC 406, [1965] 3 All ER 619, HL; *Johnson v Agnew* [1980] AC 367, HL at 401; and generally Treitel *Law of Contract* (6th edn) Stevens, 722.

Unmerchantable goods

It is almost universal for Conditions of Sale to attempt to exclude faults and imperfections in goods sold. As has already been explained, the implied condition of merchantable quality is likely otherwise to apply, subject to certain qualifications. These qualifications are best explained by examining the position of a successful buyer wishing to bring an action against the seller for subsequently discovered defects in the goods sold. He must first overcome the following hurdles:

(a) If the seller is a private seller, the buyer must show that he did not know this and that no reasonable steps were taken to bring this fact to his notice before the contract was made (s 14(5)).

(b) Since the implied condition of merchantable quality only applies where the defects in question were not specifically drawn to the buyer's attention before the contract was made, he must show that this did not occur.

(c) If, as normally happens, he examined the goods before bidding, he must show that the defects in question were not such as that examination ought to have revealed.[1]

(d) Finally, the buyer must show that the defects do render the goods 'unmerchantable'. Section 14(6) of the Sale of Goods Act 1979 provides that 'goods of any kind are of merchantable quality... if they are as fit for the purpose or purposes for which goods of that kind are commonly bought as it is reasonable to expect having regard to any description applied to them, the price (if relevant) and all the other relevant circumstances.' This definition has caused problems and is under reconsideration by the Law Commission who may recommend in the foreseeable future a revised definition to take into account such matters as reasonable durability. However, with regard to second-hand goods, a more relaxed meaning is given to 'merchantable quality'. As Lord Denning stated, merchantability 'means, that on the sale of a second-hand car, it is merchantable if it is in usable condition, even though not perfect... A buyer should realise that when he buys a second-hand car, defects may appear sooner or later; and in the absence of express warranty, he has no redress.'[2] Should the buyer actually succeed in showing that the goods are unmerchantable and that there has been a breach of the implied condition, the seller will then have to rely on the disclaimer of liability in the Conditions of Sale. This is subject to the reasonableness test under the Unfair Contract Terms Act 1977, as explained above.[3] However auction sales are not consumer sales and so long as such disclaimers are subject to the test of reasonableness they are likely to continue to figure prominently in standard Conditions of Sale until it is unequivocally established that in *all* circumstances this is unreasonable, a rather unlikely proposition.

1 See *Thornett and Fehr v Beers & Sons* [1919] 1 KB 486, 88 LJKB 684 (inspection of outside only of glue barrels held to impute notice of their internal condition). Despite that decision, it is now thought that 'that examination' is the examination actually made by the buyer, however superficial.
2 *Bartlett v Sidney Marcus Ltd* [1965] 2 All ER 753, CA, at 755.
3 See above, p 119. Such a clause is both void and criminally illegal in a *consumer* sale — see Consumer Transactions (Restrictions on Statements) Order 1976.

Similar remarks apply pari passu to the implied condition of fitness for purpose in the unlikely case of its being implied in these circumstances.

THE BUYER'S PREMIUM

In 1975 both Sotheby's and Christie's introduced the buyer's premium. Sotheby's Condition 3 runs, accordingly, thus:

> Except in respect of 'special category items', the buyer shall pay to Sotheby's a premium of 10 per cent on the 'hammer price' together with Value Added Tax at the standard rate on the premium, and agrees that Sotheby's, when acting as agent for the seller, may also receive commission from the seller in accordance with Condition 19.

The right to extract the additional 10 per cent on the hammer price from the buyer is thus imposed by a contractual condition. Some aspects of the auctioneer's position vis-à-vis the seller in this respect, are examined elsewhere.[4] The practice of imposing a buyer's premium is now widespread throughout the UK, though its introduction was not unattended by controversy, it being alleged that the introduction of the buyer's premium was as a result of collusion between Sotheby's and Christie's and consequently this agreement was registrable as a restrictive practice under the Restrictive Trade Practices Act 1976. It is understood that this allegation, made by a group of dealers, was rejected by the Office of Fair Trading on the grounds that there was insufficient evidence of actual collusion.[5] A further controversial point regarding the buyer's premium is whether it should correctly attract Value Added Tax since, it could be argued, the auctioneers supply no service to the *buyer*, and VAT is a tax (inter alia) on services supplied. This argument has also proved unsuccessful.

Value Added Tax is also in issue where goods are sold by vendors registered for VAT and who wish to pass on the VAT on the eventual hammer price to the buyer. Sotheby's Condition 4 states:

> Lots on which Value Added Tax is payable by the Buyer on the 'hammer price' are indicated in the catalogue with the sign † (where the tax is payable at the standard rate) and with the sign †† (where the tax is payable at a different rate). Value Added Tax, the rates of which are subject to alteration by law, is payable at the rates prevailing on the date of the auction.

Where there is no indication that the hammer price is subject to VAT, the buyer is under no obligation to pay it and the seller, if registered for VAT, must treat the net proceeds of sale as including VAT. Under powers conferred by s 18 of the Value Added Tax Act 1983, the Treasury has power to mitigate the impact of VAT on the supply of second-hand goods which would normally attract VAT on their full re-sale price. The Treasury has made orders which,

4 See ch 5. Attention is also drawn to the provisions of s 11(2) of the Trade Descriptions Act 1968 (see Appendix 2) which makes it an offence when offering to supply any goods to indicate a price less than that at which they are in fact being offered. Avoidance of this offence will depend upon the buyer's knowledge of any buyer's premium which is to be charged to him.

5 In 1983 Andrew Faulds MP unsuccessfully introduced a Private Member's Bill (the Buyer's Premium (Abolition) Bill) to abolish the premium.

subject to certain conditions, restrict the amount chargeable to VAT to the *dealer's margin* as opposed to the whole of the sale price. The special scheme in question applies to a number of second-hand goods, but for present purposes the main items likely to be in issue are used motor cars, antiques, second-hand works of art, and scientific collections. The dealer's margin on re-sale is deemed to include VAT and the scheme works, therefore, in the following way. If, for example an item cost £600 and was then sold for £692, the selling margin is £92. VAT included in the margin is represented by the fraction 15/115(3/23). Accordingly, the VAT due to Customs and Excise on the transaction is 3/23 × 92 = £12.[6]

The implications of the buyer's premium and the VAT thereon, were considered by the London VAT Tribunal in *Jocelyn Feilding Fine Arts Ltd v Customs and Excise Comr.*[7] The appellants carried on business as dealers in fine art and sold articles through Christie's and Sotheby's subject to the buyer's premium. The Customs and Excise contended that on sale the buyer's premium formed part of the sale consideration and accordingly was liable to VAT even though the seller never received it. Under both Christie's and Sotheby's conditions, the buyer's premium was stated to be part of the purchase price. The tribunal, however, considered that the buyer's premium was not part of the purchase price as it was expressly retained by the auctioneer. Instead, the tribunal analysed the transaction as consisting of:

(a) the consideration for which the goods are supplied by the seller, this being the *final bid price*;
(b) the buyer's premium, being the consideration not for the supply of goods by the seller but for the services provided by the auctioneer.

Accordingly, the consideration for the supply of goods would exclude the buyer's premium. Following this decision the Commissioners of Customs and Excise decided to treat the final bid price as the buying price for all sales by auction, whether outside or under the special scheme. Accordingly, the following principles apply:

(a) VAT is charged at the standard rate on any buyer's premium charged (Value Added Tax Act 1983, s 3, replacing previous similar provisions).
(b) Any VAT paid on the buyer's premium by a registered dealer may be treated as input tax under the normal rules.
(c) The final bid price is the consideration for which goods sold under the special scheme are supplied by the seller and acquired by the buyer. This will therefore be the figure to be entered in either the seller's or buyer's special scheme stock-book, and the margin must be calculated on that basis.[8]

Payment by the buyer

Auction sales continue to depend to a large degree on trust between auctioneer and buyer. Nevertheless standard Conditions of Sale will seek to secure as far

6 Most items in normal chattel auctions thus fall within the special scheme, but items such as plant and machinery do not and are likely to be auctioned subject to VAT. If buyers are registered for VAT, they will treat the VAT so paid as input tax. Other articles outside the special scheme are paintings created after 1 April 1973 and sold by or on behalf of the painter, and modern jewellery.
7 [1978] VATTR 164, London VAT Tribunal.
8 See VAT leaflet no 712/1/78. The EEC Draft Seventh Directive on VAT, proposing a common system of VAT on works of art and antiques etc, could have serious implications for the UK auction market.

as possible that the buyer identifies himself and pays for the goods as soon as possible. This effect is usually achieved by stipulations, broadly as follows:

(a) The buyer on making a successful bid must forthwith supply his name and address and, if so required, his bank or other suitable references.
(b) The buyer may be required to pay forthwith the whole or part of the purchase price, and if he fails to do so the lot or lots may at the auctioneer's absolute discretion be put up again and resold. In other words, failure to pay would be regarded as a fundamental breach of contract.
(c) Various reserve rights may also be secured against the purchaser. These might include later resale of the goods with liability by the buyer to meet any deficiency; the right to store the lots at the expense of the buyer until collection; the right to charge interest at a stipulated rate on the purchase price to the extent that it remains unpaid for more than (say) seven days from the date of the sale.[9]

Collection of purchases and passing of the property

Property in goods passes according to the rules contained in s 18 of the Sale of Goods Act 1979 unless otherwise agreed. In the absence of such agreement the property will pass to the buyer when the contract is made, that is, on the fall of the hammer.[10] Most Conditions of Sale contract out of this general position by stating that the ownership of any lot purchased shall not pass to the buyer until he has made payment in full to the auctioneers. Furthermore, the buyer is put under a liability to take away the lot at his own expense within a stipulated period (often 5 working days after the auction).[11]

Buyer's responsibilities for lots purchased

In practice the safekeeping of goods bought by buyers during the auction, and the prevention of damage thereto, can give rise to problems. In a crowded auction-room accidents can all too easily happen or goods purchased may be stolen. Under the Sale of Goods Act 1979 the risk remains with the seller until the property in the goods has transferred to the buyer. Where a dispute arises as to this, the first step is therefore to assess whether the property has passed to the buyer or not (which may depend on whether the buyer has paid for the goods) and then prima facie responsibility for loss or damage lies with whoever at the time is the owner. This rule, laid down by s 20 of the Sale of Goods Act 1979, is specifically subject to variation of the position: (a) where delivery has been delayed through the fault of the seller, and (b) where the law of bailment affects the position by imposing duties of care on the bailee (in this case the auctioneer). This latter point has been discussed elsewhere in detail.[12] Its significance here is that should the Conditions of Sale of the Auctioneer attempt to contract out of an existing duty of care, once again the clause is likely to be regarded as an exclusion clause whose validity will be judged by reference to the Unfair Contract Terms Act 1977 and its requirement of reasonableness.

9 See Sotheby's Conditions 6 and 15, and Christie's Conditions of Sale, 5 and 8.
10 See s 18, r 1, Sale of Goods Act 1979.
11 See Sotheby's Condition 9, and Christie's Conditions 7 and 9.
12 See p 93.

Sotheby's Condition 12 states:

> The buyer will be responsible for loss or damage to lots purchased from the time of collection or the expiry of 5 working days after the day of the auction, whichever is the sooner, and neither Sotheby's nor its servants or agents shall thereafter be responsible for any loss or damage of any kind, whether caused by negligence or otherwise, while any lot is in its custody or under its control.[13]

Christie's Condition 9 simply states that: 'The property in a lot shall not pass to the buyer until he has paid the purchase price in full, but the lot shall be at the buyer's risk in all respect from the fall of the hammer.'

CONDITIONS GOVERNING THE CONDUCT OF THE AUCTION

Definition of buyer

For the auction room contract to fall into place, 'the buyer' must obviously be defined. To put the matter beyond doubt, Conditions of Sale normally define 'the buyer'. In the case of Sotheby's Condition 1, the buyer is defined as follows:

> The highest bidder shall be the buyer at the 'hammer price', and any dispute shall be settled at the auctioneer's absolute discretion. Every bidder shall be deemed to act as principal unless there is in force a written acknowledgement by Sotheby's that he acts as agent on behalf of a named principal.

Christie's Condition of Sale 2, defines the buyer as 'the highest bidder acceptable to the auctioneer'.[14] This condition goes on to state that if

> during or immediately after the sale of the lot, the auctioneer considers that a dispute has arisen or that there is any other reason for so doing, he may at his absolute discretion immediately put up the lot again for sale.

In practice, identification of experienced bidders can take a great deal of skill on the auctioneer's part. The *Auction Companion*[15] relates that a dealer wishing to bid for a Rembrandt at Christie's in 1965 made the following arrangement:

> When Mr S is sitting down he is bidding. If he bids openly he is bidding. When he stands up he has stopped bidding. If he sits down again he is not bidding until he raises his finger. Having raised his finger, he is bidding until he stands up again.

Not surprisingly, the Rembrandt was knocked down to another bidder, at

13 Facilities exist for insurance of the goods at the seller's expense and at his option per Sotheby's Condition 20. However cover is expressed to cease at 'the earlier of the ownership of the property passing from the seller or the seller or consignor becoming bound to collect the property'. Presumably such insurance would cover uncollected goods for those five working days where the property has not passed to the buyer because he has not paid for the goods (see Sotheby's Condition 9).

14 The auctioneer will exercise his discretion where e g the highest bid in the salesroom matches the highest bid left in advance of the sale by an absent potential buyer.

15 Daniel and Katherine Leab *The Auction Companion* (1981) Macmillan.

which Mr S loudly complained and the picture was again put up for sale when Mr S was successful by openly bidding 760 000 guineas. It will be seen from this saga that there is a need for a condition which attempts to allow the auctioneer to settle disputes as to the highest bidder. Nevertheless, the gentlemanly practice which occurs in some circles where an auctioneer has closed the bidding by fall of the hammer and is then confronted with a further bidder whom he has not previously identified, at which he proceeds — with the successful bidder's permission — to reoffer the lot, is open to grave objection. The contract is completed at the fall of the hammer, it cannot be said to be vitiated by any material mistake,[16] and there is no consideration (although there may be moral pressure) for the hitherto successful bidder to abandon his contractual rights as buyer. In this situation (certainly in law, and, it is strongly suggested, in ethics), the auctioneer ought to accept the position and not attempt to reopen the bidding where there is no genuine dispute.

CONDITIONS AFFECTING THE CONDUCT OF THE AUCTION

Minimum increment

Problems can arise in practice where bidders attempt to control incremental increases from the floor. Some Conditions of Sale will forbid this practice altogether by making the right to bid conditional on acceptance of the increments suggested by the auctioneer. This is however somewhat inflexible, and Sotheby's Condition 2 states: 'The auctioneer shall have the right to refuse any bid which does not exceed the previous bid by at least 5 per cent or by such other proportion as the auctioneer shall in his absolute discretion direct.' Problems can in practice arise as to what increment has been offered by a particular bidder, especially where two or more bidders are bidding simultaneously. Again, much depends on the skill of the auctioneer who should make it clear to each bidder at what price he is bidding. The practice at some fine art sales, or sales of commodities with much above average value, can be to allocate to a particular bidder who is indicating interest a suggested price representing a conventional incremental or percentage increase. In other words, the auctioneer calls out the increments after he has purported to accept a bid. An analysis of this situation would cause considerable difficulties in the law of contract since offers must be made at an ascertainable price. The best

16 An operative mistake in law cannot generally arise where the parties agree in the same terms on the same subject matter. But a 'mutual' mistake, annulling their contract, may occur where e g a bidder bids for what he believes to be bales of tow whereas the auctioneer is in fact offering bales of hemp, though his catalogue description is not clear. This occurred in *Scriven Bros v Hindley & Co* [1913] 3 KB 564, 83 LJKB 40, where it was held that there was no genuine agreement between the parties and no binding contract. Mistaken judgment or motive is irrelevant; see *Bell v Lever Bros Ltd* [1932] AC 161, HL, at 224, per Lord Atkin, and, in equity, *Tamplin v James* (1879) 15 Ch D 215, CA, at 217, per Baggally LJ. In *Friedrich v A Monnickendam Ltd* (1973) 228 EG 1311, the Court of Appeal considered the auctioneer's duty where questionable bids are made. The case concerned a jewellery sale held by Christie's in Geneva. The facts arose out of confusion by the English highest bidder as to whether the auctioneer had called 290 000 Swiss francs for some diamond pendants, or, as he thought, 190 000. 'The auctioneer should therefore have assured himself by the clearest words in English that Mr Monnickendam appreciated that the figure was 290 000 Swiss francs' (per Lord Denning). The Court of Appeal held the contract to be vitiated by mistake (among other factors).

that can be suggested is that the bidder, in making a bid for a lot at an unidentified increment, is making a conditional offer which he must be allowed to withdraw should the increment then prove unacceptable to him (unless, of course, it can be shown that an experienced bidder knew by convention the price of the invitation being made by the auctioneer).

Admission to premises

Bidders are licensees on the premises of the auctioneers. There is no reason in law why such licence should not be withdrawn unilaterally since it is not obviously granted for any consideration. Sotheby's Condition 25 accordingly states that the company 'shall have the right, at its discretion, to refuse admission to its premises or attendance at its auctions to any person.'

Refusal to accept bids etc

Similarly, auctioneers may have good reason to refuse to accept a bid from a bidder whose integrity is in doubt. Whilst no condition is strictly needed to give the auctioneer this right, since the bidder can at best only make an offer, Conditions of Sale can make the matter clear. For instance, Sotheby's Condition 26 states that the company 'has absolute discretion without giving any reason to refuse any bid, to divide any lot, to combine any 2 or more lots, to withdraw any lot from the auction and in case of dispute put up any lot for auction again.'

GENERAL COMMENT ON CONDITIONS OF SALE

It can be seen from the selective analysis in this chapter that Conditions of Sale attempt to deal with a wide variety of problems concerning actual and potential buyers. In some cases these conditions, if binding contractually, will — either by modifying the Sale of Goods Act 1979 or by filling a gap in the law — govern the contractual situation without further ado. Other conditions will be in the nature of exemption or exclusion clauses and their validity is likely to be tested, sooner or later, under the general requirement of reasonableness imposed by the Unfair Contract Terms Act 1977. The standard conditions used by Sotheby's and Christie's are appropriate for large London auction-rooms but may not be appropriate in their entirety to country auctioneers or estate agents whose business includes occasional auctions. Appendix 1(a) therefore includes a list of suggested minimum Conditions of Sale which should appear in any chattel auction catalogue, though in the light of the effect of the Unfair Contract Terms Act 1977 in particular it must be appreciated that any clause which removes legal liability from the auctioneers which might otherwise exist is open to attack.

Chapter 7

Export licensing

The Department of Trade and Industry has general powers to regulate the exportation of goods, these powers being derived from the Import Export and Customs Powers (Defence) Act 1939. Although this Act was originally designed primarily to regulate trading with the enemy at the beginning of the second world war, it continues to provide the authority for orders made by Parliament regulating, amongst other things, the export of antiques, collectors' items and the like.

The fundamental sanction supplied by the 1939 Act is that if goods are exported in contravention of an order made under the Act, those goods are deemed to be prohibited goods and are liable to forfeiture; furthermore the exporter of the goods or his agent, or the shipper of the goods, is liable, in addition to any other penalty under the enactments relating to customs, to a further penalty formerly of £500 but now on Level 5 of the standard scale laid down by the Criminal Justice Act 1982.

A large number of orders have been made successively under this Act both to control exports to particular States or to provide a general prohibition on exportation without an export licence.[1] What follows is a short description of the way this control is exercised together with some practical advice on the obtaining of export licences.

SCOPE OF THE CONTROL

The law at present in force in the United Kingdom and in the Isle of Man provides that a licence is needed to export from the UK and from the Isle of Man to any destination:

(a) Photographic positives and negatives produced more than 60 years before the date of exportation and valued at £400 or more per item, but not including any photographic positive or negative exported by, and being the personal property of, the manufacturer or producer thereof, or the spouse, widow or widower of that person.

(b) Any other goods manufactured or produced more than 50 years before the

1 See the Export of Goods (Control) Order SI 1985/849

date of exportation, but not including:

(i) postage stamps or other articles of philatelic interest;

(ii) birth, marriage or death certificates or other documents relating to the personal affairs of the exporter or the spouse of the exporter;

(iii) letters or other writings written by or to the exporter or the spouse of the exporter;

(iv) any goods exported by, and being the personal property of, the manufacturer or producer thereof, or the spouse, widow or widower of that person.[2]

Open general export licence

An open general export licence has been made permitting the export freely to any destination of most categories of antiques and other collectors items, manufactured or produced more than 50 years before the date of exportation, if the value per article, or matching set of articles, is less than £16000. The following items are expressly excluded from the licence:

(a) Documents, manuscripts and archives, other than printed books, printed pamphlets or similar printed matter, newspapers, periodicals, magazines, or papers relating to the personal affairs of the exporter or spouse of the exporter.

(b) Articles which have been recovered at any time from the soil of the United Kingdom (including the bed of the sea within the United Kingdom territorial waters) other than:

  (i) coin; or

  (ii) articles recovered only after burial or concealment less than fifty years before the date of exportation; and

(c) Any other goods falling within a description in Sch 1 to the Export of Goods (Control) Order, manufactured or produced more than 50 years but not more than 100 years before the date of exportation.

A further exception occurs with regard to the exportation of any representation of a British historical personage unless:

(a) its value is less than £4000; or

(b) its value is £4000 or more but less than £16000 and the exporter produces to the proper officer of Customs and Excise at the place of exportation a certificate from either the Director of the National Portrait Gallery or the Keeper of the Scottish National Portrait Gallery stating that in his opinion the object concerned is not a work of national importance.

The restriction applies to items consisting of or including any representation of the likeness of any person, made otherwise than by photography and

2 There are problems relating to the sale of non-antique firearms (see ch 8) and export restrictions on items incorporating animal material from endangered species. Thus, items containing e g ivory, whalebone, or tortoiseshell need export licences granted by the Department of the Environment. Some auctioneers (e g Christie's) hold a bulk licence for African elephant ivory and items incorporating this material. See generally the Endangered Species (Import and Export) Act 1976, s 1 and Sch 3 (listing restricted items derived from endangered species).

excluding a coin, in respect of whom an entry appears in the *Dictionary of National Biography* (or any supplements thereto), *Who's Who* or *Who Was Who*.

Specific licences

Items within the scope of the control and not covered by the open general export licence or bulk licences will need a specific licence. Applications must be made for such licence to the export licensing branch of the Department of Trade. Each application is then referred by the Department of Trade to an appropriate expert adviser who may either:

(a) raise no objection to the export, or
(b) recommend that an export licence be refused for the object because of its national importance.

Cases under (b) are referred by the Department of Trade to the Reviewing Committee on the Export of Works of Art.

Cases referred to the Reviewing Committee

The Committee considers such case as is stated in writing by the applicant along with a written statement from the Department of Trade's expert adviser. These statements are exchanged before the meeting and both parties are invited to attend or be represented at the committee's meeting. The object in question is normally required to be brought to the meeting as well.

The committee's decision

The criteria which the committee adopt are indicated by the following questions:

(a) Is the object so closely connected with our history and national life that its departure would be a misfortune?
(b) Is it of outstanding aesthetic importance?
(c) Is it of outstanding significance for the study of some particular branch of art, learning or history?

The final decision is notified to the applicant without reasons. If an export licence is refused, this is normally subject to an offer by a public institution (which the exporter is not obliged to accept) being made within a specified time for the purchase of the object; failing such an offer, an export licence is granted. The price recommended is that which the reviewing committee considers reasonable, after taking advice if necessary. The committee takes account of exemptions from capital transfer tax and capital gains tax which may apply if the object is sold to one of the bodies listed in para 12 of Sch 6 to the Finance Act 1975. These bodies include national, university or local authority museums and galleries.

Bulk licences

Regular exporters may obtain a bulk licence in lieu of individual export licences for documents, manuscripts or archives, except the following:

(a) (i) manuscript books of hours, missals, psalters, antiphoners and graduals; and
(ii) illuminated or illustrated manuscripts in Arabic, Persian, Turkish, Urdu and other oriental languages, and miniature paintings by Persian, Chinese and other eastern artists, whether in or extracted from books or albums;
valued at more than £16000 each;
(b) any item or group of associated items recognised by the holder of the bulk licence as being of national importance, irrespective of value;
(c) papers and memoranda of those who have held public office relating to that office; or
(d) official papers, manorial and tithe documents; or
(e) any other document, manuscript or archive, or a group of associated such documents etc, valued at more than £250 per article, or, as the case may be, per group.

Comments

The export licensing system has come into particular prominence because of the huge buying power, in particular, of American museums and collectors, and a tendency for works of art to be bought at auction by such buyers.[3]

The history of the matter was that in 1950 the then Chancellor of the Exchequer appointed a committee under the chairmanship of Lord Waverley 'To consider and advise on the policy to be adopted by His Majesty's Government in controlling the exporting of works of art, books, manuscripts, armour and antiques and to recommend what arrangement should be made for the practical operation of policy.' In 1952, this committee recommended that there should be an age limit for articles requiring special scrutiny (and also objects should generally not be subject to special scrutiny on grounds of national importance if they were worth less than a stated figure). The criteria for the granting or refusal of a licence as explained above were devised by the Waverley Committee in 1952. About 20 cases are considered by the committee each year, and the application of the criteria combined with a temporary refusal of an export licence has in fact achieved the effect of keeping most of the items considered important within the UK. However in 1983, when some 50 cases were considered, the 5 most expensive items reviewed left the country since funds were not available to keep them.[4]

This rather obscure field of law and administration poses economic and ethical problems. On the face of it an owner of a valuable object should not be prohibited from selling to the highest buyer for external considerations

3 See Geraldine Norman 'Put Art in a New Framework' (1984) Times, April 14; and Leslie Geddis-Brown 'Must Treasures Go to the Highest Bidder?' (1984) Sunday Times, 15 July.
4 See Geraldine Norman (n 3, above). See also 'The Getty Factor' (1984) Sunday Times, 7 October.

without, at least, compensation. On the other hand it is clearly important to keep objects of national importance within the UK and this is a policy adopted by most States. France, Italy and West Germany have systems which permit a total ban on the export of a work, whether or not a local institution has the money to buy it. This, however, does amount to confiscation of a proportion of the wealth of the owner. The policy is nevertheless presumably compatible with Article 1 of the First Protocol (1952) to the European Convention of Human Rights (1950) which provides that 'No-one shall be deprived of his possessions except in the public interest.'[5]

Procedure

Exportation of goods should not be arranged until a licence has been granted. When granted, the licence may be modified or revoked by the Department of Trade and Industry at any time without reason given; it may not be altered except by the Department of Trade and Industry and it is not transferable.

Application for an export licence is obtainable from the Department of Trade and Industry, Export Licensing Branch.[6] Except for items claimed to have been imported within the last 50 years, applications for licences in respect of archaeological items, British historical portraits and any other antique, collectors item etc more than 50 years old and valued at £16000 or more must be accompanied by a non-returnable monochrome photograph of specified size. In the case of British historical portraits valued between £4000 and £16000, the buyer may instead apply to the Director of the National Portrait Gallery[7] or the Keeper of the Scottish National Portrait Gallery[8] for a certificate stating that the item is not of national importance.

The application form requires a full description of the object in question. For instance, in the case of a work of art, antique or collector's item, the description should state the style or class to which the object belongs (e g by Raphael, style of Adam, Chelsea cloisonné, mezzotint, Sheffield Plate etc), the nature of the material, the general colour, period, country of origin and exact measurements. In the case of a painting, the full title by which it is usually known should be given and an indication as to whether it is signed and, if dated, the date. Gold and silver articles require details of the hallmark and photographic positives or negatives, the name of the photographer and the particulars of the subject.

Leading auctioneers often make administrative arrangements to obtain export licences for successful bidders along with other arrangements for consignment of the goods abroad.[9]

5 The Labour Party's shadow Minister for the Arts is reported to be in favour of a total ban on specified works, coupled with power to delay export for up to two years in other cases. Opponents of this policy, which could severely affect London's central position for art-dealing in pre-Impressionist works, argue that a better answer is to modify VAT, so as to equate sales to museums with export sales, increase CTT incentives for donors to public bodies and introduce American-style income tax deductions for monetary donations to museums, thus increasing museums' ability to compete in the market.

6 Application for an export licence is made on ELB form C (revised June 1983) obtainable from the Department of Trade and Industry, Export Licensing Branch, Millbank Tower, Millbank, London SW1P 4QU (tel 01 211 3115).

7 Director of the National Portrait Gallery, 2 St Martins Place, London WC2H 0HE.

8 Keeper of the Scottish National Portrait Gallery, 17 Ainslie Place, Edinburgh EH3 6AU.

9 The authors are grateful for the help given by the Export Licensing Branch of the Department of Trade and Industry. The Department's Notice to Exporters provides additional detailed guidance, and is available on application to the Export Licensing Branch.

Chapter 8

Criminal practices at auctions

MOCK AUCTIONS

Mock auctions have little to do with the activities of genuine auctioneers. A hall is hired, a carnival atmosphere created, and as Kenneth Jones J stated in *R v Ingram*:[1]

> The average holiday-maker going into one of these premises with his eyes open would realise that these proceedings were as much to do with a true auction as visiting a shooting gallery further down the street is to do with participation in the rifle championships at Bisley.

In a short but useful article, A T H Smith[2] describes the history of mock auctions and the reasons for a protective legislation. Drawing on the debates which have taken place from time to time on this matter, he describes a typical mock auction as follows:

> A man working outside a booth (the 'pitchgetter') would encourage passers-by to enter. When a large enough crowd had gathered inside, another man (the 'top man') would sell (either genuinely, or to an accomplice) a comparatively valuable article at a give-away price. The audience were showered with gifts and then invited to show their willingness to participate in an auction by buying an unopened packet (a 'nailer') — those unwilling to do so were then sent away. A considerable amount of junk was then sold, sometimes by the use of the suggestion that the seller would return some of the purchase price — the suggestion being implanted by one or two samples in which money was then returned. This was known as 'gazoomping the Sarkers'.

Apparently problems caused by mock auctions are of long-standing. In 1924 it was estimated that there were some 1500 mock auctions in operation and that over £8m was being spent at them. The activities involved were thought to be beyond the reach of the criminal law at the time. The Mock Auctions Act 1961 was introduced as a Private Member's Bill specifically designed to prevent fraudulent practices at auctions of this sort. On reading the Act it is not entirely clear against which mischief in particular the Act is aimed and its provisions have been sufficiently ambiguous to give rise to a number of reported cases. A summary of the Act and the main cases thereon now follows.

1 (1976) 64 Cr App Rep 119.
2 (1981) NLJ 49.

It is an offence, punishable by sentences of a fine of the statutory maximum and/or imprisonment of three months on summary conviction (unlimited fine or two years on conviction on indictment), to promote or conduct or assist in the conduct of a mock auction.

A sale of goods by way of competitive bidding is a mock auction if during the course of sale: (a) a lot is sold to a person bidding for it at a price lower than the amount of his higher bid for that lot, or part of the price is repaid or credited to him or stated to be so (unless the goods are found to be defective); or (b) the right to bid is or is stated to be restricted to persons who have bought or agreed to buy one or more articles; or (c) any articles are given away or offered as gifts (Mock Auctions Act 1961, s 1).

'Competitive bidding' is defined in the Mock Auctions Act 1961, s 3(1), as including:

> any mode of sale whereby prospective purchasers may be enabled to compete for the purchase of articles whether by way of increasing bids or by the offer of articles to be bid for at successively decreasing prices or otherwise.

In *Lomas v Rydeheard*,[3] it was held by the Divisional Court (on appeal from the Crown Court) that where the defendant offered articles for sale to customers assembled in his salerooms, calling out a series of progressively decreasing prices, but not asking for bids until his final price when he offered the item to an individual in the crowd who bought it without bargaining, this was still 'competitive bidding' since it could be inferred that prices would have been reduced further if people had been unwilling to buy. The Mock Auctions Act 1961 applies to lots comprising plate, linen, china, glass, books, pictures, prints, furniture, jewellery, articles of household or personal use or ornament or any musical or scientific instruments or apparatus (s 3).

In *Clements v Rydeheard*,[4] the defendant held sales at which he offered, at a fixed price, a number of boxes with undisclosed contents and selected the purchasers from those who put up their hands. Purchasers of later lots were similarly selected but only from those who had purchased boxes. The Divisional Court held that this was a sale by competitive bidding.

Competitive bidding includes any mode of sale whereby persons can compete for the purchase of articles in any way, whether or not by reference to price. In *Allen v Simmons*,[5] the audience was asked by the respondent who would pay him 30p for a set of glasses. Hands were raised. There was only one set of glasses. The successful 'bidder' was sold the glasses for 1p and a similar performance took place relating to an offer for sale of an undisclosed item for 50p.

In the view of Melford Stevenson J[6] it was difficult to form a precise view of the meaning of the word 'otherwise' in s 3(1) of the Mock Auctions Act 1961, but the subsection did contemplate bidding in what was or appeared to be

3 (1975) 119 Sol Jo 233, 237 EG 801.
4 [1978] 3 All ER 658, 143 JP 25.
5 [1978] 3 All ER 662, [1978] 1 WLR 879.
6 *Allen v Simmons* [1978] 3 All ER 662 at 667, [1978] 1 WLR 879.

competition with other bidders. The mere fact that the effect of the bid depended on the whim of the person conducting the so-called auction did not matter. Following *Clements v Rydeheard*,[7] the court in effect construed s 3(1) (set out above) as stopping at the words 'may be enabled to compete for the purchase of articles', and the offence had accordingly been committed. As has been pointed out[8] there seems to be no point, and indeed no justification in law, in construing s 3(1) in this curtailed way. Either decision could be justified by simply relying on the words 'or otherwise'.[9]

In addition to prosecutions, normally brought by trading-standards departments of local authorities , the Office of Fair Trading has also taken action and given warnings in a number of cases. In 1979 the Office of Fair Trading wrote to all chief trading-standards officers suggesting local Codes of Practice to protect consumers in this area. The assumption is that all hirers-out of public halls in a particular area can guard against abuses by incorporating appropriate conditions in the letting contract.

In April 1982 publicity was given to the fact that written assurances had been given by a mock auctioneer to the Director General of Fair Trading under Part III of the Fair Trading Act 1973. Breach of such assurances can lead to court orders, which if not complied with, could lay the offender open to a fine or imprisonment for contempt of court. The assurances in question were in respect of nine offences under the Bargain Offers Orders and for conducting mock auctions contrary to the Mock Auctions Act 1961 in respect of which the trader was convicted in various magistrates' courts during the preceding year.

In December 1982 a press release was issued by the Director General of Fair Trading to the following effect:[10]

> 'The busy pre-Christmas shopping period is a time of year when hundreds of one-day sales are being held. Many such sales turn out to be mock auctions, which are not only against the law, but can only be described — in today's slang — as a rip off. Be on your guard.
>
> 'Once enticed by the prospect of a bargain, people can only too easily be caught up in an atmosphere which is skilfully created and manipulated by the salesman. And they are highly likely to be persuaded to part with large sums of money for items of little value,' said Sir Gordon [Borrie].
>
> 'I have evidence of people handing over £50 for a sealed, plain cardboard box. They had seen others in the audience getting bargains and expected the same. But what they hadn't realised was... those other people were working hand-in-glove with the salesman! Once the victims left the sale and opened their boxes, they realised they had spent £50 on a cheap watch or radio they could have bought elsewhere for £5.'
>
> Sir Gordon advised, 'Don't be tricked into parting with good money for inferior goods. If you go to a one-day sale, keep your wits about you and watch for the danger

7 Above, n 4.
8 [1978] Crim LR at 363.
9 It was confirmed by the Court of Appeal (Criminal Division) in *R v Pollard* (1983) 148 JP 679, CA (sales of goods from a lorry in Petticoat Lane, goods being thrown into the crowd and sold at reducing prices etc) that the words 'or otherwise' should not be construed ejusdem generis with the preceding words involving bidding on an increasing or reducing basis. The element of competition can be e g by reference to the first buyer to raise a hand.
10 OFT, London EC 4A 1PR.

signals. If the salesman sells goods to someone who is not the highest bidder, if you can only bid for certain goods after you have agreed to buy other articles, or if the salesman is giving goods away or offering gifts, you may be at a mock auction – the salesman is breaking the law, and almost certainly intends you no good, so beat a hasty retreat.

'Of course not all one day sales are swindles – at some you can find a bargain. And you can look after your interests by examining the goods before you buy them and by making sure you have a note of the seller's address. But beware of the offer that is too good to be true — "mock auctioneers" are looking for victims, not customers!'

AUCTION RINGS

The activity of auction rings gives more concern to auctioneers, private buyers and apprehensive sellers than any other phenomenon encountered in the ordinary auction-room.[11]

As to the prevalence of the practice, in one[12] of only two of the known successful prosecutions under the Auctions (Bidding Agreements) Act 1927,[13] Lewis-Bowen J at the Swansea Crown Court in passing sentence against ten antique dealers stated that rings were 'part and parcel of the antiques world'. Counsel appearing for five of the dealers had argued that the Act was applied so rarely that it must be a matter of public policy not to use it. He stated that his clients were doing something that had become a pattern of life in the trade.

A typical ring works in the following way. A group of buyers who are generally in trade as dealers agree to buy articles at auctions at less than the value such articles would otherwise probably fetch, by not competing against each other. When one of the 'ring' has successfully bid for the article, there follows afterwards a 'knock-out' which normally takes the form of a second auction held privately by the members of the ring. The article is then sold to the highest bidder within the ring, and the difference between the price actually paid to the auctioneer and that paid by the highest member of the ring at the second auction is distributed between all members according to an agreed formula.

There are several aspects to this practice which require comment. Firstly, its economic effect is to deprive the seller, as the consumer of the auctioneer's services, of the true value of his goods. One of the points in favour of an auction as a market for selling goods is that where the market value for such goods is unascertained, a free auction should normally supply that market value. Many a seller has been pleasantly surprised by the high value realised for an article, the value of which he had not appreciated. Equally, if a survey were done, there would probably be many sellers who obtain substantially less than the true value of their goods as compared with the price realised at the 'knock-out'. In other words, an auction is a forum in which free competition should reign. The existence of an auction ring prevents true competition and is

11 For an excellent general survey of the position see ATH Smith 'Auction Rings' [1981] Crim LR 86, to which article the authors are much indebted.

12 See the account of this case in (1983) Sunday Times, 4 September. The other case is *R v Jordan* [1981] CLY 131, Swansea Crown Ct.

13 *R v Barnett* [1951] 2 KB 425, CCA, concerned an unsuccessful charge of conspiracy to contravene the Act.

associated with parallel objectionable practices, such as members of the ring 'discouraging' private buyers by bidding such a private buyer up beyond the limit on one article in order to inhibit him from bidding for others, or even sometimes by various veiled threats and bad behaviour securing the non-participation of private buyers.

The second aspect of auction rings which requires comment is that, by their nature, they are difficult to detect and to prove. Both the successful prosecutions brought to date have been the work of one particular Welsh detective who specialises in this type of operation. He is quoted as commenting:[14]

> Dealers who refuse to join the ring can find the others ganging up on them so they are unable to buy anything... The crooked auction is flawed. Sometimes the auctioneer can be in on the ring himself and gets a cut from the knock-out. It can be a difficult racket to break. You have to have the co-operation of the auctioneer. Some of them don't like offending dealers because it interferes with sales.

In the second Swansea case,[15] proof was only possible by virtue of the fact that the knockout was spotted by the detective in question as taking place on a remote Welsh beach where the proceedings were recorded by a police photographer.

Having regard to the nature of the auction-ring operation it is scarcely useful to point out that technically an auction ring is a restrictive practice and should be registered as such under the Restrictive Trade Practices Act 1956. In addition, s 3(2) of the Auction (Bidding Agreements) Act 1969 gives the seller the right to avoid a contract where one of the purchasers is a dealer in a ring. He has an alternative right to bring an action for damages. The problem of a private seller proving the existence of a ring is even more acute than that facing the police authorities.

Auctions (Bidding Agreements) Acts 1927 and 1969[16]

The key sections of these Acts (as amended) run as follows.

Auctions (Bidding Agreements) Act 1927

> 1. *Certain bidding agreements to be illegal*
> (1) If any dealer agrees to give, or gives, or offers any gift or consideration to any other person as an inducement or reward for abstaining, or for having abstained, from bidding at a sale by auction either generally or for any particular lot, or if any person agrees to accept, or accepts, or attempts to obtain from any dealer any such gift or consideration as aforesaid, he shall be guilty of an offence under this Act, and shall be liable on summary conviction to a fine not exceeding [the statutory maximum], or to a term of imprisonment for any period not exceeding six months, or to both such fine and imprisonment:

14 See above, n 12.
15 See above, n 12.
16 See Appendix 2 for full text.

Provided that, where it is proved that a dealer has previously to an auction entered into an agreement in writing with one or more persons to purchase goods at the auction bona fide on a joint account and has before the goods were purchased at the auction deposited a copy of the agreement with the auctioneer, such an agreement shall not be treated as an agreement made in contravention of this section.

3. *Copy of Act to be exhibited at sale*
The particulars which, under s 7 of the Auctioneers Act 1845, are required to be affixed or suspended in some conspicuous part of the room or place where the auction is held shall include a copy of this Act, and that section shall have effect accordingly.

Auctions (Bidding Agreements) Act 1969

2. *Persons convicted not to attend or participate in auctions*
(1) On any such summary conviction or conviction on indictment as is mentioned in s 1 above,[17] the court may order that the person so convicted or that the person and any representative of him shall not (without leave of the court) for a period from the date of such conviction —
(a) in the case of a summary conviction, of not more than one year, or
(b) in the case of a conviction on indictment, of not more than three years,
enter upon any premises where goods intended for sale by auction are on display or to attend or participate in any way in any sale by auction.

(2) In the event of a contravention of an order under this section, the person who contravenes it (and, if he is the representative of another, that other also) shall be guilty of an offence and liable —
(a) on summary conviction, to a fine not exceeding [the statutory maximum];
(b) on conviction on indictment, to imprisonment for a term not exceeding two years or to a fine or to both.

(3) In any proceedings against a person in respect of a contravention of an order under this section consisting in the entry upon premises where goods intended for sale by auction were on display, it shall be a defence for him to prove that he did not know, and had no reason to suspect, that goods so intended were on display on the premises, and in any proceedings against a person in respect of a contravention of such an order consisting in his having done something as the representative of another, it shall be a defence for him to prove that he did not know, and had no reason to suspect, that that other was the subject of such an order.

(4) Any person shall not be guilty of an offence under this section by reason only of his selling property by auction or causing it to be so sold.

Notes

(a) In England and Wales, a prosecution for an offence under s 1 of the Auctions (Bidding Agreements) Act 1927 cannot be instituted without the consent of the Attorney-General or the Solicitor-General (s 1(3)).

(b) Section 2 of the 1927 Act enabled vendors to treat sales the subject matter

17 See Appendix 2.

of a conviction under s 1 as induced by fraud. As from the commencement of the 1969 Act, s 3 thereof substitutes the simpler remedy of allowing affected purchasers to avoid the contract without the necessity for a conviction (for full text, see Appendix 2).

(c) By s 1(1) of the Auctions (Bidding Agreements) Act 1969, offences under the 1927 Act are also triable on indictment and the penalty on conviction on indictment is imprisonment not exceeding two years or a fine or both.

(d) The reference in s 3 of the 1927 Act to s 7 of the Auctioneers Act 1845 is to the requirement which states that, 'if any auctioneer... begins any auction or acts as auctioneer at any auction at any room or place where his name and residence is not painted, printed or written on a ticket or board affixed or suspended as required by this section, an offence is committed. The penalty is not exceeding level 2 on the standard scale' (Auctioneers Act 1845, s 7, as amended by the Criminal Law Act 1977, s 31, and Criminal Justice Act 1982, s 46, discussed further in ch 2).

(e) Section 4 of the Auctions (Bidding Agreements) Act 1969 requires a copy of that Act also to be displayed.

(f) The subject matter of s 1 of the 1927 Act is 'any dealer'. A 'dealer' is a person who in the normal course of his business attends sale by auction for the purposes of purchasing goods with a view to reselling them (s 1(2)).

(g) The 'statutory maximum' fine is in 1985 £2000, but this sum may be altered from time to time by virtue of the Magistrates' Courts Act 1980, s 32, and the Criminal Justice Act 1982, s 74.

Interpretation of the statutory provisions

Section 1 of the Auctions (Bidding Agreements) Act 1927 poses a number of difficulties. Section 1(1) clearly imposes the giving of consideration of some kind by one person to another as an inducement to the latter for abstaining, or having abstained, from bidding. Presumably most auction-ring agreements or arrangements involve: (a) an understanding as to which member should bid, (b) an understanding that the other members should not bid, and (c) an understanding as to the maximum bid that should be offered. It is probable that this mutual exchange of implied promises constitutes consideration within the group. It has been pointed out that on the analogy of criminal conspiracy, there need be proof of no more than a 'tacit understanding between conspirators as to what should be done'.[18]

The second difficulty is the interpretation of the proviso as to the registration of partnership agreements. Clearly if there is a genuine partnership it would be nonsensical to treat this partnership as an illegal ring. On the other hand the Act implicitly distinguishes the genuine partnership from the ad hoc arrangement between rival dealers which may be arrived at to form a ring at an individual auction. The economic consequences of the ring are essentially

18 ATH Smith 'Auction Rings' [1981] Crim LR 86 at 88. But proving 'inducement' may be a problem.

the same as those which would accrue to a genuine partnership — i e the partners have a share in the accretion of value. On the other hand, in a genuine partnership, this accretion of value would only be arrived at on the eventual resale of the item from a partnership to an outsider. In a ring, the accretion occurs at an intermediate stage, and it is this accretion which, it can be argued, really belongs to the seller at the auction. The proviso to s 1 adopts the fairly blunt weapon of excluding from the provisions of s 1 the case where a dealer has previously to an auction entered into an agreement in writing with one or more persons to purchase goods at the auction bona fide on a joint account. Before the goods are purchased he is required to deposit a copy of the agreement with the auctioneer. Presumably only where such an agreement is in *writing* can it be exempted from its prima facie illegality if the further condition relating to its deposit is fulfilled. This could, however, result in the rather ludicrous situation of two longstanding partners attending the same auction without thinking of entering into any written agreement relating to their activity at that particular auction, not bidding against each other, and subsequently apparently committing a criminal offence since the consideration for the passive partner's non-participation is the prospect of a share in the resultant profit on sale of the item.

Possible reform

The fact that two successful prosecutions have been known to have been brought demonstrates that the offence is not 'only ever honoured in its breach'.[19] However, there remain formidable difficulties in the way of the prosecutor, and the event of two successful prosecutions since 1927 hardly inspires confidence that the Auction (Bidding Agreements) Acts 1927 and 1969 are effective in protecting the public from auction rings, if it is desired to do so.

There is an argument of policy that auction rings should be recognised as legal. Provided the seller fixes a realistic reserve, this is his primary insurance in not parting with his goods at a gross undervalue. Furthermore, the fact that a ring is operating does not necessarily mean that a satisfactory price was not obtained. It must be a matter of fortune as to whether there is a rival ring, an individual dealer or a private collector who is prepared to bid the goods up. Furthermore, dealers must be allowed to exploit their expertise and recognition of a valuable piece lying undiscovered by other experts is all part of the trade.

On the other hand, it can be argued, the existence of auction rings threatens to bring the auction process into considerable disrepute when private sellers subsequently find their goods resold at a hugely inflated price. It is patently in the auctioneer's own interests that this practice is at least regulated. One suggestion for reforming the law is to abolish the offence created by the 1927 Act and, instead, simply direct that collective bidding is permitted, but the agreement to do so must be in writing and notified to the auctioneer. Similarly the auctioneer who has a financial stake in the article for sale should disclose this fact to those bidding. The alternative would be to abolish the offence

19 See ATH Smith 'Auction Rings' [1981] Crim LR 86 at 91.

altogether but also to enforce the registration of 'ring' partnerships as restrictive practices and for this registration to be well publicised. The public dislike of rings might well discourage their ready formation if the necessity to register were better enforced.

OTHER DISHONEST PRACTICES AT AUCTIONS

It goes without saying that fraud by the auctioneer or his staff which adversely affects his principal, the seller, involves a breach of the civil fiduciary duty owed by agent to principal (fully discussed in ch 5). The question arising here is whether any fraudulent practices that might occur constitute *criminal* offences.

We will not spend much space here discussing the more obvious case of theft by someone if the principal's (or purchaser's) property is stolen from the auction premises. A person is guilty of theft if he dishonestly appropriates property belonging to another with the intention of permanently depriving the other of it.[20] 'Belonging' is widely defined in s 5 (1) of the Theft Act 1968 as including 'belonging to any person having possession or control of it or having in it any proprietary right or interest'. Section 5 (3) specifically states that where a bailee is under an obligation to deal with goods in a particular way, the property is regarded (as against him) as belonging to the bailor, but for technical reasons the auctioneer-bailee who steals his principal-bailor's goods is regarded as being within s 5 (1) above, since the principal is still the proprietary owner. In the auction-room, however, if a *third party* steals a particular lot before the auction takes place, the theft is the loss of the vendor. If the theft takes place after the sale, the loss is likely to fall upon the purchaser. The owner who is unable to recover his property will be advised to scrutinise the Conditions of Sale carefully. A typical one reads: 'Until sold, each lot shall be at the Vendor's risk and it shall be his duty to preserve the same. After the fall of the hammer such risk and duty shall devolve upon the Purchaser'.[1] Assuming the validity of this type of condition, whether the owner recovers his loss may depend upon whether he has effected insurance cover. This can sometimes be the case under an ordinary domestic chattels policy; in other cases the auction-house will effect cover for the vendor, charging him with the premium. It is usual for such insurance to cover against the risks of fire, burglary and water damage but not accidental damage or breakage. It is not the usual practice to insure the property in favour of a *purchaser* during such time as the goods are at his risk.

On a more sophisticated level, the trust inherent in the auction situation can easily be abused. For example, before cataloguing, a member of the auctioneer's staff may spot an item in a deceased's estate which his expertise teaches him is of some value. If the chattel sale contains numerous miscellaneous lots, the item in question may be secreted along with other items being sold as a single lot in a container. The member of staff then agrees with a colleague that the colleague shall bid up to a certain amount for what

20 Theft Act 1968, s 1.
1 Where the theft is facilitated by the auctioneer's negligence, this type of condition is subject to the requirement of reasonableness (and is thus open to challenge on this ground) by virtue of the Unfair Contract Terms Act 1977, s 2. See also Sale of Goods Act 1979, ss 17, 18 and 20 (Appendix 2).

appears to be an uninteresting lot, and thus obtains it. If neither the deceased's executors nor the auctioneer is aware of what has been going on, the ruse will probably succeed (in the absence of a sharp-eyed competing dealer). This conduct is likely to amount to a conspiracy to defraud at common law and possibly a statutory conspiracy to obtain property by deception contrary to s 15 of the Theft Act 1968. (The secreting, itself, could also be theft.)

A point which gives rise to a great deal of difficulty (but perhaps not as much concern by auctioneers as it deserves, since the practice is widespread) is whether an offence is committed when the auctioneer secures a higher price for a lot by taking imaginary bids 'off the wall'.

Assuming that a right to bid on behalf of the vendor has been properly provided for in the Conditions of Sale (and in the case of goods if such has not been notified to a buyer he may set the sale aside as fraudulent), what is the position when the auctioneer takes such imaginary bids? The auctioneer will doubtless assert that he is merely exercising the right to bid; but the better opinion is that this practice may, in appropriate circumstances, constitute the offence of 'obtaining property by deception'. Direct authority for this is somewhat lacking no doubt in part due to the formidable difficulties of proof involved.

Obtaining property by deception is defined by s 15 of the Theft Act 1968 as follows:

> (1) A person who by any deception dishonestly obtains property belonging to another, with the intention of permanently depriving the other of it, shall on conviction on indictment be liable to imprisonment for a term not exceeding ten years.
>
> (2) For purposes of this section a person is to be treated as obtaining property if he obtains ownership, possession or control of it, and 'obtain' includes obtaining for another or enabling another to obtain or to retain.
>
> (3) Section 6 shall apply for purposes of this section with the necessary adaptation of the reference to appropriating, as it applies for purposes of section 1.
>
> (4) For purposes of this section 'deception' means any deception (whether deliberate or reckless) by words or conduct as to fact or as to law, including a deception as to the present intentions of the person using the deception or any other person.

In this section 'property' is defined as including money,[2] and the meaning of 'belonging to another' is discussed above. Section 6 enlarges the natural meaning of the phrase 'intention of permanently depriving'.

Of the various elements of the offence, firstly there is a 'deception' if the successful bidder is misled by the conduct of the auctioneer so as to believe that he is bidding against genuine competition; and secondly, in these circumstances the deception is undoubtedly deliberate. Thirdly, the deception affects property of another, i e the successful bidder's money. Fourthly, the

2 See Theft Act 1968, s 4.

defendant obtains that property from the successful purchaser. Two further elements must be shown: the obtaining must have arisen as a result of the deception and, finally, the obtaining must be dishonest and accompanied by an intention to deprive the owner permanently. These latter two important aspects require some elaboration.[3]

Causation

Whether the deception causes the obtaining depends upon the circumstances. If, for example, to take the simplest case, an auctioneer takes bids 'off the wall' and a single bidder, X, then successfully enters a bid, there is only one link in the chain and the deception clearly operates to trigger the successful bid at the higher price. Where, however, there are other intervening bids the postion is more doubtful: suppose the auctioneer take a fictitious bid which is followed by a bid from X; Y then bids higher and X ultimately over-tops this bid and the property is knocked down to him. Here it is much less clear that, as a matter of law, the auctioneer's deception will be said to have operated so as to obtain X's successful bid. Arguably, the intervention of Y renders the causation chain broken.

It is no answer for the auctioneer to protest that had he not taken bids 'off the wall', the reserve would not have been reached and that therefore the highest bidder would have been unsuccessful. If the buyer has as a result been persuaded to pay more than he otherwise would, or if the false appearance of competition has led him to buy when otherwise he would not have done so at all, his money (or some of it) will have been obtained by deception. But the question remains whether the actions of the auctioneer are dishonest.

Dishonesty

Dishonesty is a question of fact for the jury to decide. There are two elements to be satisfied:[4]

(a) the conduct must be such that it would be regarded as dishonest by ordinary standards of honest and reasonable people, *and*
(b) the defendant must appreciate that his conduct is so regarded.

Given this test, it is impossible to say with regard to any individual situation whether in taking bids 'off the wall' the auctioneer has acted dishonestly. Where the auctioneer has been instructed to bid on behalf of the vendor — and his right to do so has been properly notified to the public via the Conditions of Sale[5] (as required by s 57 of the Sale of Goods Act 1979 and the somewhat similar but less clear provisions of the Sale of Land by Auction Act 1867) — he may believe that the taking of bids in this way is a proper mode of bidding

3 See further on the elements of this offence in Glanville Williams *Textbook of Criminal Law* (2nd edn, 1983) Stevens, ch 34. The Sale of Goods Act 1979, s 57(4), makes it clear that it is only where such a right to bid for the seller is reserved that the seller may bid himself or employ someone to bid. This right cannot therefore be implied from the mere existence of a reserve. See further on this point *Gilliat v Gilliat* (1869) LR 9 Eq 60, 39 LJ Ch 142.

4 *R v Ghosh* [1982] QB 1053, [1982] 2 All ER 689, CA.

5 See e g Christie's General Condition 4.

for his client. If the 'reasonable man' does not, or the auctioneer does not appreciate that the reasonable man does, in fact, regard this as an improper method of bidding for the vendor, it will not be dishonest.

That the taking of bids 'off the wall' is a proper method of bidding in such circumstances, is supported by the views of the Director General of Fair Trading who in a press release of 29 October 1980 said:[6]

> Another man spends more on a car than intended because of brisk bidding only to discover later that he has been the only genuine bidder because the auctioneer has included the right to bid on behalf of the vendor in his Conditions of Auction and has been — quite legally — inventing other bids to push up the prices.

No doubt this 'official' acceptance of the practice will fortify auctioneers. However, in the absence of a genuinely held belief that the public regard it as honest, an auctioneer remains in our view potentially liable criminally under s 15 of the Theft Act 1968.[7]

If there is no successful bidder because, despite the 'puffing', the reserve is never reached, presumably the auctioneer could be convicted of an *attempt* to obtain property by deception.

Given these uncertainties, the safer course for the auctioneer to adopt is to state at the beginning that anyone interested must start the bidding at the price he stipulates, being the reserve. Although there is evidence that a few auctioneers do adopt this practice, clearly a majority do not since they regard it as in the vendor's interest to lend impetus to the bidding by starting at a bargain figure below the reserve.

If the sale is without reserve, the commission of the offence is much clearer.[8] Additionally, a seller who runs up the price by bidding without reserving his right to do so under s 57 of the Sale of Goods Act 1979 commits a similar offence if the property is sold — otherwise this could again amount to an attempt.

FALSE TRADE DESCRIPTIONS

Descriptions of lots in catalogues supplied by the auctioneer to bidders are of such critical importance that the topic deserves a section to itself. There seems to be evidence of 'folklore' in at least some auctioneering circles that

6 OFT, London EC4A 1PR

7 The Theft Act 1968, s 2(1), states, inter alia, that appropriation of another's property is not to be regarded as dishonest if the defendant appropriates the property in the belief that he has a claim of right in law to deprive the other of it. This refers to a belief in a claim of right under the civil law, not a mistake as to the effect of the *criminal* law. If the auctioneer genuinely believes that taking bids off the wall constitutes an appropriate manner of bidding for his vendor, such a belief, whilst possibly negativing dishonesty, would not amount to a belief in a claim of right under this section. See further on s 2, Glanville Williams, *Textbook of Criminal Law* (2nd edn) p 724.

8 In addition the auctioneer will have committed the civil tort of deceit and will be liable to the purchaser for damages. These would presumably be measured by the difference between the hammer price and the price at which the bidder would otherwise have been successful. If the deception operates to induce a person to buy when otherwise he would not have done so at all, the damages are prima facie the amount by which the value of the item is less than the sum paid for it.

auctioneers are somehow exempt from the penal provisions of, in particular, the Trade Decriptions Act 1968.[9] This is completely untrue and a recent, successful and much publicised prosecution under this Act of a well known and respected firm of Midlands auctioneers has perhaps done something to dispel the myth.

The section most likely to catch a false description of goods specified in a sale catalogue is s 1(1) of the Trade Descriptions Act 1968, which runs as follows:

> Any person who in the course of a trade or business
> (a) applies a false trade description to any goods; or
> (b) supplies or offers to supply any goods to which a false trade description is applied, shall, subject to the provisions of this Act, be guilty of an offence.

The clearest way in which this provision can be explained in the context of the Act as a whole,[10] and its applicability to auctioneers considered, is to postulate an imaginary case not noticeably dissimilar to that successfully prosecuted as mentioned above.

Let us assume that an auction of chattels includes a lot thus described: 'A 17th-Century 17″ × 10″ oak joint stoool with plain frieze raised on four turned baluster supports and plain cross stretchers'. The 'Standard Conditions of Sale' at the end of the catalogue (purchase price £1) state, inter alia, that 'Neither the Auctioneer nor the Vendor(s) are responsible for error in description, authenticity, or genuineness of any lot or for any fault or defect in it, giving no warranty whatsoever, the Buyers being held to have satisfied themselves as to the condition, quantity, quality and description of the lots before bidding.'

On the basis of the catalogue description a private buyer, who states that he buys antiques occasionally at auctions for investment, purchases the item for £200.[11] The facts are investigated by the local trading standards department which ascertains the following:

(a) The buyer, on trying to resell the stool to raise some money urgently, is told that it is a twentieth-century copy. This view is supported by two written statements from expert antique dealers who also state that any expert would recognise the item as a copy for various technical reasons. Its value is put at £40.

(b) On investigating the firm, it is found that a partner, AB, is responsible for chattel auctions, but the description was written by an employee who actively conducted the auction. This employee, CD, has some years of experience but admits to relatively little knowledge in some areas where it is sometimes the practice, if in doubt, to obtain an outside expert opinion. This did not occur here.

9 Relevant sections of this legislation are reproduced in Appendix 2.

10 The Trade Descriptions Act 1968 is much more extensively explained and analysed in e g Harvey *The Law of Consumer Protection and Fair Trading* (2nd edn, 1982) Butterworths. See also O'Keefe *The Law Relating to Trade Descriptions* (2nd edn) Butterworths.

11 It in fact makes no difference whether the buyer is a private one or a dealer. The Trade Descriptions Act 1968 applies equally with regard to sales to businessmen. Nor is it a defence that an experienced dealer should not have been deceived, even was not actually deceived — see *Chidwick v Beer* (1974) 138 JP Jo 210 (QBD).

The trading standards office in question then decide to bring two charges, one against the partner and one against the firm's employee, as follows:

(i) On the...day of...at..., AB, a partner in the firm of..., in the course of a business as auctioneers, supplied to [the buyer] a stool to which a false trade description, namely, [as per catalogue] was applied by means of a catalogue, contrary to s 1(1)(b) of the Trade Descriptions Act 1968

(ii) On the...day of...at...,CD, in the course of business as an auctioneer, applied by means of a catalogue a false trade description, namely, [as per catalogue] to a stool, contrary to s 1(1)(a) of the Trade Descriptions Act 1968.

Possible defences

The two defendants, the partner AB and the employee-auctioneer CD, then have to consider their possible defences. In common with many other commercial criminal statutes, the offence in issue here is one of strict liability. There can therefore be no defence that there was no intention to misdescribe (i e no *mens rea*). The offence will be found proved if in the course of a trade or business a false trade description was actually applied to goods, or goods were 'supplied' (a wider expression than 'sold' and one which includes sales by an agent auctioneer to a buyer)[12] to which a false trade description has been applied and the defendant cannot avail himself of one of the statutory defences considered next. Any doubt in a particular case as to whether a description is false, and there can be no doubt on the facts being considered, may be resolved by reference to s 3(1) of the Trade Descriptions Act 1968 which states that a false trade description is a trade description which is 'false to a material degree' or is similarly misleading (s 3(2)).

The first possible defence is that of 'disclaimer'. Over a series of cases predominantly concerning cars with false odometer readings, it has been held by the courts technically possible to negate a false trade description applied to goods by disclaiming the accuracy of that description. The catalogue here does indeed contain such a disclaimer. However the courts have held, that, to be effective, a disclaimer:[13]

> must be as bold, precise and compelling as the trade description itself and must be as effectively brought to the notice of any person to whom the goods may be supplied. In other words, the disclaimer must equal the trade description to the extent to which it is likely to get home to anyone interested in receiving the goods.

Thus a second-hand car may have its false odometer reading zeroised or completely obscured by a notice. There are powerful limitations on the effectiveness of this doctrine. One is that once a trade description has been communicated, a casual remark or 'small print' in a document are not enough to disclaim it.[14] Furthermore, it has been emphasised in two recent cases[15] that

12 In *British Car Auctions Ltd v Wright* [1972] 3 All ER 462, [1972] 1 WLR 1519 it was held that auctioneers did not 'offer to sell' unroadworthy cars contrary to the Road Traffic Act 1960, s 68. But they would undoubtedly have 'supplied' the vehicles.

13 *Norman v Bennett* [1974] 3 All ER 351 at 354 per Widgery LCJ.

14 See generally *R v Hammertons Cars Ltd* [1976] 3 All ER 758, [1976] 1 WLR 1243, CA; *R v McMillan Aviation Ltd and McMillan* [1981] Crim LR 785.

15 See *Corfield v Starr* [1981] RTR 380; *Hackney London Borough v Measureworth Ltd & Newman* [1981] Crim LR 503 (affirmed by Div Ct (1981) 80 LGR 611, [1982] RTR 296).

a person cannot normally actively falsely describe goods and then purport to disclaim the descriptions — i e disclaim his own fraud.

So, applying these principles to the facts, the partner AB might consider claiming that the Condition of Sale negating misdescriptions disclaimed the false trade description applied by his employee, but since 'small print' of this sort is unlikely to be held to be as 'bold, precise and compelling' as the catalogue description, AB would be unlikely to be successful in sheltering behind such a disclaimer. It would not appear to be an available defence to the employee CD who actually applied the false trade description, since one cannot disclaim one's own wrong. In fact, the standard Conditions of Sale in question may well have been prefaced by a statement along the following lines:

> Care is taken to ensure that any statement as to authorisation, attribution, origin, state, age, provenance and condition is reliable and accurate but all such statements are statements of opinion and are not to be taken as statements or representations of fact. The auctioneers reserve the right in forming their opinion to consult and rely upon any expert or authority reasonably considered by them to be reliable.

If this can be regarded as an additional disclaimer, it will stand or fall with the one already considered. It may, in any event, be regarded as itself a false description as to services (contrary to s 14 of the Trade Descriptions Act 1968) if it is known that no care to verify the description of the stool was taken, and can therefore be a double-edged sword.[16] Section 14 of the Trade Descriptions Act 1968 states that it is an offence for any person in the course of any trade or business: (a) to make a statement which he knows to be false; or (b) recklessly to make a statement which is false as to a specified number of matters including 'the provision in the course of any trade or business of any services, accommodation or facilities,' or the nature of any such services, or 'the examination, approval or evaluation by any person of any services, accommodation or facilities so provided.' Although the offence requires knowledge of the falsity or recklessness, 'recklessly' has been defined by the courts to catch the trader who does not have regard to the truth or falsity of the statement even though it could not be shown that he was deliberately closing his eyes to the truth, or that he had any kind of dishonest intention.[17]

In *Zawadski v Sleigh*[18] it was accepted that it was *possible* for an auctioneer to make a disclaimer on his own behalf — a rather similar one to that in the above example being set out in Conditions of Sale relating to a car auction — but the court did not authoritatively discuss the issue which it regarded as irrelevant. The case was concerned with the correctness of the conviction of the principal-sellers of the cars which had false odometer readings. The court stated that it was not relevant to ask whether such disclaimer was made on behalf of the auctioneers alone or on behalf of both agent and principal. The only test was whether the disclaimer was effective, i e 'potent enough to get through to the buyer and make him disregard the message which the odometer had previously passed on to him.'[19]

16 See *Corfield v Starr*, n 15 above.

17 See *MFI Warehouses Ltd v Nattrass* [1973] 1 All ER 762, [1973] 1 WLR 307, DC. Section 14 is of importance in the auction business in any circumstances where statements are made, in the catalogue or otherwise, as to the quality of the *service* provided, including the care with which goods are described.

18 [1975] RTR 113, DC. See also for another case where a car auction was indirectly relevant, *Tarleton Engineering Co Ltd v Nattrass* [1973] 3 All ER 699, [1973] 1 WLR 1261.

19 [1975] RTR 113 at 118 per Lord Widgery.

The doctrine of 'disclaimer' has been developed by the courts — there is no guidance on it in the Act itself. The fundamental principle is that if the stringent criteria laid down by the courts are met, a false trade description has never been applied at all, and there is therefore no possible mischief to which the Act's provisions can apply.

Mistake, accident etc

The Trade Descriptions Act 1968 does, however, give to the defendant a two-limbed defence designed to mitigate the underlying no-fault liability imposed by s 1 and s 11, relating to goods and prices respectively. (Section 14, as has been explained, does require knowledge of recklessness in relation to false trade descriptions of services.)

This two-limbed defence is contained in the Trade Descriptions Act 1968, s 24, a section which to a greater or lesser extent appears in many other criminal provisions relating to commerce. It runs:

> 24. *Defence of mistake, accident, etc.*
> (1) In any proceedings for an offence under this Act it shall, subject to subsection (2) of this section, be a defence for the person charged to prove —
> (a) that the commission of the offence was due to a mistake or to reliance on information supplied to him or to the act or default of another person, an accident or some other cause beyond his control; and
> (b) that he took all reasonable precautions and exercised all due diligence to avoid the commission of such an offence by himself or any person under his control.
>
> (2) If in any case the defence provided by the last foregoing subsection involves the allegation that the commission of the offence was due to the act or default of another person or to reliance on information supplied by another person, the person charged shall not, without leave of the court, be entitled to rely on that defence unless, within a period ending seven clear days before the hearing, he has served on the prosecutor a notice in writing giving such information identifying or assisting in the identification of that other person as was then in his possession.
>
> (3) In any proceedings for an offence under this Act of supplying or offering to supply goods to which a false trade description is applied it shall be a defence for the person charged to prove that he did ot know, and could not with reasonable diligence have ascertained, that the goods did not conform to the description or that the description had been applied to the goods.

The defence involves the *defendant's* successfully proving, on the balance of probabilities,[20] that the defendant's commission of the offence was due to (a) a mistake, or (b) reliance on information supplied to him, or (c) the act or default of another person, or an accident or some other course beyond his control, *and* (in any of these cases) he *both* took all reasonable precautions *and* exercised all due diligence to avoid the commission of such an offence by himself or any person under his control.

20 See *McGuire v Sittingbourne Co-operative Society Ltd* (1976) 140 JP 306, 120 Sol Jo 197.

There are additional points to note. Subsection (2) imposes a pre-condition to relying on pinning the blame on a third party which is self-explanatory. Subsection (3) supplies an additional defence which could be relevant to the auctioneer. Thus, if he offers goods in a chattel sale which bear false or misleading labels or some other false trade description of which he was unaware and could not with *reasonable* diligence have ascertained, this subsection supplies a defence. But it should be noted carefully that the trade description must have been affixed by someone else. When the defendant has himself falsely described the goods in his auction catalogue, the charge would be under s 1(1)(a) of the Trade Descriptions Act 1968, applying a false trade description in the active sense, as opposed to under s 1(1)(b), supplying all goods to which a false trade description is applied, in the passive sense. A comparison of the two specimen charges against CD and AB above reveals these respective differences.

There have been many judicial statements on the precise meaning of s 24 of the Trade Descriptions Act 1968. The following are the main points of possible relevance to auctioneers:

(a) Mistake. This must be that of the person charged, not that of an employee or third party.[1]

(b) 'Reliance upon information supplied to him'. This is particularly relevant where an auctioneer seeks to rely on reproducing the vendor's description as in the entry form.[2] Reliance cannot be 'blind'. It must be capable of being judged as coming from an informed source which a responsible person would accept and which would stand up to reasonable checking out.[3]

(c) 'The act or default of another person'. In *Tesco Supermarkets Ltd v Nattrass*,[4] it was held that a shop manager employed by the defendant was 'another person'. He was not sufficiently senior to be the *ego* or *alter ego* of the company, which could therefore pin the blame on its subordinate successfully *provided* it could also comply with the second limb of the section and show that its supervisory and training system was such that it could be said to have taken all the precautions to avoid the commission of an offence and shown all due diligence in making the system work (which was held to be the case here). This defence would be much less likely to succeed in the case of auctioneers practising from one place (or a small number of places) where whilst it is conceivable that an employee responsible for the offence might be regarded as 'another person' from the auctioneering firm, the duty of close and effective supervision is such as to make it unlikely to allow its breakdown to be regarded is consistent with due diligence. In any case where the defence is pleaded, the 'other person' must be identified.[5]

1 *Birkenhead and District Co-operative Society Ltd v Roberts* [1970] 3 All ER 391, [1970] 1 WLR 1497.

2 If this practice is followed, e g in car auctions, trading standards departments are in practice much less likely to prosecute. Such prosecution in any event requires the prior notification of the Director General of Fair Trading under s 130 of the Fair Trading Act 1973. However, the legal basis for this policy seems tenuous, as explained in the text. It would be better to regard such auctioneers as having a better chance of successfully using the defence in the Trade Descriptions Act 1968, s 24(3), as also explained.

3 See e g *Barker v Hargreaves* (1981) 125 Sol Jo 165, [1981] RTR 197 (MOT certificate bearing printed warning not sufficient); also *Sutton London Borough v Perry Sanger & Co Ltd* (1971) 135 JP Jo 239 (information relied upon did not stand up to checking out). Note also the *additional* requirement of 'due diligence' in the second limb.

4 [1972] AC 153, [1971] 2 All ER 127, HL.

5 *McGuire v Sittingbourne Co-operative Society Ltd* (1976) 140 JP 306, 120 Sol Jo 197.

(d) 'An accident' etc. There is little authority on this, but it must clearly be something so unexpected that normal precautions would not have prevented it.

(e) 'All reasonable precautions and exercised all due diligence'. The meaning of these joint requirements has already been indicated under (c) above. The many authorities[6] stress the need for an efficient system actively operated to prevent the offences arising. Thus where watch retailers sold a 'waterproof' watch which filled with water after immersion in a bowl for one hour, it was held when they were charged with selling goods to which a false trade description was applied that they had not taken all due precautions and exercised all due diligence within s 24 (1)(b). No precautions at all had been exercised, such as dipping the watch in water. The retailer had simply relied on the wholesaler's reputation.[7] On the other hand, if an auctioneer is selling a quantity of used watches some of which may be described on the watch case as 'waterproof', the auctioneer might rely instead on the defence in s 24(3) (discussed above). But this would only cover him if he *himself* had not applied the false trade description — e g by a catalogue description 'waterproof watch'.

Though not strictly another defence, it must be noted for the sake of completeness that s 23 makes provision for any third party whose act or default has caused the commission of the offence to be charged instead of or jointly with the original defendant.

Applying the various principles explained in the points above, to the example charges against AB and CD, it seems most unlikely that any statement in the Conditions of Sale would be regarded as a disclaimer. The catalogue description of the lot clearly conveys the false description, and even if the General Conditions are as 'bold, precise and compelling' or as 'potent' as that unequivocal description of the soi-disant seventeenth-century stool, the courts are increasingly tending to deny the possibility of a disclaimer where the defendant has himself applied the false trade description, as is the case with CD, the actual cataloguer and auctioneer. Furthermore, s 24 offers neither defendant much comfort in this situation. Even if a mistake etc could be proved, the evidence showed a lack of any reasonable precautions and due diligence, in that no outside expert opinion was taken. In the case on which the example is founded,[8] the equivalents of AB and CD both pleaded guilty in the event. They were each fined £100 and ordered to pay compensation to the buyer and to pay costs. The case received considerable publicity.

We cannot leave this critical matter without failing to qualify any impression that such cases are necessarily as straightforward as the above. Where reputable auctioneers undertake to sell specialist items such as old master paintings or musical instruments there is normally at least one member of staff highly qualified to assess items or, at least, available for consultation. In order to accommodate doubts, the practice of Sotheby's in their musical instruments catalogue is to include a preliminary Glossary. It is explained that an instrument described as 'by' a named maker means that 'the instrument is in

6 See O'Keefe *The Law Relating to Trade Descriptions* (2nd edn) Butterworths, (3) 250 f.
7 *Sherratt v Geralds the American Jewellers Ltd* (1970) 114 Sol Jo 147, 68 LGR 256, DC.
8 See p 149, above.

our opinion of the named maker'. Thereafter progressive degrees of doubt are conveyed by the expressions 'ascribed to', 'attributed to', 'School of', 'Workshop of', and 'labelled' — 'the instrument is not in our opinion by the maker indicated'.[9]

Should it occur that a buyer can establish that such an item has been misattributed in the catalogue,[10] it is thought that the defence of 'mistake' etc together with proof of having taken 'all reasonable precautions and exercised all due diligence' is readily available. In addition many auctioneers include a general condition to the effect that any lot which proves to be a 'deliberate forgery' (as defined in those conditions) may be returned within a specified time (e g five years) to the auctioneers and the sale may then be set aside and the money refunded to the buyer (see e g Sotheby's Condition 16). Whilst this does not in fact negate a trade descriptions offence if committed, it nevertheless renders prosecution unlikely if the buyer is treated fairly.

There are other offences akin to those provided by the Trade Descriptions Act. An example is afforded by the Hallmarking Act 1973, s 1(1) of which provides as follows:

> Subject to the provisions of this Act, any person who, in the course of a trade or business —
> (a) applies to an unhallmarked article a description indicating that it is wholly or partly made of gold, silver or platinum, or
> (b) supplies, or offers to supply, an unhallmarked article to which such a description is applied,
> shall be guilty of an offence.

It has recently been decided in *Chilvers v Rayner*[11] that this offence, like that provided by s 1(1) of the Trade Descriptions Act 1968, is an absolute one and that the honest belief that the article was hallmarked is no defence. It should be pointed out that in the Hallmarking Act 1973 there is no equivalent to s 24 of the Trade Descriptions Act 1968.

PROHIBITION ON SALES

Whereas the Trade Descriptions Act 1968 and the Hallmarking Act 1973 are aimed essentially at false descriptions, there is in addition a number of statutes which create offences in respect of *what* is sold or to *whom*. A comprehensive treatment of these is beyond the scope of this book, but one or two examples may be mentioned.

Wild birds, animals and endangered species

The sale or the offering or exposing for sale of certain live or dead wild birds or part of such or their eggs is made a criminal offence by s 6 of the Wildlife and

9 See also Christie's Notice, para 4, below p 233. For a fuller account of the difficulties of attributing stringed instruments and possible contraventions of the Trade Descriptions Act 1968, see Brian Harvey 'Violin Frauds, Fakes and Misdescriptions' (1982) 93 The Strad 93f.

10 This is often difficult, since it involves one expert opinion against another. In the case of antique items the judge can legitimately ask the dissenting expert, 'Were you there when it was made?'

11 [1984] 1 All ER 843, [1984] 1 WLR 328.

Countryside Act 1981. The relevant birds are listed in Sch 3 to the Act. Similarly, by s 9, it is an offence to sell or to offer or expose for sale or to possess those wild animals, whether live or dead, listed in Sch 5 to the Act.

As regards the import or export of certain species, the Endangered Species (Import and Export) Act 1976, as amended by the Wildlife and Countryside Act 1981, restricts the import and export of certain animals and plants and renders it an offence to sell or offer or expose them for sale to the public unless they have been imported or exported in accordance with the terms of a licence.

The main difficulty with these offences may lie simply in identification. The average auctioneer may have difficulty in successfully identifying the particular item concerned. He would be wise to take expert advice.

Firearms

Somewhat less esoteric (since there is an established auction tradition in this area) but at least as problematic, may be the legislation relating to the sale of firearms. The possession and sale of firearms is now largely controlled by the Firearms Act 1968.[12] Section 1 of the Act provides that it is an offence to possess certain firearms without a firearms certificate. Section 3 provides two separate offences:

> (1) A person commits an offence if, by way of trade or business he —
>
> (a) manufactures, sells, transfers,...any firearm or ammunition to which section 1 of this Act applies, or a shotgun; or
> (b) exposes for sale or transfer or has in his possession for sale, transfer,...any such firearm or ammunition or a shotgun,
>
> without being registered under this Act as a firearms dealer.
>
> (2) It is an offence for a person to sell or transfer to any other person in the United Kingdom, other than a registered firearms dealer, any firearm or ammunition to which section 1 of this Act applies, or a shotgun, unless that other produces a firearms certificate authorising him to purchase or acquire it or, as the case may be, his shotgun certificate, or shows that he is by virtue of this Act entitled to purchase or acquire it without holding a certificate.

Thus it is an offence to sell etc any firearm[13] or shotgun without being registered as a dealer. An auctioneer can quite easily guard against commission of this offence by being so registered. Moreover, if he is not a regular seller of such chattels, he is protected under s 9 of the Firearms Act 1968: first as regards *possession* in the ordinary course of business, and second as regards *sale* or *exposure for sale* even if he is not so registered if he follows the expedient of obtaining a permit therefor from the Chief Officer of Police for the Area.

The real difficulty lies with s 1(2) of the Firearms Act 1968, in that it is an offence to sell *to* anyone other than a dealer unless that other holds a certificate authorising him to purchase the weapon. Under the Sale of Goods Act 1979

12 See Appendix 2.
13 Including an imitation firearm. See the Firearms Act 1982.
14 See *Dennant v Skinner and Collom* [1948] 2 KB 164, [1948] 2 All ER 29.

there is a contract of sale where under a contract the property in the goods is transferred to the buyer. However there is no sale but only an agreement to sell where the transfer of the property in the goods is to take place at a future time or subject to some condition to be fulfilled. In the absence of such pre-conditions the sale would normally be complete and the property passed to the buyer on the fall of the hammer, subsequently-imposed conditions not being effective to prevent the property in the goods passing to the buyer.[14] Most auctioneers' general conditions do provide that ownership in property is not to pass to the buyer until the full purchase price has been paid. In the case of sales of firearms and shotguns it would be expedient to include a contractual provision whereby no ownership would pass to the buyer unless and until he produces the requisite certificate.

Section 3(2) of the Firearms Act 1968 also makes it an offence to *transfer* a firearm, ammunition or a shotgun to anyone who fails to show he is entitled to purchase or acquire it. 'Transfer' is defined in s 57(4) of the Act as including 'let on hire, give lend and part with possession'. Thus it would seem that an offence is committed by an auctioneer who returns a firearm to his vendor client who has not a permit to possess it, for example, after an unsuccessful sale; in practice auctioneers should retain such unsold guns until they can find a registered dealer willing to acquire them.

Excepted from the rigors of this regulatory statute are antique firearms. Section 58(2) of the Firearms Act 1968 provides: 'Nothing in this Act relating to firearms shall apply to an antique firearm which is sold, transferred, purchased, acquired or possessed as a curiosity or ornament.' Thus it would not be an offence to sell an antique firearm for that purpose to a person who failed to produce the requisite certificate, but there are several problems with this exemption.

Honest belief irrelevant

It has been held that s 1 of the Firearms Act 1968 creates an absolute offence. That is to say that if the prosecution proves that a person has in his possession what is in fact a firearm, as defined in s 57 of the Act, then he is guilty of the offence regardless of whether he knew it was such a proscribed weapon.[15] In *R v Howells*,[16] the defendant was charged and convicted of offences under s 1 in respect of a number of firearms including a Colt .31 muzzle-loading percussion revolver which he had bought from a gun dealer as a genuine 1860 Colt. He argued, inter alia, that his conviction was wrong in that the judge had failed to direct the jury that it was a defence to a charge under s 1 if the appellant reasonably and honestly believed the firearm to be an antique and he possessed it as a curiosity or ornament. On this point the Court of Appeal upheld that conviction. The argument that the exemption provided by s 58(2)[17] was necessary to protect *bona fide* dealers and collectors of antique firearms, and that it would be substantially lost if a collector who was the genuine victim of a fake could not escape liability by showing that he honestly

15 See *R v Hussain* [1981] 2 All ER 287, [1981] 1 WLR 416, CA; *R v Howells* [1977] QB 614, [1977] 3 All ER 417, CA.
16 See n 15 above.
17 This sub-section is reproduced above and in Appendix 2.

and reasonably believed it was an antique, was rejected by the court. Brown L J said:[18]

> This sub-section relates to facts and not beliefs; what is excluded is that which is an antique which is sold or possessed as a curiosity or ornament. There is no room, in our opinion, for any other exclusions such as those firearms that are believed by the possessor to be antiques.

The court took the view that the intention of Parliament in passing this legislation was to provide an absolute prohibition against the possession of lethal firearms without proper authority, and that to allow in a defence of honest belief that the firearm was an antique would defeat this intention.

Although in this case we were concerned with an s 1 offence of possession, the same arguments apply to the offences of sale etc contained in s 3.

What is an antique?

Age

If then, whatever the state of mind or belief of an auctioneer, it is an offence to sell or transfer a firearm but there is a defence only if it is, in fact, an antique, it becomes crucially important to determine what is an antique.

Unfortunately Parliament has not seen fit to define an antique, and the judges have been loth to do so themselves. In *Richards v Curwen*[19] a defendant was charged with offences relating to his possession of two revolvers which he bought as antiques and hung on his living-room walls as ornaments. He possessed no firearms certificate for either of them. One revolver was German and had been manufactured sometime after 1891. It could be fired if the hammer was hit hard. The other was Belgian, made after 1893 and was in poor condition but could be rendered capable of being fired. The case against him was brought in 1975 but he was acquitted by the magistrates on the ground that the firearms were antiques and possessed as a curiosity or ornament. The prosecutor appealed but the Divisional Court dismissed the appeal, failing to find that the magistrates had approached the matter improperly. The proper approach in deciding whether a particular item was or was not an antique was, said the court, to recognise that it is 'a question of fact and degree in all the circumstances of the case'.[20] Referring to a dictionary definition might have been of some limited assistance, but essentially it was a matter to be decided by the magistrates or the jury charged with the responsibility of adjudicating upon matters of the fact. The judges declined to lay down what age a firearm had to be before it could be regarded as an antique. These weapons were not more than 83 and 85 years old and the court did not accept that to be antiques they needed to be 100 years old.[1]

Decisions holding firearms of that age as antiques must be treated with some caution. They cannot simply be cited as precedents in subsequent cases. In

18 [1977] QB 614 at 620, CA.
19 [1977] 3 All ER 426, [1977 1 WLR 747.
20 [1977] 3 All ER 426 at 430, [1977] 1 WLR 747 at 750, per Wien J.
1 Although it was recognised that, in auctions of furniture and china, that is generally the test.

Bennet v Brown,[2] the Divisional Court did not disturb a finding by magistrates that a revolver dated circa 1886 was an antique. But is must be stressed that in all these appeals the court's duty was to see whether the tribunal of fact had reached a conclusion properly and would only overturn it if it was felt that no reasonable bench or jury could come to that conclusion. It does not by any means follow that the court approved the finding or would itself have found the same way.[3]

Firing ability

In *Richards v Curwen*[4] both the weapons were capable of being fired. It was suggested by the prosecution that such weapons should not be regarded as antiques. This negative partial definition had been provided in s 2 of the Pistols Act 1903, a forerunner of the present Firearms Act but dropped in the Firearms Acts of 1920, 1937 and 1968. In the light of this it was not felt appropriate to adopt such a criterion.

However, usability did feature in the test of antiquity in the subsequent case of *Bennett v Brown*,[5] where the items in question were a post-1905 Mauser rifle in working order and a Mauser pistol, circa 1910, modified but capable of firing a .22 cartridge. The defendant was a genuine collector and it was found that he had these weapons for ornament. The only question was whether they were antiques. Eveleigh L J observed:[6]

> But turning to the weaponry in the present case, what does one find? One finds that the rifle was manufactured post 1905 and the pistol 1910 onwards. Both of these weapons therefore could rightly be envisaged as weapons used in the 1914-1918 war. That I think is not drawing upon any particular judicial knowledge but upon public and general knowledge. One would not expect an army to be equipped with weapons that were only manufactured some six or seven years before the war and would expect even modern armies to use weapons of much greater age than seven, eight or ten years. It seems that it would be quite impossible to say that any weapon that could reasonably be envisaged as available for use in a war in this century could be properly regarded as an antique.
>
> I therefore am of the opinion that the evidence does not support the conclusion that the 8 mm rifle and the Mauser self-loading pistol were antique within the meaning of section 58(2).

Watkins J went further:[7]

> Justices must feel entitled to receive practical guidance upon such a difficult matter as whether a firearm is deemed to be of the description antique within the meaning of that word as it is used in the Firearms Act 1968. Whilst it is not possible to be of specific assistance, which can be applied generally when asked a question of the kind that is asked in the instant case, I think this court should be able to say if not what

2 (1980) 71 Cr App Rep 109, DC.
3 See *Bennett v Brown* (1980) 71 Cr App Rep 109, DC, especially per Eveleigh J at 112.
4 [1977] 3 All ER 426, [1977] 1 WLR 747.
5 (1980) 71 Cr App Rep 109.
6 (1980) 71 Cr App Rep 109 at 112.
7 See n 6, above.

> does, then what does not make good sense in attempting to define the word antique. Thus I am prepared to say that no reasonable bench of justices could conclude, regardless of whether or not a firearm could be used in a war at any time, that a firearm which has been manufactured during this century is an antique. To that limited extent I offer with humility some assistance to justices who will continue to be faced with difficulty when called upon to decide the seemingly insoluble problem created by Parliament.

In the absence of a willingness on the part either of Parliament or of the courts to grasp this particular nettle, there is little of a positive nature which can be said about identification of antiques in this area; if it is 100 years old it will be; if it is close to that age it may be; if it has been manufactured this century it apparently will not be; and perhaps, its continuing usability as a weapon of war will militate against it being an antique. But it must be reiterated that every case will depend on its own facts and circumstances and expert evidence will be crucial. There is some burden on the defendant to raise the issue that he bought them as antiques but thereafter it is for the prosecution to establish, beyond a reasonable doubt, that they are, in fact, not antiques.[8]

'As a curiosity or ornament'

It will have been seen that for s 58(2) of the Firearms Act 1968 to afford a defence, the firearm must not only be antique but must be possessed, or as far as auctioneers are concerned, sold, as a curiosity or ornament. In *R v Howells* the judge at first instance said to the jury:[9]

> Now I'm not going to attempt to go to a dictionary and define for you what keeping something as a curiosity means and what keeping something as an ornament means. I am going to assume that you know perfectly well what it means.

It is obvious that this involves a subjective element and auctioneers might be well advised to stipulate expressly with antique firearms that they are sold for those purposes only.

Other offences

There is a number of other statutes which create offences relating to the sale of substances or goods which may be harmful:

(a) Food Act 1984, s 8 — sale of food rendered unfit for human consumption.
(b) Agriculture Act 1970, s 73 — sale of material for use as a feeding stuff which is discovered to be unwholesome or dangerous to animals or human beings.
(c) Medicines Act 1968, ss 52 and 53 — proscribing the retailing of drugs.
(d) Various Regulations made under the Consumer Protection Act 1961 and Consumer Safety Act 1978. These regulations cover a wide range of goods (e g oil heaters, toys with toxic paint or sharp edges etc, electrical appliances, in each case not conforming to prescribed standards) and the Consumer Protection Act 1961 makes it an offence to sell or have in

8 *R v Burke* (1978) 67 Cr App Rep 220, CA..
9 [1977] QB 614, CA, at 619.

possession for the purposes of sale any article contravening a regulation. This potentially very serious threat to the legality of sales of a wide variety of elderly 'household clutter' is somewhat lessened by an express exception in favour of sellers selling other than in a course of a business *or the agent of such a seller* (s 2(5)). Most of the Regulations have been made under the Consumer Protection Act 1961. The Consumer Safety Act 1978 is wider in scope, and contains no similar exception.[10] However both statutes provide a defence that the defendant took all reasonable steps and exercised all due diligence to avoid committing the offence, and this type of defence is further discussed in its trade descriptions context above. This area of consumer safety law is under review and standards of safety are likely to be tightened up.

10 For further details see Miller *Product Liability and Safety Encyclopaedia* Butterworths, divn IV; and Harvey *Law of Consumer Protection and Fair Trading* (2nd edn, 1982) Butterworths, ch 9.

Chapter 9

Sales of land by auction or tender

AUCTIONS

Practice and procedure

Land is probably the one commodity which, when sold by auction, poses special problems of law and practice. This is partly because there are specific statutory requirements applicable to the sale of *land* by auction and by other means, and partly because a sale of land which is commenced by an auction has to be dovetailed into standard conveyancing practice. Conveyancing practice involves far more careful preliminary enquiries and, usually, much more attention to the details of the description, than in the case of an auction of chattels.

The preliminary decision as to whether to sell land by auction or otherwise involves economic criteria which are outlined in ch 1. This chapter will proceed on the basis that the vendor has accepted the advice of his agent that the most effective way of realizing the value of the land to be sold is by selling it at auction.

So far as the auctioneer is concerned, the preparation for the auction will not be dissimilar to the preparation of land sold by private treaty.[1] Particulars of the land (including, of course, any buildings thereon) to be sold will be carefully prepared for dissemination to all those expressing an interest. The auctioneer will communicate with the solicitor for the vendor who will be charged with the drawing up of the contract. The contract will normally incorporate Standard Conditions of Sale which are examined later. The successful bidder will be required to sign the contract, or possibly have it signed on his behalf as also explained later, and the transaction then proceeds in a similar way to sales of land by private treaty.

It must be appreciated that the sale of land by auction poses particular problems for potential purchasers. These stem from the fact that the purchaser will not have known whether he has been successful until the auction is held. Meanwhile he must be prepared for the consequences of a successful bid. This will involve, normally, making all the standard local searches preceding the

1 See Brahams 'A Better Deal for Buyers?' (1982) 261 EG 847.

signing of a binding contract and, of course, ensuring that the finance is available for the purchase. It is, therefore, usually impracticable for a purchaser to proceed with a purchase by auction where he is still relying on the possible sale of his existing property unless he is prepared to effect bridging facilities through his bank. This, in itself, can attract heavy interest charges. Furthermore many purchasers of domestic property will be dependent upon the provision of a mortgage, and it is not always easy to secure the offer of a mortgage before it is known whether the potential morgagor has been successful in the auction. The vendor and his auctioneer must take these factors into account when deciding whether to employ the auction as the best means of sale.

Some steps can be taken in practice to ease the path of the potential purchaser. For instance, it is quite common for the vendor's solicitors to effect a local search of the vendor's property before the auction and to make the result of this available to potential purchasers. Similarly, standard enquiries before contract may be answered on a pro-forma basis. Occasionally the standard form of contract for land auctions incorporates a provision allowing the purchaser to make his local searches after the auction and rescind if the certificate of search discloses adverse entries which have not been revealed as special conditions in the contract. There is no reason why a survey commissioned by the vendor, and including a timber survey, should not be open for inspection. However, conveyancing practitioners acting for potential buyers view auctions less than enthusiastically owing to the strong possibility of wasting their time and their client's money on carrying out work which turns out to be fruitless.[2]

The auction itself is normally either held on the property to be sold or at premises designated by the auctioneer. The vendor's solicitor will normally be present in order to answer any enquiries which may be made as to the accuracy or completeness of the particulars drawn up by the auctioneer or arising out of General or Special Conditions in the contract. It is not normal current practice, as used to be the case, for the whole contract and General Conditions to be read out before the auction takes place. It is assumed that all potential purchasers have perused the contract and, if necessary, obtained a copy of it. The contractual position of the auction itself is that once the highest bid has been accepted the purchaser is obliged to sign the contract. It is the signed contract which, of course, gives the binding effect to the sale.

There is one possible legal difficulty arising. It is standard form in the General Conditions of Sale for land to include a condition which stipulates that the purchaser shall forthwith complete and sign the contract and pay the deposit in accordance with the General Conditions.[3] However, this condition can be of no effect until the contract itself is signed. Should the successful purchaser refuse to sign the contract, the action against him would, in theory, be for this failure rather than for failure to buy the land as such.[4] This is because the general condition requiring him to sign the contract is in the very contract which he has not signed. This problem is, however, largely theoretical

2 See P H Halstead 'Auctions: Suggested Code of Practice' (1984) Law Soc Gaz 2357.
3 See the Law Society's General Condition of Sale 25(5) in Appendix 2.
4 It was held, however, in *Daulia Ltd v Four Millbank Nominees Ltd* [1978] Ch 231, [1978] 2 All ER 557, that such a unilateral contract to enter into a formal written contract for sale of land must itself be evidenced in writing.

because, by ancient authority,[5] the auctioneer may sign the contract on the purchaser's behalf. This authority resides with the auctioneer himself unless the purchaser has in some tangible way authorised the auctioneer's clerk to sign as agent.[6] The question can arise as to how long this authority to sign on behalf of the purchaser lasts. The general rule is that the signature must be made at the auction or within a short time thereafter. Thus, in *Chaney v Macklow*,[7] a freehold house was knocked down to the defendant as the highest bidder, but he afterwards refused to sign the contract because one of the Conditions of Sale required the purchaser to pay certain road-making charges. On the same day the auctioneer, as soon as he was informed of the defendant's refusal, signed the contract as the defendant's agent. The vendor brought an action for specific performance. It was held that an auctioneer had authority to sign a contract conforming with s 40 of the Law of Property Act 1925 (see below), provided he signed it at such a time and in such circumstances that the signature could be said to be part of the transaction of sale. This was a question of fact and in this particular case the auctioneer's signature could fairly be said to be part of the transaction of sale.[8]

In practice the formal contract for sale of land is prepared in duplicate: one copy will be signed by the purchaser and the other, already prepared, will have been signed by the vendor or the auctioneer as his agent. In this connection, the auctioneer is also the agent of the vendor and has authority to sign a contract on his behalf. The authority to do so on behalf of the vendor is derived from the contract between the vendor and the auctioneer. It is not as limited as the authority to sign on behalf of the purchaser and is not conditional on receipt of the deposit from him.[9] The purchase price will, of course, have to be inserted where the documents have been prepared in advance and, in accordance with standard conveyancing practice, the documents are prepared in duplicate and become binding when exchanged by the purchaser taking the part signed by the vendor and vice versa. General conditions will normally stipulate that the date of the contract is that of the auction,[10] and that a ten per cent deposit is immediately payable by the purchaser.

General statutory requirements

Law of Property Act 1925, s 40

It will be inferred from the comments on practice and procedure above, that the existence of a properly formed memorandum in writing is essential for there to be an enforcable contract of sale in the case of land. This requirement stems from s 40 of the Law of Property Act 1925 (replacing the Statute of

5 *Emmerson v Heelis* (1809) 2 Taunt 38; *White v Proctor* (1811) 4 Taunt 209.
6 *Bell v Balls* [1897] 1 Ch 663, 66 LJ Ch 397; and see further, under discussion of 'capacity and authority', p 34.
7 [1929] 1 Ch 641, 98 LJ Ch 345, CA.
8 See also *Sims v Landray* [1894] 2 Ch 318, 63 LJ Ch 535, where it was held that the action of the auctioneer's clerk in filling in the purchaser's name and address in the form of contract, but not signing it on his behalf, was nevertheless a sufficient signature on behalf of the highest bidder to constitute a memorandum for the purposes of the Statute of Frauds. In *Bells v Balls* (n 6 above), where the memorandum was signed on behalf of the purchaser seven days after the auction, it was held that by this time the auctioneer's authority had ceased and the signing was of no effect.
9 See *Phillips v Butler* [1945] Ch 358 [1945] 2 All ER 258; *Leeman v Stocks* [1951] Ch 941, [1951] 1 All ER 1043.
10 See e g National Conditions of Sale 1(5), reproduced in Appendix 2.

Frauds 1677, s 4). A detailed commentary on this section is beyond the scope of this book since it forms part of the substantive topics of land law and conveyancing. Section 40(1) of the Law of Property Act 1925, however, so far as material, provides as follows:

> No action may be brought upon any contract for the sale or other disposition of land or any interest in land, unless the agreement upon which such action is brought, or some memorandum or note thereof is in writing, and signed by the party to be charged or by some other person thereunto by him lawfully authorised.

It will be appreciated that the width of this statutory provision is such that it would include a contract not only for the sale of freehold or leasehold property, but also for the sale of interests in land such as easements or profits (including, for example, fishing rights) and anything else within the definition of 'land' contained in s 205(1)(ix) of the Law of Property Act 1925.

There is a great deal of case law on what constitutes a memorandum, and considerable latitude has been vouchsafed by the courts to a wide variety of documents in order to hold them memoranda within the meaning of the section. The memorandum itself must contain the essential terms of the contract, that is to say the names of the parties, a description of the property and the nature of the consideration. In the case of the sale of leaseholds additional matters would also be regarded as essential, such as the length of the term, the date of its commencement and the rent.

It is almost invariable practice in the auction room, as indicated above, to provide the statutory memorandum in the form of a standard form contract. This will normally have been prepared by the vendor's solicitors and is likely to be in the printed form incorporating either the Law Society's General Conditions of Sale or the National Conditions of Sale. In complex cases a special form of contract may well be prepared by the vendor's solicitors but it is still usual to incorporate by reference one or other of the standard sets of conditions. These General Conditions, besides indicating what the correct procedure when a sale by auction occurs is, will also deal with such matters as the payment of the deposit, the title to be shown and the date for completion.

In the unlikely case that there is no written memorandum sufficient to satisfy s 40 of the Law of Property Act 1925, in so far as there may be an oral contract to purchase an interest in land, this is in itself not invalid. However, the effect of s 40 is to make the contract unenforceable by action. The party seeking to enforce the contract is thus disabled from suing for damages or making a claim for specific performance of the contract.[11]

Sale of Land by Auction Act 1867

This venerable and somewhat obscure statute needs some explanation. The mischief against which it was aimed was the possible fraud committed on a purchaser where the vendor of land attended the auction and bid for the property without disclosing his intention of doing so. Alternatively, and perhaps with a little more subtlety, the vendor might employ a puffer to inflate

11 See *Leroux v Brown* (1852) 12 CB 801, 22 LJCP1; and generally Cheshire and Burn *Modern Law of Real Property*(13th edn, 1982) Butterworths, p 117.

the price on his behalf. The attitude of the common law courts to this practice was stated by Byles J in *Green v Baverstock* as follows: 'Upon a sale by auction where the highest bidder is to be the purchaser, the secret employment of a puffer by the vendor is a fraudulent act. The sale is vitiated by the fraud and void, unless the vendee, with knowledge of the fact, has acted upon it so as to deprive himself of the right to complain.'[12]

This decision came at a time when there was a pronounced division between the administration of law and equity, and the courts of equity adopted a modified version of this principle. Unless the sale was stated to be 'without reserve', equity would not avoid a sale where the vendor appointed one person to bid for him since the vendor had a legitimate interest in preventing a sale at an undervalue.[13] The Sale of Land by Auction Act 1867 was designed to resolve this conflict of views and the Act was intended to give priority to the common law rule. The material sections run as follows:

> 4. *Sales of land invalid in law from employment of a puffer to be also invalid in equity*
> And whereas there is at present a conflict between Her Majesty's courts of law and equity in respect of the validity of sales by auction of land where a puffer has bid, although no right of bidding on behalf of the owner was reserved, the courts of law holding that all such sales are absolutely illegal, and the courts of equity under some circumstances giving effect to them but even in courts of equity the rule is unsettled: And whereas it is expedient that an end should be put to such conflicting and unsettled opinions: Be it therefore enacted, that from and after the passing of this Act whenever a sale by auction of land would be invalid at law by reason of the employment of a puffer, the same shall be deemed invalid in equity as well as at law.
>
> 5. *Rule respecting sale without reserve, etc.*
> The particulars or conditions of sale by auction of any land shall state whether such land will be sold without reserve, or subject to a reserved price, or whether a right to bid is reserved; if it is stated that such land will be sold without reserve, or to that effect, then it shall not be lawful for the seller to employ any person to bid at such sale, or for the auctioneer to take knowingly any bidding from any such person.
>
> 6. *Rule respecting sale subject to right of seller to bid*
> And where any sale by auction of land is declared either in the particulars or conditions of such sale to be subject to a right for the seller to bid, it shall be lawful for the seller or any one person on his behalf to bid at such auction in such manner as he may think proper.

The intended effect of s 4 is self-explanatory. 'With regard to the statute, it seems to me that the object of the 4th section is not to restrict the legal doctrine, but to leave it as it was and to make the equitable doctrine correspond with it,' as Lindley J remarked in *Parfitt v Jepson*.[14]

The effect of s 5 is more doubtful.[15] It seems clear, despite dicta to the contrary,[16] that it is not necessary in the Conditions of Sale to state whether the

12 (1863) 14 CBNS 204, 32 LJCP 181.
13 See *Mortimer v Bell* (1865) 1 Ch App 10, 35 LJ Ch 25, CA, and the other authorities cited in Bateman's *Law of Auctions* (11th edn, 1953) Estates Gazette, p 142.
14 (1877) 46 LJQB 529 at 533.
15 See the discussion of this section and s 6 in Murdoch *The Law of Estate Agency and Auctions* (2nd edn, 1984) Estates Gazette, p 488 f.
16 See per Lord Romilly M R in *Gilliat v Gilliat* (1869) LR 9 Eq 60, 39 LJ Ch 142.

sale is subject to, or without, a reserve. But such conditions must state either that the sale is without reserve, *or* that the land is subject to reserved price, *or*, if neither of these two things is stated, whether a right to bid is reserved. The better opinion is that so long as one of these three alternatives is stated in the Conditions of Sale, the requirements of the Act are satisfied.[17] Section 5 goes on to state that where the sale is stipulated to be without reserve, it is unlawful for the seller to employ a puffer or for the auctioneer knowingly to take a bid from any such person. Provided the National Conditions of Sale or the Law Society's Conditions of Sale (discussed below) are used, no difficulty will arise since both make specific provision for a reserve price and the right of the vendor or his agent to bid up to any reserve price, unless this General Condition is specifically negated.[18] (It may be added that some auctions of land are made subject to 'upset prices' where the reserve price is openly disclosed to bidders.)

Section 6 of the Sale of Land by Auction Act 1867 is intended to be complementary to s 5 by providing that *where* the conditions stipulate that the sale is to be subject to a right for the seller to bid, it is lawful for the seller to do so personally or by his agent 'in such manner as he may think proper'.

It will be appreciated that if a standard set of General Conditions of Sale is used and consequently the right to bid by the vendor or on his behalf is reserved up to the reserve price, where the vendor does not choose to bid personally (and this may be inadvisable if he is known in the area) the auctioneer should obtain a specific authority to do so on his behalf.[19]

The decision of the Court of Common Pleas in *Parfitt v Jepson*[20] emphasises that any rights reserved under s 5 of the Sale of Land by Auction Act 1867 must be strictly exercised as reserved. In that case land was sold by public auction under conditions which stated that the highest bidder should be the purchaser, and which reserved to the vendor the right to bid once by himself or his agent. The auctioneer bid three times with the vendor's permission and then the vendor stated what the reserve price was, when a person bid beyond that sum and was thereupon declared the purchaser. It was held that by reason of the biddings of the auctioneer, the vendor had exceeded the limited right reserved to him by the condition of bidding once by himself or his agent. The sale was therefore voidable at the option of the purchaser, both at law and under the 1867 Act.[1] The paucity of cases within the last 50 years on the 1867 Act seems to suggest that the obvious incompetence of its draftsmanship has not caused significant problems in practice. This is no doubt attributable to the widespread use of General Conditions of Sale which cater for the Act's provisions satisfactorily.[2]

17 See Bateman *Law of Auctions* (11th edn, 1953) Estates Gazette, p 143.
18 See National Condition of Sale 1(2) and Law Society's General Condition of Sale 25(3) (Appendix 2). See also *Dimmock v Hallett* (1866) 2 Ch App 21, 36 LJ Ch 146.
19 Various model letters concerning the auctioneer's authority to act on behalf of the vendor in the conduct of the auction will be found in 2 Encyclopaedia of Forms and Precedents (4th edn).
20 (1877) 46 LJQB 529.
1 This decision was distinguished in *Hills & Grant Ltd v Hodson* [1934] Ch 53, 103 LJ Ch 17, where it was emphasized that the words 'with reserve' or 'without reserve' need not specifically be used provided it is made plain in some way that the sale is subject to a reserve where that is the case.
2 Similar, but better drafted, provisions apply to chattel auctions by virtue of the Sale of Goods Act 1979, s 57.

General Conditions of Sale as to the conduct of land auctions

Where, as is standard practice, the auction of land is by reference to either the National Conditions of Sale (20th edn) or the Law Society's General Conditions of Sale (1984 revn), these sets of General Conditions both contain provision for the general conduct of the auction. It follows that there is no need for the auctioneer to have his separate *conditions*, although it is good practice to make it clear in the *particulars* of the property that the sale will be subject to the stipulated General and Special Conditions of Sale in the contract[3] and also to announce this at the commencement of the auction. This is because there are some provisions in the above-mentioned General Conditions of Sale which apply to all bidders whether successful or not. The remainder of the contract will, however, only bind the purchaser.[4]

The relevant National General Conditions are as follows:[5]

1. *The sale: by auction: by private treaty*

(1) Paragraphs (2) to (5) of this Condition apply on a sale by auction and paragraphs (6) and (7) on a sale by private treaty.

(2) Unless otherwise provided in the Special Conditions, the sale of the property and of each lot is subject to a reserve price and to a right for the vendor or any one person on behalf of the vendor to bid up to that price.

(3) The auctioneer may refuse any bid and no person shall at any bid advance less than the amount fixed for that purpose by the auctioneer.

(4) If any dispute arises respecting a bid, the auctioneer may determine the dispute or the property may, at the vendor's option, either be put up again at the last undisputed bid, or be withdrawn.

(5) Subject to the foregoing provisions of this Condition, the highest bidder shall be the purchaser and shall forthwith complete and sign the contract, the date of which shall be the date of the auction.

. . .

The parallel General Condition contained in the Law Society's General Conditions of Sale is as follows:[6]

3 A typical clause in the auctioneer's particulars might run: The property will, unless previously withdrawn, be sold subject to General and Special Conditions of Sale which may be inspected during usual office hours at the offices of the vendor's solicitors and the Auctioneers, during the seven days (excluding Saturday and Sunday) immediately before the day of the auction. The Conditions of Sale may also be inspected in the Sale Room but they will not then be read out. Purchasers shall be deemed to have notice of each Condition and all bidders to have bid on the basis that they have inspected the said Conditions (whether they have in fact done so or not).

4 Failure to distinguish between the auctioneer's particulars, which are primarily for information only, and the contract which, apart from the specific General Conditions dealing with the conduct of the auction, is binding but only on the highest accepted bidder, causes some confusion in practice. The clause suggested in the footnote above must be given contractual effect as regards *all* bidders if the two complementary documents are to be properly linked. Yet some auctioneer's particulars specifically deny that they constitute 'an offer or a contract'. The clause in the preceding footnote must in fact, be construed as a collateral contract with all bidders and is not within the Law of Property Act 1925, s 40 (above).

5 This extract and others from the National Conditions of Sale (20th edn) are reproduced in this book by kind permission of the Solicitors' Law Stationery Society plc.

6 This extract and others from the Contract and Conditions of Sale (1984 revn) are reproduced in this book by kind permission of the Law Society.

25. *Auctions*

(1) This condition applies if the property is sold by auction.

(2) The sale is subject to a reserve price for the property and, when the property is sold in lots, for each lot.

(3) The vendor reserves the right —
(a) to divide the property into lots and to sub-divide, re-arrange or consolidate any lots
(b) to bid personally or by his agent up to any reserve price
(c) without disclosing any reserve price, to withdraw from the sale any property or lot at any time before it has been sold, whether or not the sale has begun.

(4) The auctioneer may —
(a) refuse to accept a bid
(b) in the case of a dispute as to any bid, forthwith determine the dispute or again put up the property or lot at the last undisputed bid.

(5) The purchaser shall forthwith complete and sign the contract and pay, but not necessarily by the means specified in condition 9(1), the normal deposit.

With regard to these standard General Conditions, the following points should be noted.

Both sets of General Conditions contain a paragraph governing the conduct of the auction. In both cases the auctioneer has the right to refuse any bid. Under the National Conditions, bidders are required to accept the auctioneer's bid advances. Under the Law Society's Conditions, 25(4)(b) states that in the case of a dispute as to a bid, the auctioneer may forthwith determine the dispute or again put up the property at the last undisputed bid. Under the National Conditions, 1(4) gives the auctioneer the additional option of withdrawing the property altogether.

Under both sets of General Conditions it is specifically stipulated that the sale is subject to a reserve price and the right to bid up to *any reserve price* is reserved to the vendor or his agent. Under the National Conditions, 1(5) specifically stipulates that the highest bidder shall be the purchaser. Under both sets of General Conditions the purchaser is under a duty forthwith to complete and sign the contract and pay the deposit.

Neither set of General Conditions contains a provision, formerly quite commonly found, that no bid shall be retracted. On the face of it, such a stipulation would be of no effect since the bid is merely an offer and on general contractual principles may be retracted before acceptance by fall of the hammer. On the other hand it has been pointed out that there are a number of stipulations in the Sale of Land by Auction Act 1867 (see above), as to e g the reserve price, which are intended to regulate the conduct of the auction and to bind all bidders.[7] It has been ingeniously argued that on similar principles a provision that no bid shall be retracted should be regarded as binding.[8]

7 See Barnsley *Conveyancing Law and Practice* (2nd edn, 1982) Butterworths, p 244 and the authorities therein cited.
8 Barnsley (n 7 above). Such a provision might be regarded as a separate unilateral contract with bidders, but could the principal-plaintiff show any consideration?

As may be inferred from above, the deposit of ten per cent of the purchase price is paid by the purchaser on signing the contract. The National Conditions of Sale have a specific General Condition, which runs as follows:[9]

> 2. *Deposit*
>
> (1) Unless the Special Conditions otherwise provide, the purchaser shall on the date of the contract pay a deposit of 10 per cent of the purchase price, on a sale by auction, to the auctioneer, or on a sale by private treaty, to the vendor's solicitor and, in either case, as stakeholder.
>
> (2) In case a cheque taken for the deposit (having been presented, and whether or not it has been re-presented) has not been honoured then and on that account the vendor may elect —
> either (i) to treat the contract as discharged by breach thereof on the purchaser's part
> or (ii) to enforce payment of the deposit as a deposit, by suing on the cheque or otherwise.

The Law Society's General Conditions of Sale relating to auctions (above) cross-refer to General Condition 9, which runs as follows:[10]

> 9. *Deposit*
>
> (1) The purchaser shall on or before the date of the contract pay by way of deposit to the vendor's solicitors as stakeholders the normal deposit,[11] or such lesser sum as the vendor shall have agreed in writing. On a sale by private treaty, payment shall be made by banker's draft or by cheque drawn on a solicitor's bank account.
>
> (2) Upon service by the vendor of a completion notice, the purchaser shall pay to the vendor any difference between the normal deposit and any amount actually paid (if less).
>
> (3) If any draft, cheque or other instrument tendered in or towards payment of any sum payable under this condition is dishonoured when first presented the vendor shall have the right by notice to the purchaser within seven working days thereafter to treat the contract as repudiated.

There are interesting differences between the two General Conditions but they also have much in common. If the National Conditions of Sale are used, the ten per cent deposit cheque should be made out in favour of the auctioneer. It is clear that he then holds the deposit as stakeholder for both parties. This means that the vendor cannot use this deposit for his own purchase. Under the Law Society's General Conditions of Sale, Condition 9 states that the purchaser's cheque shall be paid to the *vendor's solicitors* as stakeholders. It is envisaged here that the cheque is likely to be the purchaser's own cheque, in contrast with a sale by private treaty where the deposit must specifically be paid by banker's draft or a cheque drawn upon a solicitor's bank account. This will be the position in practice, as well, if the National Conditions of Sale are used. It will also be noted that both sets of General Conditions make specific provision for

9 Extract from the National Conditions of Sale (20th edn) Solicitors' Law Stationery Society plc.
10 Extract from the Contract and Conditions of Sale (1984 revn) Law Society.
11 'Normal deposit' is defined in Condition 1 as meaning 'the sum which together with any preliminary deposit paid by the purchaser, amounts to ten per centum of the purchase money (excluding any separate price to be paid for any chattels, fixtures or fittings).'

a case where the cheque taken for the deposit is not honoured. In either event the vendor may choose to treat the contract as repudiated. The previous edition (1980) of the Law Society's Conditions made reference to a vendor's right to elect to treat dishonour of a cheque 'as a fundamental breach of the purchaser's obligations under the contract' but the wording has been changed to refer instead to automatic repudiation. This reflects the decision in *Millichamp v Jones*[12] where non-payment of the deposit must be treated, it was held, as breach of a fundamental term.

Both sets of General Conditions contain specific provision for errors, mis-statements or omissions with regard to descriptions of the property. These conditions are considered specifically under the next heading.

PROBLEMS REGARDING MISREPRESENTATION AND MISDESCRIPTIONS

Misrepresentations prior to the sale

As already indicated, in a typical auction-sale of land, particulars of sale will have been prepared initially by the auctioneer. The function of these is to advertise the property to all potential purchasers and the particulars will essentially contain a description of the property, including a detailed description of buildings on the property, facilities and services enjoyed by the property and any other general remarks which may or may not be statements of fact rather than opinion. More often than not the particulars are accompanied by a photograph of the property (showing it in its best light on a sunny day). The difference between land auctions and chattel auctions is that the description of the property which is formally the subject of the sale will not be in the auctioneer's particulars but in the contract normally prepared by the vendor's solicitors. The contractual description of the land will normally be taken from the documents of title. It will not describe in detail the buildings on the land but will, or should, define the area of land to be sold accurately and deal with such matters as the grant and reservation of easements over neighbouring land. The contract will also reveal all matters which under general conveyancing law must be revealed to the purchaser relating to latent defects, incumbrances etc; and, since the auctioneer will not normally include these in his own particulars, it is good practice for the auctioneer's particulars to cross-refer to the more detailed description in the draft contract.

With regard to the auctioneer's particulars, potential liability exists if there is a factual statement which misrepresents the position. In this connection there have been many cases in the law of contract on the difference between a statement of opinion (or 'puff') and a statement of fact. Thus, describing land as 'uncommonly rich watermeadow'[13] or as 'fertile and improvable'[14] were held to be expressions of opinion only. Particulars for the sales of land, whether by private treaty or auction, are renowned for eulogistic descriptions of the property to be sold. The usual type of phrase such as 'a most desirable

12 [1983] 1 All ER 267, [1982] 1 WLR 1422.
13 *Scott v Hanson* (1829) 1 Russ & M 128.
14 *Dimmock v Hallett* (1866) 2 Ch App 21, 36 LJ Ch 146.

property' or 'a substantial and convenient dwelling-house' are all likely to be held as merely puffs.[15] However, where the statement is essentially factual, such as that the property is in good repair[16] or, as in the well-known case of *Smith v Land and House Property Corpn*[17] where a hotel was sold by auction and described as let to 'a most desirable tenant' (the tenant being in arrears with rent and generally undesirable), the Court of Appeal held that the purchasers were entitled to rescind the contract, the description being one of fact rather than one of opinion. There was an implicit assertion that nothing had occurred which could be regarded as rendering the tenant undesirable.[18]

Misrepresentations prior to the sale can also be made by inaccurate replies to the standard form Enquiries Before Contract, submitted by the purchaser's solicitors to the vendor's solicitors. As has been mentioned, it is normal practice to issue interested potential purchasers with prepared forms containing answers to the standard enquiries. This variation from private-treaty sales does not appear to affect the contractual situation, in that anyone proceeding to purchase the property and having been induced to do so by misrepresentations of fact would be in the same position here as if the sale had been by private treaty.

The law of contract governs the situation where a material misrepresentation has been made, and a full discussion of this topic is outside the scope of this book. Suffice it to say here that where a representation is made which is a false statement of fact by one party to the contract to the other, and which does not technically form a term of that contract, but in whole or in part induces the person to whom it is made to enter into the contract, the law permits two remedies. Whether the misrepresentation is fraudulent, negligent or, more commonly, innocent, the purchaser may normally exercise the equitable remedy of rescission. In these circumstances the contract is in effect nullified and the parties returned to their former position. If the misrepresentation is fraudulent or, in some cases, negligent, the purchaser may in addition be entitled to damages. The common law position relating to misrepresentation generally has been radically altered as regards parties to the contract by the Misrepresentation Act 1967 (as amended)[19] and as to the position in tort of those making false statements on which others rely, by the decision of the House of Lords in *Hedley-Byrne & Co Ltd v Heller & Partners Ltd*.[20]

The implications of the *Hedley-Byrne* decision for professional people are wide. Thus, for instance, in *Yianni v Edwin Evans & Sons*[1] a surveyor negligently reported that a house was worth a certain sum of money. The report was to the purchaser's building society which offered to lend that amount of money for the purchase of the house and this was in fact worth much less. The property was subject to serious defects and the report of the surveyors was described by the judge as 'grossly incompetent and negligent'. It was held that the firm of surveyors in this case knew the purpose of their report to the building society and they had a duty of care to the buyers. Damages were awarded against the

15 See *Johnson v Smart* (1860) 2 Giff 151, 2 LT 307; *Watson v Burton* [1956] 3 All ER 929.
16 See *Dyer v Hargrove* (1805) 10 Ves 505.
17 (1884) 28 ChD 7, 51 LT 718.
18 An 'opinion' implies that the representor believes it to be soundly based. If the 'opinion' is not really held at all, it would give rise to an actionable misrepresentation.
19 The relevant legislation can be found in Appendix 2.
20 [1964] AC 465, [1963] 2 All ER 575, HL. See above, p 95f.
1 [1982] QB 438, [1981] 3 All ER 592.

firm, related to the worth of remedial work (£8 000) which was required. The implications of this type of development to auctioneers who make statements negligently to potential purchasers are obvious. But for present purposes, this part of this chapter will concentrate on the contractual position only and in particular the purchaser's right to rescind the contract as against the vendor through whom the misrepresentation has occurred, particularly where the vendor relies on some sort of disclaimer.

As an illustration of a simple misrepresentation made in the auctioneer's particulars of sale which was held to entitle the purchaser to rescind the sale, the decision of the Court of Appeal in *Brown v Raphael*[2] is helpful (though the facts do not involve a sale of real property). What occurred was that in a sale by auction held in 1955, lot 11 was described as an absolute reversion in a trust fund on the death of an annuitant who was 'believed to have no aggregable estate'. The significance of the latter words is that, at the time, whether or not the annuitant had an aggregable estate would affect the estate duty payable on the absolute reversion and hence its net value. The statement in question was made honestly by the solicitors for the vendor, but they had no reasonable grounds for so believing. Lord Evershed MR emphasised that the purchaser seeking to rescind must establish three things: first, he must show that the language relied upon does import or contain a representation of some material fact; second, he must show that the representation is untrue; and, third, he must show that in entering into the contract he was induced so to do in reliance upon it. The Court of Appeal went on to hold the purchaser entitled to rescind on the ground of an innocent misrepresentation. The statement was one obviously and vitally affecting the subject matter being offered and the vendor was in a far stronger position than the purchaser to ascertain the relevant facts; it must accordingly be imported into the representation that the vendor had reasonable grounds to support his belief. Accordingly the purchaser was entitled to rescind the contract.

It must be emphasised that the defendant will be the principal who has expressly or impliedly authorised the misrepresentation. The decision of Mustill J in *Resolute Maritime Inc v Nippon Kaiji Kyokai, The Skopas*[3] makes it clear that the agent in this situation incurs no personal liability under s 2(1) of the Misrepresentation Act 1967 to the purchaser though he may be so liable in tort or for breach of a collateral warranty.[4]

Exclusion clauses and disclaimers

In modern practice it is common for both auctioneers' and estate agents' particulars and replies to enquiries by solicitors to contain written disclaimers of legal responsibility. Estate agents often use a form of disclaimer which runs in this way:

> These Particulars do not constitute any part of an offer or contract and any intending purchaser must satisfy himself by inspection or otherwise as to the

2 [1958] Ch 636, [1958] 2 All ER 79, CA.
3 [1983] 2 All ER 1, [1983] 1 WLR 857.
4 On liability under these heads, see ch 5.

correctness of each of the statements contained herein. The vendor and his agents make or give no representation or warranty whatever in relation to this property and no responsibility can be taken for the statements contained in these Particulars which are not to be relied on as statements or representations of fact on the part of either of them.

Printed forms of enquiry used by solicitors contain a warning that the replies are believed to be correct though their accuracy is not guaranteed and the replies do not obviate the need for the purchaser to make appropriate searches, enquiries and inspections. Furthermore, both the National Conditions of Sale and the Law Society's Conditions of Sale contain a provision negativing the right to rescind. The Law Society's Condition of Sale 7(1) states that 'no error, omission or mis-statement herein or in any plan furnished or any statement made in the course of negotiations leading to the contract shall annul the sale or entitle the purchaser to be discharged from the purchase'.[5]

These disclaimers must now be read in the light of modern consumer protection legislation. The statutory provisions likely to be most applicable are contained in the Misrepresentation Act 1967, s 3, and the Unfair Contract Terms Act 1977, s 2.[6]

We will take first the position where a misrepresentation is made prior to the contract by the auctioneer.

In these circumstances the vendor's first line of defence might well be to look at any disclaimer incorporated into his particulars. These might include a statement that 'neither the auctioneers nor any person in the employment of the auctioneers has any authority to make or give any representation or warranty in relation to these properties.'[7]

The validity of a somewhat similar disclaimer came before the Court of Appeal in *Overbrooke Estates Ltd v Glencombe Properties Ltd*.[8] The issue in this case was whether the disclaimer of authority in the particulars of sale which stated that 'neither the auctioneers nor any person in the employment of the auctioneers has any authority to make or give any representation or warranty' was effective to negate liability for a misrepresentation which would have allowed the defendants to refuse to complete the purchase from the plaintiff-vendors. The misrepresentation alleged was that the defendants, who were the highest bidders at the auction, had asked the auctioneers questions about the development plans of the local authorities to which inaccurate replies had been made. Brightman J held that even if the allegations could be proved, the misrepresentations could not be relied upon. The auctioneers had effectively disclaimed their authority to make such statements. This was so despite the terms of s 3 of the Misrepresentation Act 1967 which, in its current version, runs as follows:[9]

5 Contract and Conditions of Sale (1984 revn) Law Society. See also the National Conditions of Sale (20th edn) Solicitors' Law Stationery Society plc, Condition 17.

6 These two sections are reproduced in Appendix 2.

7 See a similar disclaimer published in October 1981 by the Royal Institution of Chartered Surveyors, reproduced in (1981) Conv 8006/3. The auctioneer's own possible liability under a collateral contract, as in *Shanklin Pier Ltd v Detel Products Ltd* [1951] 2 KB 854, [1951] 2 All ER 471, and a long line of subsequent cases, must also be borne in mind, as also liability for negligence.

8 [1974] 3 All ER 511, [1974] 1 WLR 1335.

9 The decision in this case was based on an earlier version of s 3, but it is thought that the amendments would have made no difference. See also the similar decision in *Collins v Howell-Jones* (1980) 259 EG 331, CA. See also Murdoch (1981) LQR 522.

3. If a contract contains a term which would exclude or restrict —
(a) Any liability to which a party to a contract may be subject by reason of any misrepresentation made by him before the contract was made; or
(b) Any remedy available to another party to the contract by reason of such misrepresentation,

that term shall be of no effect except in so far as it satisfies the requirement of reasonableness as stated in section 11(1) of the Unfair Contract Terms Act 1977; and it is for those claiming that the term satisfies the requirement to show that it does.

Brightman J went on to hold that the terms of s 3 of the Misrepresentation Act 1967 were not relevant since the disclaimer in question in the particulars did not 'exclude or restrict any liability'. The disclaimer merely imposed a limitation on the apparent authority of the auctioneers. It should also be noted in this context that s 3 refers to terms in a 'contract'. Disclaimers in auctioneers' or estate agents' particulars are normally a preliminary to, and not a part of, the contract itself.[10] Although Sch 1 of the Unfair Contract Terms Act 1977 excludes 'any contract' relating to the creation or transfer of an interest in land, the 'notice' or disclaimer of the type being discussed here does not appear in a contract but in the preliminary particulars. It is therefore open to possible attack on this ground and would then have to comply to the definition of 'reasonableness' in the Unfair Contract Terms Act 1977.

Where a disclaimer forms part of a contractual document, as is the position where one of the main sets of Conditions of Sale imposes the disclaimer or exclusion clause, quite apart from the question of whether such disclaimers are caught by the Unfair Contract Terms Act 1977, it may be possible for the vendor to show, at the least, that the purchaser did not rely on the misrepresentation.

Misdescriptions in the contract

The situation to be considered here is where the contract itself contains a misdescription. It will be recalled that the purchaser must sign this on making his successful bid. A number of cases in conveyancing law contain the situation where the contract itself misdescribes a property or contains some other material misrepresentation. As already explained, the purchaser potentially has the equitable remedy of rescision available to him in these circumstances. Even if the misrepresentation is non-fraudulent, following the passing of the Misrepresentation Act 1967 it has been possible for the purchaser to claim, in addition, damages where there has been negligence in the contract's making (which the maker must *disprove*) (s 2(1)).[11] It is no longer material that the contract has been completed by conveyance before the action is started.

10 This decision was made before the passing of the Unfair Contract Terms Act 1977. Section 2 of that Act refers to 'any contract term or to a notice' excluding or restricting liability for negligence. The decision in *The Skopas* [1983] 2 All ER 1, [1983] 1 WLR 857, discussed above (p 173), emphasises that the liability imposed by s 2(1) of the Misrepresentation Act 1967 (damages for innocent misrepresentation) attaches to the *principal* rather than to his authorised agent. An agent may be liable for negligence under the principle in *Hedley Byrne & Co Ltd v Heller & Partners Ltd* [1964] AC 465, [1963] 2 All ER 575, HL, and it is this liability against which any exemption clause will be aimed.

11 This also applies where the representation is made by an agent on behalf of his contracting principal — see *Gosling v Anderson* (1972) 223 EG 1743, CA.

Since we are now dealing with misdescriptions in the contract, the blame for these will usually lie with the vendor's solicitors rather than the auctioneers. Admittedly the auctioneers, in their capacity as surveyors, may have drawn up an inaccurate plan for which separate liability may lie to the vendor (in contract) or to the purchaser (in tort, under the *Hedley Byrne* principle).[12] But the situation most likely to arise is where the contract contains some material misdescription, omission or error in respect of which the purchaser wishes to exercise his remedy of rescision.

A contract for the sale of land, unlike the more general particulars drawn up for all potential purchasers by the auctioneers, must be a precise document. The contract will normally contain at least the following matters:

(a) a physical description of the property with its boundaries;

(b) a statement as to the tenure of the property (i e freehold or leasehold, and if leasehold, with particulars of the terms of the lease);
(c) a statement of any easements or other appurtenant rights affecting the property;
(d) a statement as to incumbrances including easements, restrictive covenants and mortgages to which the property is subject;
(e) if the property is let, the terms of the lease subject to which the purchaser must take.

The vendor is under an obligation to prove that the identity of the property matches the description in the document of title. If there is a misdescription of the property, there will be a breach of contract in respect of which the purchaser may either rescind or claim compensation according to the seriousness of the misdescription. In addition, the vendor is under an obligation to disclose all latent defects in his title and in the property. An example of the latter might be a defect which renders the property valueless for the purpose for which the purchasers are likely to require it. It will be seen from this that the vendor is under the dual duty to avoid misdescribing the land and actively to disclose certain matters. Of these two duties, that of description is the most commonly broken. In *Flight v Booth* it was stated that[13]

> where the description, although not proceeding from fraud, is in a material and substantial point so far affecting the subject matter of the contract that it may reasonably be supposed, but for the misdescription, the purchaser might never have entered the contract at all, in such a case the contract is voided altogether.

Thus if property is stated in the particulars in the contract to amount to approximately 3 920 square yards, but in fact contains only 2 360 square yards, a misstatement of the area to the extent of 40 per cent is likely to be held to be substantial. In *Watson v Burton*,[14] where similar facts arose, the vendor's action for specific performance was dismissed and judgment given for the purchaser for rescission and return of the deposit. Similarly, a misdescription of use such as 'valuable business premises' which was applied to business premises unusable for a number of ordinary trades was held not to be a fair

12 Explained above, p 172.
13 (1834) 1 Bing NC 370 at 377.
14 [1956] 3 All ER 929, [1957] 1 WLR 19.

description and to entitle the purchaser to rescission and recovery of the deposit.[15]

Having outlined the general law relating to misdescription and non-disclosure, it is now necessary to examine the position in the context of the auction-room.

Oral attempts to modify written terms

As explained at the beginning of this chapter, it is common practice for the auctioneer and vendor's solicitor to invite questions about properties before they are actually auctioned. This raises the question of whether oral corrections of written terms are likely to be effective. The 'parole evidence' rule serves generally to exclude all evidence which adds to, varies or contradicts a written document. Thus in *Powell v Edmunds*[16] printed Conditions of Sale concerning timber growing in a certain close did not state anything about the quantity. It was held that parol evidence that the auctioneer at the time of sale warranted a certain quantity was not admissible, as varying the written contract.[17]

The practical lesson is that where variations or amendments are found to be desirable prior to the auction, the contract ought to be amended before the auction takes place. However, where this practice is not followed, the fact that the auctioneer or vendor's solicitor has corrected a misleading description or statement, and that the purchaser was aware of this correction, may enable the vendor fully to enforce the contract on the basis that the purchaser was not *induced* to sign the contract on the basis of a misrepresentation,[18] or that an ambiguity has been clarified orally so that the purchasers knew the facts.[19]

Damping the sale

It is convenient here also briefly to discuss the practice known as *'damping the sale'*. This essentially consists of a bidder or bidders making audible derogatory statements or comments about the lot to be sold, prior to the bidding beginning. Although this can occur in any sale it is, in the authors' experience, more likely to happen in sales of land. This is because, normally, a specific opportunity is given to ask questions and it is not uncommon to find some of those present taking the opportunity of querying such matters as the status of the planning permission enjoyed by development land, the feasibility of access to that land, or the structural state of the property as contrasted with the description in the auction particulars. If this process results in either a sale at a price reduced from the true value or no sale at all, the vendor may have remedies.

Where there is a sale, but the purchaser has 'damped' it, he may not be entitled to the equitable remedy of a specific performance. Being a discretionary

15 *Charles Hunt Ltd v Palmer* [1931] 2 Ch 287, 100 LJ Ch 356.
16 (1810) 12 East 6.
17 See also *Ogilvie v Foljambe* (1817) 3 Mer 53; *Heywood v Mallalieu* (1883) 25 Ch D 357, 53 LJ Ch 492.
18 See *Farebrother v Gibson* (1875) 1 De G & J 602; contrast *Manser v Back* (1848) 6 Hare 443 and *Re Hare and O'More's Contract* [1901] 1 Ch 93, 70 LJ Ch 45, where, in neither case, was it thought equitable for the contract to be enforced against the purchaser since the purchaser did not hear or appreciate the corrections.
19 *Re Edwards to Daniel Sykes & Co Ltd* (1890) 62 LT 445.

remedy, the plaintiff's conduct will be in issue, and it seems from the very elderly authorities on this matter that the conduct in question may fall short of actual fraud, though it must presumably be in some way unconscionable.[20]

If a person present maliciously makes statements which are untrue as to the vendor's property and consequently no sale results, the vendor has an action against him for the tort of malicious falsehood (or slander of title).[1] There seems no reason in principle why this should not also be the case where the property is sold at a proven depreciated price as a result of the public pronouncement of untrue and malicious statements or innuendoes.

It might be thought that an agreement between two interested potential purchasers not to bid against each other would be equivalent to 'damping' the sale, since the vendor is unlikely to get the same value as if there were unfettered competition. But it was clearly held in the more modern case of *Harrop v Thompson*[2] that this was not contrary to public policy as being in restraint of trade. In that case the plaintiff had agreed to buy the defendant's farm at a public auction, and applied to the court under RSC Ord 86 for specific performance of the agreement. The defendants resisted the application on the grounds that the plaintiff had acquired the farms cheaply because the plaintiff had agreed with a potential bidder that he should stay away from the auction. The court ruled that the plaintiff was entitled to specific performance, there being no vitiating factor as explained above. Even an agreement for a subsequent 'knock out' sale has been held not to be illegal,[3] but if the parties to such an agreement are 'dealers' this principle must now be read subject to the Auctions (Bidding Agreements) Acts 1927 and 1969 and the right of the vendor to set such a sale aside for fraud.[4]

General conditions attempting to disclaim written particulars or special conditions

Both the National Conditions of Sale and the Law Society's Conditions of Sale contain, as already has been mentioned, attempts to disclaim the consequences of omissions and misdescriptions. These must now be read in the light of s 3 of the Misrepresentation Act 1967 (already considered) and also the material provisions of the Unfair Contract Terms Act 1977.

As an illustration of the current position, the decision in *Walker v Boyle*[5] provides useful guidance. In that case the vendor of a property, in answering the usual preliminary enquiries before contract, stated to the purchaser that to the vendor's knowledge there were no disputes regarding the boundaries of the property. There was in fact a boundary dispute and the purchaser claimed

20 See *Twining v Morrice* (1788) 2 Bro CC 326; *Manson v Armitage* (1806) 13 Ves 25; *Fuller v Abrahams* (1821) 3 Brod & Bing 116, 6 Moore CP 316 (a barge was stated by the plaintiff not to have been paid for).
1 See *Mayer v Pluck* (1971) 223 EG 33, 219 (the defendant, who had unsuccessfully negotiated for the plaintiff's house, publicly asked the auctioneer if he knew the house was built on an underground stream and that the cellar was waterlogged).
2 [1975] 2 All ER 94, [1975] 1 WLR 545.
3 *Leopard v Litoun* (1897) 41 Sol Jo 545; *Rawlings v General Trading Co* [1921] 1 KB 635, 90 LJKB 404, CA.
4 Discussed in ch 8.

rescission of the contract against the vendor. The vendor relied on Condition 17(1) of the National Conditions of Sale (19th edn) which then provided that 'no error, mis-statement or omission in any preliminary answer concerning the property... shall annul the sale'. Dillon J held that a vendor who made an innocent representation about his property when the true facts were within his knowledge was not entitled to rely on this condition, but even if Condition 17(1) were to apply, it would only exclude the vendor's liability for the misrepresentation if it satisfied the requirement of reasonableness[6] as set out in s 11(1) of the Unfair Contract Terms Act 1977: that 'the term shall have been a fair and reasonable one to be included having regard to the circumstances which were, or ought reasonably to have been, known to or in the contemplation of the parties when the contract was made.' It was held in this case that in all the circumstances Condition 17(1) (which has since been re-drafted) did not satisfy the requirement of reasonableness. Furthermore, the standard warning on the preliminary enquiries form that the 'replies on behalf of the vendor are believed to be accurate but accuracy is not guaranteed and they do not obviate the need to make appropriate searches, enquiries and inspections' could not prevent the answers given on the form from being *representations of fact*.

Since this decision, Condition 17 of the National Conditions of Sale has been modified by providing that the exclusion shall not apply to fraudulent or reckless statements. It remains to be decided whether the courts would hold this condition fair and reasonable so as to allow the vendor to rely upon it.

A further illustration of a purported disclaimer which became a casualty of s 3 of the Misrepresentation Act 1967 is illustrated by the decision of Croom-Johnson J in *South Western General Property Co Ltd v Marton*.[7] In 1979 the plaintiffs sold some land by auction to the defendant. The defendant's action was to rescind the contract on the grounds of innocent misrepresentation. The land was sold by description in the auctioneer's catalogue, lot 82 being described as 'long leasehold building land'. The particulars went on to imply that planning consent for the land had been refused. This was because the proposed development was out of character with the area. In fact it was unlikely that planning consent for a dwelling would ever be given on the site, as this would have been detrimental to visual amenities and with the character of a conservation area. Furthermore, by implication, various other conditions were incorporated into the contract similar to those found in the Standard Conditions of Sale of the Law Society and the National Conditions. Amongst these conditions was a statement that any error or omission found in the Particulars or Conditions of Sale should not annul the sale or entitle the purchaser to be discharged from the purchase. There was a further condition which stated that all statements in the particulars were made without responsibility on the part of the auctioneers or the vendor and were statements of opinion and were not to be taken as or implying a statement or representation of fact and that any intending purchaser must satisfy himself by inspection or otherwise as to the correction of each statement contained in the particulars.

5 [1982] 1 All ER 634, [1982] 1 WLR 495.
6 As required by s 3 of the Misrepresentation Act 1967 (see Appendix 2).
7 (1982) 263 EG 1090.

In fact the purchaser, who was a builder, attended the auction at short notice. He acquired the catalogue only the day before. The only enquiries he made as to the property were informal ones at the auction (the effect of which, if any, the judge ignored).

In the event it was held that the particulars contained a false, though innocent, representation which had been acted upon by the purchaser. The various disclaimer clauses did not in the circumstances satisfy the requirement of reasonableness (as stated in s 11(1) of the Unfair Contract Terms Act 1977) as required by s 3 of the Misrepresentation Act 1967. The judge concluded:[8]

> The words of s 11 of the Unfair Contract Terms Act are very wide. I have to deal with this contract, with the parties to this contract and the circumstances in which the contract was made. The conclusion I have come to is that the plaintiffs have not satisfied me that these are terms which are fair and reasonable and have been included in the contract between the plaintiffs and defendant at the time of the auction. These terms, if they were included, would exclude liability for the failure to tell the purchaser more than only a part of the facts which were among the most material to the whole contract of sale. In the result the plaintiffs are unable to rely upon the condition in the auctioneer's catalogue, and there must be judgment for the defendant [i e the purchaser].

It is not clear how far the facts of this case render the judge's conclusion generally applicable. Some weight appears to have been attached to 'the circumstances in which this contract was made' and these were unusual. The buyer does not normally enter into a contract for the sale of land, even by auction, at such very short notice and without making his own searches and enquiries. Had this purchaser done so it is conceivable that more weight might have been put on the relevant disclaimer clauses. Nevertheless, the case is a salutary warning that the prevailing tendency of the courts is to scrutinise carefully the reasonableness of such disclaimers and where the bargaining powers are unequal or the state of knowledge of the vendor is much greater than that of the purchaser, the court's sympathies seem to lie with the purchaser. The power to negate exclusion and disclaimer clauses is, as the learned judge points out, a very wide one. In practice, though, solicitors and auctioneers will no doubt take the view that nothing is lost by putting them in if in some circumstances they could remain effective.

TENDERS

Practice and procedure

The background and contractual situation where the sale of land takes place by tender has already been explained in ch 1. That chapter also contains a brief description of the advantages and disadvantages of adopting this method of sale.

Whilst there is no 'standard' procedure, the following describes the practice that is often adopted.

8 (1982) 263 EG 1090 at 1092.

The auctioneers in this instance will fulfil approximately the same function as if the sale were at auction. In other words, their function is to disseminate the tender documents to all potential tenderers, and generally act as agents for the vendor. Tenders sent in response to the invitation to tender may either be sent to the auctioneers or to the vendor's solicitors or, in some cases, to the vendor direct. The auctioneers will be responsible for drawing up the tender documentation in conjunction with the vendor's solicitors. Essentially the transaction takes place in three stages. The first stage involves dissemination of the invitation to tender to all potential purchasers, notice being given therein that tenders must be submitted by a stipulated date. The second stage involves consideration of the tenders and notification of acceptance by the vendor to the successful tenderer by a further stipulated date. The third stage will be handled by the vendor's solicitors and will involve the normal post-contractual conveyancing procedure with completion taking place by a further stipulated date.

The content of tender documents[9]

The tender documentation — which is prepared by the auctioneers in conjunction with the vendor's solicitors — normally commences with a detailed description of the property. Particulars here will be similar to those involved in a sale by private treaty or by auction. Information with regard to services, rateable value, town planning, fixtures and fittings and viewing arrangements is normally included together with a standard disclaimer as to absence of responsibility for statements made in the particulars or as to the authority of the auctioneers to make or give warranties in relation to the property. The status of this type of disclaimer in a contract for the sale of land by tender was discussed by the Court of Appeal in *Cremdean Properties Ltd v Nash*,[10] and this case is discussed below. Accompanying the particulars prepared by the agents there will often be a detailed plan.
There then is likely to follow a statement of the conditions of tender and sale. The purpose of these conditions is to explain the procedure to be adopted for the sale. Standard Conditions of Tender will contain the following clauses:

(a) A condition that each tenderer will send his tender on the appropriate form. This will contain his name, address, the amount of his offer and other relevant details. The condition will also stipulate that the completed form must be placed in a sealed envelope and addressed to the stipulated recipient — i e the vendor's agent or the vendor personally. The envelope should be appropriately marked to make it clear that it is a tender, and if sent by post, it should be sent by recorded delivery. The condition also imposes the deadline by which tenders must have arrived — e g 'to arrive [at the stipulated address] at or before noon on the Tender Date' (the latter being defined as a particular date).

(b) The second condition may make specific provision for tenders being made jointly, in which case full names of those involved should be given; or where the tender is made on behalf of a company, the full name and

9 There is a convenient precedent in *The Conveyancer and Property Lawyer*, vol 2: *Precedents for the Conveyancer*, 16-24. See also 18 Encyclopaedia of Forms & Precedents (4th edn) 601.
10 (1977) 244 EG 547, CA.

registered office of the company should be stipulated. If made on behalf of a partnership, the tender should be signed by duly authorised signatory. If an offer is made by an agent, he should be required to give the full name and address of his principal or principals as well as his own and it can be made clear that no tender will be accepted from undisclosed principals. The purpose of this condition is to give the vendor the fullest information as to the nature and standing of the potential purchaser.

(c) The next condition may stipulate that the amount tendered should be a fixed sum in sterling and not e g a reference to a stipulated amount above other offers.[11]

(d) As explained in ch 1, the invitation to tender is not normally regarded as an offer. The vendor can therefore reserve the right not to accept an offer, even though it be the highest bid. This condition may thus state: 'The Vendor does not undertake to accept the highest or any Tender.'

(e) The next condition may make arrangements for the payment of the deposit. This will normally be ten per cent of the amount of the tender payable by cheque or banker's draft. In the case of cheques it is wise to provide that the vendor may present the cheque prior to the date on which he undertakes to notify the successful bidder. If the cheque is not met upon first presentation, provision may be made for the vendor to reject the tender forthwith.

(f) Next, a condition is necessary to settle the situation with regard to notification of the successful tenderer. This condition will stipulate that by a certain date (usually approximately 14 days after the deadline for tenders) the vendor or his agent will indicate acceptance of the tender to the successful tenderer by letter sent by recorded delivery at the address inserted in the tender form. The cheque or banker's draft accompanying the successful tender will then be retained by the vendor as a deposit on account of the purchase price in accordance with the above conditions. This condition will also stipulate that the cheques or banker's drafts of unsuccessful Tenderers will then be returned forthwith.

(g) Finally, a condition should be inserted making it clear that each person who submits a tender is deemed to accept the Conditions of Tender and Sale contained in the documentation and to undertake that his tender will remain unvaried and open for acceptance until, and will not be withdrawn before, a stipulated time (usually two days) after the date specified for notification of the successful bid. Although there must be some doubt as to the validity of this provision in the absence of consideration supplied by the tenderer, it is conceivable it could be upheld as a collateral contract.

The next part of the document will contain the 'Conditions of Sale'. These will correspond to the Special Conditions inserted in normal standard form contracts for the sale of land, and will be prepared by the vendor's solicitors. The conditions will deal with such matters as the date for completion, the position if there is delay on completion, the title of the vendor to the property,

11 'If the offeror wishes to rule out referential bids, he should say so' — per Waller LJ in *Harvela v Royal Trust Co* [1985] 1 All ER 261 at 267.

the matters subject to which the property is sold and, often, a further disclaimer with regard to errors, omissions or misdescriptions of the property whether contained in the Conditions of Tender or of Sale. The Special Conditions will also normally indicate whether or not vacant possession is to be given on completion. The Conditions of Sale are then normally followed by a schedule describing the land by reference to its description in the documents of title. In addition it is normal practice to 'fill the gaps' by incorporating by reference one of the two standard sets of General Conditions discussed above, the contractual position being that these General Conditions will apply except in so far as they may be varied by the Special Conditions, here entitled 'Conditions of Sale'.

Finally, a form of tender designed to be separated from the documentation and returned by tenderers will be appended. This takes the form of a simple statement that 'the Tenderer hereby submits a Tender to purchase the [property in question], the Tender being in the sum of £...' (usually in figures and words to avoid possible ambiguities) and a statement that a banker's draft or cheque for ten per cent of the sum tendered is enclosed.

It is wise also to append a formal acknowledgement that the tender is submitted in accordance with the 'Conditions of Tender and Sale' annexed. It is essential that the tender is signed by the tenderer and that it should contain his address and be dated. The form of tender should indicate to whom cheques or banker's drafts should be payable.

In principle the combination of the signed offer to purchase by the successful bidder together with the vendor's notification of acceptance will jointly form a sufficient memorandum of agreement to satisfy s 40 of the Law of Property Act 1925. There have been queries in practice as to whether either the vendor or purchaser may change his mind after this stage, but since there is from this stage onwards a binding contract (if the form discussed above is used), there can then be no question of going back. This point was reaffirmed by Goff J in *Michael Richards Properties Ltd v Corporation of Wardens of St Saviour's Parish Church, Southwark*[12] where the vendors mistakenly accepted the successful tender 'subject to contract'. Goff J rejected the latter words as meaningless. The learned judge emphasised that the tender documents set out all the terms of the contract and nothing further needed to be negotiated.

Mention was made above of the decision in *Cremdean Properties Ltd v Nash*.[13] The decision involved consideration of a tender, and the judge describes at some length the documents involved which are similar to those described above.

The facts were that the appellants decided to sell an important block of property in Bristol for redevelopment mainly as offices, outline planning permission having been secured. The position was slightly complicated by the fact that there were two vendors; one was the owner of part of the property and the other was a body of trustees of a charity who owned the remaining part. They instructed agents jointly, and the agents invited prospective purchasers to tender for the whole block. The stipulated date by which tenders had to be

12 [1975] 3 All ER 416.
13 (1977) 244 EG 547, CA. See also JE Adams [1981] Conv 326.

received was 14 November 1973. On 13 November 1973 the plaintiffs put in a tender for £552 500, which was accepted. This represented the price based on values at the height of the then property boom. The acceptance of the plaintiffs' tender resulted in the conclusion of two separate contracts, the tendered sum being apportioned between the two vendors. One contract was completed by conveyance; the other contract (with the charity trustees) was never completed but this part of the action was compromised.

The plaintiffs claimed rescission of both contracts on the ground of misrepresentation. The misrepresentation alleged was that the agent's particulars described the property as consisting of 'approximately 17 900 square feet of offices, a new Church Hall and 8 car parking spaces'. The document also incorporated a plan. Two pages of the document were then headed 'Special Conditions of Sale by Tender' and these consisted of 18 numbered clauses and two schedules. A footnote to the Special Conditions of Sale by Tender read as follows:

> Messrs ... [the agents acting for the defendants in relation to the sale] for themselves, for the vendors or landlords whose agents they are give notice that (a) these particulars are prepared for the convenience of an intending purchaser or tenant and although they are believed to be correct their accuracy is not guaranteed and any error, omission or misdescription shall not annul the sale or be grounds on which compensation may be claimed and neither do they constitute any part of an offer of a contract; (b) any intending purchaser or tenant must satisfy himself by inspection or otherwise as to the correctness of each of the statements contained in these particulars.

The main issue in the case was the consequences of the alleged misrepresentation, in that the amount of office-space permitted was much less than the 17 900 square feet, in the light of the purported disclaimers. Bridge LJ stated that the statement in the Conditions of Sale that 'any error, omission or misdescription shall not annul the sale will be grounds on which compensation may be claimed' was nothing more or less than a purported exclusion of liability which would otherwise accrue on the ground of the misrepresentations in the statements to be found in the document. Bridge LJ regarded the decision in the *Overbrooke Estates Ltd* case[14] as not material to this issue. The agents had the full authority of their principals to say what they did in the document. As already discussed above, s 3 of the Misrepresentation Act 1967 makes any purported disclaimer of liability of this sort subject to a test of reasonableness.

The court was in fact concerned with trying the preliminary issue as to whether the existence of the condition in question conclusively negated any misrepresentation. The Court of Appeal rejected this view. Section 3 of the Misrepresentation Act 1967 applied to the purported disclaimer and at the trial proper the court would have to decide whether it was fair and reasonable to allow the defendants, in the circumstances of the case, to rely on their disclaimer.

The court also dealt with another problem. It is not always clear whether disclaimers such as these are part of the contract (as will normally be the case

14 [1974] 3 All ER 511, [1974] 1 WLR 1335, discussed on p 174f above.

in tender documents) or merely a preliminary misrepresentation not being a term of the contract. Bridge LJ summarised the position in this case by saying that if the disclaimer was a term of the contract binding as between the parties, then it was a term which is counter to s 3 of the Act and therefore ineffective, unless the court trying the action thought it fair and reasonable to give it effect. If it was not part of the contract, then it was not binding on the purchaser and it would therefore not help the vendor in any case.

The issue in this case is of general importance in property sales, whether they take place by auction, tender or private treaty. It again emphasises the modern judicial tendency to view with great suspicion attempts by the vendor or his agents to disclaim responsibility for matters which are within their knowledge and within their power to control. If the purchaser is induced by a misrepresentation to enter into a contract, whether formed at an auction, as a result of a tender or by private treaty, s 3 of the Misrepresentation Act 1967 is a formidable hurdle for the vendor to jump, in so far as he hopes to rely on this type of disclaimer. Where sales of chattels are concerned, the same type of issue arises and is discussed in some detail in ch 6.

Chapter 10

Vehicle auctions and specialised auctions of other property

VEHICLE AUCTIONS

Introduction

Sales by auction of motor vehicles have rapidly increased in popularity in recent years. Currently some 750 000 vehicles per annum are estimated as being sold in this way. Although the majority of vehicles are far from new, dealers also use this method for selling new stock unsold for 60 days for cash-flow reasons. About one in five of vehicles sold at auction are bought by private purchasers. Auctioneers range from small firms or single proprietors who, typically, organise weekly or monthly evening auctions at a series of towns in a given geographical area, to the large specialist concerns such as British Car Auctions at Measham, Leicestershire and Central Motor Auctions. In addition, the non-specialist auctioneer may find that, for instance, a deceased's chattels to be disposed of by auction include a car. Auctions of motor vehicles give rise to specific problems, whatever the status of the auctioneer. Some of these problems concern the laxity with which conditions of sale are drawn up. Others concern possible infringements of the criminal law, particularly under s 60 of the Road Traffic Act 1972 (selling unroadworthy vehicles) or under s 1 of the Trade Descriptions Act 1968 (fully discussed in ch 8).[1]

Conditions of Sale

The first consideration here is whether the conditions bind the purchasers of the vehicles sold and bind bidders generally. The same considerations apply here as were fully discussed in ch 6, and the party seeking to rely on the conditions will need to show that the actual or potential defendant has notice of the conditions. Much will depend on the circumstances. For instance, it is quite common for less formal vehicle auctions to accept entries up to a few minutes before the start of the auction, not to issue catalogues (scarcely practicable in these circumstances) and to print Conditions of Sale on the *entry* form. This obviously does not as such affect buyers with notice of relevant protective and exclusion clauses unless the Conditions of Sale are also on

1 See Appendix 2 for the full text of these sections.

prominent display at the auction site. It is also common to find conditions affecting sellers (e g rates of commission) intermingled with Conditions of Sale affecting bidders and buyers. It is with the latter type of condition that problems of this character could arise; for example, a buyer purporting to reject an unmerchantable car where its merchantability has been purportedly excluded by a non-binding clause.

The content of the Conditions of Sale affecting *buyers* is dissimilar only in a few important details to conditions appropriate for the sale of chattels generally, but it is suggested that specific clauses should be added, namely:

(a) A clause giving purchasers the right to reject a materially defective vehicle purchased within one hour (or other appropriate time) of the sale of it to him *if* the vehicle is specifically sold by the auctioneer on 'pre-trial' terms. It is sensible to qualify the right to reject by excluding from consideration defects specifically revealed by the seller on the entry form.[2] Examples have been seen of very loosely-drawn clauses along these lines and used in practice, but it is nevertheless likely that disputes could arise, even with the above qualification, as to whether a vehicle is 'materially defective'. However, this phrase is an improvement on an unqualified right to reject 'trial before payment' cars, which gives ample scope for purchasers to reject for no good reason in law.

(b) A clause excluding all express and implied conditions and warranties relating to the vehicle. This clause can be along similar lines to clause 6 in the specimen Conditions of Sale (Appendix 1).

(c) A clause making it clear that any written or oral reference to the year of a motor vehicle refers to the date of its first registration in the UK. The reason for this is that there can be discrepancies between the date of manufacture and date of registration, the latter being the only date readily discoverable from the registration documents. There has been litigation under the Trade Descriptions Act 1968 on this point. Thus in *Routledge v Ansa Motors (Chester le Street) Ltd*[3] a Ford manufactured in 1972 was converted into a caravanette and registered on 1 August 1975. In November 1975 it was sold and described as 'one used 1975 Ford Escort Fiesta'. In allowing an appeal against the justices' finding that there was no case to answer to a charge under ss 1 and 2(1)(h) of the Trade Descriptions Act 1968,[4] the court stated that the justices should have considered whether '1975' was likely to be taken as an indication of the *age* of the vehicle and if so whether this was false or misleading to a material degree under s 3 of the Trade Descriptions Act 1968.

(d) A clause making it clear that vehicles are sold with the benefit of any unexpired vehicle excise licences attached thereto and current MOT certificate relating thereto.

2 The clause could thus run: 'The Purchaser shall have the right to reject vehicles specifically sold by the Auctioneer on 'Pre-Trial' terms if found to be materially defective, such rejection taking place within one hour of the Purchaser's successful bid, except that there is no right to reject in respect of defects revealed on the Entry Form relating to a vehicle available for inspection by the Purchaser in advance.'

3 (1979) 123 Sol Jo 735, [1980] RTR 1.

4 See Appendix 2.

(e) A clause stating that the purchaser of any motor vehicle is responsible for complying with all legal requirements as to the roadworthiness, construction and use of that vehicle and for obtaining all certificates, permits or other authorisation necessary before that vehicle can be used on any road. The purpose of this clause is to mitigate the possibility of prosecution of the auctioneer for contravention of s 60 of the Road Traffic Act 1972, and for other legislative provisions requiring current excise licences, MOT certificates etc. The clause should be tied in with a clause on the entry form affecting sellers under which all sellers are required to warrant that, unless previously disclosed to the auctioneer, any vehicle consigned by the seller for sale is in a roadworthy condition and complies with the regulations made under s 40 of the Road Traffic Act 1972 (relating to construction and use) or any statutory modification thereof. (An additional clause relating to the currency of licences will be required if the auctioneer or his staff will need to drive the vehicle on a highway.)

(f) A clause indemnifying the auctioneer against the cost of insurance, the desirability of which is explained below.

Some special features of motor auctions

Vehicle auctions seem to be the main type to employ the use of the 'provisional bid' which is in effect a fall-back procedure where a vehicle attracts a bid less than its reserve. The practice was examined in *RH Willis & Son v British Car Auctions Ltd,*[5] and during the course of his judgment Lord Denning MR described the provisional bid system as an established feature of the vehicle auction trade. The case also highlights problems of title to vehicles subject to hire-purchase agreements or not otherwise owned by the seller.

The facts were that RHW, the plaintiffs, were car dealers who 'sold' a car to C on hire-purchase terms, a deposit being paid. The hire-purchase agreement contained the usual warning that the goods could not be sold before all instalments were paid. Instead, C took the car to the defendant auctioneers BCA, with a reserve agreed of £450. The highest bid, made by W, was £410. BCA then contacted C, either by telephone or through their 'provisional bid office' and having ascertained that W would 'stand by' the bid of £410 (i e not withdraw it) asked C if he would accept it. C agreed provided BCA reduced their commission, which they did. The auctioneers checked with Hire Purchase Information (HPI)[6] who stated that no information was registered against that vehicle. The deal therefore went through, and shortly afterward C became bankrupt and the facts came to light.

The issue was whether the loss (the £275 balance on the hire-purchase agreement) should fall on RHW, the dealers, or BCA, the auctioneers. The auctioneers could only be liable if they had committed the tort of conversion.[7]

5 [1978] 2 All ER 392, [1978] 1 WLR 438, CA.

6 HPI and the status of answers supplied by HPI to enquiries were discussed in *Moorgate Mercantile Co Ltd v Twitchings* [1977] AC 890, [1976] 2 All ER 641, HL; see also discussion in Harvey *Law of Consumer Protection and Fair Trading* (2nd edn, 1982) Butterworths, p 263.

7 This aspect of *R H Willis & Son v British Car Auctions Ltd* [1978] 2 All ER 392, [1978] 1 WLR 438, CA, is discussed further on p 104 above.

Lord Denning had no doubt that under the present state of the law, sales under the hammer of goods to which the vendor has no title give rise to liability in conversion, on behalf of both the auctioneer and the buyer, to the true owner.[8] The question was whether a sale by 'provisional bid' was any different. The Court of Appeal was satisfied that it was not different. Decisive factors included the auctioneer's own evidence that the 'provisional bid' system was to facilitate sales 'because we are in commerce to make money and we are delighted if a sale can be agreed so that we can earn the negotiating fee'.[9] The court equated the negotiating fee with conventional commission. In addition, each purchaser under the 'provisional bid' system was required, under clause 20 of the relevant Conditions of Sale for auctions, to pay £2 premium to an insurance company associated with the auctioneers against losses suffered through any defect in title of the seller. Since this was a system applying to hammer sales as well as provisional bid sales, the same consequences should ensue in either case. Lord Denning was particularly swayed by the policy point that the innocent acquirer (here, W) and the innocent handler (here, the auctioneers BCA) were both protected against claims by the true owner through the insurance policy 'so that the loss is not borne by any single individual but is spread through the community at large'.[10] But even if the vehicle auctioneer did not avail himself and purchasers of insurance protection, it is to be assumed that the provisional bid procedure would still be indistinguishable in its essential nature and legal consequences from sales under the hammer. The decision underlines the good sense of such auctioneers taking out insurance against the consequences of the vendor's vehicle having been stolen or being subject to an undischarged hire-purchase agreement, and purchasers at such sales checking that valid insurance exists.[11]

Selling unroadworthy cars

Criminal liability

Criminal liability now depends on s 60 of the Road Traffic Act 1972 which (as amended) runs as follows:

> 60. *Vehicles not to be sold in unroadworthy condition or altered so as to be unroadworthy*
>
> (1) Subject to the provisions of this section it shall not be lawful to sell, or to supply, or to offer to sell or supply, or to expose for sale, a motor vehicle or trailer for delivery in such a condition that the use thereof on a road in that condition would be unlawful by virtue of any provision made by regulations under section 40 of this Act as respects brakes, steering gear or tyres or as respects the construction, weight or equipment of vehicles, or as respects the maintenance of vehicles, their parts and accessories in such a condition that no danger is likely to be caused, or in such a condition, as respects lighting equipment or reflectors or the maintenance thereof, that it is not capable of being used on a road during the hours of darkness without contravention of the requirements imposed by law as to obligatory lamps or reflectors.

8 See *Barker v Furlong* [1891] 2 Ch 172 at 181.
9 [1978] 2 All ER 392 at 398.
10 [1978] 2 All ER 392 at 397.
11 The court did not analyse the provisional bid procedure in terms of offer and acceptance, but presumably the 'provisional bid' is a conditional offer which must first be made unconditional by the buyer. The auctioneer then accepts or rejects it having received fresh instructions from the vendor.

(2) Subject to the provisions of this section it shall not be lawful to alter a motor vehicle or trailer so as to render its condition such that the use thereof on a road in that condition would be unlawful by virtue of any provision made as respects the construction, weight or equipment of vehicles by regulations under the said section 40.

(3) If a motor vehicle or trailer is sold, supplied, offered, exposed for sale, or altered in contravention of the provisions of this section, any person who so sells, supplies, or offers it, exposes it for sale, or alters it, or causes or permits it to be so sold, supplied, offered, exposed for sale, or altered, shall be guilty of an offence.

(4) A person shall not be convicted of an offence under this section in respect of the sale, supply, offer, exposure for sale, or alteration of a motor vehicle or trailer if he proves —
(a) that it was sold, supplied, offered, exposed for sale, or altered, as the case may be, for export from Great Britain, or
(b) that he had reasonable cause to believe that the vehicle or trailer would not be used on a road in Great Britain, or would not be so used until it had been put into a condition in which it might lawfully be so used, or
(c) in the case of a vehicle or trailer the sale, supply, offer or exposure for sale, of which is alleged to be unlawful by reason of its condition as respects lighting equipment or reflectors or the maintenance thereof, that he had reasonable cause to believe that the vehicle or trailer would not be used on a road in Great Britain during the hours of darkness until it had been put into a condition in which it might be so used during those hours without contravention of the requirements imposed by law as to obligatory lamps or reflectors.

(5) Nothing in the foregoing provisions of this section shall affect the validity of a contract or any rights arising under a contract.

(6) In this section 'obligatory lamps or reflectors' means, in relation to a motor vehicle or trailer, the lamps or reflectors required by law to be carried thereon while it is on a road during the hours of darkness and when it is neither drawing nor being drawn by another vehicle, except that the said expression does not, in the case of a motor vehicle, include any lamps or reflectors required to be carried by virtue of section 79 of this Act, or, in the case of a trailer, include any lamps or reflectors so required to be carried or any lamps showing a white light to the front.

There are a number of points to note about this widely-drafted section, which catches sales of defective vehicles by private sellers as well as by business sellers. These are:

(a) In *British Car Auctions Ltd v Wright*[12] it was held that an auctioneer, when he stood on his rostrum, does not make an 'offer to sell' the goods in question; he merely invites those present at the auction to make offers to buy them. Accordingly the auctioneers were not guilty of an offence under the predecessor of this section, which referred to its being unlawful 'to sell, or to supply, or to offer to sell or supply' unroadworthy vehicles. The current legislation adds, by virtue of the Road Traffic Act 1974 amending the original text, the significant words 'or to expose for sale'. Vehicles in course of being auctioned are clearly exposed for sale. (The possiblity that the auctioneer had nevertheless 'sold' the car was not examined.)

12 [1972] 3 All ER 462, [1972] 1 WLR 1519, QBD, following *Fisher v Bell* [1961] 1 QB 394, [1960] 3 All ER 731 and *Partridge v Crittenden* [1968] 2 All ER 421, [1968] 1 WLR 1204. The more colloquial meaning was rejected in this particular context.

(b) If an auctioneer does 'expose for sale' an unroadworthy vehicle, the offence is of 'strict liability'. Absence of knowledge of the defects is irrelevant.[13] The defence to the charge is likely to be under s 60(4)(b) of the Road Traffic Act 1972 (as amended). The auctioneer must show that he had reasonable cause to believe that the vehicle would not be used on a road in Great Britain, or would not be so used until it had been put into a condition in which it might lawfully be so used. In this latter connection, a clause such as Condition (e) above[14] (putting the onus on the purchaser to ensure that the vehicle is roadworthy before using it on any road) will be helpful. The question of whether the auctioneer did have 'reasonable cause to believe' involves satisfying the court that he did so actually believe and had reasonable cause so to do.[15]

(c) Section 60(5) of the Road Traffic Act 1972 (as amended) makes it clear that infringement of this section does not invalidate, by reason of illegality, any civil contract made between seller and buyer for the sale of the car. The purchaser will still be bound to pay the price, though in any consequential criminal proceedings the court has discretion to make a compensation order under s 35 of the Powers of Criminal Courts Act 1973 (as amended) in addition to or instead of a fine. Compensation is limited to £2 000 (in 1984) in magistrates' courts.

(d) The offence is a summary one carrying a maximum fine of level 5 on the standard scale (see s 46(1) of the Criminal Justice Act 1982).

Civil liability

Contract

It is not proposed to repeat in detail here the analysis provided in ch 6 of the conditions of fitness for purpose and merchantable quality contained in s 14 of the Sale of Goods Act 1979, and the validity of any clause attempting to exclude these implied conditions. Suffice it to say that an unroadworthy car is, on the face of it, likely neither to be fit for the purpose of the buyer nor of merchantable quality. But these statements must be qualified by re-emphasising that the condition of merchantable quality does not apply as regards defects first drawn to the buyer's attention, or as regards defects which ought to have been revealed on the examination made by the buyer; the condition as to fitness for purpose may equally not be implied if, for instance, the buyer's purpose is purely to buy the car for spares or to 'cannibalise' (see *Hurley v Dyke*,[16] discussed below).

Even if such a sale is in breach of one or both these conditions, the Conditions of Sale are likely to contain an exemption clause. Assuming that this clause has been effectively brought to the notice of the buyer or is otherwise contractually

13 *Sandford Motor Sales v Habgood* [1962] Crim LR 487; see also the note following the report which questions the Divisional Court's assumption that no mens rea is necessary in these circumstances. The question is whether the section's wording clearly or by implication rules out the requirement of guilty knowledge.
14 See above, p 188.
15 See *Nakkuda Ali v M F de S Jayaratne* [1951] AC 56; *McArdle v Egan* (1933) 150 LT 412, 98 JP 103, CA; and *R v Harrison* [1938] 3 All ER 134, 159 LT 95.
16 [1979] RTR 265, HL.

binding, the buyer's only line of attack could be that the exemption clause does not satisfy the requirement of reasonableness as laid down by s 6 of the Unfair Contract Terms Act 1977 (discussed in ch 6).

Tort

Suppose that a buyer of a car at auction drives it away and is injured as a result of an accident caused by the car's unroadworthy condition. Most defendants would prefer to sue the seller on the basis of a breach of the implied conditions in s 14 of the Sale of Goods Act 1979, since if a breach can be proved, the seller's liability is strict i e there is no need to prove that the seller was negligent.[17]

However, as shown above, a contractually-based action may not be available to the plaintiff either because there is in fact no breach of contract or because there is no privity of contract between the buyer of the car who is injured and the seller at auction. This latter situation occurred in *Hurley v Dyke*[18] which is worth careful study in this area and will now be examined. It illustrates the possibilities of and limitations surrounding a possible action in tort against the seller, and this in turn can have implications for the auctioneer.

The facts were that D, a small-garage owner, bought a Reliant three-seater car from an owner when it broke down near his garage. He paid £10 for it (in 1971) and though it was obvious that the car was in very bad structural condition, the House of Lords found as a fact that the extent of D's knowledge of the defects was that he 'was aware of the very real danger of driving the car without further examination and the doing of any necessary repairs which that examination revealed'.[19]

Some days later, without any material work being done on the car, it was driven by D's mechanic to a local auction held by British Car Auctions Ltd. D also drove over and entered the car at a reserve of £40 and subject to the auctioneer's conditions. There was both an entry condition and Condition of Sale stipulating that vehicles offered 'as seen' or realising £200 or less 'are sold and bought for what they are and with all their faults' and all conditions and warranties were excluded. In addition, Condition of Sale 16(a) stipulated that if a vehicle sold was in a condition to make its use on the road unlawful 'there shall be deemed to be incorporated in the contract between the seller and the purchaser an undertaking on the part of the purchaser that it will not be used on a road until a valid Test Certificate has been obtained' or it is otherwise made roadworthy.

When the car was sold, the auctioneer repeated what was written on the entry form: namely, that it was sold 'As seen and with all its faults and without warranty'.

The car was knocked down to J for £40, J's intention being to cannibalise it. C had also attended the auction, but had been an unsuccessful bidder. But he

17 See *Randall v Newsom* (1876) 45 LJQB, 364; and generally, Harvey *Law of Consumer Protection and Fair Trading* (2nd edn, 1982) Butterworths p 97.
18 [1979] RTR 265, HL.
19 [1979] RTR 265, HL, at 302.

succeeded in getting J to re-sell it to him (C) for a slightly enhanced price. Having driven the car apparently without serious incident for eight days, C was then involved in a catastrophic accident when the chassis snapped due to corrosion beneath the passenger seat. C was killed and the plaintiff, H, was seriously injured. H would have been entitled to claim £45 000 damages if he could show D was responsible in negligence (there being no passenger insurance). D would be liable for the tort of negligence if it could be shown that he was in breach of his duty of care to a foreseeable purchaser. Lord Denning had found D so liable in a dissenting judgment in the Court of Appeal,[20] the essence of his judgment being that (a) clearly a duty of care was owed, (b) D knew the car to be a 'death-trap' and (c) in these circumstances the auctioneer's warning was insufficient.

Although the House of Lords disagreed with Lord Denning (and Jones J at first instance) in finding D liable, there seems to have been general agreement at all levels that the vendor at an auction of an article which he knows to be dangerous owes a duty of care to potential buyers of the article.[1] The nub of the issue was whether D had discharged this duty of care by the giving of the warning at the auction. Having regard to the fact of D's limited knowledge of the fatal defect, the House of Lords held that he had.[2]

The hypothetical question then arises: what would the position have been if it could have been established that the seller knew the car to be dangerous? Both Viscount Dilhorne and Lord Scarman agreed that it should not be assumed that the seller had discharged such duty as lay upon him by selling it 'as seen and with all its faults and without warranty'.

Although the position of the *auctioneer* was nowhere discussed in this litigation, it is apparent that there is a strong likelihood of his incurring civil liability, jointly with the vendor or exclusively, in a variety of circumstances. For instance, if the auctioneer was *aware* of the dangerous condition of the vehicle and had not given any effective warning to the buyer, there seems no reason in principle why the buyer should not succeed against the auctioneer in negligence — a duty of care clearly exists in this situation, as explained in *Hurley v Dyke*.[3] An attempted negation of this duty of care via a Condition of Sale or notice would be nullified by s 2(1) of the Unfair Contract Terms Act 1977, which states: 'A person cannot by reference to any contract term or to a notice given to persons generally or to particular persons exclude or restrict his liability for death or personal injury resulting from negligence.'[4] The obvious moral is that auctioneers should be scrupulous in: (a) requiring a full declaration by the seller as to any feature of the vehicle rendering it unroadworthy, and if this is so, (b) passing on explicitly an appropriate warning to all bidders in the form found adequate in *Hurley v Dyke*.[5]

20 [1979] RTR 265 at 276

1 See per Lord Diplock [1979] RTR 265, HL, at 301.

2 *Ward v Hobbs* (1878) 4 App Cas 13, 48 LJQB 281, HL, where a similar warning was held by the House of Lords to be effective in the case of the sale of pigs known by the seller to be diseased, was considered. There is some doubt whether this 'shocking decision' (Lord Denning's words in *Hurley v Dyke* (1979] RTR 265 at 281) would be followed today in the light of the development of the law of negligence in and after *Donoghue v Stevenson* [1932] AC 562, 101 LJPC 119, HL.

3 [1979] RTR 265, HL.

4 There is also the possibility of an action for breach of statutory duty. There is no authority on whether such an action would lie in these circumstances, but there is a presumption against its availability where the statute does not expressly confer the right to sue. Section 60 of the Road Traffic Act 1972 merely confirms that the civil *contract* is not vitiated by the criminal illegality of the sale.

5 Above, n 3.

Trade descriptions

Offences capable of being committed by auctioneers under the Trade Descriptions Act 1968 are extensively discussed in ch 8. Here we concentrate purely on the position of the vehicle auctioneer.

Prima facie any materially false description of a vehicle sold (or exposed for sale) at an auction, and which is not effectively disclaimed, constitutes an offence under s 1 of the Trade Descriptions Act 1968. A false trade description can relate purely to the catalogue description, or be made orally, or can be applied by means of a false odometer reading — there being an abundance of authority on this point.

The offence may be committeed by the auctioneer or by the seller via the entry form.

As an example of the first, in the Scottish case of *Aitchison v Reith & Anderson (Dingwall & Tain) Ltd*,[6] the respondents were long-established auctioneers but had not before auctioned a motor vehicle. They described the vehicle in writing as in 'Good Condition' without taking any technical advice. The description was false. The qualified auctioneer who conducted the sale checked the particulars from the registration book, and relying on the presence of an MOT certificate and its good external appearance assumed it was worthy. The High Court of Justiciary instructed the conviction of the respondents under s 1(1)(a) of the Trade Descriptions Act 1968, finding that there was no valid defence to the charge under this section by virtue of s 24 of that Act — taking all reasonable precautions and exercising all due diligence. An MOT certificate did not cover the defects from which the car suffered, and it was important to take technical advice on a sale outside the auctioneers' normal competence and experience. Although a director had apparently instructed that no descriptions should be issued, he had not ensured that these instructions were carried out.

The second situation, where a false trade description can be applied by the seller, is illustrated by *Zawadski v Sleigh*.[7] This decision also illustrates the principle, discussed in ch 8, that a trader can avoid commission of an offence by an effective disclaimer of what would otherwise be a false trade description applied to goods contrary to s 1(1)(b) of the Trade Descriptions Act 1968. In the case of vehicles, the most common case of this is the display of a false odometer reading, and it has been held in *Norman v Bennett*[8] that in order to negative such a false trade description the disclaimer must be as bold, precise and compelling as the odometer reading itself.

In *Zawadski v Sleigh*[9] the defendants were not the auctioneers but the motor dealers who had entered through British Car Auctions at Measham three cars whose odometer readings were incorrect, the mileage being substantially in excess of that indicated. The auctioneers used a comprehensive exemption

6 (1973) unreported, High Court of Justiciary; see O'Keefe *Law Relating to Trade Descriptions* (Butterworths) 3/80.
7 (1975) 119 Sol Jo 318, [1975] RTR 113, DC.
8 [1974] 3 All ER 351, [1974] 1 WLR 1229, followed and refined in numerous other decisions.
9 Above, n 7.

clause in their Conditions of Sale which negated any warranty condition description or representation on the part of the auctioneers affecting any vehicle sold through them together with all statutory or other warranties as to condition, roadworthiness or mileages otherwise given on the part of the auctioneers. The auctioneers' practice was to give regular oral warnings that mileage was not guaranteed, but no specific disclaimer was made as to the three cars in question.

The Divisional Court upheld the justices' conviction of the defendant dealers on a charge under s 1 of the Trade Descriptions Act 1968 on the basis that the disclaimers made by the auctioneers were on these facts insufficiently potent to remove the false impression given by the mileometer readings. Lord Widgery CJ emphasised that the correct question was not whether the disclaimer was made on the defendants' behalf by the auctioneers. It was 'whether the disclaimer would be potent enough to get through to the buyer and make him disregard the message which the odometer had previously passed on to him.'[10]

This case has some unsatisfactory features as regards the potential liability of the auctioneers. Their position was not clearly considered, but the possibility of an effective disclaimer as to their own potential liability under the Trade Descriptions Act 1968 was clearly accepted.

MISCELLANEOUS AUCTIONS OF OTHER COMMODITIES

Introduction

Auctions of commodities other than those specifically considered in this book, such as motor cars, are many and various. Sales by auction of fruit, vegetables and fish are a world-wide phenomenon. The same applies to auctions of other commodities in which there is a daily market such as tea, coffee and certain minerals. Each commodity auction is likely to have some special features, but to deal with them specifically is beyond the scope of this book. We do, however, now consider briefly three additional types of auction which take place in the UK and discuss their special features.

Plant and machinery

Sales of factory or commercial plant and machinery by auction have increased in frequency over recent years, no doubt owing to economic problems caused by the recession and the need for liquidators and receivers to turn plant into cash as quickly and efficiently as possible.

With regard to the General Conditions which could be applicable in these circumstances, the Royal Institution of Chartered Surveyors has published

10 [1975] RTR 113 at 118.

recommended Conditions of Sale for auctions of plant and machinery held on the vendor's premises.[11] It is not proposed, therefore, to discuss the form which these conditions might otherwise take since the professionally-approved model is readily available.

There are, however, a few specific problems concerned with the nature of the commodity sold which can only be guarded against if properly appreciated.

Firstly, plant and machinery can be very heavy (e g grinding machines, lathes, milling machines) and may be firmly affixed to the factory floor. The situation may arise where the land and factory building either belongs to a landlord or a creditor-mortgagee has a charge over the same. There can then arise a distinction between that land and premises which the owner of the business may not sell, and those items of plant and machinery which, being separate chattels, the business owner or his agent may be free to sell. To decide whether heavy plant fixed to the floor is a 'fixture' going with the land, or a chattel, depends upon the law of fixtures as developed as part of the law of real property. A general test involves consideration of both the *degree* of annexation and the *purpose* of that annexation. An article fixed to the floor is prima facie a fixture — the more so if it would cause difficulty to remove. But machinery standing by its own weight normally remains a chattel.[12] The 'purpose' test sometimes removes from the category of what would otherwise be a fixture an article affixed to the land because there is no other way to 'enjoy' it — e g a tapestry nailed to the wall.[13] But the courts have not been entirely consistent in applying either of these tests and the following, for example, have been held to be fixtures: looms in a worsted mill fixed by nails to wooden beams in the floor,[14] seats in a cinema,[15] machinery fixed by bolts,[16] and an electric light generating machine fixed by bolts.[17]

If it is apparent that a piece of machinery is a fixture (the fact that it has been installed by the business owner being, of course, irrelevant), the law must again be examined to see if the business proprietor nevertheless has the right to remove the fixture. This right attaches in particular to tenants of factories or other land where the fixture has been attached by the tenant for the purpose of his trade or business. A number of fixtures such as vats, fixed steam engines and boilers have come into this category of 'tenant's fixtures'. But if the fixture is to be removed, this must occur during the currency of the lease or, if the lease has not been forfeited or surrended, within a reasonable time after expiry.[18] Once this time elapses, the fixture becomes the absolute property of the landlord and may, therefore, not properly be sold without his consent.

There are special rules relating to the removal of agricultural fixtures where the tenant may, subject to certain conditions, remove fixtures within two months after the determination of the term.[19]

11 (1981) Royal Institution of Chartered Surveyors.
12 *Hulme v Brigham* [1943] KB 152, [1943] 1 All ER 204.
13 *Leigh v Taylor* [1902] AC 157, 71 LJ Ch 272, HL.
14 *Holland v Hodgson* (1872) LR 7CP 328, 41 LJCP 146.
15 *Vaudeville Electric Cinema Ltd v Muriset* [1923] 2Ch 74, 92 LJ Ch 558; but contrast *Lyon & Co v London City and Midland Bank* [1903] 2KB 135, 72 LJKB 465 (seats fixed for temporary use held to be chattels).
16 *Reynolds v Ashby & Son* [1904] AC 466, 73 LJKB 946, HL.
17 *Jordan v May* [1947] KB 427, [1947] LJR 653, CA (but the batteries were chattels).
18 See *Lavies, ex p Stephens* (1877) 7 Ch D 127, 47 LJ Bcy 22, CA.
19 Agricultural Holdings Act 1948, s 13.

Enough has been stated to show that great care must be taken by the auctioneer to ensure that the machinery and plant in question is the vendor's unencumbered property. This includes consideration of Romalpa[20] clauses under which the vendor of goods delivered to the purchaser reserves, or purports to reserve, his title to those goods until some condition (usually full payment) has been met. Difficult problems of priority can also arise where, for instance, hired machinery is fixed to a mortgaged factory,[1] but whoever may then have the best title to the machinery, it is certainly not the hirer's property to sell.

Problems can also arise with machinery not complying with safety legislation, such as the Health and Safety at Work etc Act 1974, either with regard to its safe functioning or because it contains toxic chemicals such as asbestos. The best than can be done here is to emphasise by notice in the Conditions of Sale that such machinery may not comply with current safety legislation and is sold on the basis that it is the buyer's responsibility to ensure that the machine's subsequent use is in compliance with this legislation.

The sale of large, heavy plant may cause serious administrative problems with regard to its removal. Again, Conditions of Sale should deal with the buyer's obligations on this point and bind him to reinstate any damage after removal at his own expense within a reasonable time. The buyer may need police or other permission to transport wide loads on a public highway and a warning as to this could be a wise precaution.

Sales of reversions and future property interests

As Messrs H E Foster and Cranfield[2] state in their Conditions of Sale

> H E Foster & Cranfield's periodical sales of absolute and contingent reversions to funded property, annuities, policies of assurance, life interests, ... and all descriptions of present or prospective property were established in the year 1843 and have been continued successfully since that date.

The auctions in question take place normally once a month throughout the year in London.

There is clearly a market for sales and purchases of reversions — or more accurately 'remainders' in most cases[3] — and other property to which there is a present right to future enjoyment (i e a vested future interest) or a contingent right to future enjoyment (contingent future interest). A straight forward example of a vested future interest is where a testator has left his estate to his wife for life with remainder to his only son. The son's interest is a vested one to which he will either succeed on the death of the mother, or if he predeceases his mother the remainder then falls to be distributed amongst those entitled to

20 See *Aluminium Industrie Vaassen BV v Romalpa Aluminium Ltd* [1976] 2 All ER 552, [1976] 1 WLR 676. Creditors of a company may not be bound by such a clause unless it is registered as a charge under Companies Act 1985, s 395.

1 See generally, Megarry and Wade *The Law of Real Property* (5th edn, 1984) Stevens, p 738.

2 Auctioneers, Valuers and Estate Agents, 6 Poultry, London EC2.

3 A reversion technically reverts to the original donor — e g a gift by X to A for life, X retaining the reversionary interest. A remainder is illustrated in the example in the text.

the son's estate. The value of the remainder (or 'reversion' as it is loosely called) will depend on such factors as: (a) the present capital value of the fund; (b) liability, if any, to capital transfer tax on the death of the mother as it affects the fund; (c) the trustee's future investment policy; and (d) the life expectation of the mother. The greater the latter is, the more the value of the 'reversion' will be discounted. The attraction of an immediate sale to the son is the capital prematurely in hand. The attraction to a purchaser is that the difference between the price immediately paid and the value of the interest when it falls in could represent a considerable capital gain, though the factors enumerated above introduce a heavy element of chance. A *contingent* interest is considerably more risky.

Similarly there is a market for life policies not yet matured, annuities which the annuitant wishes to sell in return for a capital sum (and in this case the annuitant's longevity is at a premium for the buyer) and other property interests of this sort which the owner wishes to convert into a capital sum in possession.

There can be very considerable legal complexities in these transactions and it is interesting to note that in Messrs H E Foster and Cranfield's General Conditions of Sale there are included conditions which entitle the purchasers to proof of the vendor's title and all proper conveyances, transfers, and assignments, the cost of the latter falling on the purchaser. Under these conditions, ten per cent deposit is payable at the successful bid (evidenced by a signed memorandum), the remaining money being payable on completion of the transaction.

Livestock sales

The selling of livestock, from the regular market sales of cattle and sheep for slaughter, to the more specialised annual sales of thoroughbred horses is almost exclusively effected by auction. Indeed, in the case of fatstock sales it is difficult to see how they might otherwise be organised. These auction market sales have certain particular features which should be noted. There exist statutory controls, and detailed specialist Conditions of Sale are normally employed.[4]

Statutory controls

The main statutory control of livestock auction markets is in the field of weighing cattle. An auctioneer must not sell cattle[5] at any market where such are habitually sold unless facilities for weighing them are provided at the market. Fines of up to £100[6] may be levied and if the offence is a continuing one, the penalty is £10 per day for every day it continues.

4 The Livestock Auctioneers' Market Committee for England and Wales has produced a standard set of Conditions of Sale for Cattle, Calves, Sheep and Pigs at Livestock Auction Market. These are in general use in such auctions and the conditions are registered with the Office of Fair Trading in accordance with the Restrictive Practices Act 1976. The authors are grateful to the committee for their kind permission to utilise and reproduce these conditions.

5 'In this Act the word "cattle" includes ram, ewe, wether, lamb, and swine': Markets and Fairs (Weighing of Cattle) Act 1887, s 3. But see n 7, below.

6 Markets and Fairs (Weighing of Cattle) Act 1891, s 4, as amended by the Criminal Justice Act 1982, s 37. The scale corresponds to level 2: ss 37 and 46 of the Criminal Justice Act 1982.

If an auctioneer sells cattle[7] fit for slaughter where such weighing facilities are provided and he fails either to weigh them or to notify the bidder of their weight at the time the cattle are offered for sale, he commits an offence under s 2 of the Markets and Fairs (Weighing of Cattle) Act 1926. The penalty for breach of this provision is £2 per head of cattle so sold.

The penalties for infringement of these provisions are not very great. However the controls are effective. Fatstock is sold by weight (today, prices usually being calculated per kilogram) and the organisers of the market ensure that proper and accurate weighing machines are used. If, as is usually the case, the market is run by the local authority for the area, the authority will ensure compliance by installing and inspecting machines. Alternatively, if, as the case in Hereford, for example, the market is run by a company formed by a consortium of auctioneer firms, the company will obtain certification as to the accuracy of the machines from the local authority's trading standards department.

Conduct of the sale

As we have already observed, livestock auctioneers are well served by standard Conditions of Sale and we do not attempt to provide our own alternative terms. However it might be useful to consider a few of the conditions commonly utilised.

Diseased etc animals

As we have seen in ch 5, an auctioneer may be under a duty to care for the goods of his vendor, as bailee and possibly also those of the purchaser either in a similar capacity or generally in negligence. One obvious risk in livestock auctions is that a diseased animal may infect those belonging to others whilst under the care and control of the auctioneer. It is sensible to guard against this potential liability and an appropriate condition is that supplied by Condition 4(a) of the Standard Conditions recommended by the Livestock Auctioneer's Market Committee. The condition places the liability for losses occasioned directly upon the person bringing such diseased animal onto the auction premises. It also permits the auctioneer at his discretion to exclude or dispose of any such animal.

Dangerous animals

An auctioneer will also be potentially liable in negligence for any injury to other animals or persons caused by an animal under his control. Whilst the female of the species may sometimes be regarded as being deadlier than the male, there is obviously a particular risk in relation to bulls. The Standard Conditions provide that no bull over ten months of age is to be brought onto the auction premises unless properly ringed and haltered.

7 The Markets and Fairs (Weighing of Cattle) Act 1926, s 1(3): 'In this section [Disclosure of weight of fat cattle on sale by auction] the expression "cattle" means bulls, cows, oxen and heifers.'

Sales of heifers by weight

Heifers and other animals sold for slaughter are sold by weight. It is obvious that if sold as warranted free of calf or lamb as the case may be and it transpires that the animal was not so free, the purchaser will have paid an excessive price for the fatstock. He will be entitled to damages for misdescription and conditions are included to ensure that the purchaser's rights under the contract of sale are exercised promptly and reasonably. Thus Condition 43 of the Standard Conditions provides:[8]

> Unless stated to the contrary in the catalogue or at the time of sale all heifers are warranted to be free of calf. If:
>
> (a) within 48 hours after the slaughter of a heifer to which the aforegoing warranty applies notice in writing is given to the auctioneers that she was carrying a calf weighing at the time of slaughter more than 9 kg, and
>
> (b) such notice is supported by a certificate signed by the slaughter-house manager or a veterinary surgeon or other competent person and stating the identity number of the heifer, the date of slaughter and the weight of the calf at that date,
>
> then the vendor shall pay to the purchaser, as and for ascertained and agreed liquidated damages, to cover all expenses, depreciation in value and other damages whatsoever, a sum equal to one-and-a-half times the value of the calf alone, calculated as a proportionate part of the value of the heifer ascertained from its purchase price per live kg at the sale. No compensation for damages shall be payable in respect of a calf weighing, at the time of slaughter, 9 kg or less.

The restrictions on the right to reject are thus of two kinds: one relates to the time in which notice is to be given, and the other limits the right to those cases where the calf is at the relevant time in excess of 9 kg in weight. Moreover the clause goes on to provide what is known as a liquidated damages provision which will be upheld only if it is found to represent a reasonable pre-estimate of the loss likely to flow from the breach. Such a clause does not come within the ambit of the Unfair Contract Terms Act 1977. The provision excluding compensation for calves of less than 9 kg is an exclusion clause within the Unfair Contract Terms Act 1977, but apart from the probability that it would be regarded as not unreasonable, it is not likely to be a matter on which litigation would be pursued.

On the other hand, Condition 28 (quoted below)[9] which amounts to an omnibus exclusion clause, will be subject to the test of reasonableness under the Unfair Contract Terms Act 1977. The ramifications of this are discussed fully in ch 6.

Milking of cows

An unusual 'perk' is provided for in Condition 72, namely that, unless the owner wishes to do so, the auctioneers shall authorise the milking of cows on the sale premises and the milk in that event shall belong to the auctioneers.

8 Conditions of Sale for Cattle, Calves, Sheep and Pigs at Livestock Auction Market, Livestock Auctioneers' Market Committee for England and Wales.

9 See below, p 203.

Conditions relating to fatstock premium schemes

The European Economic Community has introduced regimes whereby member states may establish systems for the payment of premiums for producers of certain animals. There are currently in operation schemes relating to beef and sheep meat.[10] The essence of these schemes is that a weekly target price is fixed, and when the average market price (calculated from live-weight auction sales) falls below the target or guide price, a premium will be paid. The owner of the cattle or sheep must present the animals for certification and examination by the Meat and Livestock Commission and such animals will be marked. It is a condition of these schemes that any animal certified live must be slaughtered within 21 days of the date of certification or, in the case of sheep, exported or placed in quarantine prior to export, within that period.

There is one matter relating to these detailed schemes which is of concern to auctioneers of such fatstock, and that relates to the slaughter requirements. Article 8 of the Beef Premiums (Protection of Payments) Order 1978 provides that no person shall knowingly sell a certified animal on or before the date by which it is to be slaughtered without informing the buyer of these requirements in writing. Thus if an animal so certified is sold in the ring, the auctioneer should first ensure that he has obtained such details from the vendor before accepting them for sale, and second, should note on the purchaser's invoice the date by which such an animal must be slaughtered. Moreover, once the slaughter date has passed it is an offence for a person to sell such a certified animal or, indeed, have it in his possession. There are similar provisions relating to sheep contained in Article 6 of the Sheep Variable Premium (Protection of Payments) (2) Order 1980.[11]

If any animal which has been presented for certification is bought in by or on behalf of the vendor at auction, then the animal ceases to qualify under the scheme until fresh application is made.

There are several general requirements as to the keeping of records relating to sales of particular commodities and wide powers are vested in the Intervention Board for Agricultural Produce to enter premises and inspect books etc. Failure to comply with these regulations renders a person liable to criminal penalties.[12]

10 These schemes are explained in leaflets provided by the Intervention Board for Agricultural Produce. The relevant Regulations and Statutory Provisions are as follows:
(a) *Beef*
EEC Regulation 1063/84 of 16 April 1984; EEC Regulation 1355/84 of 16 May 1984; Beef Premiums (Protection of Payments) Order 1978, SI 1978/17.
(b) *Sheep*
EEC Regulation 1837/80 of 27 June 1980; EEC Regulation 2661/80 of 17 October 1980; EEC Regulation 1238/82 of 20 May 1982; EEC Regulation 1689/83 of 24 June 1983; Sheep Variable Premium (Protection of Payments) (2) Order 1980, SI 1980/1811; Sheep Variable Premium (Protection of Payments) (Amendment) Order 1981, SI 1981/751; Sheep Variable Premium (Protection of Payments) (Amendment) Order 1982, SI 1982/726; Sheep Variable Premium (Protection of Payments) (Amendment) Order 1983, SI 1983/1009.

11 Provided by SI 1983/1009.

12 The Regulations are laid down by the Common Agricultural Policy (Protection of Community Arrangements) Regulations 1973; the penalties laid down in Article 10 provide for a fine not exceeding £100 and/or imprisonment for three months.

Meat and Livestock Commission schemes

The Meat and Livestock Commission is a statutory corporation having members appointed by the Minister of Agriculture, Fisheries and Food and the Secretary of State for Wales whose function is to promote greater efficiency in the livestock industry. The commission is partly financed by levy schemes which from time to time are instituted. Currently there is a levy scheme relating to cattle, sheep and pigs whereby charges are levied on the slaughter of such livestock. The scheme is set out in the Meat and Livestock Commission Levy Scheme (Confirmation) Order 1979, as amended.[13]

The levy is initially payable by slaughterers of the livestock, but where a slaughterer slaughters livestock on the instructions of the owner, he can recover the whole of the levy from the latter. Where on the other hand, the slaughterer kills livestock which he has in whole or in part purchased himself, he can recover half of the levy from the vendor.

How does all this affect auctioneers? The answer is provided in art 5 of the Principal Order, the proviso to sub-para (2)(a)(i) of which provides that where the slaughterer purchases the livestock slaughtered at auction he may recover half of the levy from the auctioneer. In addition, if the slaughterer defaults, the commission may recover the levy directly from the person from whom the slaughterer could have recovered it — including the auctioneer where appropriate (sub-para (iv)).

Thus auctioneers should ensure that they have the right to recover the levy or part of it where livestock sold for slaughter is within the scheme. Condition 16 of the Livestock Auctioneers' Market Committee for England and Wales provides for this situation.

Sales outside the ring

The above matters have all concerned fatstock sales. Pedigree cattle and horses are also commonly sent to auction for sale. Not infrequently in such cases (and occasionally in respect of fatstock too) a vendor may effect a sale of the livestock 'outside the ring', that is to say, within the auction premises but either before the goods have gone under the hammer or after an abortive auction sale. In such a case the practice is that the sale is 'booked' with the auctioneer.

The legal significance of this procedure was explained by Diplock J (as he then was) in *Murphy v Jonathan Howlett (a firm)* as follows:[14]

13 SI 1979/393 as amended by SI 1981/1066.
14 (1960) 176 EG 311 at 312. This case has also been considered above in ch 4.

> The seller and the intending buyer, ... agree upon the price and agree to book the sale with the auctioneer ... The auctioneer is entitled either to accept or to reject the booking ... If the auctioneer accepts the booking he pays the seller ... the amount of the price agreed between the seller and the intending buyer ... As regards the cattle, the subject-matter of the booked sale, the seller upon receiving his cheque or cash from the auctioneer is no longer interested in the transaction [and] the auctioneer ... exercises all the rights of the owner ... including the right of retaking possession if he has parted with it, and the right of resale ... The evidence as to the practice upon the booking of a sale suggests strongly that what the parties in fact do is to exercise rights and perform obligations which are identical with the legal rights and obligations which would flow from concurrent sales of the cattle (1) by the seller to the auctioneer at the agreed price less commission and (2) by the auctioneer to the buyer at the agreed price. It is the simplest explanation of the way in which the parties act after the booking and I think it is the correct legal analysis.

The significance of this analysis, that there are two concurrent sales, is that the auctioneer in law sells his *own* goods to the purchaser. He acts not as agent but as principal. In consequence the auctioneer in respect of these sales is liable *qua* seller for breaches of the conditions as to title, and as regards merchantability and fitness for purpose and the like implied by the Sale of Goods Act 1979.

In this context one must consider again the effectiveness of any purported exclusion of these implied terms. We have seen in ch 6 that these conditions cannot be excluded in any consumer sale (and that the implied condition as to title cannot be excluded in *any* sale) but that for various reasons sales by auctions are deemed not to be consumer sales. In non-consumer sales, exclusion of the conditions is permitted to the extent that it is regarded as reasonable, and certain criteria are supplied by statute. However the question arises whether a sale booked with the auctioneer is a 'sale by auction' within s 12(2) of the Unfair Contract Terms Act 1977 and it is argued that it is not; there is no element of competitive bidding involved. However, and in any event, it is ultimately unlikely that many such sales would be regarded as consumer sales because, save perhaps for certain horses, the goods are not 'of a type ordinarily supplied for private use or consumption' within s 12(1)(c) of the Act. If therefore the implied conditions are excludable then one must consider the aptness of the particular exclusion clause. Let us take the exclusion clause provided by the Livestock Auctioneers' Committee by way of example. Condition 28 provides:[15]

> The auctioneers act in all respects only as agents for the vendor and it shall be deemed that no condition or warranty expressed or implied has in any circumstance been given by the auctioneers, or any servant of the auctioneers, whether as to title, description, the quality of any lot sold or otherwise. The auctioneers and their servants shall not incur any liability to the purchaser in respect of any defect of title, error of description or imperfection or in respect of any announcement or statement relating to or affecting any lot offered for sale whether made orally or in writing and whether given before, during or after the auction, nor shall they incur any liability in relation to any dispute between any purchaser and vendors.

15 Conditions of Sale for Cattle, Calves, Sheep and Pigs at Livestock Auction Market, Livestock Auctioneers' Market Committee for England and Wales.

The opening words present an immediate difficulty. The assertion that the auctioneer acts only as agent is false in law in so far as these sales are concerned. It might be open to a court therefore to construe this condition as only applying when the auctioneer *does* act as agent. For the avoidance of doubt it might be safer for auctioneers to insert an exclusion provision directed specifically to private sales booked with them where they acknowledge that they act *qua* sellers and then purport to exclude their liability as appropriate. If auctioneers fail to exclude liability for e g misdescriptions or unmerchantability, then these private sales booked with the auctioneer may render the auctioneer exposed to legal risks to which, as agent, he is normally immune.

The major advantage enuring to the benefit of auctioneers out of the 'booking' procedure, is that it provides them with commission in respect of a private treaty sale which factually they have not effected (though the presence of a market has of course facilitated it).

Moreover, as we have pointed out in ch 4, the auctioneers can sue the buyer for the price as sellers in their own right, but if for any reason the sale to the buyer is vitiated (e g by mistake or otherwise) and the auctioneers are unable to recover against the buyer, this in no way affects the first contract of sale between the seller and the auctioneer. In *Murphy v Howlett*[16] therefore the auctioneers were held unable to avoid their contract with the vendor when doubts arose as to the identity (not to mention the solvency) of the buyer.

16 Above, n 14.

Chapter 11

Sales by vendors in special positions

INTRODUCTION

In normal cases there is a choice open to the buyer. He may either proceed to dispose of his goods by private treaty or by auction. For the vendor who is in a fiduciary or quasi-fiduciary position, this choice may not exist, or, if it does, the choice may be circumscribed. In some cases a sale by auction may be prescribed by statute. Trustees, mortgagees, pawnbrokers and public and court authorities are all examples of vendors who do not own the property beneficially (at least in its entirety) and may be under a fiduciary duty to obtain the best price reasonably obtainable.[1] Each will be taken in turn.

TRUSTEES AND OTHER FIDUCIARIES

Trustees are under an overriding duty to obtain for their beneficiaries the best price reasonably obtainable. Under modern law trustees are not, however, obliged to sell by auction. For instance, s 12 of the Trustee Act 1925 states that trustees may 'sell or concur with any other person in selling all or any part of the property, either subject to prior charges or not, and either together or in lots, by public auction or by private contract.' Nevertheless, particularly in the case of collections of chattels which are trust property, trustees (and executors and administrators) will be likely to choose the auction method so as to demonstrate that they have obtained the best possible price. This applies both to trustees of private trusts and of charitable trusts. (In the case of the latter, an order of Charity Commissioners may be a prerequisite to the sale by virtue of the provisions of the Charities Act 1960, s 29, particularly where the subject matter forms part of the permanent endowment of the charity or is land.)

There is an important corollary to the above. This arises from the principle that a purchase of trust property by a trustee from himself and any co-trustee is voidable at the instance of any beneficiary.[2] There is even elderly authority

1 See e g *Buttle v Saunders* [1950] 2 All ER 193.
2 See Snell's *Equity* (28th edn, 1982) Sweet & Maxwell, 248; *Holder v Holder* [1968] Ch 353, [1968] 1 All ER 665, CA. The purchase by the trustee of the beneficiary's interest is, however, unimpeachable in the absence of some form of fraud or undue influence.

to the effect that the principle includes the case where the sale is at a public auction.[3] If the sale is voidable in these circumstances, any beneficiary has the right to set it aside within a reasonable time after discovery of the facts. The rule will not apply where the trustee has long been retired from the trust,[4] nor to an executor (who is in a similar fiduciary position to that of a trustee for present purposes) who has renounced executorship or disassociated himself from the management of the deceased's estate. Thus, in *Holder v Holder*,[5] a testator appointed his widow, a daughter and his third son Victor to be his executors. The testator died leaving his landed estate to be equally divided between his widow and his children. Victor purported to renounce his executorship, but this renunciation was ineffective since he had intermeddled with the estate. However, he took no part in instructing the valuer who fixed the reserves for the farmland which was to be sold by auction. Victor's bid was successful at the auction and the farms were knocked down to him at a fair price. It was held by the Court of Appeal that in the special circumstances of the case Victor, although an executor, was not precluded from purchasing the property.

Similar principles apply to all persons in a fiduciary position. The rule arises from the fundamental rule that a fiduciary should not profit from his position and his special knowledge. Such persons include agents, solicitors, company directors, employees, guardians, partners, receivers, and members of a Committee of Inspection in Bankruptcy.[6]

There are exceptions to the rule. For instance the trust instrument may expressly authorise a trustee to purchase, and the court has jurisdiction to give the trustee leave to bid at an auction.[7] Under the Settled Land Act 1925, s 68, there is specific provision for a tenant for life of settled land to purchase property which he holds on trust.

MORTGAGEES

A mortgagee of land has a statutory power of sale conferred upon him by s 101 of the Law of Property Act 1925 provided the mortgage has been made by deed. The power is, when the mortgage money has become due, to sell, or to concur with any other person in selling, the mortgaged property or any part thereof, either subject to prior charges or not, and either together or in lots, by public auction or by private contract. The power may not be exercised until the conditions specified in s 103 have been satisfied. These are:

(a) Notice requiring payment of the mortgage money has been served on the mortgagor and default has been made for three months after such service; or
(b) Interest under the mortgage is in arrear and unpaid for two months after becoming due; or
(c) There has been a breach of some other provision in the mortgage deed

3 *Ex p Lacey* (1802) 6 Ves 625 at 629. The reason given appears to be that the trustee-vendor might be recognised and thus discourage bidding by others. This hardly seems convincing.
4 *Re Boles and British Land Co's Contract* [1902] 1 Ch 244, 71 LJ Ch 130.
5 [1968] Ch 353, [1968] 1 All ER 665, CA.
6 See generally Snell (n 2 above) pp 250-51.
7 See RSC Ord 85, r 2.

> imposed by the Law of Property Act 1925 (as amended) 'other than and besides a covenant for payment of the mortgage money or interest thereon'.

The mortgagee exercising his power of sale is in a less onerous position than the trustee considered above. He is not regarded as a trustee for the mortgagor, though he owes a duty to the mortgagor to act in good faith and take reasonable care to obtain the true market value of the mortgaged property on the date that he decides to sell it. The position was summarized cogently by Salmon LJ in *Cuckmere Brick Co Ltd v Mutual Finance Ltd* where it was said:[8]

> It is well settled that a mortgagee is not a trustee of the power of sale for the mortgagor. Once the power has accrued, the mortgagee is entitled to exercise it for his own purposes whenever he chooses to do so. It matters not that the moment may be unpropitious and that by waiting a higher price could be obtained. He has the right to realise his security by turning it into money when he likes. Nor, in my view, is there anything to prevent a mortgagee from accepting the best bid he can get at an auction, even though the auction is badly attended and the bidding exceptionally low. Provided none of those adverse factors is due to any fault of the mortgagee, he can do as he likes.

However this case is a warning that the mortgagee must still take reasonable care. Here, the plaintiffs had mortgaged 2.6 acres of land to the defendants. The defendants put the property up for sale by public auction without advertising the fact that there existed planning permission for 100 flats, and as a result the sale fetched some £21 000 less than the trial judge estimated the land to be worth. The majority of the Court of Appeal held that there had been a breach of the mortgagee's duty to take reasonable precautions to obtain the true market value of the mortgaged property at the date on which it was decided to sell it.

An example of where an auction of mortgaged land took place in such extraordinary circumstances that the court would have set the sale aside had not the mortgagor inordinately delayed in pursuing the remedies occurred in *Tse Kwong Lam v Wong Chit Sen*.[9] Here, commercial property in Hong Kong was mortgaged and on the default of the mortgagor the mortgagee exercised his power of sale by auction. The property was somewhat modestly advertised and the conditions of sale gave notice that there would be a reserve price and that the vendor-mortgagee reserved the right to bid. The auctioneer was informed of the reserve figure on the day of the auction. At the auction the only bidder was the mortgagee's wife, bidding on behalf of the mortgagee's family company. She put in a single bid at the reserve price and the property was knocked down to her. The borrower, with 'inexcusable delay', eventually applied for the sale to be set aside.

The Judicial Committee of the Privy Council held that whilst the mortgagee's company was not debarred from purchasing the property in the present case, the sale could 'only be supported if the mortgagee proves that he took reasonable precautions to obtain the best price reasonably obtainable at the time of sale'. Lord Templeman added: 'An auction which only produces one

8 [1971] Ch 949 at 965.
9 [1983] 3 All ER 54, [1983] 1 WLR 1349, PC.

bid is not necessarily an indication that the true market value has been achieved.' He continued by stating that expert advice ought to have been taken as to the method of sale, as to the steps which ought reasonably to have been taken to make the sale a success, and as to the amount of the reserve.[10] Because of the mortgagor's delay the sale was not set aside, but the borrower's right to sue the mortgagee for damages for failure of the mortgagee to secure the best price was confirmed.

Building society mortgagees have a specific *statutory* duty to take reasonable care to ensure that the price is the best price which can be reasonably obtained.[11]

PAWNBROKERS

For many years the sale of unredeemed pledges in respect of loans not exceeding £50 had been governed by the Pawnbrokers Act 1872 as amended by the Pawnbrokers Act 1960. These statutory provisions required that a pledge pawned for above £2, when disposed of by the pawnbroker, should be disposed of by sale by public auction and not otherwise; and the regulations prescribed by the Act should be observed with reference to the sale. A pawnbroker was permitted to bid for and purchase at a sale by auction, and on such purchase was deemed to be the absolute owner of the pledge purchased. The regulations required by the Act as to the conducting of auctions included that all pledges had to be exposed to public view, the catalogue had to show the pawnbroker's name and business address etc, advertisements in newspapers had to be placed, and valuable items had to be sold as separate lots.

The Pawnbrokers Acts 1872 and 1960 were prospectively repealed by s 121 of the Consumer Credit Act 1974. This section is set out below and it will be seen that as regards those transactions within the ambit of the section there is no particular method of sale prescribed. Those transactions not within the section will be governed by the ordinary law of contract in this respect. Regulations which have a commencement date of 19 May 1985 have been made pursuant to this section.[12] The section runs as follows:

> *121. Realisation of pawn*
> (1) When a pawn has become realisable by him, the pawnee may sell it, after giving to the pawnor (except in such cases as may be prescribed) not less than the prescribed period of notice of the intention to sell, indicating in the notice the asking price and such other particulars as may be prescribed.
> (2) Within the prescribed period after the sale takes place, the pawnee shall give the pawnor the prescribed information in writing as to the sale, its proceeds and expenses.
> (3) Where the net proceeds of sale are not less than the sum which, if the pawn had been redeemed on the date of the sale, would have been payable for its redemption, the debt secured by the pawn is discharged and any surplus shall be paid by the pawnee to the pawnor.
> (4) Where subsection (3) does not apply, the debt shall be treated as from the date

10 [1983] 3 All ER 54 at 60, 63.
11 Building Societies Act 1962, s 36.
12 See Commencement Order No 8.

of sale as equal to the amount by which the net proceeds of sale fall short of the sum which would have been payable for the redemption of the pawn on that date.
(5) In this section the 'net proceeds of sale' is the amount realised (the 'gross amount') less the expenses (if any) of the sale.
(6) If the pawnor alleges that the gross amount is less than the true market value of the pawn on the date of sale, it is for the pawnee to prove that he and any agents employed by him in the sale used reasonable care to ensure that the true market value was obtained, and if he fails to do so subsections (3) and (4) shall have effect as if the reference in subsection (5) to the gross amount were a reference to the true market value.
(7) If the pawnor alleges that the expenses of the sale were unreasonably high, it is for the pawnee to prove that they were reasonable, and if he fails to do so subsections (3) and (4) shall have effect as if the reference in subsection (5) to expenses were a reference to reasonable expenses.

Note

In sub-s(1) above, the 'prescribed period' is 14 days, and in sub-s(2) it is 20 working days. Furthermore, the section only applies to articles taken in pawn under a regulated consumer credit agreement, so the financial limits prescribed from time to time under the Act (£50 to £15 000 as from 20 May 1985) must be borne in mind. See generally the Consumer Credit (Regulation of Pawn) Regulations 1983.

SALES UNDER WRIT OF FIERI FACIAS

Where a creditor has obtained judgment in the High Court against a debtor there are a number of ways in which the money judgment may be enforced. For present purposes we are concerned with the case where it is decided to levy execution against chattels belonging to the debtor.

In these circumstances, the practice in respect of a High Court judgment is to issue a writ of fieri facias (fi fa). A form of request known as a praecipe is delivered to the court together with copies of the judgment and two copies of the writ of fieri facias. The writ is sealed and sent to the under sheriff for the county in which the debtor has goods to be seized, together with the appropriate sheriff's fee. The under sheriff's officer then executes the writ. He is empowered to take possession of sufficient goods belonging to the debtor to cover the amount for which the writ is issued plus his charges and costs of sale. The technicalities of the seizure of the debtor's goods by the sheriff's officer are beyond the scope of this book.[13]

With regard to the sale of the goods seized, the Bankruptcy Act 1883, s 145, enacts that

> where the Sheriff sells the goods of a debtor under an execution for a sum exceeding £20 (including legal incidental expenses), the sale shall, unless the court from which the process issued otherwise orders, be made by public auction and not by Bill of Sale or private contract, and shall be publicly advertised by the Sheriff on and during three days next preceding the day of sale.

13 For the procedure, see RSC Ords 46 and 47. In the USA it is understood that sales in such circumstances are normally by auction with, in effect, the reserve placed at the amount of the judgment debt.

If the sheriff desires to sell otherwise than by auction he may apply to the court under RSC Ord 47, r 6. Such an application must be made by summons and is attended by various other formalities. It is the sheriff's duty to get the best price possible for the goods and it is he that must make the application for sale otherwise than by auction on the basis that he is in the best position to know how to maximise the sale proceeds.

In the county court similar rules apply to the enforcement by the county court of a warrant of execution.[14] Section 97 of the County Courts Act 1984 makes similar provision for goods sold under an execution for a sum exceeding £20 (including legal incidental expenses), to be sold by public auction publicly advertised by the Registrar on, and during three days next preceding, the day of sale. The court has power to order otherwise. A sale not in conformity with the section is voidable only; it stands until set aside.[15]

SALES OF LAND BY ORDER OF THE COURT

By virtue of RSC Ord 31, where in any cause or matter in the Chancery Division relating to land it appears necessary or expedient for the purposes or the cause or matter that the land or any part thereof should be sold, the court may order that land or part to be sold. In carrying out the sale the court may permit the party or person having the conduct of the sale to sell the land in such manner as he thinks fit, or may direct that the land be sold in such manner as the court may either by the order or subsequent directions lay down, for the best price that can be obtained. The usual practice is to order a sale of land out of court, with liberty to apply to the court for any necessary directions should there be disagreement. Depending on the state of the property market, an auction may well be dispensed with, particularly if a price below which the property should not be sold is agreed between the parties.

With regard to the remuneration of the auctioneer, the Vice-Chancellor and judges of the Chancery Division have approved a scale of remuneration. The position is set out in the following Practice Direction:[16]

Practice Direction

Chancery Division
Family Division

1. The charges of estate agents and auctioneers selling freehold or leasehold property pursuant to orders of the Chancery Division, the Family Division, the Court of Protection or divorce county courts will normally be considered reasonable by the court if they do not exceed the rate of commission which that agent would normally charge on a sole agency basis, and they do not exceed 2½% of the sale price, exclusive of value added tax.

14 See County Courts Act 1984, s 105(1), and CCR 1981, Ord 25, r 11; also County Courts Act 1984, s 85, and CCR 1981, Ord 25.
15 See *Crawshaw v Harrison* [1894] 1 QB 79, 63 LJQB 94.
16 [1983] 1 All ER 160, [1983] 1 WLR 86.

2. These charges are to include all commission, valuations, expenses and other disbursements, including making affidavits, the cost of advertising and all other work except surveys. The allowance for a survey will be at the court's discretion.

3. If (a) an agent's charges do not fall within the limits set out in para 1 or (b) there is a sale of any investment property, business property or farm property or (c) a property is sold in lots or by valuation, an application must be made to the court to authorise the fee to be charged.

4. The limits set out in paras 1 and 2 above do not apply to sales of property for patients of the Court of Protection where an agreement has been concluded with the estate agent before the jurisdiction of the court has been invoked.

5. In matrimonial cases, either where the party who has been condemned in these costs has not agreed to the increased rate or where the costs fall to be paid out of the legal aid fund, the higher charges will be subject to the discretion of the taxing officer.

6. This Practice Direction applies to all instructions for sale which are placed with estate agents and auctioneers after 1 January 1983.

The Practice Directions of 26 July 1972 ([1972] 3 All ER 256, [1972] 1 WLR 1431) and 18 October 1972 ([1972] 3 All ER 910, [1972] 1 WLR 1471) are hereby revoked.

By direction of the Vice-Chancellor and the President of the Family Division and with the concurrence of the Lord Chancellor.

E R Heward
Chief Chancery Master
A B McFarlane
Master, Court of Protection
B P Tickle
Senior Registrar, Family Division.

22 December 1982

If there is a dispute as to the auctioneer's remuneration, the auctioneer is entitled to be represented before the master when the amount of the remuneration is fixed.[17] Under a sale directed by the court, if the solicitor to the auction or any party thereto desires to participate as a bidder at the auction, he must obtain leave to bid before the sale. No special conditions of sale are laid down for the sale by auction of land pursuant to a court order. Normally one of the forms of General Conditions discussed in ch 9 will be appropriate.[18]

Similar provisions exist in the county court by virtue of Ord 22, r 11 of the County Court Rules 1981. This rule applies the same provisions as the rules of the Supreme Court considered above.

SALES UNDER DISTRESS FOR RENT

The right of distress has its origin in feudal times and was used by a lord to enforce the rendering of services by his tenant, subject to which services the

17 *Re Wolfe, Heller v Wolfe* [1952] 2 TLR 388.

18 In *Re Walford, Walford v Walford* (1889) 5 TLR 251, CA, where a testator's land was sold by auction under a power of sale in the mortgage but the mortgagees had taken directions from the chief clerk the sale was regarded as if directed by the court and the auctioneer limited to the appropriate scale charge.

tenant held the land. The remedy is now limited to when a landlord and tenant relationship exists as to land and where the rent is in arrear. Although the remedy has not fallen into complete dissuetude, and although in 1975 the government announced that it had no intention of abolishing it,[19] this area of law is rightly regarded as 'highly complex, technical and archaic'.[20]

Distress is essentially a self-help remedy by the landlord, no court order being necessary unless the tenant is protected by the Rents Acts. Essentially, either the landlord or, in practice, a duly certificated bailiff, enters onto the tenant's land and takes possession of a sufficient amount of the teant's non-privileged goods to provide reasonable security for outstanding rent and expenses. The bailiff is certificated by the county court and should be given a distress warrant by the landlord authorising him to levy the distress. The goods may not be sold for five days, and this period can be extended to fifteen days if the tenant so applies in writing. Until the sale the tenant has the right to 'replevy' them i e tender the rent owing and expenses.

If the goods are sold, there is an ancient duty to sell at the best price obtainable for the goods. Thus a public auction is desirable if not essential. The tenant may expressly request in writing that the goods be removed to a public auction room or some other fit and proper place to be there sold.[1]

SALES UNDER OTHER MISCELLANEOUS POWERS

The following persons have powers of sale over goods in their possession, though these powers may not necessarily be exercised by auctions:

(a) A *repairer* who has expended money on uncollected goods. The position here is that following the 18th Report of the Law Reform Committee (Conversion and Detinue) the Disposal of Uncollected Goods Act 1952 (which prescribed sale by public auction) was repealed and replaced by the Torts (Interference With Goods) Act 1977. The bailee – repairer now has a general power to sell the goods by the best method of sale reasonably available in the circumstances. Various obligations are imposed upon him, particularly as to notice to the owner, before this right may be exercised.

(b) *Innkeepers*. An innkeeper enjoys the right, by virtue of the Innkeepers Act 1878, to detain under a lien a guest's goods brought to the hotel until the cost of food and lodging is met. If the goods are detained for six weeks the goods may be sold if the sale is advertised as specified by the Act at least a month beforehand. Section 1 of the Act specifically prescribes that the sale shall be by public auction.[2]

19 HC Official Report (5th series) written answer.
20 See Report of Payne Committee on the Enforcement of Judgment Debts (1969) Cmnd 3909, paras 912-932 — abolition was recommended; also similar remarks of Lord Denning MR in *Abingdon RDC v O'Gorman* [1968] 2 QB 811, CA, at 819.
1 Law of Distress Amendment Act 1888.
2 The definitions of 'Innkeeper' and 'Hotel' are now contained in the Hotel Proprietors Act 1956.

(c) *Certain warehousemen.* Under ss 497 and 498 of the Merchant Shipping Act 1894, wharfingers and warehousemen mentioned in these sections may sell either perishable goods, or in other cases, after 90 days, general goods on which they have an undischarged item for storage charges, by public auction. The sections impose preconditions including the giving of notice by advertisement and specific notice to the owner, though the title of a bona fide purchaser is not affected by omission to send the latter notice.[3]

(d) *Trustees in bankruptcy* have power to sell the bankrupt's property by virtue of s 55(I) of the Bankruptcy Act 1914.

(e) *Liquidators* of companies are empowered to sell the company's property under s 539(2) of the Companies Act 1985.

PROPERTY IN THE POSSESSION OF THE POLICE

Property can come into the possession of the police either because it is being used or is intended for use for purposes of crime or, more usually, because it is connected with the investigation of a suspected offence.

In the former case, s 43 of the Powers of Criminal Courts Act 1973 empowers the court to make an order depriving an offender of such property, and if it is claimed that the offender does not own the property, no claim may be made to it after six months from the date of such order. In the latter case, above, the Police (Property) Act 1897 empowers the Secretary of State to make regulations for the disposal of such property. There is also a general power to sell perishable property or property whose custody involves unreasonable expense and inconvenience. In this case, the proceeds of sale must be kept for a year; in other cases, the goods must be retained for a year.

The Police (Disposal of Property) Regulations 1975[4] provide that property in the possession of the police either by virtue of s 43 of the Powers of Criminal Courts Act 1973, or when the owner has not been ascertained and no court order is made, 'shall be sold'. No method of sale is specified but, again, a public auction is normally chosen. The regulations go on to deal with the application of the proceeds of sale which are kept in the Police Property Act Fund, but these details are not relevant to the subject matter of this book.[5]

PROBLEMS OF TITLE

Section 21 of the Sale of Goods Act 1979 makes specific provision for sales under statutory powers. Having stated the *nemo dat* rule (that the buyer acquires no better title than the seller), s 21(2) goes on to state that 'nothing

3 Agents of necessity also have common law powers of sale in limited cases of emergency.
4 Made primarily under the Police (Property) Act 1897 mentioned above.
5 In the case of stolen property whose owner cannot be traced, it will be seen that there can be no identifiable person with a direct interest in obtaining the best possible price. Nevertheless, auction sales of 'unclaimed property by direction of the Police' are commonplace and offer the best proof of a bona fide sale should this ever be questioned.

in this Act affects... the validity of any contract of sale under any special common law or statutory power of sale or under the order of a court of competent jurisdiction.'

Specific statutes also protect bona fide purchasers in limited circumstances. Thus in the case of sales by distraining landlords, where the goods are unprotected from distress, the purchaser from the distraining landlord gets a good title as against the true owner – e g where the tenant possessed the goods on hire-purchase.[6]

Sales by trustees in bankruptcy pass a good title to the purchaser, even if the goods are only in the reputed ownership of the bankrupt (with the owner's consent). Here the true owner must prove in the bankruptcy for their value.[7]

Section 15 of the Bankruptcy and Deeds of Arrangement Act 1913 specifically provides that where goods of a debtor are sold by a sheriff etc 'without any claim having been made to the same, the purchaser of the goods so sold shall acquire a good title to the goods so sold,' though this statement is followed by an apparently contradictory proviso. It was, however, confirmed by the Court of Appeal in *Curtis v Maloney*[8] that a purchaser gets a good title as against the true owner to the goods (in this case, a motor cruiser possessed by the debtor under a hire-purchase agreement).

6 Law of Distress Amendment Act 1908, s 4.
7 *Re Button, ex p Haviside* [1907] 2 KB 180, 76 JKB 833, CA.
8 [1951] 1 KB 736, [1950] 2 All ER 982, CA. See also s 40(3) of the Bankruptcy Act 1914.

Appendix 1

Conditions of Sale

Suggested miniumum Conditions of Sale: specimen
Conditions of Sale of Sotheby's
Conditions of Sale of Christie Manson & Woods Ltd

SUGGESTED MINIMUM CONDITIONS OF SALE: SPECIMEN

EXPLANATORY INTRODUCTION TO OUR AUCTIONS

The Auctioneer acts only as agent for the Seller (unless otherwise specifically declared). Accordingly Sellers are not paid until payment is received from the Buyer, nor is the Auctioneer necessarily in a position to know the history of or assess the quality of lots sold on behalf of these principals. In addition, lots sold are likely to have been subject to wear and tear caused by user or the effects of age and may therefore have faults and imperfections. Buyers are given ample opportunity at viewing times to examine lots to be sold and will be assumed to have done so. They must rely solely on their own skill or judgment as to whether lots are fit for any particular purpose, and as to compliance with the catalogue description or illustrations — see Condition 6.

1. Bids
All bids made shall be treated as offers made upon these Conditions of Sale and all persons present are admitted to attend a sale on the basis that they have notice of these Conditions.

2. Ascertainment of the buyer
The Buyer shall be the person making the highest bid which is acceptable to the Auctioneer as signified by fall of the hammer. In the case of a dispute as to the highest bidding during or immediately after the sale of the lot, the Auctioneer may if he thinks fit put up the lot again for sale.

3. Auctioneer's discretion
The Auctioneer has sole discretion (a) to refuse any bid, (b) to advance the bidding as he may decide, (c) to decide whether there has been a dispute as to the bidding and under Condition 2 to resell the lot in question, (d) to withdraw or divide any lot or combine one lot with another or others, and (e) to exclude any person from the auction room.

4. Reserves and seller's right to bid.
Lots put up for sale are subject (a) to any reserve price imposed by the Seller, (b) the right of the Auctioneer to bid on behalf of the Seller, and (c) where no reserve price has been imposed (but in no other case) for the Seller to bid personally or through any one agent.

5. Buyer's duties
The Buyer shall forthwith or as soon as reasonably possible after the sale of the relevant

lot (a) supply his name and address, (b) supply, if so required, bank or other suitable references, (c) pay the full purchase price in a way acceptable to the Auctioneer, and (d) on proof of payment clear the lots purchased by him not later than the end of normal working hours during the day of the sale.

6. Liability of the auctioneer and sellers
Subject to Condition 8, (a) lots are sold with all faults and imperfections and neither the Seller nor the Auctioneer is responsible for any defects whatsoever; (b) no warranty is given or authorised to be given by the Seller or the Auctioneer with regard to any lot other than that the Seller had the right to sell it; (c) any express or implied conditions or warranties whether relating to description or quality, are hereby excluded.

7. Catalogue descriptions
The Auctioneer undertakes that care has been taken to see that catalogue descriptions are accurate and reliable, but these are necessarily matters of opinion only and shall not be taken to be statements of fact. Subject to Condition 8, neither the Seller nor the Auctioneer are responsible for the correctness of any description of any lot or its attribution in any manner to any particular originator.

8. Forgeries
Notwithstanding Condition 6 and 7, if the Auctioneer receives notice in writing from the Buyer within 10 days of the sale that in his opinion a lot is a forgery (as defined in Condition 11) and on giving such notification the lot in question is returned to the Auctioneer at his working premises in the same condition as when bought, then if on considering such evidence as the Buyer supplies to prove his assertion, the Auctioneer decides that the lot is a forgery the sale of the lot will be rescinded and the purchase price repaid to the Buyer.

9. Property in lots and risk
The Buyer shall not become the owner of any lot, and the Auctioneer shall have a lien thereon, until the Buyer had discharged the purchase price, but after the fall of the hammer the risk of damage or loss shall nevertheless be the Buyer's.

10. Default by buyer
If the Buyer fails to pay for or remove any lot bought by him or in any other material respect fails to comply with these Conditions, the Auctioneer shall have the right (a) to resell the lot by public auction or otherwise without notice to the Buyer, and if any deficiency arises on such resale after deducting the Auctioneer's full costs and expenses, the Buyer shall be responsible to the Seller and Auctioneer therefor (but any net surplus to be the Seller's) or, alternatively, (b) to store the lot at the Auctioneer's premises or elsewhere and to release the lot to the Buyer only after payment in full of all reasonable storage and removal expenses incurred (in addition to the purchase price).

11. Definitions and interpretation
In these Conditions: (a) References to 'the Auctioneer' shall be taken to mean, as the context so admits, the firm of [insert name of auctioneer's firm] or any director, partner or employee thereof at the time of the sale; (b) 'Buyer' shall have the meaning ascribed to it in Condition 2 and for the purpose of these Conditions all Buyers shall be deemed to be principals unless to the knowledge of the Auctioneer they are acting as agent on behalf of a named principal; (c) 'Forgery' means a lot (i) which is so constituted as deliberately to deceive when considered in the light of its catalogue description, and (ii) whose value as such is materially less than if it had complied with the catalogue description; (d) The Interpretation Act 1978 shall apply to the general constructionof terms and expressions used in these Conditions as if contained in a statute, and these Conditions shall be governed by English law.

Name and address of auctioneer's firm.

Notes

1. These Conditions of Sale are intended to be as short and simple as is compatible with securing, so far as possible, avoidance of the more predictable legal problems that can occur. They are designed to be used for general sales of chattels (including paintings, antiques and jewellery) and to be reproduced, with appropriate adaptations, in catalogues issued to bidders and to be on permanent public display in the auction room. The 'Introduction' has been partly chosen to show, more than is usually the case, the reason for a particular provision (particularly Condition 6). The inclusion of the 'Introduction' must be a matter of choice, but it is likely to be regarded as helpful to the buyer when assessing reasonableness. The precedent is not suitable for specialist sales such as of land, livestock, motor cars, plant etc.

2. Conditions purporting to disclaim legal liability which might otherwise arise must be read in the light of the detailed analysis of the law in the text. It must be borne in mind that in criminal law false trade descriptions applied by the auctioneer may not be effectively disclaimed by him, and other exemption clauses are likely to be subject to the test of reasonableness. In the light of this, and the civil court's wide discretion in this area, it is recommended that a reasonable balance between the rights of the seller and the buyer strongly indicates that the buyer's right to reject 'forgeries' be expressly conferred. The time limit for giving notice of this is designed to be within the period normally taken for the administration of the sale's completion and subsequent payment of sellers. This Condition in its present form is therefore unsuitable to specialist auctioneers where forgeries may legitimately be first discovered over a greater time scale. This problem is discussed in the text.

3. The position as to the right for the seller to bid or for the auctioneer to bid on his behalf should be carefully observed. The legal background to this is discussed in the text.

4. No Condition has been drafted to require the buyer to pay a premium in addition to the purchase price. If this is desired, it must specifically be added.

5. It is perhaps obvious that these Conditions are designed to be included with catalogues and bind, so far as possible, buyers. Separate conditions of business need to be negotiated with sellers dealing with such matters as commission and other charges, insurance of goods, warranty of title, reserves, unsold lots, prohibition of bidding by the seller personally except when there is no reserve, etc. These must be negotiated when it is agreed with the seller to accept his goods for sale by auction. There is little point in including any of these matters in sale catalogues issued to buyers, except perhaps for information purposes.

CONDITIONS OF SALE[1] OF SOTHEBY'S[2]

SOTHEBY PARKE BERNET & CO[3]
CONDITIONS OF BUSINESS

(EXCEPT THOSE CONCERNING THE FAST SALE SERVICE)

Conditions mainly concerning buyers

1. The buyer
The highest bidder shall be the buyer at the 'hammer price' and any dispute shall be settled at the auctioneer's absolute discretion. Every bidder shall be deemed to act as principal unless there is in force a written acknowledgment by Sotheby's that he acts as agent on behalf of a named principal.

2. Minimum increment
The auctioneer shall have the right to refuse any bid which does not exceed the previous bid by at least 5 per cent or by such other proportion as the auctioneer shall in his absolute discretion direct.

3. The premium
Except in respect of 'special category items', the buyer shall pay to Sotheby's a premium of 10 per cent on the 'hammer price' together with Value Added Tax at the standard rate on the premium, and agrees that Sotheby's, when acting as agent for the seller, may also receive commission from the seller in accordance with Condition 19.

4. Value Added Tax (VAT)
Lots on which Value Added Tax is payable by the buyer on the 'hammer price' are indicated in the catalogue with the sign † (where the tax is payable at the standard rate) and with the sign ‡ (where the tax is payable at a different rate). Value Added Tax, the rates of which are subject to alteration by law, is payable at the rates prevailing on the day of the auction.

5. Currency converter
A currency converter will be operated at some auctions but only for the guidance of bidders. Sotheby's will not accept any responsibility in the event of error on the currency converter whether in the foreign currency equivalent of bids in pounds sterling or otherwise.

6. Payment
Immediately a lot is sold the buyer shall:

(a) give to Sotheby's his name and address and, if so requested, proof of identity; and

(b) pay to Sotheby's the 'total amount due' (unless credit terms have been agreed with Sotheby's before the auction).

7. Sotheby's may, at its absolute discretion, agree credit terms with the buyer before an auction under which the buyer will be entitled to take possession of lots purchased up to an agreed amount in value in advance of payment by a determined future date of the 'total amount due'.

1 As at June 1984.
2 These Conditions are the copyright of Sotheby's and are reproduced with their kind permission.
3 Sotheby Parke Bernet & Co changed the firm's name to 'Sotheby's' in September 1984.

8. Any payments by a buyer to Sotheby's may be applied by Sotheby's towards any sums owing from that buyer to Sotheby's on any account whatever without regard to any directions of the buyer or his agent, whether express or implied.

9. Collection of purchases
The ownership of the lot purchased shall not pass to the buyer until he has made payment in full to Sotheby's of the 'total amount due'.

10. (a) The buyer shall at his own expense take away the lot purchased not later than 5 working days after the day of the auction but (unless credit terms have been agreed in accordance with Condition 7) not before payment to Sotheby's of the 'total amount due'.

(b) The buyer shall be responsible for any removal, storage and insurance charges on any lot not taken away within 5 working days after the day of the auction.

11. For wines, spirits and cigars not available for collection from Sotheby's premises, the supply of a release order authorising the release of the lot to the buyer will constitute delivery by Sotheby's.

12. Buyers responsibilities for lots purchased
The buyer will be responsible for loss or damage to lots purchased from the time of collection or the expiry of 5 working days after the day of the auction, whichever is the sooner, and neither Sotheby's nor its servants or agents shall thereafter be responsible for any loss or damage of any kind, whether caused by negligence or otherwise, while any lot is in its custody or under its control.

13. The buyer of a 'motor vehicle' is responsible for complying with the provisions of the Road Traffic Act 1972 and all relevant regulations made under section 40 thereof (including the Motor Vehicles (Construction and Use) Regulations 1973) and any statutory modification thereof.

14. The buyer of a firearm is responsible for obtaining a valid firearm certificate, shot gun certificate or certificate of registration as a firearms dealer and for conforming with the regulations in force in Great Britain relating to firearms, notice of which is published in catalogues of firearms. Sotheby's will not deliver lots to buyers without production of evidence of compliance with this condition.

15. Remedies for non-payment or failure to collect purchases
If any lot is not paid for in full and taken away in accordance with Conditions 6 and 10, or if there is any other breach of either of those Conditions, Sotheby's as agent of the seller shall at its absolute discretion and without prejudice to any other rights it may have, be entitled to exercise one or more of the following rights and remedies:

(a) to proceed against the buyer for damages for breach of contract;

(b) to rescind the sale of that or any other lots sold to the defaulting buyer at the same or any other auction;

(c) to re-sell the lot or cause it to be re-sold by public auction or private sale and the defaulting buyer shall pay to Sotheby's any resulting deficiency in the 'total amount due' (after deduction of any part payment and addition of re-sale costs) and any surplus shall belong to the seller;

(d) to remove, store and insure the lot at the expense of the defaulting buyer and, in the case of storage either at Sotheby's premises or elsewhere;

(e) to charge interest at a rate not exceeding 1.5 per cent per month on the 'total amount due' to the extent it remains unpaid for more than 5 working days after the day of the auction;

(f) to retain that or any other lot sold to the same buyer at the same or any other auction and release it only after payment of the 'total amount due';

(g) to reject or ignore any bids made by or on behalf of the defaulting buyer at any future auctions or obtain a deposit before accepting any bids in future;

(h) to apply any proceeds of sale then due or at any time thereafter becoming due to the defaulting buyer towards settlement of the 'total amount due' and to exercise a lien on any property of the defaulting buyer which is in Sotheby's possession for any purpose.

16. Liability of Sotheby's and sellers[4]

(a) Goods auctioned are usually of some age. All goods are sold with all faults and imperfections and errors of description. Illustrations in catalogues are for identification only. Buyers should satisfy themselves prior to sale as to the condition of each lot and should exercise and rely on their own judgment as to whether the lot accords with its description. Subject to the obligations accepted by Sotheby's under this Condition, none of the seller, Sotheby's, its servants or agents is responsible for errors of description or for the genuineness or authenticity of any lot, no warranty whatever is given by Sotheby's, its servants or agents, or any seller to any buyer in respect of any lot and any express or implied conditions or warranties are hereby excluded.

(b) Any lot which proves to be a 'deliberate forgery' may be returned by the buyer to Sotheby's within 5 years of the date of the auction in the same condition in which it was at the time of the auction, accompanied by a statement of defects, the number of the lot, and the date of the auction at which it was purchased. If Sotheby's is satisfied that the item is a 'deliberate forgery' and that the buyer has and is able to transfer a good and marketable title to the lot free from any third party claims, the sale will be set aside and any amount paid in respect of the lot will be refunded: Provided that the buyer shall have no rights under this Condition if:
(i) the description in the catalogue at the date of the sale was in accordance with the then generally accepted opinion of scholars and experts or fairly indicated that there was a conflict of such opinion; or
(ii) the only method of establishing at the date of publication of the catalogue that the lot was a 'deliberate forgery' was by means of scientific processes not generally accepted for use until after publication of the catalogue or a process which was unreasonably expensive or impractical; or

(c) A buyer's claim under this Condition shall be limited to any amount paid in respect of the lot and shall not extend to any loss or damage suffered or expense incurred by him.

(d) The benefit of this Condition shall not be assignable and shall rest solely and exclusively in the buyer who, for the purpose of this Condition, shall be and only be the person to whom the original invoice is made out by Sotheby's in respect of the lot sold.

Conditions mainly concerning sellers and consignors

17. Warranty of title and availability

(a) The seller warrants to Sotheby's and to the buyer that he is the true owner of the property or is properly authorised to sell the property by the true owner and is able to transfer good and marketable title to the property free from any third party claims.

(b) The seller of property not held by Sotheby's on its premises or under its control, warrants and undertakes to Sotheby's and the buyer that the property will be available and in a deliverable state on demand by the buyer.

(c) The seller will indemnify Sotheby's, its servants and agents and the buyer against any loss or damage suffered by either in consequence of any breach of (a) or (b) above on the part of the seller.

4 See pp 224-227 for alternative Conditions 16 for sales of: (i) Impressionist, modern and contemporary art; (ii) 'books'; (iii) gemstones and perals; (iv) numismatic items; (v) postage stamps; (vi) wines, spirits and cigars, and motor vehicles; (vii) musical instruments.

18. Reserves
The seller shall be entitled to place prior to the auction a reserve on any lot, being the minimum 'hammer price' at which that lot may be treated as sold. A reserve once placed by the seller shall not be changed without the consent of Sotheby's. Sotheby's may at their option sell at a 'hammer price' below the reserve but in any such cases the sale proceeds to which the seller is entitled shall be the same as they would have been had the sale been at the reserve. Where a reserve has been placed, only the auctioneer may bid on behalf of the seller. Where no reserve has been placed, the seller may bid, either personally or through the agency of any one person.

19. Authority to deduct commission and expenses
The seller authorises Sotheby's to deduct commission at the 'stated rates' and 'expenses' from the 'hammer price' and acknowledges Sotheby's right to retain the premium payable by the buyer in accordance with Condition 3.

20. Insurance[5]
Unless otherwise instructed, Sotheby's will insure property (other than 'motor vehicles') consigned to it or put under its control for sale and may, at its discretion, insure property put under its control for any other purpose. In all cases save where Sotheby's is required to insure, the property shall remain at all times at the risk of the seller or consignor and neither Sotheby's nor its servants or agents will be responsible for any loss or damage whether caused by negligence or otherwise. Such insurance will be at the expense of the seller or consignor, will be for the amount estimated by Sotheby's to be, from time to time, the current value of the property at auction and will subsist until whichever is the earlier of the ownership of the property passing from the seller or the seller or consignor becoming bound to collect the property.

21. Electrical and mechanical goods
The seller or consignor of electrical or mechanical goods warrants and undertakes to Sotheby's that at the date on which the same are consigned to Sotheby's or put under Sotheby's control and except as previously disclosed to Sotheby's the same are safe if reasonably used for the purpose for which they were designed and free from any defect not obvious on external inspection which could prove dangerous to human life or health, and will indemnify Sotheby's its servants and agents against any loss or damage suffered by any of them in consequence of any breach of the above warranty and undertaking.

22. Rescission of the sale
If before Sotheby's remit the 'sale proceeds' to the seller, the buyer makes a claim to rescind the sale under Condition 16 if appropriate and Sotheby's is of the opinion that the claim is justified, Sotheby's is authorised to rescind the sale and refund to the buyer any amount paid to Sotheby's in respect of the lot.

23. Payment of sale proceeds
Sotheby's shall remit the 'sale proceeds' to the seller not later than one month (or, in the case of numismatic items, 14 days) after the auction, but if by that date Sotheby's has not received the 'total amount due' from the buyer then Sotheby's will remit the 'sale proceeds' within five working days after the day on which the 'total amount due' is received from the buyer. If credit terms have been agreed between Sotheby's and the buyer, Sotheby's shall remit to the seller the sale proceeds not later than one month (or, in the case of numismatic items, 14 days) after the auction unless otherwise agreed by the seller: Provided that where in the case of postage stamps Sotheby's has granted an extension it shall remit the 'sale proceeds' when a certificate of genuineness is received by Sotheby's or sixty-five days after the auction, whichever is the sooner, but if by then Sotheby's has not received the 'total amount due' from the buyer then Sotheby's will

5 See p 228 below for alternative Conditions 20 for sales of motor vehicles.

remit the 'sale proceeds' within five working days after the day on which the 'total amount due' is received from the buyer.

24. If the buyer fails to pay to Sotheby's the 'total amount due' within 3 weeks after the auction, Sotheby's will endeavour to notify the seller and take the seller's instructions as to the appropriate course of action and, so far as in Sotheby's opinion is practicable, will assist the seller to recover the 'total amount due' from the buyer. If circumstances do not permit Sotheby's to take instructions from the seller, the seller authorises Sotheby's at the seller's expense to agree special terms for payment of the 'total amount due', to remove, store and insure the lot sold, to settle claims made by or against the buyer on such terms as Sotheby's shall in its absolute discretion think fit, to take such steps as are necessary to collect moneys due by the buyer to the seller and if necessary to rescind the sale and refund money to the buyer.

25. If, notwithstanding that the buyer fails to pay to Sotheby's the 'total amount due' within three weeks after the auction, Sotheby's remits the 'sale proceeds' to the seller, the ownership of the lot shall pass to Sotheby's.

26. Charges for withdrawn lots
Where a seller cancels instructions for sale, Sotheby's reserves the right to charge a fee of 10 per cent of Sotheby's then latest estimate or middle estimate of the auction price of the property withdrawn, together with Value Added Tax thereon and 'expenses' incurred in relation to the property.

27. Rights to photographs and illustrations
The seller gives Sotheby's full and absolute right to photograph and illustrate any lot placed in its hands for sale and to use such photographs and illustrations and any photographs and illustrations provided by the seller at any time at its absolute discretion (whether or not in connection with the auction).

28. Unsold lots
Where any lot fails to sell, Sotheby's shall notify the seller accordingly. The seller shall make arrangements either to re-offer the lot for sale or to collect the lot and to pay the reduced commission under Condition 29 and 'expenses'. If such arrangements are not made:

(a) within 7 days of notification, the seller shall be responsible for any removal, storage and insurance expenses;

(b) within 3 months of notification, Sotheby's shall have the right to sell the lot at public aucion without reserve and to deduct from the 'hammer price' any sum owing to Sotheby's including (without limitation) removal, storage and insurance expenses, the 'expenses' of both auctions, reduced commission under Condition 29 in respect of the first auction as well as commission at the 'stated rates' on the sale and all other reasonable expenses before remitting the balance to the seller or, if he cannot be traced, placing it in a bank account in the name of Sotheby's for the seller.

29. Sotheby's reserves the right to charge commission up to one-half of the 'stated rates' calculated on the 'bought-in price' and in addition, 'expenses' in respect of any unsold lots.

General conditions and definitions

30. Sotheby's sells as agent for the seller (except where it is stated wholly or partly to own any lot as principal) and as such is not responsible for any default by seller or buyer.

31. Any representation or statement by Sotheby's , in any catalogue as to authorship, attribution, genuineness, origin, date, age, provenance, condition or estimated selling price is a statement of opinion only. Every person interested should exercise and rely on his own judgment as to such matters and neither Sotheby's nor its servants or agents are responsible for the correctness of such opinions.

32. Whilst the interests of prospective buyers are best served by attendance at the auction, Sotheby's will if so instructed execute bids on their behalf, neither Sotheby's nor its servants or agents being responsible for any neglect or default in doing so or for failing to do so.

33. Sotheby's shall have the right, at its discretion, to refuse admission to its premises or attendance at its auctions by any person.

34. Sotheby's has absolute discretion without giving any reason to refuse any bid, to divide any lot, to combine any two or more lots, to withdraw any lot from the auction and in case of dispute to put up any lot for auction again.

35. (a) Any indemnity under these Conditions shall extend to all actions proceedings costs expenses claims and demands whatever incurred or suffered by the person entitled to the benefit of the indemnity.

(b) Sotheby's declares itself to be a trustee for its relevant servants and agents of the benefit of every indemnity under these Conditions to the extent that such indemnity is expressed to be for the benefit of its servants and agents.

36. Any notice by Sotheby's to a seller, consignor, prospective bidder or buyer may be given by first class mail or airmail and if so given shall be deemed to have been duly received by the addressee 48 hours after posting.

37. These Conditions shall be governed by and construed in accordance with English law. All transactions to which these Conditions apply and all matters connected therewith shall also be governed by English law. Sotheby's hereby submits to the exclusive jurisdiction of the English courts and all other parties concerned hereby submit to the non-exclusive jurisdiction of the English courts.

38. In these Conditions:
(a) 'Sotheby's' means Sotheby Parke Bernet & Co ;

(b) 'catalogue' includes any advertisement, brochure, estimate, price list and other publication;

(c) 'hammer price' means the price at which a lot is knocked down by the auctioneer to the buyer;

(d) 'total amount due' means the 'hammer price' in respect of the lot sold together with any premium, Value Added Tax chargeable and additional charges and expenses due from a defaulting buyer under Condition 15, in pounds sterling:

(e) 'special category items' means numismatic items, wines, spirits and cigars;

(f) 'book' means any item included or proposed to be included in a sale of books and includes a manuscript or print;

(g) 'deliberate forgery' means an imitation made with the intention of deceiving as to authorship, origin, date, age, period, culture or source which is not shown to be such in the description in the catalogue and which at the date of the sale had a value materially less than it would have had if it had been in accordance with that description;

(h) 'sale proceeds' means the net amount due to the seller being the 'hammer price' of the lot sold less commission at the 'stated rates' and 'expenses' and any other amounts due to Sotheby's by the seller in whatever capacity and howsoever arising;

(i) 'stated rates' means Sotheby's published rates of commission for the time being and Value Added Tax thereon;

(j) 'expenses' in relation to the sale of any lot means Sotheby's charges and expenses for insurance, illustrations, special advertising, packing and freight of that lot and any Value Added Tax thereon;

(k) 'motor vehicle' means any item included or proposed to be included in a sale of motor vehicles;

(l) 'bought-in price' means 5 per cent more than the highest bid received below the reserve.

39. Special terms may be used in catalogues in the description of a lot. Where terms are not self-explanatory and have special meanings ascribed to them, a glossary will appear before Lot 1 in the catalogue of the auction.

40. The headings in these Conditions do not form part of the Conditions but are for convenience only.

(i)
Alternative Condition 16 for catalogues for sales of Impressionist, modern and contemporary art

16. Liability of Sotheby's and sellers

(a) Goods auctioned are usually of some age. All goods are sold with all faults and imperfections and errors of description. Illustrations in catalogues are for identification only. Buyers should satisfy themselves prior to sale as to the condition of each lot and should exercise and rely on their own judgment as to whether the lot accords with its description. Subject to the obligations accepted by Sotheby's under this Condition, none of the seller, Sotheby's, its servants or agents is responsible for errors of description or for the genuineness or authenticity of any lot, no warranty whatever is given by Sotheby's, its servants or agents, or any seller to any buyer in respect of any lot and any express or implied conditions or warranties are hereby excluded.

(b) Any lot which was executed by someone other than the person described in the catalogue as the artist may be returned by the buyer to Sotheby's within five years of the date of the auction, in the same condition in which it was at the time of the auction, accompanied by a statement of defects, the number of the lot and the date of the auction at which it was purchased. If Sotheby's is satisfied that the lot was so executed and that the buyer has and is able to transfer a good and marketable title to the lot free from any third party claims the sale will be set aside and any amount paid in respect of the lot wil be refunded.

(c) A buyer's claim under this Condition shall be limited to any amount paid in respect of the lot and shall not extend to any loss or damage suffered or expense incurred by him.

(d) The benefit of this Condition shall not be assignable and shall rest solely and exclusively in the buyer who, for the purpose of this Condition, shall be and only be the person to whom the original invoice is made out by Sotheby's in respect of the lot sold.

(ii)
Alternative Condition 16 for catalogues for sales of 'books'

16. Liability of Sotheby's and sellers

(a) Goods auctioned are usually of some age. All goods are sold with all faults and imperfections and errors of description. Illustrations in catalogues are for identification only. Buyers should satisfy themselves prior to sale as to the condition of each lot and should exercise and rely on their own judgment as to whether the lot accords with its description. Subject to the obligations accepted by Sotheby's under this Condition, none of the seller, Sotheby's, its servants or agents is responsible for errors of description or for the genuineness or authenticity of any lot, no warranty whatever is given by Sotheby's, its servants or agents, or any seller to any buyer in respect of any lot and any express or implied conditions or warranties are hereby excluded.

(b) If within 21 days of the auction, the buyer gives notice to Sotheby's in writing that an item is defective in text or illustration and returns the lot to Sotheby's in the same condition in which it was at the time of the auction indicating the number of the lot and the date of the auction at which it was purchased, and it is established that the lot is defective, Sotheby's will rescind the sale and refund any amount paid in respect of the lot: Provided that such an item may not be returned nor will its sale be set aside or refund made if:
(i) it is described in the catalogue as sold not subject to return; or
(ii) it is sold un-named in a lot; or
(iii) it comprises an atlas, an extra-illustrated book, a volume with fore-edge paintings, a periodical publication or a print or drawing; or
(iv) in the case of a manuscript, it was not described in the catalogue as complete; or
(v) the defect in question was mentioned in the catalogue; or
(vi) the defect complained of is other than in text or illustration. For example (but without limitation) an item may not be returned nor will its sale be set aside on account of damage to bindings, stains, foxing, marginal wormholes, lack of blank leaves, or other conditions not affecting the completeness of the text or illustration, lack of list of plates, inserted advertisements, cancels or any subsequently published volume, supplement, appendix or plates or error in the enumeration of the plates.

(c) A buyer's claim under this Condition shall be limited to any amount paid in respect of the lot and shall not extend to any loss or damage suffered or expense incurred by him.

(d) The benefit of this Condition shall not be assignable and shall rest solely and exclusively in the buyer who, for the purpose of this Condition, shall be and only be the person to whom the original invoice is made out by Sotheby's in respect of the lot sold.

(iii)
Alternative Condition 16 for catalogues for sales of gemstones and pearls

16. Liability of Sotheby's and seller

(a) Goods auctioned are usually of some age. All goods are sold with all faults and imperfections and errors of description. Illustrations in catalogues are for identification only. Buyers should satisfy themselves prior to sale as to the condition of each lot and should exercise and rely on their own judgment as to whether the lot accords with its description. Subject to the obligations accepted by Sotheby's under this Condition, none of the seller, Sotheby's, its servants or agents is responsible for errors of description or for the genuineness or authenticity of any lot, no warranty whatever is given by Sotheby's, its servants or agents, or any seller to any buyer in respect of any lot and any express or implied conditions or warranties are hereby excluded.

(b) Gemstones, and pearls are sold as genuine, untreated and of natural origin, unless stated to be otherwise in the catalogue or by the auctioneer at the sale. If within 21 days of an auction the buyer of a gemstone or pearl gives notice in writing to Sotheby's that an item purchased is not genuine, untreated, or of natural origin, and returns the lot to Sotheby's in the same condition as it was at the date of the sale, and it is established by a test carried out by a competent authority that the defect complained of is justified, Sotheby's will rescind the sale and refund any amount paid in respect of the lot, together with the testing fee, if paid by the buyer:

(c) A buyer's claim under this Condition shall be limited to any amount paid in respect of the lot and shall not extend to any loss or damage suffered or expense incurred by him.

(d) The benefit of this Condition shall not be assignable and shall rest solely and exclusively in the buyer who, for the purpose of this Condition, shall be and only be the person to whom the original invoice is made out by Sotheby's in respect of the lot sold.

(iv)
Alternative Condition 16 for catalogues for sales of numismatic items

16. Liability of Sotheby's and sellers

(a) Goods auctioned are usually of some age. All goods are sold with all faults and imperfections and errors of description. Illustrations in catalogues are for identification only. Buyers should satisfy themselves prior to sale as to the condition of each lot and should exercise and rely on their own judgment as to whether the lot accords with its description. Subject to the obligations accepted by Sotheby's under this Condition, none of the seller, Sotheby's, its servants or agents is responsible for errors of description or for the genuineness of authenticity of any lot, no warranty whatever is given by Sotheby's, its servants or agents, or any seller to any buyer in respect of any lot and any express or implied conditions or warranties are hereby excluded.

(b) If within eight days of the auction the buyer gives notice in writing to Sotheby's that an item purchased is a 'deliberate forgery' and returns the lot to Sotheby's in the same condition as it was at the date of the sale and it is established that the item is a 'deliberate forgery', Sotheby's will rescind the sale and refund any amount paid in respect of the lot.

(c) A buyer's claim under this Condition shall be limited to any amount paid in respect of the lot and shall not extend to any loss or damage suffered or expense incurred by him.

(d) The benefit of this Condition shall not be assignable and shall rest solely and exclusively in the buyer who, for the purpose of this Condition, shall be and only be the person to whom the original invoice is made out by Sotheby's in respect of the lot sold.

(v)
Alternative Condition 16 for catalogues for sales of postage stamps

16. Liability of Sotheby's and sellers

(a) Subject to the obligations accepted by Sotheby's under this Condition, none of the seller, Sotheby's, its servants or agents is reponsible for errors of description or for the genuineness or authenticity of any lot, no warranty whatever is given by Sotheby's, its servants or agents, or any seller to any buyer in respect of any lot and any express or implied conditions or warranties are hereby excluded.

(b) If within 21 days of the auction Sotheby's receives notice in writing from the buyer of a postage stamp lot claiming that an item is not genuine or does not correspond with the description in the catalogue and the lot is returned to Sotheby's by a date agreed by Sotheby's in the same condition as it was at the time of sale and on the original lot folder and Sotheby's agrees that the buyer's claim is justified, Sotheby's will rescind the sale and refund any amount paid to Sotheby's in respect of the lot: Provided that no return will be accepted nor sale rescinded nor refund made if:
(i) the lot is described in the catalogue or is announced by the auctioneer at the sale as being not subject to return or as being defective; or
(ii) the lot is a collection or mixed lot containing more than four items, in which case the lot is purchased by the buyer with all (if any) faults, lack of genuineness and errors of description including the number of stamps in the lot; or

(iii) the lot has been illustrated and the defect complained of is apparent in the illustrations; or
(iv) there is a conflict of opinion between the Royal Philatelic Society London and BPA Expertising Limited or either is unable to express a conclusive opinion.

(c) Where an extension has been granted under (d) below on an item which is proved not to be genuine then Sotheby's will rescind the sale and refund any amount paid to Sotheby's in respect of that item: Provided that:
(i) within the extension period of 60 days Sotheby's receives back the item together with the certificate stating that it is not genuine; and
(ii) the buyer has paid for the lot in accordance with Conditions 6 or 7.

(d) If Sotheby's receives a written application for an extension on a lot not later than 24 hours before an auction from an intending buyer, Sotheby's may grant an extension for a maximum of 60 days from the date of the auction during which the buyer may obtain a certificate of genuineness or non-genuineness from the Royal Philatelic Society of London or BPA Expertising Limited: Provided that no extension will be granted on:
(i) a collection or mixed lot containing more than four items or a single item contained in such a lot; or
(ii) an item which is described as accompanied by a specified certificate of opinion dated within ten years of the sale.

(e) Sotheby's reserve the right on behalf of the seller to withdraw a lot on which an extension has been requested under (d) above.

(f) (i) The certificate of either the Royal Philatelic Society London or BPA Expertising Limited obtained under (d) above is conclusive;
(ii) All costs in connection with obtaining such certificate are the responsibility of the buyer regardless of the opinion received.

(g) A buyer's claim under this Condition shall be limited to any amount paid in respect of the lot and shall not extend to any loss or damage suffered or expense incurred by him.

(h) The benefit of this Condition shall not be assignable and shall rest solely and exclusively in the buyer who, for the purpose of this Condition, shall be and only be the person to whom the original invoice is made out by Sotheby's in respect of the lot sold.

(vi)
Alternative Condition 16 for sales of wines, spirits and cigars, and for sales of motor vehicles

16. Liability of Sotheby's and sellers
Goods auctioned are usually of some age. All goods are sold with all faults and imperfections and errors of description. Illustrations in catalogues are for identification only. Buyers should satisfy themselves prior to sale as to the condition of each lot and should exercise and rely on their own judgment as to whether the lot accords with its description. None of the seller, Sotheby's, its servants or agents is responsible for errors of description or for the genuineness or authenticity of any lot, no warranty whatever is given by Sotheby's, its servants or agents, or any seller to any buyer in respect of any lot and any express or implied conditions or warranties are hereby excluded.

(vii)
Alternative Condition 16 for sales of musical instruments

16. Liability of Sotheby's and sellers
(a) Goods auctioned are usually of some age. All goods are sold with all faults and imperfections and errors of description. Illustrations in catalogues are for identification

only. Buyers should satisfy themselves prior to sale as to the condition of each lot and should exercise and rely on their own judgment as to whether the lot accords with its description. Subject to the obligations accepted by Sotheby's under this Condition, none of the seller, Sotheby's, its servants or agents is reponsible for errors of description or for the genuineness or authenticity of any lot, no warranty whatever is given by Sotheby's, its servants or agents, or any seller to any buyer in respect of any lot and any express or implied conditions or warranties are hereby excluded.

(b) Any lot which proves to be a 'deliberate forgery' may be returned by the buyer to Sotheby's within 5 years of the date of the auction in the same condition in which it is was at the time of the auction, accompanied by a statement of defects, the number of the lot, and the date of the auction at which it was purchased. If Sotheby's is satisfied that the item is a 'deliberate forgery' and that the buyer has and is able to transfer a good and marketable title to the lot free from any third party claims, the sale will be set aside and any amount paid in respect of the lot will be refunded: Provided that the buyer shall have no rights under this Condition if:
(i) the description in the catalogue at the date of the sale was in accordance with the then generally accepted opinion of scholars and experts or fairly indicated that there was a conflict of such opinion; or
(ii) the only method of establishing at the date of publication of the catalogue that the lot was a 'deliberate forgery' was by means of scientific processes not generally accepted for use until after publication of the catalogue, or a process which was unreasonably expensive or impractical; or
(iii) in the case of musical instrument bows, where it is established on removal of the lapping that the bow is a composite piece.

(c) in the case of musical instrument bows if within 21 days of the auction the buyer gives notice to Sotheby's in writing that at the time of the auction the bow was broken in a place other than underneath the lapping and returns the bow to Sotheby's in the same condition in which it was at the time of the auction and it is established that such a claim is justified, Sotheby's will rescind the sale and refund any amount paid in respect of such bow: Provided that such a bow may not be returned nor will its sale be set aside or refund made if: (i) it is described in the catalogue as having been repaired; (ii) the lot also contains items other than musical instrument bows.

(d) A buyer's claim under this Condition shall be limited to any amount paid in respect of the lot and shall not extend to any loss or damage suffered or expense incurred by him.

(e) The benefit of this Condition shall not be assignable and shall rest solely and exclusively in the buyer who, for the purpose of this Condition, shall be and only be the person to whom the original invoice is made out by Sotheby's in respect of the lot sold.

Alternative Condition 20 for motor vehicle catalogues

20. (a) Insurance
Unless otherwise instructed, Sotheby's will insure property (other than 'motor vehicles') consigned to it or put under its control for sale and may at its discretion insure property put under its control for any other purpose. In all cases save where Sotheby's is required to insure, the property shall remain at all times at the risk of the seller or consignor and neither Sotheby's nor its servants or agents will be responsible for any loss or damage whether caused by negligence or otherwise. Such insurance will be at the expense of the seller or consignor, will be for the amount estimated by Sotheby's to be, from time to time, the current value of the property at auction and will subsist until whichever is the earlier of the ownership of the property passing from the seller or the seller or consignor becoming bound to collect the property.

(b) 'Motor vehicles'
The seller or consignor of a 'motor vehicle' warrants and undertakes to Sotheby's that at the date on which it is consigned to Sotheby's or put under Sotheby's control and

except as previously disclosed to Sotheby's:
(i) such vehicle is in roadworthy condition and complies with the provision of all relevant regulations made under section 40 of the Road Traffic Act 1972 (including the Motor Vehicles (Construction and Use) Regulations 1973) and any statutory modification thereof; and
(ii) there is, and will whilst the vehicle remains in Sotheby's custody be in force in respect of the vehicle such test certificate and insurance complying with the provisions of the said Act and any statutory modification thereof as will enable it to be driven lawfully by servants and agents of Sotheby's on any highway, and will indemnify Sotheby's, its servants and agents against any loss or damage suffered by any of them in consequence of any breach of the above warranty and undertaking.

CONDITIONS OF SALE[6] OF CHRISTIE MANSON & WOODS LTD[7]

Terms for selling works of art by auction at our Great Rooms

Our Commission from the Seller (except on wine, coins and medals) is 10 per cent of the final bid price on lots selling for £1 000 and above and 12.5 per cent on lots selling for less than £1 000. Commission from the Seller on wine, coins and medals is 15 per cent of the final bid price. There is a Buyer's premium of 8 per cent of the final bid price (together with any VAT chargeable thereon) except for wine, coins and medals on which there is no Buyer's premium. In the case of lots failing to reach their reserve a charge of 5 per cent will be made on the last bid on lots on which the last bid price is less than £500, and 2½ per cent on the last bid on all other lots.

VAT at the standard rate is payable on all Sellers' commission.

Private foreign residents, except those within the EEC, are exempt from VAT on Sellers' commission and illustration charges.

CONDITIONS OF ACCEPTANCE

1. Christie's act only as agent save as hereinafter appears of the person or persons (in these Conditions called the Seller) sending property to or leaving property with Christie's for sale. The Seller warrants to Christie's that he is entitled to sell.
Christie's accept property for sale only on the basis that if they sell the same they will be entitled in addition to commission from the Seller to retain that part of the purchase price representing the premium payable by the Buyer as set out in Conditions 5 and 9 of their Conditions of Sale as follows:
5. The purchase price payable by the Buyer shall be the aggregate of the final bid and a premium of 8 per cent of the final bid (together with any VAT chargeable on the final bid and such premium). 'The final bid' means the price at which a lot is knocked down to the Buyer.
9. The property in a lot shall not pass to the Buyer until he has paid the purchase price in full, but the lot shall be at the Buyer's risk in all respects from the fall of the hammer. Notwithstanding that Christie's act only as agents for the Seller, they shall be entitled

6 As at June 1983.
7 These Conditions are the sole copyright of Christie Manson & Woods Ltd and are reproduced with their kind permission.

to retain the premium referred to in Condition 5 hereof, irrespctive of and in addition to such remuneration as they may receive from the Seller. Christie's shall be entitled to a lien on any lot sold until the purchase price is paid in full by the Buyer.
Similarly in the event of the failure by a Buyer to pay the purchase price, and on a resale there being a surplus over the purchase price after payment of all expenses Christie's shall be entitled to retain the premium. All sums received by Christie's by way of purchase price shall as between the Seller and Christie's be appropriated exclusively to purposes other than the payment of the premium until the Seller's and all other claims upon such sums shall have been fully discharged.

2. Christie's shall have complete discretion as to whether to offer for sale or not and as to:
(a) whether the property is suitable for sale by them and if so as to the place and date of sale and as to the Conditions of Sale and as to the manner in which such sale is conducted;
(b) the description of the property in their catalogues or other literature;
(c) seeking the views of any expert;
(d) illustrating the property in their catalogues at the expense of the Seller up to a maximum of £35 for black and white and £350 for colour (together with any VAT chargeable thereon).

3. The Seller shall not bid for his property or employ any person to bid for him save that he may impose a reserve in which case the Auctioneer alone shall have the right to bid on behalf of the Seller. If a reserve is imposed in a currency other than sterling such reserve will be calculated at the closing rate obtainable by Christie's on the London Foreign Exchange Market on the last business day before the sale, the certificate in writing of Christie's as to such rate being conclusive.

4. (a) The net proceeds of sale less the premium, Christie's commission and any charges to the Seller's debit will become due and payable to the Seller at the expiration of one month after the date of sale provided that Christie's have by then been paid the purchase price in full by the Buyer and that no notice has been given by the Buyer that in his view the lot is a deliberate forgery.
(b) If before the purchase price has been paid in full by the Buyer, Christie's pay an amount equal to the net proceeds of sale to the Seller, property in the lot shall pass to Christie's.
(c) In the case of overseas Sellers, whose property has been sent to the United Kingdom for sale, the net proceeds of sale will be paid to the Seller in such currency available to Christie's as may be agreed providing that the Seller specifies to Christie's in writing prior to the date of sale the currency required. Such sum shall be calculated at the spot rate available for the net proceeds on the London Foreign Exchange Market on the date of sale, the certificate in writing of Christie's as to such spot rate being conclusive. If no currency is specified as aforesaid the net proceeds will be paid in the currency of the country where the Seller has his address as notified to Christie's or at Christie's discretion in sterling.

5. Once the catalogue including the property has been printed the property may be withdrawn by the Seller but only on payment of 10 per cent of the reserve (together with any VAT chargeable thereon) and expenses, or if there is no reserve on payment of 10 per cent of the figure at which the property has been valued for Insurance (as determined by Christie's), together with any VAT chargeable thereon and expenses.

6. If before the net proceeds of sale have been paid to the Seller Christie's have received from the Buyer of any lot notice in writing that in his view the lot is a deliberate forgery and within 14 days after such notification the Buyer ensures that the lot is in the possession of Christie's in the same condition as at the time of sale and within a reasonable period thereafter by producing evidence, the burden of proof to be upon the Buyer, satisfies Christie's that considered in the light of the description in the catalogue the lot is a deliberate forgery then Christie's are authorised to set aside the sale and refund to the Buyer the amount paid by the Buyer for the lot. 'A deliberate forgery' means a lot made or substantially made with an intention to deceive, when considered in the light of the description in the catalogue, and which at the date of sale had a value materially less than it would have had if it had been in accordance with that description.

7. Unless otherwise instructed by the Seller, all property being held by Christie's whether on Christie's premises or elsewhere will automatically be covered by insurance under Christie's own Fine Arts Policy which excludes responsibility for items damaged by woodworm, or by changes in atmospheric conditions, or for the disintegration of gesso-covered picture frames. The rate of premium payable by the Seller is 0.75 per cent of the last bid made for the property. The sums for which property is covered for insurance under this Condition will be estimated by Christie's from time to time and shall not constitute and shall not be relied upon by the Seller as a representation, warranty or guarantee that the property will if and when sold by Christie's be sold for such amount. Provided that in the event that the Seller instructs Christie's not to insure under this Condition (a) the property shall at all times until sold by Christie's remain at the risk of the Seller who hereby agrees to indemnify Christie's against all proceedings, liability, claims, damages and expenses which may be made against Christie's by or incurred by Christie's to the Seller or any insurer of the Seller in respect of loss or damage to the property of whatever nature however and wheresoever occurring and in any circumstances even where negligence is alleged or proven and to reimburse Christie's on demand for all payments, losses, costs and expenses made suffered or incurred by Christie's in consequence thereof or arising therefrom: (b) any payment which Christie's shall make in respect of such loss or damage shall be binding upon the Seller and shall be accepted by the Seller as conclusive evidence that Christie's were liable to make such payment, (c) the Seller further undertakes to notify any insurer of his of the existence of the indemnity contained in this Condition.

8. Lots bought in and property not being kept for sale must be collected at the Seller's expense within two months after notice requiring the Seller to collect. After such two months Christie's are authorised to sell such property in such manner and on such terms as they think fit. Property returned at the request of the Seller shall be returned at his risk and expense and will not be insured in transit unless Christie's have received special directions.

9. Christie's reserve the right at their discretion to arrange for storage in a warehouse of any property sent to or left with them.

10. The Seller must give Christie's all relevant information as to his VAT status with regard to the article to be sold which he warrants to be correct and upon which Christie's shall be entitled to rely. Once a lot has been designated in the sale catalogue on the basis of such information no alteration so as to affect the liability to VAT can be made.

11. Modern firearms: supplement available on request.

12. Any notice given hereunder shall be in writing and if given by post to the address of the Seller any such notice shall be deemed to have been delivered in the ordinary course of post.

13. (a) These Conditions constitute together with the matters set out on the receipt form the entire agreement between Christie's and the Seller.
(b) The respective rights and obligations of the parties shall be governed and interpreted by English law and the Seller hereby submits to the non-exclusive jurisdiction of the English Courts.

Old master pictures
Engraving and prints
Topographical pictures
Drawings
Impressionist pictures
Contemporary pictures
Miniatures
Watercolours

NOTICE

Your attention is drawn to the following:

1. All sales take place on the Conditions of Sale set out below and subject to reserves.

2. Certain terms are used in this Catalogue for your guidance with the meanings ascribed to them below. The description of each lot, however, is an opinion only. Many lots are of an age and nature which precludes their being in pristine condition and some catalogue descriptions make reference to damage and/or restoration. The absence of such a reference does not imply that a lot is free from defects nor does any reference to particular defects imply the absence of others. Such information is given for guidance only and the condition of any lot and the nature and extent of any damage or restoration should be confirmed by examination prior to the sale. In this conection you are specifically requested to read Condition 6 of the Conditions of Sale.

3. Notwithstanding any terms of the Conditions of Sale and subject to the provisions of (a), (b) and (c) below, if, within five years of the sale (1) Christie's have received notice in writing from the buyer of any lot that in his view the lot is a deliberate forgery and (2) within 14 days from such notification the buyer ensures that the lot is in the possession of Christie's in the same condition as at the date of sale and (3) within a reasonable time thereafter, by producing evidence (the burden of proof to be upon the buyer), satisfies Christie's that the lot is a deliberate forgery then Christie's will set aside the sale and refund to the buyer the amount paid by the buyer for the lot.

For the purposes of this guarantee:

(a) 'a deliberate forgery' means a lot made or substantially made with an intention to deceive when considered in the light of the description in the catalogue and which at the date of the sale had a value materially less than it would have had if it had been in accordance with the description.
(b) notwithstanding that the lot is a deliberate forgery as above, the buyer shall have no rights against Christie's under this guarantee where:
   (i) the catalogue description at the date of sale was in accordance with the then generally accepted opinion of scholars or experts or fairly indicated there to be a conflict of such opinion; or

(ii) it can be established that the lot is a deliberate forgery only by means of a scientific process not generally accepted for use until after publication of the catalogue or by means of a process which at the date of the sale was unreasonably expensive or impractical or likely to have caused damage to the lot;

(c) the benefit of this guarantee, which shall not be assignable, shall rest solely and exclusively in the buyer who shall be and only be the person to whom the original invoice was made out by Christie's in respect of the lot when sold and who has since the sale retained uninterrupted, unencumbered ownership thereof.

4. Explanation of cataloguing practice.

Terms referred to in paragraph 2 [of this Notice] are as follows:

A work catalogued with the name(s) or recognised designation of an artist, without any qualification, is, in our opinion, a work by the artist.

In other cases, the following expressions, with the following meanings are used:

'Attributed to . . .'	in our opinion probably a work by the artist in whole or in part.
'Studio of . . .' 'Workshop of . . .'	in our opinion a work executed in the studio or workshop of the artist, possibly under his supervision
'Circle of . . .'	in our opinion a work of the period of the artist and showing his influence.
'Follower of . . .'	in our opinion a work executed in the artist's style but not necessarily by a pupil.
'Manner of . . .'	in our opinion a work executed in the artist's style but of a later date.
'After . . .'	in our opinion a copy (of any date) of a work of the artist.
'Signed . . .' 'Dated . . .' 'Inscribed . . .'	in our opinion the work has been signed/dated/inscribed by the artist. The addition of a question mark indicates an element of doubt.
'With signature . . .' 'With date . . .' 'With inscription . . .'	in our opinion the signature/date/inscription is by a hand other than that of the artist.

CONDITIONS OF SALE

All bids shall be treated as offers made upon the following Conditions of Sale

1. Christie, Manson & Woods Limited ('Christie's') act in all respects, save where otherwise appears, only as agents for the Seller of each lot.

2. The highest bidder acceptable to the Auctioneer shall be the Buyer, but if, during or immediately after the sale of the lot, the Auctioneer considers that a dispute has

arisen or that there is any other reason for so doing, he may at his absolute discretion immediately put up the lot again for sale.

3. The Auctioneer has the right at his absolute discretion to refuse any bid and to advance the bidding as he may decide.

4. (a) The Seller shall be entitled to place a reserve on any lot, and the Auctioneer shall have the right to bid on behalf of the Seller for any lot on which a reserve has been placed.

   (b) Christie's have the right at their absolute discretion to withdraw or divide any lot or to combine any two or more lots.

5. (a) The purchase price payable by the Buyer shall be the aggregate of the final bid and a premium of 8 per cent of the final bid (together with any VAT chargeable on the final bid and such premium). 'The final bid' means the price at which a lot is knocked down to the Buyer.

   (b) The Buyer shall forthwith supply his name and address and if so required by Christie's his bank or other suitable references.

   (c) The Buyer may be required to pay forthwith the whole or any part of the purchase price, and if he fails to do so the lot or lots may at the Auctioneer's absolute discretion be put up again and resold.

6. (a) All statements in the Catalogues, advertisements or brochures of forthcoming sales as to any of the matters specified in (b) and (c) below are statements of opinion and are not, nor are they to be relied upon as statements or representations of fact. Illustrations in the Catalogues, advertisements or brochures of forthcoming sales are solely for the guidance of intending purchasers and are not to be relied upon in terms of tone or colour or necessarily to reveal imperfections in any lot. Intending buyers must satisfy themselves by inspection or otherwise as to all such matters, as to the physical description of any lot and as to whether or not any lot has been repaired.

   (b) Neither the Seller nor Christie's are responsible for the correctness of any statement as to the authorship, origin, date, age, attribution, genuineness or provenance of any lot, or any other errors of description.

   (c) Neither the Seller nor Christie's are responsible for any faults or defects in any lot.

   (d) Neither the Seller nor Christie's nor any person in their employ, make or have any authority to make any representation or warranty nor are they responsible for any representation or warranty, or for any statement in the Catalogues, advertisements or brochures of forthcoming sales or illustrations therein.

7. (a) No lot can be taken away during the auction, nor can any lot be taken away until the purchase price has been paid in full.

   (b) All lots are to be paid for and taken away at the Buyer's expense within SEVEN days from sale.

8. If a Buyer fails either to pay for or take away any lot in accordance with Condition 7, Christie's shall be entitled at their absolute discretion and without prejudice to any other right or remedies to exercise one or more of the following rights:

   (a) without notice to the Buyer to resell the lot or cause it to be resold by public or private sale. Any deficiency in the purchase price attending such resale (after giving credit for any payment and after deducting full costs incurred in connection with the lot) to be made good by the defaulting Buyer, and any surplus (after retention by Christie's of the premium) to be the Seller's;

(b) to store the lot or cause it to be stored whether at their own premises or elsewhere at the sole expense of the Buyer, and to release the lot only after payment in full of the purchase price, the accrued cost of removal, storage and insurance (if any) and all other costs incurred in connection with the lot;

(c) to charge interest at a rate of 2 per cent over Lloyds Bank plc base rate on the purchase price to the extent it remains unpaid for more than 7 days from the date of the sale.

9. The property in a lot shall not pass to the Buyer until he has paid the purchase price in full, but the lot shall be at the Buyer's risk in all respects from the fall of the hammer. Notwithstanding that Christie's act only as agents for the Seller, they shall be entitled to retain the premium referred to in Condition 5(a) hereof, irrespective of and in addition to such remuneration as they may receive from the Seller. Christie's shall be entitled to a lien on any lot sold until the purchase price is paid in full by the Buyer.

10. The respective rights and obligations of the parties in respect to the Conditions of Sale shall be governed and interpreted by English Law and the Buyer hereby submits to the non-exclusive jurisdiction of the English Courts.

INFORMATION FOR SELLERS AND BUYERS

Terms of Sale

Seller's Commission:
Our commission from the seller (except on wine, coins and medals) is 10 per cent of the final bid on lots selling for £1 000 and above and 12.5 per cent on lots selling for less than £1 000. Our commission from the seller on wine, coins and medals is 15 per cent of the final bid.

Buyer's Premium:
Buyers are reminded that there is an 8 per cent premium payable on the final bid of each lot (see clause 5(a) of the Conditions of Sale), except for wine, coins and medals.

Value Added Tax (VAT)

VAT at the standard rate is payable on the seller's commission. Private foreign residents, except those within the EEC, are exempt.

VAT is payable in all cases on the premium.

In the case of a lot marked with a dagger (†) in the catalogue, VAT is payable in addition on the final bid.
In the case of second-hand goods which are dealt with for VAT purposes under the Special Scheme described in VAT Notice 712, HM Customs & Excise treat the final bid as the seller's selling price and the buyer's purchase price.

Sellers overseas

There are no auction taxes in the United Kingdom.

Paintings, drawings, prints, sculpture disposed of by the creator or as part of his estate before 1st April 1973, collections and collector's pieces and antiques more than 100 years old all enter the United Kingdom free of duty and without payment of VAT (explanatory leaflet on request).

It is essential that all items imported for sale must be declared to H M Customs at the point of entry into the United Kingdom.

Commission bids
Christie's are always pleased to advise Clients and to execute bids on their behalf, but if successful the purchase price payable will be the final bid price and the premium of 8 per cent together with any VAT chargeable thereon (see clause 5(a) of the Conditions of Sale).

Bids must always be made or confirmed in writing or by telex, reference being made to each sale through the code name printed on the title page of each catalogue. A form for written bids is printed at the back of the catalogue. To ensure that bids will be accepted and the delivery of lots is not delayed, intending buyers should supply bank or other suitable references to Christie's. The references should be supplied in good time to be taken up before the sale.

Valuations
Charges for supplying valuations with inventories for probate, insurance, family division or other purposes totalling more than £50 000 will be arranged by negotiation. The charge up to a total of £50 000 is 1½ per cent. VAT will be added to these charges. Minimum fee: £25 in London and £50 in the country.

Inspections
There will be no charge for calling upon owners and advising with a view to possible sale by auction in our rooms, except for travel and out-of-pocket expenses.

Appendix 2

Statutory and other material: selected extracts

Appendix 2 is in four parts, as follows:
Sale of goods
Criminal law
Land
Supplies of a service

SALE OF GOODS

This section of Appendix 2 contains individual sections etc of Acts, as follows:
Sale of Goods Act 1979, ss 12-25 and 57
Factors Acts 1889, s 2(1)
Misrepresentation Act 1967, ss 1-3
Unfair Contract Terms Act 1977, ss 2, 3, 6, 10-12 and Sch 2
Torts (Interference with Goods) Act 1977, s 8
Civil Liability (Contribution) Act 1978, ss 1-8

SALE OF GOODS ACT 1979

12. Implied terms about title, etc
(1) In a contract of sale, other than one to which subsection (3) below applies, there is an implied condition on the part of the seller that in the case of a sale he has a right to sell the goods, and in the case of an agreement to sell he will have such a right at the time when the property is to pass.

(2) In a contract of sale, other than one to which subsection (3) below applies, there is also an implied warranty that—

(a) the goods are free, and will remain free until the time when the property is to pass, from any charge or encumbrance not disclosed or known to the buyer before the contract is made, and
(b) the buyer will enjoy quiet possession of the goods except so far as it may be disturbed by the owner or other person entitled to the benefit of any charge or encumbrance so disclosed or known.

(3) This subsection applies to a contract of sale in the case of which there appears from the contract or is to be inferred from its circumstances an intention that the seller should transfer only such title as he or a third person may have.

(4) In a contract to which subsection (3) above applies there is an implied warranty that all charges or encumbrances known to the seller and not known to the buyer have been disclosed to the buyer before the contract is made.

(5) In a contract to which subsection (3) above applies there is also an implied warranty that none of the following will disturb the buyer's quiet possession of the goods, namely—

(a) the seller;
(b) in a case where the parties to the contract intend that the seller should transfer only such title as a third person may have, that person;
(c) anyone claiming through or under the seller or that third person otherwise than under a charge or encumbrance disclosed or known to the buyer before the contract is made.

(6) . . .

13. Sale by description
(1) Where there is a contract for the sale of goods by description, there is an implied condition that the goods will correspond with the description.

(2) If the sale is by sample as well as by description it is not sufficient that the bulk of the goods corresponds with the sample if the goods do not also correspond with the description.

(3) A sale of goods is not prevented from being a sale by description by reason only that, being exposed for sale or hire, they are selected by the buyer.

(4) . . .

14. Implied terms about quality or fitness
(1) Except as provided by this section and section 15 below and subject to any other enactment, there is no implied condition or warranty about the quality or fitness for any particular purpose of goods supplied under a contract of sale.

(2) Where the seller sells goods in the course of a business, there is an implied condition that the goods supplied under the contract are of merchantable quality, except that there is no such condition —

(a) as regards defects specifically drawn to the buyer's attention before the contract is made; or
(b) if the buyer examines the goods before the contract is made, as regards defects which that examination ought to reveal.

(3) Where the seller sells goods in the course of a business and the buyer, expressly or by implication, makes known —

(a) to the seller, or
(b) where the purchase price or part of it is payable by instalments and the goods were previously sold by a credit-broker to the seller, to that credit-broker,

any particular purpose for which the goods are being bought, there is an implied condition that the goods supplied under the contract are reasonably fit for that purpose, whether or not that is a purpose for which such goods are commonly supplied, except where the circumstances show that the buyer does not rely, or that it is unreasonable for him to rely, on the skill or judgment of the seller or credit-broker.

(4) An implied condition or warranty about quality or fitness for a particular purpose may be annexed to a contract of sale by usage.

(5) The preceding provisions of this section apply to a sale by a person who in the course of a business is acting as agent for another as they apply to a sale by a principal in the course of business, except where that other is not selling in the course of a business and either the buyer knows that fact or reasonable steps are taken to bring it to the notice of the buyer before the contract is made.

(6) Goods of any kind are of merchantable quality within the meaning of subsection (2) above if they are as fit for the purpose or purposes for which goods of that kind are commonly bought as it is reasonable to expect having regard to any description applied to them, the price (if relevant) and all the other relevant circumstances.

(7) . . .

(8) . . .

15. Sale by sample

(1) A contract of sale is a contract for sale by sample where there is an express or implied term to that effect in the contract.

(2) In the case of a contract for sale by sample there is an implied condition —

(a) that the bulk will correspond with the sample in quality;
(b) that the buyer will have a reasonable opportunity of comparing the bulk with the sample;
(c) that the goods will be free from any defect, rendering them unmerchantable, which would not be apparent on reasonable examination of the sample.

(3) In subsection (2)(c) above 'unmerchantable' is to be construed in accordance with section 14(6) above.

(4) . . .

16. Goods must be ascertained

Where there is a contract for the sale of unascertained goods no property in the goods is transferred to the buyer unless and until the goods are ascertained.

17. Property passes when intended to pass

(1) Where there is a contract for the sale of specific or ascertained goods the property in them is transferred to the buyer at such time as the parties to the contract intend it to be transferred.

(2) For the purpose of ascertaining the intention of the parties regard shall be had to the terms of the contract, the conduct of the parties and the circumstances of the case.

18. Rules for ascertaining intention

Unless a different intention appears, the following are rules for ascertaining the intention of the parties as to the time at which the property in the goods is to pass to the buyer.

Rule 1.—Where there is an unconditional contract for the sale of specific goods in a deliverable state the property in the goods passes to the buyer when the contract is made, and it is immaterial whether the time of payment or the time of delivery, or both, be postponed.

Rule 2.—Where there is a contract for the sale of specific goods and the seller is bound to do something to the goods for the purpose of putting them into a deliverable state, the property does not pass until the thing is done and the buyer has notice that it has been done.

Rule 3.—Where there is a contract for the sale of specific goods in a deliverable state but the seller is bound to weigh, measure, test, or do some other act or thing with reference to the goods for the purpose of ascertaining the price, the property does not pass until such act or thing be done, and the buyer has notice thereof.

Rule 4.—When goods are delivered to the buyer on approval or 'on sale or return' or other similar terms the property therein passes to the buyer —

(a) When he signifies his approval or acceptance to the seller or does any other act adopting the transaction;
(b) If he does not signify his approval or acceptance to the seller but retains the goods without giving notice or rejection then, if a time has been fixed for the return of the goods, on the expiration of such time, and, if no time has been fixed, on the expiration of a reasonable time. What is a reasonable time is a question of fact.

Rule 5.—(1) Where there is a contract for the sale of unascertained or future goods by description, and goods of that description and in a deliverable state are unconditionally appropriated to the contract, either by the seller with the assent of the buyer or by the buyer with the assent of the seller, the property in the goods then passes to the buyer; and the assent may be express or implied, and may be given either before or after the appropriation is made.
(2) Where, in pursuance of the contract, the seller delivers the goods to the buyer or to a carrier or other bailee or custodier (whether named by the buyer or not) for the purpose of transmission to the buyer, and does not reserve the right of disposal, he is to be taken to have unconditionally appropriated the goods to the contract.

19. Reservation of right of disposal
(1) Where there is a contract for the sale of specific goods or where goods are subsequently appropriated to the contract, the seller may, by the terms of the contract or appropriation, reserve the right of disposal of the goods until certain conditions are fulfilled; and in such a case, notwithstanding the delivery of the goods to the buyer, or to a carrier or other bailee or custodier for the purpose of transmission to the buyer, the property in the goods does not pass to the buyer until the conditions imposed by the seller are fulfilled.

(2) Where goods are shipped, and by the bill of lading the goods are deliverable to the order of the seller or his agent, the seller is prima facie to be taken to reserve the right of disposal.

(3) Where the seller of goods draws on the buyer for the price, and transmits the bill of exchange and bill of lading to the buyer together to secure acceptance or payment of the bill of exchange, the buyer is bound to return the bill of lading if he does not honour the bill of exchange, and if he wrongfully retains the bill of lading the property in the goods does not pass to him.

20. Risk prima facie passes with property
(1) Unless otherwise agreed, the goods remain at the seller's risk until the property in them is transferred to the buyer, but when the property in them is transferred to the buyer the goods are at the buyer's risk whether delivery has been made or not.

(2) But where delivery has been delayed through the fault of either buyer or seller the goods are at the risk of the party at fault as regards any loss which might not have occurred but for such fault.

(3) Nothing in this section affects the duties or liabilities of either seller or buyer as a bailee or custodier of the goods of the other party.

21. Sale by person not the owner
(1) Subject to this Act, where goods are sold by a person who is not their owner, and who does not sell them under the authority or with the consent of the owner, the buyer acquires no better title to the goods than the seller had, unless the owner of the goods is by his conduct precluded from denying the seller's authority to sell.

(2) Nothing in this Act affects —

(a) the provisions of the Factors Acts or any enactment enabling the apparent owner of goods to dispose of them as if he were their true owner;
(b) the validity of any contract of sale under any special common law or statutory power of sale or under the order of a court of competent jurisdiction.

22. Market overt
(1) Where goods are sold in market overt, according to the usage of the market, the buyer acquires a good title to the goods, provided he buys them in good faith and without notice of any defect or want of title on the part of the seller.

(2) This section does not apply to Scotland.

(3) . . .

23. Sale under voidable title
When the seller of goods has a voidable title to them, but his title has not been avoided at the time of the sale, the buyer acquires a good title to the goods, provided he buys them in good faith and without notice of the seller's defect of title.

24. Seller in possession after sale
Where a person having sold goods continues or is in possession of the goods, or of the documents of title to the goods, the delivery or transfer by that person, or by a mercantile agent acting for him, of the goods or documents of title under any sale, pledge, or other disposition thereof, to any person receiving the same in good faith and without notice of the previous sale, has the same effect as if the person making the delivery or transfer were expressly authorised by the owner of the goods to make the same.

25. Buyer in possession after sale
(1) Where a person having bought or agreed to buy goods obtains, with the consent of the seller, possession of the goods or the documents of title to the goods, the delivery or transfer by that person, or by a mercantile agent acting for him, of the goods or document of title, under any sale, pledge, or other disposition thereof, to any person receiving the same in good faith and without notice of any lien or other right of the original seller in respect of the goods, has the same effect as if the person making the delivery or transfer were a mercantile agent in possession of the goods or documents of title with the consent of the owner.

(2) For the purposes of subsection (1) above —

(a) the buyer under a conditional sale agreement is to be taken not to be a person who has bought or agreed to buy goods, and
(b) 'conditional sale agreement' means an agreement for the sale of goods which is a consumer credit agreement within the meaning of the Consumer Credit Act 1974 under which the purchase price or part of it is payable by instalments, and the property in the goods is to remain in the seller (notwithstanding that the buyer is to be in possession of the goods) until such conditions as to the payment of instalments or otherwise as may be specified in the agreement are fulfilled.

(3) . . .

(4) . . .

57. Auction sales
(1) Where goods are put up for sale by auction in lots, each lot is prima facie deemed to be the subject of a separate contract of sale.

(2) A sale by auction is complete when the auctioneer announces its completion by the fall of the hammer, or in other customary manner; and until the announcement is made any bidder may retract his bid.

(3) A sale by auction may be notified to be subject to a reserve or upset price, and a right to bid may also be reserved expressly by or on behalf of the seller.

(4) Where a sale by auction is not notified to be subject to a right to bid by or on behalf of the seller, it is not lawful for the seller to bid himself or to employ any person to bid at the sale, or for the auctioneer knowingly to take any bid from the seller or any such person.

(5) A sale contravening subsection (4) above may be treated as fraudulent by the buyer.

(6) Where, in respect of a sale by auction, a right to bid is expressly reserved (but not otherwise) the seller or any one person on his behalf may bid at the auction.

FACTORS ACT 1889

2. Powers of mercantile agent with respect to disposition of goods
(1) Where a mercantile agent is, with the consent of the owner, in possession of goods or of the documents of title to goods, any sale, pledge, or other disposition of the goods, made by him when acting in the ordinary course of business of a mercantile agent, shall, subject to the provisions of this Act, be as valid as if he were expressly authorised by the owner of the goods to make the same; provided that the person taking under the disposition acts in good faith, and has not at the time of the disposition notice that the person making the disposition has not authority to make the same.

(2) . . .

(3) . . .

(4) . . .

MISREPRESENTATION ACT 1967

1. Removal of certain bars to rescission for innocent misrepresentation
Where a person has entered into a contract after a misrepresentation has been made to him, and

(a) the misrepresentation has become a term of the contract; or
(b) the contract has been performed; or both, then, if otherwise he would be entitled to rescind the contract without alleging fraud, he shall be so entitled, notwithstanding the matters mentioned in paragraphs (a) and (b) of this section.

2. Damages for mispresentation
(1) Where a person has entered into a contract after a misrepresentation has been made to him by another party thereto and as a result thereof he has suffered loss, then, if the person making the misrepresentation would be liable to damages in respect thereof had the mispresentation been made fraudulently, that person shall be so liable notwithstanding that the misrepresentation was not made fraudulently, unless he proves that he had reasonable ground, to believe and did believe up to the time the contract was made that the facts represented were true.

(2) Where a person has entered into a contract after a mispresentation has been made to him otherwise than fraudulently, and he would be entitled, by reason of the misrepresentation, to rescind the contract, then, if it is claimed, in any proceedings

arising out of the contract, that the contract ought to be or has been rescinded, the court or arbitrator may declare the contract subsisting and award damages in lieu of rescission, if of opinion that it would be equitable so to do, having regard to the nature of the misrepresentation and the loss that would be caused by it if the contract were upheld, as well as to the loss that rescission would cause to the other party.

(3) Damages may be awarded against a person under subsection (2) of this section whether or not he is liable to damages under sub-section (1) thereof, but where he is so liable any award under the sub-section (2) shall be taken into account in assessing his liability under the said sub-section (1).

3. Avoidance of certain provisions excluding liability for misrepresentation
If a contract contains a term which would exclude or restrict —

(a) Any liability to which a party to a contract may be subject by reason of any misrepresentation made by him before the contract was made; or
(b) Any remedy available to another party to the contract by reason of such a misrepresentation,

that term shall be of no effect except in so far as it satisfies the requirement of reasonableness as stated in section 11(1) of the Unfair Contract Terms Act 1977; and it is for those claiming that the term satisfies the requirement to show that it does.

UNFAIR CONTRACT TERMS ACT 1977

2. Negligence liability
(1) A person cannot by reference to any contract term or to a notice given to persons generally or to particular persons exclude or restrict his liability for death or personal injury resulting from negligence.

(2) In the case of other loss or damage, a person cannot so exclude or restrict his liability for negligence except in so far as the term or notice satisfies the requirement of reasonableness.

(3) Where a contract term or notice purports to exclude or restrict liability for negligence a person's agreement to or awareness of it is not of itself to be taken as indicating his voluntary acceptance of any risk.

3. Liability arising in contract
(1) This section applies as between contracting parties where one of them deals as consumer or on the other's written standard terms of business.

(2) As against that party, the other cannot by reference to any contract term—

(a) when himself in breach of contract, exclude or restrict any liability of his in respect of the breach; or
(b) claim to be entitled—
   (i) to render a contractual performance substantially different from that which was reasonably expected of him, or
   (ii) in respect of the whole or any part of his contractual obligation, to render no performance at all,

except in so far as (in any of these cases mentioned above in this subsection) the contract term satisfies the requirement of reasonableness.

6. Sale and hire-purchase
(1) Liability for breach of the obligations arising from —

(a) section 12 of the Sale of Goods Act 1979 (seller's implied undertakings as to title etc);
(b) section 8 of the Supply of Goods (Implied Terms) Act 1973 (the corresponding thing in relation to hire-purchase),

cannot be excluded or restricted by reference to any contract term.

(2) As against a person dealing as a consumer, liability for breach of the obligations arising from —

(a) section 13, 14, or 15 of the 1979 Act (seller's implied undertakings as to conformity of goods with description or sample, or as to their quality or fitness for a particular purpose);
(b) section 9, 10 or 11 of the 1973 Act (the corresponding things in relation to hire-purchase),

cannot be excluded or restricted by reference to any contract term.

(3) As against a person dealing otherwise than as consumer, the liability specified in subsection (2) above can be excluded or restricted by reference to a contract term, but only in so far as the term satisfies the requirement of reasonableness.

(4) The liabilities referred to in this section are not only the business liabilities defined by section 1(3), but include those arising under any contract of sale of goods or hire-purchase agreement.

10. Evasion by means of secondary contract

A person is not bound by any contract term prejudicing or taking away rights of his which arise under or in connection with the performance of, another contract, so far as those rights extend to the enforcement of another's liability which this Part of this Act prevents that other from excluding or restricting.

11. The 'reasonableness' test

(1) In relation to a contract term, the requirement of reasonableness for the purposes of this Part of this Act, section 3 of the Misrepresentation Act 1967 and section 3 of the Misrepresentation Act (Nothern Ireland) 1967 is that the term shall have been a fair and reasonable one to be included having regard to the circumstances which were, or ought reasonably to have been, known to or in the contemplation of the parties when the contract was made.

(2) In determining for the purposes of section 6 or 7 above whether a contract term satisfies the requirement of reasonableness, regard shall be had in particular to the matters specified in Schedule 2 of this Act; but this subsection does not prevent the court or arbitrator from holding, in accordance with any rule of law, that a term which purports to exclude or restrict any relevant liability is not a term of the contract.

(3) In relation to a notice (not being a notice having contractual effect) the requirement of reasonableness under this Act is that it should be fair and reasonable to allow reliance on it, having regard to all the circumstances obtaining when the liability arose or (but for the notice) would have arisen.

(4) Where by reference to a contract term or notice a person seeks to restrict liability to a specified sum of money, and the question arises (under this or any other Act) whether the term or notice satisfies the requirement of reasonableness, regard shall be had in particular (but without prejudice to subsection (2) above in the case of contract terms) to—

(a) the resources which he could expect to be available to him for the purposes of meeting the liability should it arise; and

(b) how far it was open to him to cover himself by insurance.

(5) It is for those claiming that a contract term or notice satisfies the requirement of reasonableness to show that it does.

12. 'Dealing as consumer'
(1) A party to a contract 'deals as consumer' in relation to another party if—

(a) he neither makes the contract in the course of a business nor holds himself out as doing so; and
(b) the other party does make the contract in the course of a business; and
(c) in the case of a contract governed by the law of sale of goods or hire-purchase, or by section 7 of this Act, the goods passing under or in pursuance of the contract are of a type ordinarily supplied for private use or consumption.

(2) But on a sale by auction or by competitive tender the buyer is not in any circumstances to be regarded as dealing as consumer.

(3) Subject to this, it is for those claiming that a party does not deal as consumer to show that he does not.

Schedule 2
'Guidelines' for application of reasonableness test
The matters to which regard is to be had in particular for the purposes of section 6(3), 7(3) and (4), 20 and 21 are any of the following which appear to be relevant—

(a) the strength of the bargaining positions of the parties relative to each other, taking into account (among other things) alternative means by which the customer's requirements could have been met;
(b) whether the customer received an inducement to agree to the term or in accepting it had an opportunity of entering into a similar contract with other persons, but without having to accept a similar term;
(c) whether the customer knew or ought reasonably to have known of the existence and extent of the term (having regard, among other things, to any custom of the trade and any previous course of dealing between the parties);
(d) where the term excludes or restricts any relevant liability if some condition is not complied with, whether it was reasonable at the time of the contract to expect that compliance with that condition would be practicable;
(e) whether the goods were manufactured, processed or adapted to the special order of the customer.

TORTS (INTERFERENCE WITH GOODS) ACT 1977

8. Competing rights to the goods
(1) The defendant in an action for wrongful interference shall be entitled to show, in accordance with rules of court, that a third party has a better right than the plaintiff as respects all or any part of the interest claimed by the plaintiff, or in right of which he sues, and any rule of law (sometimes called jus tertii) to the contrary is abolished.

(2) Rules of court relating to proceedings for wrongful interference may —

(a) require the plaintiff to give particulars of his title,
(b) require the plaintiff to identify any person who, to his knowledge, has or claims any interest in the goods.
(c) authorise the defendant to apply for directions as to whether any person should be joined with a view to establishing whether he has a better right than the plaintiff, or has a claim as a result of which the defendant might be doubly liable,

(d) where a party fails to appear on an application within paragraph (c), or to comply with any direction given by the court on such an application, authorise the court to deprive him of any right of action against the defendant for the wrong either unconditionally, or subject to such terms or conditions as may be specified.

(3) Subsection (2) is without prejudice to any other power of making rules of court.

CIVIL LIABILITY (CONTRIBUTION) ACT 1978

1. Entitlement to contribution

(1) Subject to the following provisions of this section, any person liable in respect of any damage suffered by another person may recover contribution from any other person liable in respect of the same damage (whether jointly with him or otherwise).

(2) A person shall be entitled to recover contribution by virtue of subsection (1) above notwithstanding that he has ceased to be liable in respect of the damage in question since the time when the damage occurred, provided that he was so liable immediately before he made or was ordered or agreed to make the payment in respect of which the contribution is sought.

(3) A person shall be liable to make contribution by virtue of subsection (1) above notwithstanding that he has ceased to be liable in respect of the damage in question since the time when the damage occurred, unless he ceased to be liable by virtue of the expiry of a period of limitation or prescription which extinguished the right on which the claim against him in respect of the damage was based.

(4) A person who has made or agreed to make any payment in bona fide settlement or compromise of any claim made against him in respect of any damage (including a payment into court which has been accepted) shall be entitled to recover contribution in accordance with this section without regard to whether or not he himself is or ever was liable in respect of the damage, provided, however, that he would have been liable assuming that the factual basis of the claim against him could be established.

(5) A judgment given in any action brought in any part of the United Kingdom by or on behalf of the person who suffered the damage in question against any person from whom contribution is sought under this section shall be conclusive in the proceedings for contribution as to any issue determined by that judgment in favour of the person from whom the contribution is sought.

(6) References in this section to a person's liability in respect of any damage are references to any such liability which has been or could be established in an action brought against him in England and Wales by or on behalf of the person who suffered the damage; but it is immaterial whether any issue arising in any such action was or would be determined (in accordance with the rules of private international law) by reference to the law of a country outside England and Wales.

2. Assessment of contribution

(1) Subject to subsection (3) below, in any proceedings for contribution under section 1 above the amount of the contribution recoverable from any person shall be such as may be found by the court to be just and equitable having regard to the extent of that person's responsibility for the damage in question.

(2) Subject to subsection (3) below, the court shall have power in any such proceedings, to exempt any person from liability to make contribution, or to direct that the contribution to be recovered from any person shall amount to a complete indemnity.

(3) Where the amount of the damages which have or might have been awarded in respect of the damage in question in any action brought in England and Wales by or on behalf of the person who suffered it against the person from whom the contribution is sought was or would have been subject to —

(a) any limit imposed by or under any enactment or by any agreement made before the damage occurred;
(b) any reduction by virtue of section 1 of the Law Reform (Contributory Negligence) Act 1945 or section 5 of the Fatal Accidents Act 1976; or
(c) any corresponding limit or reduction under the law of a country outside England and Wales;

the person from whom the contribution is sought shall not by virtue of any contribution awarded under section 1 above be required to pay in respect of the damage a greater amount than the amount of those damages as so limited or reduced.

3. Proceedings against persons jointly liable for the same debt or damage
Judgment recovered against any person liable in respect of any debt or damage shall not be a bar to an action, or to the continuance of an action, against any other person who is (apart from any such bar) jointly liable with him in respect of the same debt or damage.

4. Successive actions against persons liable (jointly or otherwise) for the same damage
If more than one action is brought in respect of any damage by or on behalf of the person by whom it was suffered against persons liable in respect of the damage (whether jointly or otherwise) the plaintiff shall not be entitled to costs in any of those actions, other than that in which judgment is first given, unless the court is of the opinion that there was reasonable ground for bringing the action.

5. Application to the Crown
Without prejudice to section 4(1) of the Crown Proceedings Act 1947 (indemnity and contribution), this Act shall bind the Crown, but nothing in this Act shall be construed as in any way affecting Her Majesty in Her private capacity (including in right of Her Duchy of Lancaster) or the Duchy of Cornwall.

6. Interpretation
(1) A person is liable in respect of any damage for the purposes of this Act if the person who suffered it (or anyone representing his estate or dependants) is entitled to recover compensation from him in respect of that damage (whatever the legal basis of his liability, whether tort, breach of contract, breach of trust or otherwise).

(2) References in this Act to an action brought by or on behalf of the person who suffered any damage include references to an action brought for the benefit of his estate or dependants.

(3) In this Act 'dependants' has the same meaning as in the Fatal Accidents Act 1976.

(4) In this Act, except in section 1(5) above, 'action' means an action brought in England and Wales.

7. Savings
(1) Nothing in this Act shall affect any case where the debt in question became due or (as the case may be) the damage in question occurred before the date on which it comes into force.

(2) A person shall not be entitled to recover contribution or liable to make contribution in accordance with section 1 above by reference to any liability based on breach of any

obligation assumed by him before the date on which this Act comes into force.

(3) The right to recover contribution in accordance with section 1 above supersedes any right, other than an express contractual right, to recover contribution (as distinct from indemnity) otherwise than under this Act in corresponding circumstances; but nothing in this Act shall affect —

(a) any express or implied contractual or other right to indemnity; or
(b) any express contractual provision regulating or excluding contribution;

which would be enforceable apart from this Act (or render enforceable any agreement for indemnity or contribution which would not be enforceable apart from this Act).

8. Application to Northern Ireland
In the application of this Act to Northern Ireland —

(a) the reference in section 2(3)(b) to section 1 of the Law Reform (Contributory Negligence) Act 1945 or section 5 of the Fatal Accidents Act 1976 shall be construed as a reference to section 2 of the Law Reform (Miscellaneous Provisions) Act (Northern Ireland) 1948 or Article 7 of the Fatal Accidents (Northern Ireland) Order 1977;
(b) the reference in section 5 to section 4(1) of the Crown Proceedings Act 1947 shall be construed as a reference to section 4(1) of that Act as it applies in Northern Ireland;
(c) the reference in section 6(3) to the Fatal Accidents Act 1976 shall be construed as a reference to the Fatal Accidents (Northern Ireland) Order 1977;
(d) references to England and Wales shall be construed as references to Northern Ireland; and
(e) any reference to an enactment shall be construed as including a reference to an enactment of the Parliament of Northern Ireland and a Measure of the Northern Ireland Assembly.

CRIMINAL LAW

This section of Appendix 2 contains individual sections etc of Acts, as follows:

Auctions (Bidding Agreements) Act 1927, ss 1-4
Auctions (Bidding Agreements) Act 1969, ss 1-5
Theft Act 1968, s 15
Trade Descriptions Acts 1968 and 1972, ss 1-6, 11, 13, 14 and 23-26
Road Traffic Act 1972, s 60
Firearms Act 1968, ss 1-3, 55 and 57-58

AUCTIONS (BIDDING AGREEMENTS) ACT 1927

1. Certain bidding agreements to be illegal
(1) If any dealer agrees to give, or gives, or offers any gift or consideration to any other person as an inducement or reward for abstaining, or for having abstained, from bidding at a sale by auction either generally or for any particular lot, or if any person agrees to accept, or accepts, or attempts to obtain from any dealer any such gift or consideration as aforesaid, he shall be guilty of an offence under this Act, and shall be liable on summary conviction to a fine not exceeding the statutory maximum, or to a

term of imprisonment for any period not exceeding six months, or to both such fine and such imprisonment:

Provided that, where it is proved that a dealer has previously to an auction entered into an agreement in writing with one or more persons to purchase goods at the auction bonâ fide on a joint account and has before the goods were purchased at the auction deposited a copy of the agreement with the auctioneer, such an agreement shall not be treated as an agreement made in contravention of this section.

(2) For the purposes of this section the expression 'dealer' means a person who in the normal course of his business attends sales by auction for the purpose of purchasing goods with a view to reselling them.

(3) In England and Wales a prosecution for an offence under this section shall not be instituted without the consent of the Attorney -General or the Solicitor-General.

2. Right of vendors to treat certain sales as fraudulent

Any sale at an auction, with respect to which any such agreement or transaction as aforesaid has been made or effected, and which has been the subject of a prosecution and conviction, may, as against a purchaser who has been a party to such agreement or transaction, be treated by the vendor as a sale induced by fraud:

Provided that a notice or intimation by the vendor to the auctioneer that he intends to exercise such power in relation to any sale at the auction shall not affect the obligation of the auctioneer to deliver the goods to the purchaser.

3. Copy of Act to be exhibited at sale

The particulars which under section seven of the Auctioneers Act 1845, are required to be affixed or suspended in some conspicuous part of the room or place where the auction is held shall include a copy of this Act, and that section shall have effect accordingly.

4. Short title, commencement and extent

(1) This Act may be cited as the Auctions (Bidding Agreements) Act 1927 . . .

(2) This Act shall not extend to Northern Ireland.

AUCTIONS (BIDDING AGREEMENTS) ACT 1969

1. Offences under Auctions (Bidding Agreements) Act 1927 to be indictable as well as triable summarily, and extension of time for bringing summary proceedings

(1) Offences under section 1 of the Auctions (Bidding Agreements) Act 1927 (which, as amended by the Criminal Justice Act 1967, renders a dealer who agrees to give, or gives, or offers a gift or consideration to another as an inducement or reward for abstaining, or for having abstained, from bidding at a sale by auction punishable on summary conviction with a fine not exceeding the statutory maximum or imprisonment for a term not exceeding six months, or both, and renders similarly punishable a person who agrees to accept, or accepts, or attempts to obtain from a dealer any such gift or consideration as aforesaid) shall be triable on indictment as well as summarily; and the penalty that may be imposed on a person on conviction on indictment of an offence under that section shall be imprisonment for a term not exceeding two years or a fine or both.

. . .

(5) This section applies only to offences committed after the commencement of this Act.

2. Persons convicted not to attend or participate in auctions

(1) On any such summary conviction or conviction on indictment as is mentioned in section 1 above, the court may order that the person so convicted or that person and any representative of him shall not (without leave of the court) for a period from the date of such conviction —

(a) in the case of a summary conviction, of not more than one year, or
(b) in the case of a conviction on indictment, of not more than three years,

enter upon any premises where goods intended for sale by auction are on display or to attend or participate in any way in any sale by auction.

(2) In the event of a contravention of an order under this section, the person who contravenes it (and, if he is the representative of another, that other also) shall be guilty of an offence and liable —

(a) on summary conviction, to a fine not exceeding the statutory maximum;
(b) on conviction on indictment, to imprisonment for a term not exceeding two years or to a fine or to both.

(3) In any proceedings against a person in respect of a contravention of an order under this section consisting in the entry upon premises where goods intended for sale by auction were on display, it shall be a defence for him to prove that he did not know, and had no reason to suspect, that goods so intended were on display on the premises, and in any proceedings against a person in respect of a contravention of such an order consisting in his having done something as the representative of another, it shall be a defence for him to prove that he did not know, and had no reason to suspect, that that other was the subject of such an order.

(4) A person shall not be guilty of an offence under this section by reason only of his selling property by auction or causing it to be so sold.

3. Rights of seller of goods by auction where agreement subsists that some person shall abstain from bidding for the goods

(1) Where goods are purchased at an auction by a person who has entered into an agreement with another or others that the other or the others (or some of them) shall abstain from bidding for the goods (not being an agreement to purchase the goods bona fide on a joint account) and he or the other party, or one of the other parties, to the agreement is a dealer, the seller may avoid the contract under which the goods are purchased.

(2) Where a contract is avoided by virtue of the foregoing subsection, then, if the purchaser has obtained possession of the goods and restitution thereof is not made, the persons who were parties to the agreement that one or some of them should abstain from bidding for the goods the subject of the contract shall be jointly and severally liable to make good to the seller the loss (if any) he sustained by reason of the operation of the agreement.

(3) Subsection (1) above applies to a contract made after the commencement of this Act whether the agreement as to the abstention of a person or persons from bidding for the goods the subject of the contract was made before or after that commencement.

(4) Section 2 of the Auctions (Bidding Agreements) Act 1927 (right of vendors to treat certain sales as fraudulent) shall not apply to a sale the contract for which is made after the commencement of this Act.

(5) In this section, 'dealer' has the meaning assigned to it by section 1(2) of the Auctions (Bidding Agreements) Act 1927.

4. Copy of Act to be exhibited at sale
Section 3 of the Auctions (Bidding Agreements) Act 1927 (copy of Act to be exhibited at sale) shall have effect as if the reference to that Act included a reference to this Act.

5. Short title, commencement and extent
(1) This Act may be cited as the Auctions (Bidding Agreements) Act 1969.

(2) This Act shall come into force at the expiration of one month beginning with the day on which it is passed.

(3) This Act shall not extend to Northern Ireland.

THEFT ACT 1968

15. Obtaining property by deception
(1) A person who by any deception dishonestly obtains property belonging to another, with the intention of permanently depriving the other of it, shall on conviction on indictment be liable to imprisonment for a term not exceeding ten years.

(2) For purposes of this section a person is to be treated as obtaining property if he obtains ownership, possession or control of it, and 'obtain' includes obtaining for another or enabling another to obtain or to retain.

(3) Section 6 above shall apply for purposes of this section, with the necessary adaptation of the reference to appropriating, as it applies for purposes of section 1.

(4) For purposes of this section 'deception' means any deception (whether deliberate or reckless) by words or conduct as to fact or as to law, including a deception as to the present intentions of the person using the deception or any other person.

TRADE DESCRIPTIONS ACTS 1968 AND 1972

1. Prohibition of false trade descriptions
(1) Any person who, in the course of a trade or business —

(a) applies a false trade description to any goods; or
(b) supplies or offers to supply any goods to which a false trade description is applied;

shall, subject to the provisions of this Act, be guilty of an offence.

(2) Sections 2 to 6 of this Act shall have effect for the purposes of this section and for the interpretation of expressions used in this section, wherever they occur in this Act.

2. Trade description
(1) A trade description is an indication, direct or indirect, and by whatever means given, of any of the following matters with respect to any goods or parts of goods, that is to say —

(a) quantity, size or gauge;
(b) method of manufacture, production, processing or reconditioning;
(c) composition;
(d) fitness for purpose, strength, performance, behaviour or accuracy;
(e) any physical characteristics not included in the preceding paragraphs;
(f) testing by any person and results thereof;
(g) approval by any person or conformity with a type approved by any person;
(h) place or date of manufacture, production, processing or reconditioning;

(i) person by whom manufactured, produced, processed or reconditioned;
(j) other history, including previous ownership or use.

(2) The matters specified in subsection (1) of this section shall be taken —

(a) in relation to any animal, to include sex, breed or cross, fertility and soundness;
(b) in relation to any semen, to include the identity and characteristics of the animal from which it was taken and measure of dilution.

(3) In this section 'quantity' includes length, width, height, area, volume, capacity, weight and number.

(4) Notwithstanding anything in the preceding provisions of this section, the following shall be deemed not to be trade descriptions, that is to say, any description or mark applied in pursuance of —

(a) [repealed]
(b) section 2 of the Agricultural Produce (Grading and Marking) Act 1928 (as amended by the Agricultural Produce (Grading and Marking) Amendment Act 1931) or any corresponding enactment of the Parliament of Northern Ireland;
(c) the Plant Varieties and Seeds Act 1964;
(d) the Agriculture and Horticulture Act 1964 or any Community grading rules within the meaning of Part III of that Act.
(e) the Seeds Act (Northern Ireland) 1965;
(f) the Horticulture Act (Northern Ireland) 1966; any statement made in respect of, or mark applied to, any material in pursuance of Part IV of the Agriculture Act 1970, any name or expression to which a meaning has been assigned under section 70 of that Act when applied to any material in the circumstances specified in that section any mark prescribed by a system of classification compiled under section 5 of the Agriculture Act 1967 and any designation, mark or description applied in pursuance of a scheme brought into force under section 6(1) or an order made under section 25(1) of the Agriculture Act 1970.
(g) the Consumer Safety Act 1978.

(5) Notwithstanding anything in the preceding provisions of this section —

(a) where provision is made under the Food and Drugs Act 1955, the Food and Drugs (Scotland) Act 1956 or the Food and Drugs Act (Northern Ireland) 1958, or the Consumer Safety Act 1978 prohibiting the application of a description except to goods in the case of which the requirements specified in that provision are complied with, that description, when applied to such goods, shall be deemed not to be a trade description;
(b) where by virtue of any provision made under Part V of the Medicines Act 1968 (or made under any provisions of the said Part V as applied by an order made under section 104 or section 105 of that Act) anything which, in accordance with this Act, constitutes the application of a trade description to goods is subject to any requirements or restrictions imposed by that provision, when applied to goods in circumstances to which those requirements or restrictions are applicable, shall be deemed not to be a trade description.

3. False trade description
(1) A false trade description is a trade description which is false to a material degree.

(2) A trade description which, though not false, is misleading, that is to say, likely to be taken for such an indication of any of the matters specified in section 2 of this Act as would be false to a material degree, shall be deemed to be a false trade description.

(3) Anything which, though not a trade description, is likely to be taken for an indication of any of those matters and, as such an indication, would be false to a material degree, shall be deemed to be a false trade description.

(4) A false indication, or anything likely to be taken as an indication which would be false, that any goods comply with a standard specified or recognised by any person or implied by the approval of any person shall be deemed to be a false trade description, if there is no such person or no standard so specified, recognised or implied.

4. Applying a trade description to goods
(1) A person applies a trade description to goods if he —

(a) affixes or annexes it to or in any manner marks it on or incorporates it with—
  (i) the goods themselves or
  (ii) anything in, on or with which the goods are supplied; or
(b) places the goods in, on or with anything which the trade description has been affixed or annexed to, marked on or incorporated with, or places any such thing with the goods; or
(c) uses the trade description in any manner likely to be taken as referring to the goods.

(2) An oral statement may amount to the use of a trade description.

(3) Where goods are supplied in pursuance of a request in which a trade description is used and the circumstances are such as to make it reasonable to infer that the goods are supplied as goods corresponding to that trade description, the person supplying the goods shall be deemed to have applied that trade description to the goods.

5. Trade descriptions used in advertisements
(1) The following provisions of this section shall have effect where in an advertisement a trade description is used in relation to any class of goods.

(2) The trade description shall be taken as referring to all goods of the class, whether or not in existence at the time the advertisement is published —

(a) for the purpose of determining whether an offence has been committed under paragraph (a) of section 1(1) of this Act; and
(b) where goods of the class are supplied or offered to be supplied by a person publishing or displaying the advertisement, also for the purpose of determining whether an offence has been committed under paragraph (b) of the said section 1(1).

(3) In determining for the purposes of this section whether any goods are of a class to which a trade description used in an advertisement relates regard shall be had not only to the form and content of the advertisement but also to the time, place, manner and frequency of its publication and all other matters making it likely or unlikely that a person to whom the goods are supplied would think of the goods as belonging to the class in relation to which the trade description is used in the advertisement.

6. Offer to supply
A person exposing goods for supply or having goods in his possession for supply shall be deemed to offer to supply them.

11. False or misleading indications as to price of goods
(1) If any person offering to supply goods of any description gives, by whatever means, any false indication to the effect that the price at which the goods are offered is equal to or less than —

(a) a recommended price; or

(b) the price at which the goods of the same description were previously offered by him;

or is less than such a price by a specified amount, he shall, subject to the provisions of this Act, be guilty of an offence.

(2) If any person offering to supply any goods gives, by whatever means, any indication likely to be taken as an indication that the goods are being offered at a price less than that at which they are in fact being offered he shall, subject to the provisions of this Act be guilty of an offence.

(3) For the purposes of this section —

(a) an indication that goods were previously offered at a higher price or at a particular price —
   (i) shall be treated as an indication that they were so offered by the person giving the indication, unless it is expressly stated that they were so offered by others and it is not expressed or implied that they were, or might have been, so offered also by that person; and
   (ii) shall be treated, unless the contrary is expressed, as an indication that they were so offered within the preceding six months for a continuous period of not less than twenty-eight days;

(b) an indication as to a recommended price —
   (i) shall be treated, unless the contrary is expressed, as an indication that it is a price recommended by the manufacturer or producer; and
   (ii) shall be treated, unless the contrary is expressed, as an indication that it is a price recommended generally for supply by retail in the areas where the goods are offered;

(c) anything likely to be taken as an indication as to a recommended price or as to the price at which goods were previously offered shall be treated as such an indication; and

(d) a person advertising goods as available for supply shall be taken as offering to supply them.

13. False representations as to supply of goods or services

If any person, in the course of any trade or business, gives, by whatever means, any false indication, direct or indirect, that any goods or services supplied by him are of a kind supplied to any person he shall, subject to the provisions of this Act, be guilty of an offence.

14. False or misleading statements as to services etc

(1) It shall be an offence for any person in the course of any trade or business —

(a) to make a statement which he knows to be false; or
(b) recklessly to make a statement which is false; as to any of the following matters, that is to say —
   (i) the provision in the course of any trade or business of any services, accommodation or facilities,
   (ii) the nature of any services, accommodation or facilities provided in the course of any trade or business;
   (iii) the time at which, manner in which or persons by whom any services, accommodation or facilities are so provided;
   (iv) the examination, approval or evaluation by a person of any services, accommodation or facilities so provided; or
   (v) the location or amenities of any accommodation so provided.

(2) For the purposes of this section —

(a) anything (whether or not a statement as to any of the matters specified in the preceding subsection) likely to be taken for such a statement as to any of those matters as would be false shall be deemed to be a false statement as to that matter; and
(b) a statement made regardless of whether it is true or false shall be deemed to be made recklessly, whether or not the person making it had reasons for believing that it might be false.

(3) In relation to any services consisting of or including the application of any treatment or process or the carrying out of any repair, the matters specified in subsection (1) of this section shall be taken to include the effect of the treatment, process or repair.

(4) In this section 'false' means false to a material degree and 'services' does not include anything done under a contract of service.

23. Offences due to fault of other person
Where the commission by any person of an offence under this Act is due to the act or default of some other person that other person shall be guilty of the offence, and a person may be charged with and convicted of the offence by virtue of this section whether or not proceedings are taken against the first-mentioned person.

24. Defence of mistake, accident etc
(1) In any proceedings for an offence under this Act it shall, subject to subsection (2) of this section, be a defence for the person charged to prove —

(a) that the commission of the offence was due to a mistake or to reliance on information supplied to him or to the act or default of another person, an accident or some other cause beyond his control; and
(b) that he took all reasonable precautions and exercised all due diligence to avoid the commission of such an offence by himself or any person under his control.

(2) If in any case the defence provided by the last foregoing subsection involves the allegation that the commission of the offence was due to the act or default of another person or to reliance on information supplied by another person, the person charged shall not, without leave of the court, be entitled to rely on that defence unless, within a period ending seven clear days before the hearing, he has served on the prosecutor a notice in writing giving such information identifying or assisting in the identification of that other person as was then in his possession.

(3) In any proceedings for an offence under this Act of supplying or offering to supply goods to which a false trade description is applied it shall be a defence for the person charged to prove that he did not know, and could not with reasonable diligence have ascertained, that the goods did not conform to the description or that the description had been applied to the goods.

25. Innocent publication of advertisement
In proceedings for an offence under this Act committed by the publication of an advertisement it shall be a defence for the person charged to prove that he is a person whose business it is to publish or arrange for the publication of advertisements and that he received the advertisement for publication in the ordinary course of business and did not know and had no reason to suspect that its publication would amount to an offence under this Act.

26. Enforcing authorities
(1) It shall be the duty of every local weights and measures authority as defined in section 36 of the Weights and Measures Act 1963 to enforce within their area the provisions of this Act and of any order made under this Act; and section 37 of the

Weights and Measures Act 1963 (power of local authorities to combine) shall apply with respect to the functions of such authorities under this Act as it applies with respect to their functions under that Act.

(2) Every local weights and measures authority shall, whenever the Board of Trade so direct, make to the Board a report on the exercise of their functions under this Act in such form and containing such particulars as the Board may direct.

(3) Nothing in this section shall be taken as authorising a local weights and measures authority in Scotland to institute proceedings for an offence.

ROAD TRAFFIC ACT 1972

60. Vehicles not to be sold in unroadworthy condition or altered so as to be unroadworthy

(1) Subject to the provisions of this section it shall not be lawful to sell, or to supply, or to offer to sell or supply (or to expose for sale) a motor vehicle or trailer for delivery in such a condition that the use thereof on a road in that condition would be unlawful by virtue of any provision made by regulations under section 40 of this Act as respects brakes, steering gear or tyres or as respects the construction, weight or equipment of vehicles (or as respects the maintenance of vehicles, their parts and accessories in such a condition that no danger is likely to be caused) or in such a condition as respects lighting equipment or reflectors or the maintenance thereof, that it is not capable of being used on a road during the hours of darkness without contravention of the requirements imposed by law as to obligatory lamps or reflectors.

(2) Subject to the provisions of this section it shall not be lawful to alter a motor vehicle or trailer so as to render its condition such that the use thereof on a road in that condition would be unlawful by virtue of any provision made as respects the construction, weight or equipment of vehicles by regulations under the said section 40.

(3) If a motor vehicle or trailer is sold, supplied, offered (exposed for sale) or altered in contravention of the provisions of this section, any person who so sells, supplies (or offers it, exposes it for sale) or alters it, or causes or permits it to be so sold, supplied, offered (exposed for sale) or altered, shall be guilty of an offence.

(4) A person shall not be convicted of an offence under this section in respect of the sale, supply, offer (exposure for sale) or alteration of a motor vehicle or trailer if he proves —

(a) that it was sold, supplied, offered (exposed for sale) or altered, as the case may be, for export from Great Britain, or
(b) that he had reasonable cause to believe that the vehicle or trailer would not be used on a road in Great Britain, or would not be so used until it had been put into a condition in which it might lawfully be so used; or
(c) in the case of a vehicle or trailer the sale, supply (offer or exposure for sale) of which is alleged to be unlawful by reason of its condition as respects lighting equipment or reflectors or the maintenance thereof that he had reasonable cause to believe that the vehicle or trailer would not be used on a road in Great Britain during the hours of darkness until it had been put into a condition in which it might be so used during those hours without contravention of the requirements imposed by law as to obligatory lamps or reflectors.

FIREARMS ACT 1968

1. Requirement of firearm certificate

(1) Subject to any exemption under this Act, it is an offence for a person —

(a) to have in his possession, or to purchase or acquire, a firearm to which this section applies without holding a firearm certificate in force at the time, or otherwise than as authorised by such a certificate;
(b) to have in his possession, or to purchase or acquire, any ammunition to which this section applies without holding a firearm certificate in force at the time, or otherwise than as authorised by such a certificate, or in quantities in excess of those so authorised.

(2) It is an offence for a person to fail to comply with a condition subject to which a firearm certificate is held by him.

(3) This section applies to every firearm except —

(a) a shot gun (that is to say a smooth-bore gun with a barrel not less than 24 inches in length, not being an air gun); and
(b) an air weapon (that is to say, an air rifle, air gun or air pistol not of a type declared by rules made by the Secretary of State under section 53 of this Act to be specially dangerous).

(4) This section applies to any ammunition for a firearm, except the following articles, namely:—

(a) cartridges containing five or more shot, none of which exceeds ·36 inch in diameter;
(b) ammunition for an air gun, air rifle or air pistol; and
(c) blank cartridges not more than one inch in diameter measured immediately in front of the rim or cannelure of the base of the cartridge.

2. Requirement of certificate for possession of shot guns
(1) Subject to any exemption under this Act, it is an offence for a person to have in his possession, or to purchase or acquire, a shot gun without holding a certificate under this Act authorising him to possess shot guns.

(2) It is an offence for a person to fail to comply with a condition subject to which a shot gun certificate is held by him.

3. Business and other transactions with firearms and ammunition
(1) A person commits an offence if, by way of trade or business, he —

(a) manufactures, sells, transfers, repairs, tests or proves any firearm or ammunition to which section 1 of this Act applies, or a shot gun; or
(b) exposes for sale or transfer, or has in his possession for sale, transfer, repair, test or proof any such firearm or ammunition, or a shot gun,

without being registered under this Act as a firearms dealer.

(2) It is an offence for a person to sell or transfer to any other person in the United Kingdom, other than a registered firearms dealer, any firearm or ammunition to which section 1 of this Act applies, or a shot gun, unless that other produces a firearm certificate authorising him to purchase or acquire it or, as the case may be, his shot gun certificate, or shows that he is by virtue of this Act entitled to purchase or acquire it without holding a certificate.

(3) It is an offence for a person to undertake the repair, test or proof of a firearm or ammunition to which section 1 of this Act applies, or of a shot gun, for any other person in the United Kingdom other than a registered firearms dealer as such, unless that other produces or causes to be produced a firearm certificate authorising him to have possession of the firearm or ammunition or, as the case may be, his shot gun certificate, or shows that he is by virtue of this Act entitled to have possession of it without holding a certificate.

(4) Subsections (1) to (3) above have effect subject to any exemption under subsequent provisions of this Part of this Act.

(5) A person commits an offence if, with a view to purchasing or acquiring, or procuring the repair, test or proof of, any firearm or ammunition to which section 1 of this Act applies, or a shot gun, he produces a false certificate or a certificate in which any false entry has been made, or personates a person to whom a certificate has been granted, or makes any false statement.

(6) It is an offence for a pawnbroker to take in pawn any firearm or ammunition to which section 1 of this Act applies, or a shot gun.

55. Exercise of police functions
(1) Rules made under section 53 of this Act may —

(a) regulate the manner in which chief officers of police are to carry out their duties under this Act;
(b) enable all or any of the functions of a chief officer of police to be discharged by a deputy in the event of his illness or absence, or of a vacancy in the office of chief officer of police.

(2) Without prejudice to subsection (1)(b) of this section, the functions of a chief officer of police under this Act shall be exercisable on any occasion by a person, or a person of a particular class, authorised by the chief officer of police to exercise that function on that occasion, or on occasions of that class or on all occasions.

57. Interpretation
(1) In this Act, the expression 'firearm' means a lethal barrelled weapon of any description from which any shot, bullet or other missile can be discharged and includes —

(a) any prohibited weapon, whether it is such a lethal weapon as aforesaid or not; and
(b) any component part of such a lethal or prohibited weapon; and
(c) any accessory to any such weapon designed or adapted to diminish the noise or flash caused by firing the weapon;

and so much of section 1 of this Act as excludes any description of firearm from the category of firearms to which that section applies shall be construed as also excluding component parts of, and accessories to, firearms of that description.

(2) In this Act, the expression 'ammunition' means ammunition for any firearm and includes grenades, bombs and other like missiles, whether capable of use with a firearm or not, and also includes prohibited ammunition.

(3) For purposes of sections 45, 46, 50, 51(4) and 52 of this Act, the offences under this Act relating specifically to air weapons are those under sections 22(4), 22(5), 23(1) and 24(4).

(4) In this Act —
'acquire' means hire, accept as a gift or borrow and 'acquisition' shall be construed accordingly;
'air weapon' has the meaning assigned to it by section 1(3)(b) of this Act;
'area' means a police area;
'certificate' (except in a context relating to the registration of firearms dealers) and 'certificate under this Act' mean a firearm certificate or a shot gun certificate and —

(a) 'firearm certificate' means a certificate granted by a chief officer of police under this Act in respect of any firearm or ammunition to which section 1 of this Act applies and includes a certificate granted in Northern Ireland under section 1 of the Firearms Act 1920 or under an enactment of the Parliament of Northern Ireland amending or substituted for that section; and

(b) 'shot gun certificate' means a certificate granted by a chief officer of police under this Act and authorising a person to possess shot guns;

'firearms dealer' means a person who, by way of trade or business, manufactures, sells, transfers, repairs, tests or proves firearms or ammunition to which section 1 of this Act applies, or shot guns;
'imitation firearm' means any thing which has the appearance of being a firearm (other than such a weapon as is mentioned in section 5(1)(b) of this Act) whether or not it is capable of discharging any shot, bullet or other missile;
'indictable offence' has the same meaning as in the Magistrates' Courts Act 1952, except that it does not include an offence which is triable on indictment only after one or more previous summary convictions thereof;
'premises' includes any land;
'prescribed' means prescribed by rules made by the Secretary of State under section 53 of this Act;
'prohibited weapon' and 'prohibited ammunition' have the meanings assigned to them by section 5(2) of this Act;
'public place' includes any highway and any other premises or place to which at the material time the public have or are permitted to have access, whether on payment or otherwise;
'registered', in relation to a firearms dealer, means registered either —

(a) in Great Britain, under section 33 of this Act,
or
(b) in Northern Ireland, under section 8 of the Firearms Act 1920 or any enactment of the Parliament of Northern Ireland amending or substituted for that section,

and references to 'the register', 'registration' and a 'certificate of registration' shall be construed accordingly, except in section 40;
'shot gun' has the meaning assigned to it by section 1(3)(a) of this Act and, in sections 3(1) and 45(2) of this Act and in the definition of 'firearms dealer', includes any component part of a shot gun and any accessory to a shot gun designed or adapted to diminish the noise or flash caused by firing the gun;
'slaughtering instrument' means a firearm which is specifically designed or adapted for the instantaneous slaughter of animals or for the instantaneous stunning of animals with a view to slaughtering them; and
'transfer' includes let on hire, give, lend and part with possession, and 'transferee' and 'transferor' shall be construed accordingly.

(5) The definitions in subsections (1) to (3) above apply to the provisions of this Act except where the context otherwise requires.

(6) For purposes of this Act —

(a) the length of the barrel of a firearm shall be measured from the muzzle to the point at which the charge is exploded on firing; and
(b) a shot gun or an air weapon shall be deemed to be loaded if there is ammunition in the chamber or barrel or in any magazine or other device which is in such a position that the ammunition can be fed into the chamber or barrel by the manual or automatic operation of some part of the gun or weapon.

58. Particular savings
(1) Nothing in this Act shall apply to the proof houses of the Master, Wardens and Society of the Mystery of Gun-makers of the City of London and the guardians of the Birmingham proof house or the rifle range at Small Heath in Birmingham where

firearms are sighted and tested, so as to interfere in any way with the operations of those two companies in proving firearms under the provisions of the Gun Barrel Proof Act 1868 or any other Acts for the time being in force, or to any person carrying firearms to or from any such proof house when being taken to such proof house for the purposes of proof or being removed therefrom after proof.

(2) Nothing in this Act relating to firearms shall apply to an antique firearm which is sold, transferred, purchased, acquired or possessed as a curiosity or ornament.

(3) The provisions of this Act relating to ammunition shall be in addition to and not in derogation of any enactment relating to the keeping and sale of explosives.

(4) The powers of arrest and entry conferred by Part III of this Act shall be without prejudice to any power of arrest or entry which may exist apart from this Act; and section 52(3) of this Act is not to be taken as prejudicing the power of a constable, when arresting a person for an offence, to seize property found in his possession or any other power of a constable to seize firearms, ammunition or other property, being a power exercisable apart from that subsection.

(5) Nothing in this Act relieves any person using or carrying a firearm from his obligation to take out a licence to kill game under the enactments requiring such a licence.

LAND

This section of Appendix 2 contains individual sections etc of Acts, and extracts from Conditions of Sale, as follows:

The Law Society's General Conditions of Sale (1984)
The National Conditions of Sale (1981)
Sale of Land by Auction Act, 1867, ss 4-6
Estate Agents Act 1979, ss 12-15

THE LAW SOCIETY'S GENERAL CONDITIONS OF SALE (1984)[1]

25. Auctions

(1) This condition applies if the property is sold by auction.

(2) The sale is subject to a reserve price for the property and, when the property is sold in lots, for each lot.

(3) The vendor reserves the right —

(a) to divide the property into lots and to sub-divide, re-arrange or consolidate any lots
(b) to bid personally or by his agent up to any reserve price
(c) without disclosing any reserve price, to withdraw from the sale any property or lot at any time before it has been sold, whether or not the sale has begun.

(4) The auctioneer may —

1 Reproduced by permission of the Law Society.

(a) refuse to accept a bid
(b) in the case of a dispute as to any bid, forthwith determine the dispute or again put up the property or lot at the last undisputed bid.

(5) The purchaser shall forthwith complete and sign the contract and pay ... the normal deposit.

THE NATIONAL CONDITIONS OF SALE (1981)[2]

1. The sale: by auction: by private treaty

(1) Paragraph (2) to (5) of this condition apply on a sale by auction and paragraphs (6) and (7) on a sale by private treaty.

(2) Unless otherwise provided in the Special Conditions, the sale of the property and of each lot is subject to a reserve price and to a right for the vendor or any one person on behalf of the vendor to bid up to that price.

(3) The auctioneer may refuse any bid and no person shall at any bid advance less than the amount fixed for that purpose by the auctioneer.

(4) If any dispute arises respecting a bid, the auctioneer may determine the dispute or the property may, at the vendor's option, either be put up again at the last undisputed bid, or be withdrawn.

(5) Subject to the foregoing provisions of this condition, the highest bidder shall be the purchaser and shall forthwith complete and sign the contract, the date of which shall be the date of the auction.

SALE OF LAND BY AUCTION ACT 1867

4. Sales of land invalid in law from employment of a puffer to be also invalid in equity

And whereas there is at present a conflict between Her Majesty's court of law and equity in respect of the validity of sales by auction of land where a puffer has bid, although no right of bidding on behalf of the owner was reserved, the courts of law holding that all such sales are absolutely illegal, and the courts of equity under some circumstances giving effect to them but even in courts of equity the rule is unsettled: And whereas it is expedient that an end should be put to such conflicting and unsettled opinions: Be it therefore enacted, that from and after the passing of this Act whenever a sale by auction of land would be invalid at law by reason of the employment of a puffer, the same shall be deemed invalid in equity as well as at law.

5. Rule respecting sale without reserve etc

... The particulars or conditions of sale by auction of any land shall state whether such land will be sold without reserve, or subject to a reserved price, or whether a right to bid is reserved; if it is stated that such land will be sold without reserve, or to that effect, then it shall not be lawful for the seller to employ any person to bid at such sale, or for the auctioneer to take knowingly any bidding from any such person.

6. Rule respecting sale subject to right of seller to bid

And where any sale by auction of land is declared either in the particulars or conditions of such sale to be subject to a right for the seller to bid, it shall be lawful for the seller or any one person on his behalf to bid at such auction in such manner as he may think proper.

2 Reproduced by permission of the Solicitors' Law Stationery Society plc.

ESTATE AGENTS ACT 1979

12. Meaning of 'clients' money' etc

(1) In this Act 'clients' money', in relation to a person engaged in estate agency work, means any money received by him in the course of that work which is a contract or pre-contract deposit —

(a) in respect of the acquisition of an interest in land in the United Kingdom, or
(b) in respect of a connected contract,

whether that money is held or received by him as agent, bailee, stakeholder or in any other capacity.

(2) In this Act 'contract deposit' means any sum paid by a purchaser —

(a) which in whole or in part is, or is intended to form part of the consideration for acquiring such an interest as is referred to in subsection (1)(a) above or for a connected contract; and
(b) which is paid by him at or after the time at which he acquires the interest or enters into an enforceable contract to acquire it.

(3) In this Act 'pre-contract deposit' means any sum paid by any person —

(a) in whole or in part as an earnest of his intention to acquire such an interest as is referred to in subsection (1)(a) above, or
(b) in whole or in part towards meeting any liability of his in respect of the consideration for the acquisition of such an interest which will arise if he acquires or enters into an enforceable contract to acquire the interest or
(c) in respect of a connected contract,

and which is paid by him at a time before he either acquires the interest or enters into an enforceable contract to acquire it.

(4) In this Act 'connected contract', in relation to the acquisition of an interest in land, means a contract which is conditional upon such an acquisition or upon entering into an enforceable contract for such an acquisition (whether or not it is also conditional on other matters).

13. Clients' money held on trust or as agent

(1) It is hereby declared that clients' money received by any person in the course of estate agency work in England, Wales or Northern Ireland —

(a) is held by him on trust for the person who is entitled to call for it to be paid over to him or to be paid on his direction or to have it otherwise credited to him, or
(b) if it is received by him as stakeholder, is held by him on trust for the person who may become so entitled on the occurence of the event against which the money is held.

(2) It is hereby declared that clients' money received by any person in the course of estate agency work in Scotland is held by him as agent for the person who is entitled to call for it to be paid over to him or to be paid on his discretion or to have it otherwise credited to him.

(3) The provisions of sections 14 and 15 below as to the investment of clients' money, the keeping of accounts and records and accounting for interest shall have effect in place of the corresponding duties which would be owed by a person holding clients' money as trustee, or in Scotland as agent, under the general law.

(4) Where an order of the Director under section 3 above has the effect of prohibiting a person from holding clients' money the order may contain provision —

(a) appointing another person as trustee, or in Scotland as agent, in place of the person to whom the order relates to hold and deal with clients' money held by that person when the order comes into effect; and
(b) requiring the expenses and such reasonable remuneration of the new trustee or agent as may be specified in the order to be paid by the person to whom the order relates, or if the order provides, out of the clients' money;

but nothing in this subsection shall affect the power conferred by section 41 of the Trustee Act 1925 or section 40 of the Trustee Act (Northern Ireland) 1958 to appoint a new trustee to hold clients' money.

(5) For the avoidance of doubt it is hereby declared that the fact that any person has or may have a lien on clients' money held by him does not affect the operation of this section and also that nothing in this section shall prevent such a lien from being given effect.

14. Keeping of client accounts
(1) Subject to such provision as may be made by accounts regulations, every person who receives clients' money in the course of estate agency work shall, without delay, pay the money into a client account maintained by him or by a person in whose employment he is.

(2) In this Act a 'client account' means a current or deposit account which —

(a) is with an institution authorised for the purposes of this section, and
(b) is in the name of a person who is or has been engaged in estate agency work; and
(c) contains in its title the word 'client'.

(3) The Secretary of State may make provision by regulations (in this section referred to as 'accounts regulations') as to the opening and keeping of client accounts, the keeping of accounts and records relating to clients' money and the auditing of those accounts; and such regulations shall be made by statutory instrument which shall be subject to annulment in pursuance of a resolution of either House of Parliament.

(4) As to the opening and keeping of client accounts, accounts regulations may in particular specify —

(a) the institutions which are authorised for the purposes of this section;
(b) any persons or classes of persons to whom, or any circumstances in which, the obligation imposed by subsection (1) above does not apply;
(c) any circumstances in which money other than clients' money may be paid into a client account; and
(d) the occasions on which, and the persons to whom, money held in a client account may be paid out.

(5) As to the auditing of accounts relating to clients' money, accounts regulations may in particular make provision —

(a) requiring such accounts to be drawn up in respect of specified accounting periods and to be audited by a qualified auditor within a specified time after the end of each period;
(b) requiring the auditor to report whether in his opinion the requirements of this Act and of the accounts regulations have been complied with or have been substantially complied with;

(c) as to the matters to which such a report is to relate and the circumstances in which a report of substantial compliance may be given; and
(d) requiring a person who maintains a client account to produce on demand to a duly authorised officer of an enforcement authority the latest auditor's report.

(6) Subject to subsection (7) below, 'qualified auditor' in subsection (5)(a) above means —

(a) a person who is a member of one or more bodies of accountants established in the United Kingdom and for the time being recognised by the Secretary of State for the purposes of section 389(1)(a) of the Companies Act 1985 or, in Northern Ireland, recognised by the Department of Commerce for Northern Ireland for the purposes of section 155(1)(a) of the Companies Act (Northern Ireland) 1960; or
(b) a person who is for the time being authorised by the Secretary of State under section 389(1)(b) of the Companies Act 1985 or, in Northern Ireland, by the Department of Commerce for Northern Ireland under section 155(1)(b) of the Companies Act (Northern Ireland) 1960; or
(c) in the case of a client account maintained by a company, a person who is qualified to audit the accounts of the company by virtue of section 389(2) of the Companies Act 1985 (unqualified auditors of former exempt private companies); or
(d) a Scottish firm of which all the members are qualified auditors within paragraphs (a) to (c) above.

(7) A person is not a qualified auditor for the purposes of subsection (5)(a) above if, in the case of a client account maintained by a company, he is disqualified from auditing the accounts of the company either by subsection (6), subsection (7) or subsection (8) of section 389 of the Companies Act 1985 or by subsection (2), subsection(3) or subsection (4) of section 155 of the Companies Act (Northern Ireland) 1960.

(8) A person who —

(a) contravenes any provision of this Act or of accounts regulations as to the manner in which clients' money is to be dealt with or accounts and records relating to such money are to be kept, or
(b) fails to produce an auditor's report when required to do so by accounts regulations,

shall be liable on summary conviction to a fine not exceeding £500.

15. Interest on clients' money
(1) Accounts regulations may make provision for requiring a person who has received any clients' money to account, in such cases as may be prescribed by the regulations, to the person who is or becomes entitled to the money for the interest which was, or could have been, earned by putting the money in a separate deposit account at an institution authorised for the purposes of section 14 above.

SUPPLIES OF A SERVICE

SUPPLY OF GOODS AND SERVICES ACT 1982

12. The contracts concerned
(1) In this Act 'contract for the supply of a service' means, subject to subsection (2) below, a contract under which a person ('the supplier') agrees to carry out a service.

(2) For the purposes of this Act, a contract of service or apprenticeship is not a contract for the supply of a service.

(3) Subject to subsection (2) above, a contract is a contract for the supply of a service for the purposes of this Act whether or not goods are also —

(a) transferred or to be transferred, or
(b) bailed or to be bailed by way of hire,

under the contract, and whatever is the nature of the consideration for which the service is to be carried out.

(4) The Secretary of State may by order provide that one or more of sections 13 to 15 below shall not apply to services of a description specified in the order, and such an order may make different provision for different circumstances.

(5) The power to make an order under subsection (4) above shall be exercisable by statutory instrument subject to annulment in pursuance of a resolution of either House of Parliament.

13. Implied term about care and skill
In a contract for the supply of a service where the supplier is acting in the course of a business, there is an implied term that the supplier will carry out the service with reasonable care and skill.

14. Implied term about time for performance
(1) Where, under a contract for the supply of a service by a supplier acting in the course of a business, the time for the service to be carried out is not fixed by the contract, left to be fixed in a manner agreed by the contract or determined by the course of dealing between the parties, there is an implied term that the supplier will carry out the service within a reasonable time.

(2) What is a reasonable time is a question of fact.

15. Implied term about consideration
(1) Where, under a contract for the supply of a service, the consideration for the service is not determined by the contract, left to be determined in a manner agreed by the contract or determined by the course of dealing between the parties, there is an implied term that the party contracting with the supplier will pay a reasonable charge.

(2) What is a reasonable charge is a question of fact.

Appendix 3

Rules of procedure: selected extracts

The rules given below are those applicable to procedure in the High Court. The county court has jurisdiction in respect of actions in contract and tort not exceeding £5 000. Actions relating to recovery of or in respect of title to land may be brought in the county court where the rateable value does not exceed £1 000. We have given the appropriate County Court Rule in the footnotes to the text of the Supreme Court Rule.

Appendix 3 contains the following:
RSC Ord 15, r 4
RSC Ord 16, rr 1, 2, 6-8, 10 and 11
RSC Ord 17, rr 1-3, 5, 7 and 8
RSC Ord 29, rr 2A, 4 and 6
RSC Ord 43, rr 1-8

ORDER 15. CAUSES OF ACTIONS, COUNTERCLAIMS AND PARTIES

4. Joinder of parties[1]
(1) Subject to rule 5 (1), two or more persons may be joined together in one action as plaintiffs or as defendants with the leave of the Court or where —

(a) if separate actions were brought by or against each of them, as the case may be, some common question of law or fact would arise in all the actions, and
(b) all rights to relief claimed in the action (whether they are joint, several or alternative) are in respect of or arise out of the same transaction or series of transactions.

(2) Where the plaintiff in any action claims any relief to which any other person is entitled jointly with him, all persons so entitled must, subject to the provisions of any Act and unless the Court gives leave to the contrary, be parties to the action and any of them who does not consent to being joined as a plaintiff must, subject to any order made by the Court on an application for leave under this paragraph, be made a defendant.

This paragraph shall not apply to a probate action.

1 The corresponding County Court Rule to RSC Ord 15, r 4 is CCR 1981, Ord 5, r 2.

ORDER 16. THIRD PARTY AND SIMILAR PROCEEDINGS[2]

1. Third party notice

Where in any action a defendant who has given notice of intention to defend —

(a) claims against a person not already a party to the action any contribution or indemnity; or
(b) claims against such a person any relief or remedy relating to or connected with the original subject-matter of the action and substantially the same as some relief or remedy claimed by the plaintiff; or
(c) requires that any question or issue relating to or connected with the original subject-matter of the action should be determined not only as between the plaintiff and the defendant but also as between either or both of them and a person not already a party to the action;

then, subject to paragraph (2), the defendant may issue a notice in Form No. 20 or 21 in Appendix A, whichever is appropriate (in this Order referred to as a third party notice), containing a statement of the nature of the claim made against him and, as the case may be, either of the nature and grounds of the claim made by him or of the question or issue required to be determined.

(2) A defendant to an action may not issue a third party notice without the leave of the Court unless the action was begun by writ and he issues the notice before serving his defence on the plaintiff.

(3) Where a third party notice is served on the person against whom it is issued, he shall as from the time of service be a party to the action (in this Order referred to as a third party) with the same rights in respect of his defence against any claim made against him in the notice and otherwise as if he had been duly sued in the ordinary way by the defendant by whom the notice is issued.

2. Application for leave to issue third party notice

(1) Application for leave to issue a third party notice may be made ex parte but the Court may direct a summons for leave to be issued.

(2) An application for leave to issue a third party notice must be supported by an affidavit stating —

(a) the nature of the claim made by the plaintiff in the action;
(b) the stage which proceedings in the action have reached;
(c) the nature of the claim made by the applicant or particulars of the question or issue required to be determined, as the case may be, and the facts on which the proposed third party notice is based; and
(d) the name and address of the person against whom the third party notice is to be issued

6. Setting aside third party proceedings

Proceedings on a third party notice may, at any stage of the proceedings, be set aside by the Court.

7. Judgment between defendant and third party

(1) Where in any action a defendant has served a third party notice, the Court may at or after the trial of the action or, if the action is decided otherwise than by trial, on an application by summons or motion, order such judgment as the nature of the case may require to be entered for the defendant against the third party or for the third party against the defendant.

2 The corresponding County Court Rule to RSC Ord 16 is CCR 1981, Ord 12.

(2) Where judgment is given for the payment of any contribution or indemnity to a person who is under a liability to make a payment in respect of the same debt or damage, execution shall not issue on the judgment without the leave of the Court until that liability has been discharged.

(3) For the purpose of paragraph (2) 'liability' includes liability under a judgment in the same or other proceedings and liability under an agreement to which section 1(4) of the Civil Liability (Contribution) Act 1978 applies.

8. Claims and issues between a defendant and some other party
(1) Where in any action a defendant who has given notice of intention to defend —

(a) claims against a person who is already a party to the action any contribution or indemnity; or
(b) claims against such a person any relief or remedy relating to or connected with the original subject-matter of the action and substantially the same as some relief or remedy claimed by the plaintiff; or
(c) requires that any question or issue relating to or connected with the original subject-matter of the action should be determined not only as between the plaintiff and himself but also as between either or both of them and some other person who is already a party to the action;

then, subject to paragraph (2), the defendant may, without leave, issue and serve on that person a notice containing a statement of the nature and grounds of his claim or, as the case may be, of the question or issue required to be determined.

(2) Where a defendant makes such a claim as is mentioned in paragraph (1) and that claim could be made by him by counterclaim in the action, paragraph (1) shall not apply in relation to the claim.

(3) No acknowlegement of service of such a notice shall be necessary if the person on whom it is served has acknowledged service of the writ or originating summons in the action or is a plaintiff therein, and the same procedure shall be adopted for the determination between the defendant by whom, and the person on whom, such a notice is served of the claim, question or issue stated in the notice as would be appropriate under this Order if the person served with the notice were a third party and (where he has given notice of intention to defend the action or is a plaintiff) had given notice of intention to defend the claim, question or issue.

(4) Rule 4(2) shall have effect in relation to proceedings on a notice issued under this rule as if for the words '7 days after giving notice of intention to defend' there were substituted the words '14 days after service of the notice on him'.

10. Offer of contribution
If, at any time after he has acknowledged service, a party to an action who, stands to be held liable in the action to another party to contribute towards any debt or damages which may be recovered against that other party in the action, makes (without prejudice to his defence) a written offer to that other party to contribute to a specified extent to the debt or damages, then, notwithstanding that he reserves the right to bring the offer to the attention of the Judge at the trial, the offer shall not be brought to the attention of the Judge until after all questions of liability and amount of debt or damages have been decided.

11. Counterclaim by defendant
Where in any action a counterclaim is made by a defendant, the foregoing provisions of this Order shall apply in relation to the counterclaim as if the subject-matter of the counterclaim were the original subject-matter of the action, and as if the person making the counterclaim were the plaintiff and the person against whom it is made a defendant.

ORDER 17. INTERPLEADER[3]

1. Entitlement to relief by way of interpleader

(1) Where —

(a) a person is under a liability in respect of a debt or in respect of any money, goods or chattels and he is, or expects to be, sued for or in respect of that debt or money or those goods or chattels by two or more persons making adverse claims thereto, or
(b) claim is made to any money, goods or chattels taken or intended to be taken by a sheriff in execution under any process, or to the proceeds or value of any such goods or chattels, by a person other than the person against whom the process is issued,

the person under liability as mentioned in sub-paragraph (a) or (subject to rule 2) the sheriff, may apply to the Court for relief by way of interpleader.

(2) References in this Order to a sheriff shall be construed as including references to any other officer charged with the execution of process by or under the authority of the High Court.

2. Claim to goods etc taken in execution

(1) Any person making a claim to or in respect of any money, goods or chattels taken or intended to be taken in execution under process of the Court, or to the proceeds or value of any such goods or chattels, must give notice of his claim to the sheriff charged with the execution of the process and must include in his notice a statement of his address, and that address shall be his address for service.

(2) On receipt of a claim made under this rule the sheriff must forthwith give notice thereof to the execution creditor and the execution creditor must, within 4 days after receiving the notice, give notice to the sheriff informing him whether he admits or disputes the claim.

An execution creditor who gives notice in accordance with this paragraph admitting a claim shall only be liable to the sheriff for any fees and expenses incurred by the sheriff before receipt of that notice.

(3) Where —

(a) the sheriff receives a notice from an execution creditor under paragraph (2) disputing a claim, or the execution creditor fails, within the period mentioned in that paragraph, to give the required notice, and
(b) the claim made under this rule is not withdrawn,

the sheriff may apply to the Court for relief under this Order.

(4) A sheriff who receives a notice from an execution creditor under paragraph (2) admitting a claim made under this rule shall withdraw from possession of the money, goods or chattels claimed and may apply to the Court for relief under this Order of the following kind, that is to say, an order restraining the bringing of an action against him for or in respect of his having taken possession of that money or those goods or chattels.

3. Mode of application

(1) An application for relief under this Order must be made by originating summons unless made in a pending action, in which case it must be made by summons in the action.

3 The corresponding County Court Rule to RSC Ord 17 is CCR 1981, Ord 33.

(2) Where the applicant is a sheriff who has withdrawn from possession of money, goods or chattels taken in execution and who is applying for relief under Rule 2(4), the summons must be served on any person who made a claim under that rule to or in respect of that money or those goods or chattels, and that person may attend the hearing of the application.

(3) An originating summons under this rule shall be in Form No. 10 in Appendix A.

(4) Subject to paragraph (5), a summons under this rule must be supported by evidence that the applicant —

(a) claims no interest in the subject-matter in dispute other than for charges or costs,
(b) does not collude with any of the claimants to that subject-matter, and
(c) is willing to pay or transfer that subject-matter into court or to dispose of it as the Court may direct.

(5) Where the applicant is a sheriff, he shall not provide such evidence as is referred to in paragraph (4) unless directed by the Court so to do.

5. Powers of Court hearing summons
(1) Where on the hearing of a summons under this Order all the persons by whom adverse claims to the subject-matter in dispute (hereafter in this Order referred to as 'the claimants') appear, the Court may order —

(a) that any claimant be made a defendant in any action pending with respect to the subject-matter in dispute in substitution for or in addition to the applicant for relief under this Order, or
(b) that an issue between the claimants be stated and tried and may direct which of the claimants is to be plaintiff and which defendant.

(2) Where —

(a) the applicant on a summons under this Order is a sheriff, or
(b) all the claimants consent or any of them so requests, or
(c) the question at issue between the claimants is a question of law and the facts are not in dispute,

the Court may summarily determine the question at issue between the claimants and make an order accordingly on such terms as may be just.

(3) Where a claimant, having been duly served with a summons for relief under this Order, does not appear on the hearing of the summons or, having appeared, fails or refuses to comply with an order made in the proceedings, the Court may make an order declaring the claimant, and all persons claiming under him, for ever barred from prosecuting his claim against the applicant for such relief and all persons claiming under him, but such an order shall not affect the rights of the claimants as between themselves.

7. Power to stay proceedings
Where a defendant to an action applies for relief under this Order in the action, the Court may by order stay all further proceedings in the action.

8. Other powers
Subject to the foregoing rules of this Order, the Court may in or for the purposes of any interpleader proceedings make such order as to costs or any other matter as it thinks just.

ORDER 29. INTERLOCUTORY INJUNCTIONS, INTERIM PRESERVATION OF PROPERTY, INTERIM PAYMENTS ETC

2A. Delivery of goods under s 4 of Torts (Interference with Goods) Act 1977[4]

(1) Without prejudice to rule 2, the Court may, on the application of any party to a cause or matter, make an order under section 4 of the Torts (Interference with Goods) Act 1977 for the delivery up of any goods which are the subject-matter of the cause or matter or as to which any question may arise therein.

(2) Paragraphs (2) and (3) of rule 1 shall have effect in relation to an application for such an order as they have effect in relation to an application for the grant of an injunction.

4. Sale of perishable property[5]

(1) The Court may, on the application of any party to a cause or matter, make an order for the sale by such person, in such manner and on such terms (if any) as may be specified in the order of any property (other than land) which is the subject-matter of the cause or matter or as to which any question arises therein and which is of a perishable nature or likely to deteriorate if kept or which for any other good reason it is desirable to sell forthwith.

In this paragraph 'land' includes any interest in, or right over, land.

(2) Rule 2 (5) and (6) shall apply in relation to an application for an order under this rule as they apply in relation to an application for an order under that rule.

6. Recovery of personal property subject to lien etc[6]

Where the plaintiff, or the defendant by way of counterclaim, claims the recovery of specific property (other than land) and the party from whom recovery is sought does not dispute the title of the party making the claim but claims to be entitled to retain the property by virtue of a lien or otherwise as security for any sum of money, the Court, at any time after the claim to be so entitled appears from the pleadings (if any) or by affidavit or otherwise to its satisfaction, may order that the party seeking to recover the property be at liberty to pay into court, to abide the event of the action, the amount of money in respect of which the security is claimed and such further sum (if any) for interest and costs as the Court may direct and that, upon such payment being made, the property claimed be given up to the party claiming it.

ORDER 43. ACCOUNTS AND INQUIRIES

1. Summary order for account

(1) Where a writ is endorsed with a claim for an account or a claim which necessarily involves taking an account, the plaintiff may, at any time after the defendant has acknowledged service of the writ or after the time limited for acknowledging service, apply for an order under this rule.

(1A) A defendant to an action begun by writ who has served a counterclaim, which includes a claim for an account or a claim which necessarily involves taking an account, on —

(a) the plaintiff, or
(b) any other party, or

4 There is no corresponding County Court Rule to RSC Ord 29, r 2A.
5 The corresponding County Court Rule to RSC Ord 29, r 4 is CCR 1981, Ord 13, r 7.
6 The corresponding County Court Rule to RSC Ord 29, r 6 is CCR 1981, Ord 13, r 7.

(c) any person who becomes a party by virtue of such service may apply for an order under this rule.

(2) An application under this rule must be made by summons and, if the Court so directs, must be supported by affidavit or other evidence.

(3) On the hearing of the application, the Court may, unless satisfied that there is some preliminary question to be tried, order that an account be taken and may also order that any amount certified on taking the account to be due to either party be paid to him within a time specified in the order.

2. Court may direct taking of accounts etc[7]

(1) The Court may, on an application made by summons at any stage of the proceedings in a cause or matter, direct any necessary accounts or inquiries to be taken or made.

(2) Every direction for the taking of an account or the making of an inquiry shall be numbered in the judgment or order so that, as far as may be, each distinct account and inquiry may be designated by a number.

3. Directions as to manner of taking account or making inquiry[7]

(1) Where the Court orders an account to be taken or inquiry to be made it may by the same or a subsequent order give directions with regard to the manner in which the account is to be taken or vouched or the inquiry is to be made.

(2) Without prejudice to the generality of paragraph (1) the Court may direct that in taking an account the relevant books of account shall be evidence of the matters contained therein with liberty to the parties interested to take such objections thereto as they think fit.

4. Account to be made, verified etc

(1) Where an account has been ordered to be taken, the accounting party must make out his account and, unless the Court otherwise directs, verify it by an affidavit to which the account must be exhibited.

(2) The items on each side of the account must be numbered consecutively.

(3) Unless the order for the taking of the account otherwise directs, the accounting party must lodge the account with the Court and must at the same time notify the other parties that he has done so and of the filing of any affidavit verifying the account and of any supporting affidavit.

5. Notice to be given of alleged omissions etc in account

Any party who seeks to charge an accounting party with an amount beyond that which he has by his account admitted to have received or who alleges that any item in his account is erroneous in respect of amount or in any other respect must give him notice thereof stating, so far as he is able, the amount sought to be charged with brief particulars thereof or, as the case may be, the grounds for alleging that the item is erroneous.

6. Allowances

In taking any account directed by any judgment or order all just allowances shall be made without any direction to that effect.

7 RSC Ord 43, rr 2 and 3 are expressly incorporated into the County Court Rules 1981 by virtue of the County Courts Act 1984, s 76.

7. Delay in prosecution of accounts etc

(1) If it appears to the Court that there is undue delay in the prosecution of any accounts or inquiries, or in any other proceedings under any judgment or order, the Court may require the party having the conduct of the proceedings or any other party to explain the delay and may then make such order for staying the proceedings or for expediting them or for the conduct thereof and for costs as the circumstances require.

(2) The Court may direct any party or the official solicitor to take over the conduct of the proceedings in question and to carry out any directions made by an order under this rule and may make such order as it thinks fit as to the payment of the official solicitor's costs.

8. Distribution of fund before all persons entitled are ascertained

Where some of the persons entitled to share in a fund are ascertained, and difficulty or delay has occured or is likely to occur in ascertaining the other persons so entitled, the Court may order or allow immediate payment of their shares to the persons ascertained without reserving any part of those shares to meet the subsequent costs of ascertaining those other persons.

Appendix 4

Directory of selected London sale rooms and terms of business[1]

Christie's: King Street, St James's, London SW1
Premium 8 per cent; commission 10 per cent (12½ per cent for lots sold under £1 000)

Christie's South Kensington: 85 Old Brompton Road, London SW7.
No premium; commission 15 per cent plus £1 per lot.

Christie's-Robson Lowe (stamps): 47 Duke Street, St James's, London SW1.
Premium 8 per cent; commission 10 per cent (12½ per cent for lots sold under £200).

Sotheby's: 34-35 New Bond Street, London W1, and opposite at Bloomfield Place, London W1
Premium 10 per cent; commission 10 per cent (15 per cent for lots under £500).

Sotheby's Fast Sales: 26 Conduit Street, London W1.
Premium 10 per cent; commission 10 per cent.

Phillips: Blenstock House, 7 Blenheim Street, New Bond Street, London W1.
Premium 10 per cent; commission 10 per cent (12½ per cent for lots sold under £500); minimum charge £5 per lot.

Glendining and Co (coins and medals): 7 Blenheim Street, New Bond Street, London W1.
Premium 10 per cent; commission 10 per cent.

Bonhams: Montpelier Galleries, Montpelier Street, Knightsbridge, London SW7.
Premium 10 per cent; commission 10 per cent (12 per cent for lots sold under £500); minimum charge £5 per lot sold.

Harvey's: 14-18 Neal Street, London WC2.
Premium 10 per cent; commission 10 per cent.

Frank G Bowen: 15 Greek Street, London W1.
No premium; commission 15 per cent.

Bloomsbury Book Auctions: 3 & 4 Hardwick Avenue, London EC1.
Premium 10 per cent; commission 10 per cent.

Lots Road Chelsea Auctions Galleries: 71 Lots Road, London SW10.
Premium 10 per cent; commission 15 per cent; minimum charge £9.

1 As at November 1984. Source: direct. Terms of business may be altered and should always be checked before business is transacted.

Index